1000 Recipes
Grandma's Recipes

igloobooks

Published in 2014
by Igloo Books Ltd
Cottage Farm
Sywell
NN6 0BJ
www.igloobooks.com

SHE001 0214
2 4 6 8 10 9 7 5 3
ISBN 978-1-78197-439-1

Food photography and recipe development: PhotoCuisine UK
Front and back cover images © PhotoCuisine UK

Printed and manufactured in China

1000 Recipes
Grandma's Recipes

CONTENTS

STARTERS AND LIGHT BITES

MAKES 16

Chicken and Mushroom Vol-au-Vents

PREPARATION TIME 10 MINUTES

COOKING TIME 15 - 20 MINUTES

INGREDIENTS

450 g / 1 lb all-butter puff pastry
1 egg, beaten
3 tbsp butter
100 g / 3 ½ oz / 1 ⅓ cups button
mushrooms, sliced
1 tbsp plain (all purpose) flour
300 ml / 10 ½ fl. oz / 1 ¼ cups milk
2 tsp Dijon mustard
150 g / 5 ½ oz cooked chicken breast,
chopped

- Preheat the oven to 220°C (200° fan) / 425F / gas 7 and line a baking tray with greaseproof baking paper.
- Roll out the pastry on a floured surface and use a 7cm / 3 " round pastry cutter to cut out 32 circles.
- Transfer 16 circles to a baking tray and remove the centres from the rest with a 4cm / 1 ½ " cutter.
- Attach the pastry rings to the bases with a little beaten egg then transfer the cut-out centres to the tray and brush everything with egg.
- Bake the pastry for 15 – 20 minutes.
- Heat half of the butter in a frying pan and fry the mushrooms for 5 minutes.
- Heat the rest of the butter in a pan and stir in the flour.
- Gradually add the milk and stir until it thickens.
- Stir in the mustard, chicken and mushrooms and season.
- Spoon the mix into the cases and top with a pastry lid.

Ham and Mushroom Vol-au-vents **2**

- Replace the chicken with 150 g of cooked ham in small cubes.

3

SERVES 4

Baked Potatoes with Soured Cream

PREPARATION TIME 2 MINUTES

COOKING TIME 1 HOUR

INGREDIENTS

4 medium baking potatoes
2 tbsp olive oil
125 g / 4 ½ oz / ½ cup soured cream
2 tbsp chives, chopped
4 bay leaves to garnish

- Preheat the oven to 200°C (180° fan) / 400F / gas 6.
- Rub the potatoes with olive oil and sprinkle with salt then transfer them directly to the top shelf of the oven.
- Bake the potatoes for 1 hour or until a skewer inserted slides in easily.
- While the potatoes are cooking, mix the soured cream with the chives and season to taste with salt and pepper.
- When the potatoes are ready, cut open the tops and spoon in the soured cream, then garnish each one with a bay leaf.

Sweet Potatoes with Soured Cream **4**

- Replace the baking potatoes with orange-fleshed sweet potatoes.

SERVES 4

Lamb Picadillo

- Heat the oil in a frying pan then fry the minced lamb with the chilli powder for 4 minutes.
- Add the spring onions and garlic and stir-fry for 2 more minutes, then add the tomatoes, tomato puree, lime juice and sugar.
- Simmer for 15 minutes, adding a splash of water if it gets too dry.
- Stir in the raisins and olives and cook for 2 more minutes or until the sauce is thick.
- Divide the mixture between the 4 tortillas and serve immediately.

PREPARATION TIME: 5 MINUTES

COOKING TIME 25 MINUTES

INGREDIENTS

2 tbsp olive oil
450 g / 1 lb / 2 cups minced lamb
½ tsp chilli (chili) powder
4 spring onions (scallions), chopped
2 cloves of garlic, crushed
2 medium tomatoes, chopped
2 tbsp tomato puree
1 lime, juiced
1 tbsp dark brown sugar
50 g / 1 ¾ oz / ¼ cup raisins
75 g / 2 ½ oz / ½ cup pimento-stuffed olives
4 flour tortillas

Beef Picadillo

- Replace the lamb mince with an equal quantity of beef mince.

SERVES 4

Fruit Salad with Cheese

- Using a sharp knife, cut the tops off the melons in a zigzag pattern.
- Scoop out and discard the seeds, then use a melon baller to remove the flesh and transfer the melon balls to a bowl.
- Toss the goats' cheese cubes with the crushed peppercorns and add them to the bowl with the cheddar and grapes.
- Mix everything carefully together then divide it between the 4 hollowed out melons.
- Garnish the tops with sprigs of redcurrants before serving.

PREPARATION TIME: 10 MINUTES

INGREDIENTS

4 small orange-fleshed melons
150 g / 5 ½ oz goats' cheese, cubed
1 tsp mixed peppercorns, crushed
150 g / 5 ½ oz Cheddar, julienned
200 g / 7 oz / 1 ⅓ cups seedless red grapes
100 g / 3 ½ oz / ¾ cup redcurrant sprigs

Fruit Salad with Port

- Omit the cheeses and drizzle 2 tbsp of port over each melon 30 minutes before serving.

9

SERVES 4

Tandoori Drumsticks with Raisin Pilaf

PREPARATION TIME 35 MINUTES

COOKING TIME 35 MINUTES

INGREDIENTS

1 lemon, juiced
3 tbsp tandoori spice mix
12 chicken drumsticks

FOR THE PILAF:
3 tbsp olive oil
1 onion, finely chopped
2 cloves of garlic, crushed
3 tbsp raisins
3 cardamom pods
4 cloves
½ tsp ground turmeric
445 g / 1 lb / 2 ¼ cups basmati rice
550 ml / 1 pint/ 2 ¼ cups chicken stock
2 tbsp walnuts, chopped

- Mix the lemon juice with the spice mix and a pinch of salt and rub it over the chicken. Marinate for 30 minutes.
- Preheat the grill to its highest setting.
- Heat the oil in a saucepan and fry the onion for 5 minutes without colouring. Add the garlic, raisins and spices and cook for 2 more minutes then stir in the rice.
- Add the stock and bring to the boil.
- Put the lid on the pan, turn down the heat to its lowest setting and simmer for 12 minutes.
- Turn off the heat and leave the rice to stand, without lifting the lid, for a further 15 minutes.
- Meanwhile, grill the chicken drumsticks for 15 – 20 minutes, turning regularly, until cooked through.
- Fluff up the rice with a fork and stir through the walnut pieces then serve the drumsticks with the pilaf on the side.

Tandoori Drumsticks with Yoghurt Dip

 10

- Make a dip from 150 g Greek yoghurt, 2 tbsp mango chutney, ½ tsp tandoori spice mix and half a crushed clove of garlic.

11

MAKES 4

Mini Cottage Pies

PREPARATION TIME 2 MINUTES

COOKING TIME 1 HOUR 30 MINUTES

INGREDIENTS

2 tbsp olive oil
1 small onion, finely chopped
2 cloves of garlic, crushed
200 g / 7 oz / 1 cup minced beef
200 g / 7 oz / 1 cup canned tomatoes, chopped
200 ml / 7 fl. oz / ¾ cups beef stock

FOR THE PASTRY:
100 g / 3 ½ oz / ½ cup butter, cubed
200 g / 7 oz / 1 ⅓ cups plain (all purpose) flour

FOR THE TOPPING:
450 g / 1 lb floury potatoes, peeled and cubed
100 ml / 3 ½ fl. oz / ½ cup milk
50 g / 1 ¾ oz / ¼ cup butter
50 g / 1 ¾ oz / ½ cup Cheddar cheese, grated

- Heat the oil and fry the onion and garlic for 3 minutes.
- Add the mince and fry for 2 minutes then add the tomatoes and stock and bring to a gentle simmer.
- Cook for 1 hour, stirring occasionally.
- Meanwhile, make the pastry. Rub the butter into the flour and add just enough cold water to bind.
- Chill for 30 minutes then roll out on a floured surface.
- Preheat the oven to 200°C (180° fan) / 400F / gas 6.
- Line the cases with pastry and prick with a fork.
- Line the pastry with clingfilm and fill with baking beans then bake for 10 minutes.
- Boil the potatoes for 10 minutes, then drain well.
- Return the potatoes to the saucepan, add the milk and butter, then mash. Fill the pastry cases with the mince mixture.
- Top with the mashed potato, sprinkle with cheese and bake for 15 minutes.

Mini Vegetarian Cottage Pies

12

- Process 2 carrots, 1 courgette and 10 mushrooms in a food processor until very finely chopped. Use in place of the beef mince and replace the stock with vegetable stock.

13

SERVES 4

Crêpes with Smoked Salmon

Crêpes with Salmon and Horseradish

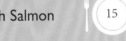

14

- Stir 1 tbsp of horseradish sauce into the cream cheese before serving.

Crêpes with Salmon and Capers

15

- Sprinkle each serving with a teaspoon of capers before serving.

PREPARATION TIME 5 MINUTES

COOKING TIME 20 MINUTES

....

INGREDIENTS

Preparation time: 5 minutes
Cooking time: 20 minutes

150 g / 5 ½ oz / 1 cup plain (all purpose) flour
1 large egg
325 ml / 11 ½ fl. oz / 1 ⅓ cups whole milk
2 tbsp butter
4 tbsp cream cheese
8 slices smoked salmon
1 lemon, halved

- Put the oven on a low setting.
- Sieve the flour into a bowl and make a well in the centre. Break in the egg and pour in the milk then use a whisk to gradually incorporate all of the flour from round the outside.
- Melt the butter in a small frying pan then whisk it into the batter.
- Put the buttered frying pan back over a low heat. Add a small ladle of batter and swirl the pan to coat the bottom.
- When it starts to dry and curl up at the edges, turn the crepe over with a spatula and cook the other side until golden brown and cooked through.
- Transfer the crêpe to a plate, cover with a clean tea towel and keep warm in the oven.
- Repeat the process until all the batter has been used, keeping the finished crepes warm under the tea towel.
- Divide the crêpes between 4 warm plates and top each one with a tablespoon of cream cheese and 2 slices of smoked salmon.
- Squeeze over the lemon at the table.

16

MAKES 6

Mini Fish Pies

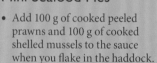

Mini Seafood Pies

17

- Add 100 g of cooked peeled prawns and 100 g of cooked shelled mussels to the sauce when you flake in the haddock.

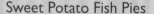

Sweet Potato Fish Pies

18

- Replace the potatoes with sweet potatoes for a sweeter flavour.

PREPARATION TIME 10 MINUTES

COOKING TIME 30-35 MINUTES

....

INGREDIENTS

450 g / 1 lb potatoes, peeled and cubed
500 ml / 17 ½ fl. oz / 2 cups milk
1 bay leaf
400 g / 14 oz smoked haddock fillet
4 tbsp butter
2 tbsp plain flour

- Preheat the oven to 200°C (180° fan) / 400F / gas 6.
- Cook the potatoes in boiling salted water for 12 minutes or until tender then drain well.
- Meanwhile, put the milk and bay leaf in a small saucepan and bring to a simmer.
- Lay the haddock in a snugly-fitting dish and pour the hot milk over the top. Cover the dish with clingfilm and leave to stand for 10 minutes.
- Heat half of the butter in a small saucepan and stir in the flour.
- Reserve 2 tablespoons of the haddock milk for the potatoes and strain the rest into the butter and flour mixture, stirring constantly. Cook until the sauce is thick and smooth.
- Remove any skin and bones from the haddock then flake the flesh into the white sauce. Season to taste with salt and black pepper then divide the mixture between 6 individual pie dishes.
- Mash the potatoes with the reserved milk and remaining butter and spoon it on top of the haddock.
- Bake the pies for 15 – 20 minutes or until the topping is golden brown.

19

SERVES 4

Crispbreads with Cream Cheese

- Top the crisp breads with the cream cheese and arrange the cucumber on top.
- Slice half of the chives on the diagonal and sprinkle over the cream cheese.
- Garnish with short lengths of the remaining chives.

PREPARATION TIME 5 MINUTES

INGREDIENTS

8 crispbreads
125 g / 4 ½ oz / ½ cup cream cheese
½ cucumber, thinly sliced
a small bunch of chives

Crispbreads with Blue Cheese

20

- Beat 100 g of crumbled Roquefort into the cream cheese and omit the cucumber.

21

SERVES 4

Creamy Cauliflower Soup

- Heat the oil and butter in a saucepan and fry the leeks for 8 minutes or until softened.
- Add the garlic and cauliflower to the pan and cook for 2 more minutes, then stir in the vegetable stock and bring to the boil.
- Simmer for 15 minutes then stir in the double cream and nutmeg.
- Blend the soup until smooth with a liquidiser or emersion blender then try the soup and adjust the seasoning with salt and pepper.

PREPARATION TIME 5 MINUTES

COOKING TIME 30 MINUTES

INGREDIENTS

2 tbsp olive oil
2 tbsp butter
3 leeks, finely chopped
2 cloves of garlic, crushed
1 cauliflower, cubed
1 litre / 1 pint 15 fl. oz / 4 cups vegetable stock
100 ml / 3 ½ fl. oz / ½ cup double (heavy) cream
¼ tsp freshly ground nutmeg
flat leaf parsley to garnish

Truffled Cauliflower Soup

22

- Add a few drops of truffle oil to the soup just before serving.

23

SERVES 4

Chunky Leek and Potato Soup

PREPARATION TIME 5 MINUTES

COOKING TIME 30 MINUTES

INGREDIENTS

2 tbsp olive oil
2 tbsp butter
3 leeks, halved and thickly sliced
2 cloves of garlic, crushed
3 medium potatoes, cubed
1 litre / 1 pint 15 fl. oz / 4 cups
vegetable stock

- Heat the oil and butter in a saucepan and fry the leeks for 8 minutes or until softened.
- Add the garlic and potatoes to the pan and cook for 2 more minutes, then stir in the vegetable stock and bring to the boil.
- Simmer for 15 minutes then adjust the seasoning with salt and pepper.

Leek, Potato and Sage Soup **24**

- Add 1 tbsp of chopped sage leaves to the leeks while they are frying.

25

SERVES 4

Smoked Salmon and Scrambled Egg

PREPARATION TIME 2 MINUTES

COOKING TIME 5 MINUTES

INGREDIENTS

8 large eggs
2 tbsp butter
3 slices smoked salmon, chopped
4 cranberry soda bread rolls to serve

- Gently beat the eggs with a pinch of salt and pepper to break up the yolks.
- Heat the butter in a non-stick frying pan until sizzling then pour in the eggs.
- Cook over a low heat, stirring constantly until the eggs start to scramble, then stir in the salmon and cook until done to your liking.
- Spoon onto the bottom half of the rolls and sandwich with the tops.

Cranberry Soda Bread Rolls **26**

- Mix together 500 g plain flour, 2 tsp bicarbonate of soda, 1 tsp salt, 50 g dried cranberries and 400 g buttermilk. Shape into 4 rolls and bake at 200°C for 25 minutes.

27

MAKES 4

Tuna Mayonnaise on Toast

- Toast the bread in a toaster or under a hot grill until golden brown.
- Meanwhile, mix the tuna with the mayonnaise and lemon juice and season to taste with salt and black pepper.
- Divide the toast between 4 plates, top with the tuna mixture and garnish with chives

PREPARATION TIME 5 MINUTES

COOKING TIME 4 MINUTES

....

INGREDIENTS

8 slices crusty bread
125 g / 4 ½ oz / ½ cup canned tuna, flaked
4 tbsp mayonnaise
1 tbsp lemon juice
chives to garnish

Tuna Melt

28

- Spread the tuna mixture on the toast and top with 100 g of grated Cheddar. Cook under a hot grill until bubbling.

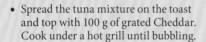

29

SERVES 4

Red Cabbage with Bacon

- Preheat the grill to its highest setting.
- Heat the oil in a sauté pan and fry the garlic and caraway for 2 minutes.
- Add the cabbage and a sprinkle of salt and pepper and sauté for 5 minutes.
- Pour in the wine, put on the lid and steam for 8 minutes.
- Meanwhile, grill the bacon for 2 minutes on each side or until cooked to your liking.
- Stir the grapes into the cabbage and sauté for 4 more minutes or until almost all the liquid has evaporated.

PREPARATION TIME 5 MINUTES

COOKING TIME 20 MINUTES

....

INGREDIENTS

2 tbsp olive oil
2 cloves of garlic, crushed
1 tsp caraway seeds
½ red cabbage, sliced
100 ml / 3 ½ fl. oz / ½ cup port
150 g / 5 ½ oz / 1 cup red grapes, halved
8 rashers smoked bacon

Red Cabbage with Mackerel

30

- Replace the bacon with 4 large mackerel fillets. Cook under the grill as before.

MAKES 16

Cheese Croquettes

31

PREPARATION TIME 20 MINUTES

COOKING TIME 4-5 MINUTES

INGREDIENTS

4 tbsp plain (all purpose) flour
1 egg, beaten
75 g / 2 ½ oz / ½ cup panko breadcrumbs
450 g / 1 lb / 2 cups leftover mashed potato
100 g / 3 ½ oz / 1 cup Cheddar, grated
sunflower oil for deep-frying
basil and sage leaves to serve

- Put the flour, egg and panko breadcrumbs in 3 separate bowls.
- Mix the mashed potato with the cheese then shape it into 16 cylinders.
- Dip the croquettes alternately in the flour, egg and breadcrumbs and shake off any excess.
- Heat the oil in a deep fat fryer, according to the manufacturer's instructions, to a temperature of 180°C.
- Lower the croquettes in the fryer basket and cook for 4 – 5 minutes or until crisp and golden brown.
- Tip the croquettes into a kitchen paper lined bowl to remove any excess oil.

Chicken Croquettes

 32

- Add 100 g of finely chopped cooked chicken breast to the potato when you add the cheese.

33

MAKES 12

Cheese Puffs

PREPARATION TIME 15 MINUTES

COOKING TIME 20 MINUTES

INGREDIENTS

2 tbsp olive oil
1 small onion, finely chopped
2 rashers streaky bacon, finely chopped
1 clove of garlic, crushed
50 g / 1 ¾ oz / ⅔ cup fresh breadcrumbs
100 g / 3 ½ oz / 1 cup Cheddar, grated
1 tsp Dijon mustard
500 g / 1 lb 2 oz all-butter puff pastry
1 egg, beaten

- Preheat the oven to 230°C (210° fan) / 450F / gas 8.
- Heat the oil in a frying pan and fry the onion, bacon and garlic for 5 minutes, stirring occasionally.
- Stir in the breadcrumbs, cheese and mustard and season to taste with salt and pepper.
- Roll out the pastry on a lightly floured surface and cut out 12 circles.
- Put a heaped teaspoon of the cheese mixture in the centre of each circle, then fold it in half and seal with beaten egg.
- Crimp the edges, transfer the pastries to a baking tray and brush the tops with egg.
- Bake the puffs for 15 minutes or until golden brown and cooked through.

Cheese and Chorizo Puffs

 34

- Add 100 g of chorizo in small cubes to the filling when you fry the onion.

35

SERVES 4

Pancakes with Bacon and Syrup

Pancakes with Sausages and Syrup

36

- Gently fry 8 chipolata sausages for 10 minutes, turning regularly, and serve with the pancakes instead of the bacon.

Pancakes with Blueberries and Maple Syrup

37

- Replace the bacon with 6 tbsp of blueberries for a fruity alternative.

PREPARATION TIME 10 MINUTES

COOKING TIME 30 MINUTES

INGREDIENTS

250 g / 9 oz / 1 ⅔ cups plain (all purpose) flour
2 tsp baking powder
300 ml / 10 ½ fl. oz / 1 ¼ cups milk
2 large eggs, beaten
2 tbsp butter
8 rashers streaky bacon
100 ml / 3 ½ fl. oz / ⅓ cup maple syrup

- Mix the flour and baking powder in a bowl and make a well in the centre.
- Pour in the milk and eggs then use a whisk to gradually incorporate all of the flour from round the outside.
- Melt the butter in a small frying pan then whisk it into the batter.
- Put the buttered frying pan back over a low heat. You will need a tablespoon of batter for each pancake and you should be able to cook 4 pancakes at a time in the frying pan.
- Spoon the batter into the pan and cook for 2 minutes or until small bubbles start to appear on the surface.
- Turn the pancakes over with a spatula and cook the other side until golden brown and cooked through.
- Repeat until all the batter has been used, keeping the finished batches warm in a low oven.
- While the pancakes are cooking, grill or fry the bacon for 2 minutes on each side or until cooked to your liking.
- Serve the pancakes with the bacon and the maple syrup drizzled over.

MAKES 12

Bacon and Egg Scones

Egg Mayonnaise and Chive Scones

- Omit the bacon and stir 2 tbsp of chopped chives into the egg mayonnaise. Add 2 tbsp of chopped chives to the scone mixture.

Cream Cheese and Chive Scones

- Fill the scones with cream cheese mashed with 2 tbsp of chopped fresh chives.

PREPARATION TIME 25 MINUTES

COOKING TIME 10-15 MINUTES

....

INGREDIENTS

225 g / 8 oz / 1 ½ cups self-raising flour
55 g / 2 oz / ¼ cup butter
150 ml / 5 fl. oz / ⅔ cup milk

FOR THE FILLING:
4 large eggs
4 rashers streaky bacon
4 tbsp mayonnaise
cress to garnish

- Preheat the oven to 220°C (200° fan) / 425F / gas 7 and oil a large baking sheet.
- Sieve the flour into a bowl and rub in the butter until the mixture resembles fine breadcrumbs.
- Stir in enough milk to bring the mixture together into a soft dough.
- Flatten the dough with your hands on a floured work surface until 2.5 cm / 1" thick.
- Use a pastry cutter to cut out 12 circles and transfer them to the prepared baking sheet.
- Bake in the oven for 10 – 15 minutes or until golden brown and cooked through.
- Transfer the scones to a wire rack to cool a little while you make the filling.
- Boil the eggs for 6 minutes then drain and plunge into cold water for 4 minutes.
- Meanwhile, grill the bacon for 3 minutes on each side or until crisp, then roughly chop.
- Peel the eggs and mash them with a fork then mix with the bacon pieces and mayonnaise.
- Split open the scones and fill with the bacon and egg mayonnaise and a sprinkle of cress.

41
MAKES 12
Toasted Teacakes

- Pour the tea over the fruit and leave to soak for 20 minutes.
- Rub the butter into the bread flour and stir in the yeast, sugar, salt and spice, followed by the tea and soaked fruit.
- Knead the mixture on a lightly oiled surface for 10 minutes or until the dough is smooth and elastic.
- Leave the dough to rest, covered with the mixing bowl, for 1 – 2 hours or until doubled in size.
- Shape the dough into 12 buns and transfer to a greased baking tray, then cover and leave to prove for 45 minutes.
- Preheat the oven to 220°C (200° fan) / 425F / gas 7.
- Bake the teacakes for 15 – 20 minutes or until golden brown and cooked through.
- Leave to cool on a wire rack then split in half and toast under a hot grill.
- Spread with butter before serving.

St Clements Buns
42

- Replace the dried fruit with chopped candied peel and add the grated zest of an orange to the bread dough.

PREPARATION TIME 2 HOURS 30 MINUTES

COOKING TIME 15-20 MINUTES

INGREDIENTS

300 ml / 10 ½ fl. oz / 1 ¼ cups freshly brewed tea
100 g / 3 ½ oz / ½ cup mixed dried fruit
55 g / 2 oz / ¼ cup butter, cubed
400 g / 14 oz / 2 ⅔ cups strong white bread flour, plus extra for dusting
½ tsp easy blend dried yeast
4 tbsp caster (superfine) sugar
1 tsp fine sea salt
softened butter for spreading

43
SERVES 6
Pineapple Fritters

- Heat the sunflower oil in a deep fat fryer, according to the manufacturer's instructions, to a temperature of 180°C.
- Mix the flour with the sugar then beat the egg with the pineapple juice and whisk enough of it into the dry ingredients to create a thick batter.
- Dip the pineapple chunks in the batter and deep-fry in batches for 2 - 3 minutes or until golden and puffy.
- Remove the fritters with a slotted spoon and leave to drain on kitchen paper for a few minutes.
- Repeat with the rest of the pineapple then sprinkle the finished fritters with caster sugar.

PREPARATION TIME 10 MINUTES

COOKING TIME 2-3 MINUTES

INGREDIENTS

300 g / 10 ½ oz / 2 cups plain (all purpose) flour
60 g / 2 oz / ¼ cup caster (superfine) sugar, plus extra for sprinkling
1 large egg
300 ml / 10 ½ fl. oz / 1 ¼ cups pineapple juice
1 pineapple, peeled and cut into large chunks
sunflower oil for deep-frying

Pineapple and Coconut Fritters
44

- Replace the pineapple juice with coconut milk and sprinkle the finished fritters with desiccated coconut.

45

MAKES 16

Sweet Potato and Cheese Croquettes

PREPARATION TIME 20 MINUTES

COOKING TIME 4-5 MINUTES

....

INGREDIENTS

4 tbsp plain (all purpose) flour
1 egg, beaten
75 g / 2 ½ oz / ½ cup panko
breadcrumbs
225 g / 8 oz / 1 cup leftover mashed
potato
225 g / 8 oz / 1 cup leftover mashed
sweet potato
100 g / 3 ½ oz / 1 cup Cheddar,
grated
sunflower oil for deep-frying

- Put the flour, egg and panko breadcrumbs in 3 separate bowls.
- Mix the mashed potato and sweet potato with the cheese then shape it into 16 cylinders.
- Dip the croquettes alternately in the flour, egg and breadcrumbs and shake off any excess.
- Heat the oil in a deep fat fryer, according to the manufacturer's instructions, to a temperature of 180°C.
- Lower the croquettes in the fryer basket and cook for 4 – 5 minutes or until crisp and golden brown.
- Tip the croquettes into a kitchen paper lined bowl to remove any excess oil.

Sweet Potato and Chorizo Croquettes

 46

- Add 100 g of finely chopped chorizo to the potatoes when you add the cheese.

47

SERVES 4

Black Pudding Scrambled Egg

PREPARATION TIME 2 MINUTES

COOKING TIME 5 MINUTES

....

INGREDIENTS

8 large eggs
2 tbsp butter
250 g / 9 oz black pudding, skinned
and crumbled
4 slices ciabatta
150 g / 5 ½ oz / ¾ cup roasted red
peppers in oil, drained
a few sprigs of parsley to serve

- Gently beat the eggs with a pinch of salt and pepper to break up the yolks.
- Heat the butter in a non-stick frying pan until sizzling then add the black pudding and stir-fry for 2 minutes.
- Pour in the eggs and cook over a low heat, stirring constantly until the eggs start to scramble.
- Spoon onto the ciabatta and top with the red peppers and parsley.

Veggie Sausage Scrambled Egg

48

- Replace the black pudding with 4 vegetarian sausages, chopped into small pieces.

49

SERVES 4

Chicken Fajitas

- Toss the chicken with the seasoning mix and leave to marinate for 30 minutes.
- Heat the oil in a large frying pan and stir-fry the chicken for 4 minutes.
- Add the onions and peppers and stir fry for a further 4 minutes, then divide the mixture between the tortillas.
- Roll up the fajitas and serve with guacamole for dipping.

PREPARATION TIME 35 MINUTES

COOKING TIME 8 MINUTES

INGREDIENTS

450 g / 1 lb chicken breast, sliced
2 tbsp fajita seasoning mix
2 tbsp sunflower oil
1 onion, sliced
1 red pepper, sliced
1 yellow pepper, sliced
1 green pepper, sliced
8 soft flour tortillas
guacamole to serve

Speedy Guacamole

50

- Remove the stone from a ripe avocado and scrape the flesh into a food processor with the juice of half a lime and a pinch of salt. Blend until smooth.

51

MAKES 18

Cherries and Pecorino on Toast

- Put the cherries and sugar in a saucepan with the vinegar
- Put a lid on the pan then cook over a gentle heat for 10 minutes, stirring occasionally, until the cherries are soft.
- Meanwhile, toast the bread until golden in a toaster or under the grill.
- Spoon the warm pickled cherries over the toast and top with the Pecorino, baby chard and thyme.
- Garnish with whole cherries and serve immediately.

PREPARATION TIME 5 MINUTES

COOKING TIME 10 MINUTES

INGREDIENTS

225 g / 8 oz / 1 ½ cups cherries, stoned
2 tbsp caster (superfine) sugar
2 tbsp white wine vinegar
4 slices white bread
150 g / 5 ½ oz young Pecorino, thinly sliced
a handful of baby chard leaves
1 tbsp thyme leaves
whole cherries with stems to garnish

Figs and Pecorino on Toast

52

- Replace the cherries with 8 figs, cut into quarters, and reduce the cooking time to 6 minutes.

SERVES 4

Sautéed Courgette with Coppa

PREPARATION TIME I MINUTES

COOKING TIME 12 MINUTES

....

INGREDIENTS

1 tbsp olive oil
2 tbsp butter
3 courgettes (zucchini), sliced
1 clove of garlic, crushed
1 tbsp basil leaves, finely chopped
4 slices coppa
a few sprigs of basil to garnish

- Heat the olive oil and butter in a large sauté pan until sizzling.
- Add the courgette, season with salt and pepper and cook for 10 minutes, stirring occasionally.
- When all of the liquid that comes out has evaporated and they start to colour, add the garlic and chopped basil and cook for 2 more minutes.
- Divide between 4 mini casserole dishes and top with the coppa and sprigs of basil.

Sautéed Courgette with Smoked Salmon   54

- Replace the coppa with thin slices of smoked salmon.

SERVES 4

Chunky Bacon and Vegetable Soup

PREPARATION TIME 5 MINUTES

COOKING TIME 30 MINUTES

....

INGREDIENTS

2 tbsp olive oil
2 tbsp butter
1 onion, finely chopped
2 cloves of garlic, crushed
2 medium potatoes, cubed
3 carrots, cubed
1 litre / 1 pint 15 fl. oz / 4 cups vegetable stock
150 g / 5 ½ oz / 1 cup peas, defrosted if frozen
4 rashers streaky bacon
a few sprigs of chervil to serve

- Heat the oil and butter in a saucepan and fry the onion for 5 minutes or until softened.
- Add the garlic, potatoes and carrots to the pan and cook for 2 more minutes, then stir in the vegetable stock and bring to the boil.
- Simmer for 12 minutes then add the peas and simmer for a further 5 minutes.
- While the peas are cooking, cook the bacon under a hot grill until crispy then chop into large pieces.
- Stir the bacon into the soup, add salt and pepper to taste and garnish with chervil.

Chunky Chorizo and Vegetable Soup   56

- Replace the bacon with 100 g of thinly sliced chorizo, fried until crispy.

57

SERVES 4

Gammon and Salad Onion Skewers

Gammon and Pineapple Skewers

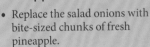

58

- Replace the salad onions with bite-sized chunks of fresh pineapple.

Red Pepper and Gammon Skewers

59

- Chop 2 large red peppers into chunks and thread onto the skewers between the gammon and onions.

PREPARATION TIME 20 MINUTES

COOKING TIME 8 MINUTES

INGREDIENTS

6 salad onions
400 g / 14 oz unsmoked gammon, cubed
4 tbsp barbeque sauce

- Put 12 wooden skewers in a bowl of water and leave to soak for 20 minutes.
- Meanwhile, cut off the green parts of the onions and reserve for garnish. Cut the bulb of the onions in half.
- Thread the gammon and onions onto the skewers and spread them out on a large grill tray.
- Brush them with barbeque sauce then grill for 4 minutes on each side or until the onions are slightly charred on the edges.
- Slice the reserved onion greens on the diagonal and scatter over the skewers.

SERVES 4

Ham Pancakes with Chive Butter

Feta Pancakes with Thyme Butter

61

- Replace the ham with cubes of Feta and use young thyme leaves instead of chives in the butter.

Ham Pancakes with Tarragon Butter

62

- Replace the chives with finely chopped tarragon.

PREPARATION TIME 45 MINUTES

COOKING TIME 4 MINUTES

INGREDIENTS

250 g / 9 oz / 1 ⅔ cups plain (all purpose) flour
2 tsp baking powder
2 large eggs
300 ml / 10 ½ fl. oz / 1 ¼ cups milk
2 tbsp butter
2 slices cooked ham, chopped

FOR THE CHIVE BUTTER:
100 g / 3 ½ oz / ½ cup butter, softened
1 tbsp chives, chopped

- First make the chive butter. Mix the butter with the chives, then roll up in a sheet of foil and chill until solid. Cut into slices.
- Mix the flour and baking powder in a bowl then break in the eggs and pour in the milk. Use a whisk to gradually incorporate all of the flour from round the outside.
- Melt the butter in a small frying pan then whisk it into the batter with the ham.
- Put the pan back over a low heat. You will need a tablespoon of batter for each pancake and you should be able to cook 4 pancakes at a time.
- Spoon the batter into the pan and cook for 2 minutes or until small bubbles start to appear on the surface.
- Turn the pancakes over with a spatula and cook the other side until golden brown and cooked through.
- Repeat until all the batter has been used, keeping the finished batches warm in a low oven.
- Pile the pancakes onto warm plates and top each one with a slice of chive butter.

63

SERVES 4

Ham, Egg and Chorizo Tapas

- Heat the oil in a large frying pan and fry the chorizo and pepper for 5 minutes, turning occasionally.
- Move the chorizo and pepper to the side of the pan and break in the eggs.
- Fry the eggs for 3 minutes or until the whites are set, but the yolks still runny.
- Arrange the ham on top of the bread and top each one with a piece of chorizo, followed by an egg.
- Top with the green peppers and garnish with parsley.

PREPARATION TIME 5 MINUTES

COOKING TIME 8 MINUTES

INGREDIENTS

2 tbsp olive oil
4 small cooking chorizo
1 green pepper, sliced
4 small eggs
4 slices Iberico ham
4 slices crusty baguette
a few sprigs of flat leaf parsley

Ham, Egg and Manchego Tapas

64

- Omit the chorizo and green pepper and top the eggs with thin shavings of Manchego instead.

65

MAKES 12

Bacon and Poppy Seed Scones

- Preheat the oven to 220°C (200° fan) / 425F / gas 7 and line a baking tray with greaseproof paper.
- Heat the oil in a small frying pan and fry the bacon for 2 minutes. Leave to cool.
- Rub the butter into the flour with your fingertips until the mixture resembles fine breadcrumbs then stir in the mustard powder.
- Add the milk and bacon pieces and mix together into a pliable dough.
- Turn the dough out onto a floured work surface and flatten it into a rectangle, 2 cm / 1 " thick.
- Use a round pastry cutter to stamp out the scones then transfer them to the baking tray.
- Brush the scones with milk, sprinkle with poppy seeds and bake for 12 – 15 minutes or until golden brown and cooked through.
- Transfer the scones to a wire rack to cool before serving.

PREPARATION TIME 10 MINUTES

COOKING TIME 12-15 MINUTES

INGREDIENTS

1 tbsp olive oil
4 rashers streaky bacon, finely chopped
2 tsp thyme leaves
75 g / 2 ½ oz / ⅓ cup butter, cubed
250 g / 9 oz / 1 ⅔ cups self-raising flour, plus extra for dusting
½ tsp mustard powder
150 ml / 5 ½ fl. oz / ⅔ cup milk, plus extra for brushing
3 tbsp poppy seeds

Bacon and Sesame Seed Scones

66

- Add 1 tbsp sesame oil to the milk and top the scones with sesame seeds instead of poppy seeds.

67

SERVES 8

Cold Roast Beef with Vinaigrette

PREPARATION TIME 15 MINUTES

COOKING TIME 45 MINUTES

INGREDIENTS

2 tbsp olive oil
1 kg / 2 lb 3 oz topside of beef
radicchio to serve

FOR THE VINAIGRETTE:
½ shallot, finely chopped
2 tbsp white wine vinegar
1 tsp Dijon mustard
1 tsp runny honey
4 tbsp olive oil
2 gherkins, finely chopped
1 tbsp flat leaf parsley, finely chopped
1 tbsp French tarragon, finely chopped

- Preheat the oven to 200°C (180° fan) / 400F / gas 6.
- Heat the oil in a large oven-proof frying pan. Season the beef well with salt and pepper then sear it on all sides.
- Transfer the pan to the oven and roast for 45 minutes.
- Leave the beef to cool completely before carving into thin slices.
- To make the vinaigrette, put the shallot, vinegar, mustard and honey in a jam jar with a big pinch of salt and stir well to dissolve the salt.
- Add the oil, put a lid on the jar and shake well to emulsify. Stir in the gherkins and herbs and season to taste with black pepper.
- Spoon the vinaigrette over the beef and serve with radicchio leaves.

68

MAKES 4

Mini Vegetable Quiches

PREPARATION TIME 1 HOUR

COOKING TIME 35-40 MINUTES

INGREDIENTS

2 tbsp olive oil
1 small onion, finely chopped
1 large carrot, diced
1 courgette (zucchini), diced
3 large eggs
225 ml / 8 fl. oz / ¾ cup double (heavy) cream

FOR THE PASTRY:
100 g / 3 ½ oz / ½ cup butter, cubed
200 g / 7 oz / 1 ⅓ cups plain (all purpose) flour
1 large egg, beaten

- To make the pastry, rub the butter into the flour until the mixture resembles fine breadcrumbs.
- Stir in enough cold water to bring the pastry together into a pliable dough and chill for 30 minutes.
- Preheat the oven to 190°C (170° fan) / 375F / gas 5.
- Roll out the pastry on a floured surface and use it to line 4 individual tart cases.
- Prick the pastry with a fork, line with greaseproof baking paper and fill with baking beans or rice.
- Bake the cases for 10 minutes then remove the paper and baking beans.
- Meanwhile, heat the oil in a frying pan and fry the onion, carrot and courgette for 5 minutes or until softened.
- Gently whisk the eggs with the cream until smoothly combined then stir in the vegetables and season generously with salt and pepper.
- Pour the filling into the pastry cases, then lower the oven temperature to 150°C (130° fan) / 300F / gas 2 and bake for 20 minutes or until just set in the centre.

Ravioli with Nettle Pesto

- Cook the ravioli in boiling salted water according to the packet instructions or until al dente.
- Meanwhile, blanch the nettles in boiling water for 10 seconds then drain well and squeeze out all the liquid.
- Put them in a blender with the garlic, lemon zest and oil and add a good pinch of salt and pepper, then blend to a smooth sauce.
- Drain the ravioli and split between 4 warm bowls. Spoon over the nettle pesto and top with the Ricotta.

PREPARATION TIME 5 MINUTES

COOKING TIME 5 MINUTES

INGREDIENTS

450 g / 1 lb fresh ravioli
30 g / 1 oz / 2 cups stinging nettles
1 clove of garlic, crushed
1 lemon, zest finely grated
4 tbsp olive oil
100 g / 3 ½ oz Ricotta Salata, crumbled

Ham and Goats' Cheese Tart

70

SERVES 4

PREPARATION TIME 10 MINUTES

COOKING TIME 25 MINUTES

INGREDIENTS

250 g / 9 oz all-butter puff pastry
7 slices goats' cheese log
8 thin slices honey roast ham
a small sprig of rosemary

- Preheat the oven to 220°C (200° fan) / 425F / gas 7.
- Roll out the pastry on a floured surface and cut out a circle.
- Transfer the pastry to a baking tray and arrange 6 of the goats' cheese slices on top.
- Lay the ham on top and finish with the final slice of cheese then garnish with the rosemary.
- Bake the tart for 25 minutes or until the pastry is golden brown and cooked through.

Cherry Tomato and Feta Tarts

71

MAKES 4

PREPARATION TIME 10 MINUTES

COOKING TIME 15 MINUTES

1 tbsp basil leaves, finely chopped
2 tbsp olive oil

INGREDIENTS

250 g / 9 oz all-butter puff pastry
100 g / 3 ½ oz Feta, cubed
150 g / 5 ½ oz cherry tomatoes, halved

- Preheat the oven to 220°C (200° fan) / 425F / gas 7.
- Roll out the pastry on a floured surface and cut out 4 circles.
- Transfer the pastry to a baking tray and arrange the Feta and tomatoes on top.
- Mix the basil with the oil and a pinch of salt and pepper and drizzle it over the tarts.
- Bake for 15 minutes or until the pastry is cooked through.

SERVES 6

Deep-Fried Camembert

PREPARATION TIME 10 MINUTES

COOKING TIME 4-5 MINUTES

INGREDIENTS

4 tbsp plain (all purpose) flour
1 egg, beaten
75 g / 2 ½ oz / ½ cup panko breadcrumbs
2 camembert, cut into large wedges
sunflower oil for deep-frying
grape and walnut relish to serve

- Put the flour, egg and panko breadcrumbs in 3 separate bowls.
- Dip the camembert wedges alternately in the flour, egg and breadcrumbs and shake off any excess.
- Heat the oil in a deep fat fryer, according to the manufacturer's instructions, to a temperature of 180°C.
- Lower the camembert in the fryer basket and cook for 4 – 5 minutes or until crisp and golden brown.
- Tip the camembert into a kitchen paper lined bowl to remove any excess oil and serve immediately with the grape and walnut relish.

Grape and Walnut Relish 73

- Cut 100 g grapes into quarters and macerate for 1 hour in 3 tbsp runny honey and 3 tbsp white wine vinegar. Drain and toss with 30 g of walnut pieces.

MAKES 12

Cheese Scones with Cottage Cheese

PREPARATION TIME 30 MINUTES

COOKING TIME 12 - 15 MINUTES

INGREDIENTS

75 g / 2 ½ oz / ⅓ cup butter, cubed
250 g / 9 oz / 1 ⅔ cups self-raising flour, plus extra for dusting
½ tsp mustard powder
¼ tsp cayenne pepper
150 ml / 5 ½ fl. oz / ⅔ cup milk, plus extra for brushing
100 g / 3 ½ oz / 1 cup Red Leicester cheese, grated
200 g / 7 oz / 1 cup cottage cheese
2 spring onions, thinly sliced

- Preheat the oven to 220°C (200° fan) / 425F / gas 7 and line a baking tray with greaseproof paper.
- Rub the butter into the flour with your fingertips until the mixture resembles fine breadcrumbs then stir in the mustard powder and cayenne pepper.
- Add the milk and ¾ of the Red Leicester and mix together into a pliable dough.
- Turn the dough out onto a floured work surface and flatten it into a rectangle, 2 cm / 1 " thick.
- Use a round pastry cutter to stamp out the scones then transfer them to the baking tray.
- Brush the scones with milk, sprinkle with the rest of the Red Leicester and bake for 12 – 15 minutes.
- Transfer the scones to a wire rack to cool a little before splitting in half.
- Mix the cottage cheese with the spring onions and season, then spoon the mixture onto the scones.

Cheese Scones with Gorgonzola 75

- Top the finished scones with soft Gorgonzola.

76

SERVES 6

Lamb with Braised Red Cabbage

- Preheat the oven to 180°C (160° fan) / 350F / gas 4.
- Heat the oil in a cast iron casserole dish and fry the onion and garlic for 5 minutes.
- Add the cabbage and a sprinkle of salt and pepper and sauté for 5 minutes.
- Add the pears then pour in the wine and port and bring to a simmer.
- Cover the dish and transfer to the oven to cook for 1 hour.
- Towards the end of the cooking time, season the lamb liberally with salt and pepper.
- Heat the oil in an oven-proof frying pan and sear the lamb on both sides. Transfer the pan to the oven and roast for 5 minutes.
- Serve 2 medallions per person with the red cabbage on the side. Garnish with coriander leaves.

PREPARATION TIME 5 MINUTES

COOKING TIME 1 HOUR 15 MINUTES

INGREDIENTS

1 lamb loin, cut into 12 medallions
2 tbsp olive oil
coriander (cilantro) leaves to garnish

FOR THE CABBAGE:
2 tbsp olive oil
1 red onion, sliced
2 cloves of garlic, crushed
½ red cabbage, sliced
2 pears, peeled and sliced
100 ml / 3 ½ fl. oz / ½ cup port
100 ml / 3 ½ fl. oz / ½ cup red wine

Braised Red Cabbage with Orange | 77

- Replace the port with orange juice and add a segmented orange to the pot 10 minutes before the end of the cooking time instead of the pears.

78

SERVES 6

Lamb and Date Meatloaf

- Preheat the oven to 190°C (170° fan) / 375F / gas 5.
- Heat the oil in a frying pan and fry the onion for 5 minutes or until softened.
- Add the garlic and cook for 2 more minutes, stirring constantly, then transfer to a large mixing bowl.
- Add the mince, sausagemeat, breadcrumbs, dates and egg yolk and mix it all together.
- Season with salt and pepper then pack the mixture into a loaf tin or baking dish.
- Transfer the dish to the oven and bake for 45 minutes or until cooked through and golden brown.
- Sprinkle with smoked paprika before slicing and serving.

PREPARATION TIME 15 MINUTES

COOKING TIME 45 MINUTES

INGREDIENTS

2 tbsp olive oil
1 onion, finely chopped
1 clove of garlic, crushed
250 g / 9 oz / 1 cup minced lamb
250 g / 9 oz / 1 cup lamb and mint sausages, skinned
50 g / 1 ¾ oz / ⅔ cup fresh white breadcrumbs
100 g / 3 ½ oz medjool dates, stoned
1 egg yolk
½ tsp smoked paprika

Spiced Lamb and Apricot Meatloaf | 79

- Replace the lamb and mint sausages with merguez and use dried apricots instead of the dates.

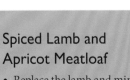

80

SERVES 4

Sardine and Egg Panini

PREPARATION TIME 5 MINUTES

COOKING TIME 3 MINUTES

....

INGREDIENTS

120 g / 4 oz canned sardines in oil
2 large ciabatta rolls, halved
2 boiled eggs, sliced
rocket (arugula) to serve

- Put an electric panini press on to heat.
- Mash the sardines into their oil with a fork and spread them over the bottom halves of the rolls.
- Top with the boiled egg slices, season with salt and pepper, then sandwich together with the top of the rolls.
- Toast the panini for 3 minutes or according to the manufacturer's instructions.
- Cut the panini into 4 pieces each and serve 2 pieces per person with some rocket on the side.

Sardine and Mozzarella Panini 81

- Replace the boiled egg with a sliced mozzarella ball.

82

SERVES 4

Roast Beef Toasted Sandwich

PREPARATION TIME 5 MINUTES

COOKING TIME 3 MINUTES

....

INGREDIENTS

8 slices white bread
4 tbsp mayonnaise
1 tsp Dijon mustard
1 tsp wholegrain mustard
8 slices rare roast beef
4 tbsp French tarragon leaves

- Toast the bread in a toaster or under a hot grill.
- Mix the mayonnaise with the mustards and season with a little black pepper.
- Spread the mustard mayonnaise over the toast and top 4 of the slices with the beef.
- Scatter over the tarragon leaves, then sandwich with the rest of the toast and cut in half on the diagonal.

Roast Pork Toasted Sandwich 83

- Replace the beef with slices of cold roast pork and use chopped chives instead of the tarragon.

84

MAKES 4

Smoked Salmon and Cucumber Bagels

Pastrami and Cucumber Bagels

85

- Replace the smoked salmon with thin slices of pastrami.

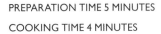

Turkey and Cranberry Bagels

86

- Replace the salmon, cucumber and lemon juice with 8 slices of turkey and a spoonful of cranberry sauce for each bagel.

PREPARATION TIME 5 MINUTES

COOKING TIME 4 MINUTES

INGREDIENTS

4 sesame bagels
125 g / 4 ½ oz / ½ cup cream cheese
2 tbsp fresh dill, finely chopped
½ lemon, juiced
½ cucumber, thinly sliced
8 slices smoked salmon

- Heat a griddle pan until smoking hot. Slice the bagels in half and toast them on the griddle for 2 minutes on each side or until nicely marked.
- Mix the cream cheese with the dill and lemon juice and season to taste with salt and pepper.
- Spread the bottom half of the bagels with the cream cheese mixture and arrange the cucumber slices and salmon on top.
- Position the other half of the bagels on top and serve while the bread is still a little warm from the griddle.

87

SERVES 6-8

Red Onion Savoury Cheesecake

Onion and Pear Savoury Cheesecake

88

- Add 2 chopped poached pears to the cream cheese mixture.

Red Onion and Cashew Cheesecake

89

- Replace the pistachios with 50g finely chopped cashew nuts.

PREPARATION TIME 25 MINUTES

COOKING TIME 40 – 50 MINUTES

INGREDIENTS

200 g / 7 oz all-butter puff pastry
3 tbsp olive oil
3 red onions, halved and sliced
450 g / 1 lb / 2 cups cream cheese
100 g / 3 ½ oz soft blue cheese, cubed
50 g / 1 ¾ oz / ½ cup pistachio nuts, chopped

- Preheat the oven to 220°C (200° fan) / 425F / gas 7 and grease a baking tray.
- Roll out the pastry on a lightly floured surface. Invert a large loaf tin on top of the pastry and cut round it, then transfer the pastry to the baking tray and prick with a fork.
- Bake the pastry for 15 minutes or until golden brown and cooked through. Leave to cool.
- Heat the oil in a large sauté pan and fry the onions over a gentle heat for 20 minutes, stirring occasionally.
- Line the loaf tin with clingfilm then spoon in the onions and level the top.
- Beat the cream cheese with the blue cheese and half of the pistachio nuts and spread it over the onions, then scatter over the rest of the pistachios.
- Put the pastry on top, press down firmly and cover with clingfilm, then chill in the fridge for 3 hours before unmoulding and slicing.

90

MAKES 18

Ham and Pineapple Toasted Sandwich

- Heat a large griddle pan until smoking hot.
- Spread the bread with butter then top 4 of the slices with the ham and pineapple.
- Top with the remaining bread slices, then transfer to the griddle pan.
- Leave the sandwiches to toast for 2 minutes, then give them a 90° turn and toast for another 2 minutes.
- Turn the sandwiches over and repeat on the other side, then serve with a jug of maple syrup for drizzling over.

PREPARATION TIME 5 MINUTES

COOKING TIME 8 MINUTES

INGREDIENTS

8 slices granary bread
4 tbsp butter, softened
8 slices ham
8 canned pineapple rings, drained
maple syrup to serve

Ham and Egg Toasted Sandwich **91**

- Replace the pineapple with a fried egg for each sandwich.

 92

SERVES 4

Tapenade and Taleggio Toasted Sandwich

- Put a panini press on to heat
- Spread 4 slices of the bread thickly with tapenade and top with the Taleggio and pine nuts.
- Top with the remaining bread slices, then toast in the panini press for 3 minutes or according to the manufacturer's instructions.
- Cut the sandwiches in half and serve immediately, garnished with basil.

PREPARATION TIME 5 MINUTES

COOKING TIME 3 MINUTES

INGREDIENTS

8 slices white bread
150 g / 5 ½ oz / ⅔ cup green olive tapenade
150 g / 5 ½ oz Taleggio, sliced
2 tbsp pine nuts, toasted
basil leaves to serve

Pesto and Taleggio Toasted Sandwich **93**

- Replace the tapenade with 4 tbsp of pesto.

94

MAKES 6

Luxury Seafood and Avocado Cocktails

PREPARATION TIME 20 MINUTES

INGREDIENTS

250 g / 9 oz sashimi-grade tuna loin, diced
2 tbsp soy sauce
1 tsp sesame oil
4 avocados, halved and stoned
2 limes, juiced
1 tsp wasabi paste
150 g / 5 ½ oz cooked crayfish tails, peeled
150 g / 5 ½ oz / ¾ cup white crabmeat
18 king prawns
250 g / 9 oz / 1 cup good quality mayonnaise
2 tbsp fresh dill, chopped, plus a few sprigs to garnish
Cayenne pepper for sprinkling

- Toss the tuna with the soy and sesame oil then divide between 6 glasses.
- Scrape the avocado flesh out of the skins and put it in a food processor with the lime juice and wasabi paste. Blend to a smooth puree and add salt to taste.
- Spoon the avocado mixture on top of the tuna and top with the crayfish tails and crabmeat.
- Arrange 3 king prawns on top of each cocktail, then pipe or spoon some mayonnaise on top.
- Sprinkle with dill and Cayenne pepper and garnish with some extra sprigs of dill.

Salmon and Crab Cocktails **95**

- Replace the tuna with sashimi-grade salmon. Omit the crayfish tails and prawns and double the amount of crabmeat. Top each one with 1 tsp of salmon roe.

96

SERVES 4

Onion Waffles with Smoked Salmon

PREPARATION TIME 10 MINUTES

COOKING TIME 25 MINUTES

INGREDIENTS

2 tbsp olive oil
1 red onion, finely chopped
250 g / 9 oz / 1 ⅔ cups plain (all purpose)flour
2 tsp baking powder
2 large eggs
300 ml / 10 ½ fl. oz / 1 ¼ cups milk
2 tbsp melted butter
sunflower oil for oiling the waffle maker
4 slices smoked salmon
a small bunch of chives

- Put the oven on a low setting and put an electric waffle maker on to heat.
- Heat the oil in a frying pan and fry the onion for 5 minutes or until softened then season with salt and black pepper.
- Mix the flour and baking powder in a bowl and make a well in the centre.
- Break in the eggs and pour in the milk and fried onions then use a whisk to gradually incorporate all of the flour from round the outside, followed by the melted butter.
- Spoon some of the batter into the waffle maker and close the lid. Cook for 4 minutes or according to the manufacturer's instructions until golden brown.
- Repeat until all the batter has been used, keeping the finished batches warm in the oven.
- Serve the waffles with the smoked salmon and chives.

Onion Waffles with Roast Beef **97**

- Serve the waffles with thinly sliced rare roast beef and horseradish sauce.

SERVES 4

Ham and Cheese Toasted Sandwich

- Put a sandwich toaster on to heat.
- Butter the bread and top 4 of the slices with the ham and Emmental.
- Top with the other slices of bread, then transfer to the sandwich toaster and toast for 3 minutes or according to the manufacturer's instructions.
- Cut in half on the diagonal and serve.

PREPARATION TIME 5 MINUTES

COOKING TIME 3 MINUTES

INGREDIENTS

8 slices wholemeal bread
4 tbsp butter, softened
8 slices cooked ham
200 g / 7 oz Emmental, sliced

Cheese and Tomato Toasted Sandwich

99

- Replace the ham with 4 thickly sliced tomatoes.

SERVES 4

Scrambled Eggs with Rocket

- Gently beat the eggs with a pinch of salt and pepper to break up the yolks.
- Heat the butter in a non-stick frying pan until sizzling then pour in the eggs.
- Cook over a low heat, stirring constantly until the eggs scramble.
- Stir in half of the rocket and divide the mixture between the halved muffins.
- Serve with extra rocket leaves on the side and a sprinkle of black pepper.

PREPARATION TIME 2 MINUTES

COOKING TIME 5 MINUTES

INGREDIENTS

8 large eggs
2 tbsp butter
50 g / 1 ¾ oz rocket leaves
4 English breakfast muffins, halved

Scrambled Eggs with Watercress

101

- Use 50 g of fresh watercress in place of the rocket leaves.

102

MAKES 4

Cream Cheese and Salad Rolls

PREPARATION TIME 5 MINUTES

INGREDIENTS

4 oat-topped wholemeal rolls, halved
125 g / 4 ½ oz / ½ cup cream cheese
1 medium tomato, sliced
½ cucumber, sliced
4 lettuce leaves

- Spread the bottom half of the rolls thickly with cream cheese and arrange the tomato, cucumber and lettuce on top.
- Sandwich with the other half of the rolls and serve immediately.

Ham, Brie and Rocket Rolls

 103

- Fill 4 seeded rolls with rocket, sliced brie and wafer-thin ham.

104

SERVES 6

Warm Potato and Bean Salad

PREPARATION TIME 10 MINUTES

COOKING TIME 55 MINUTES

INGREDIENTS

800 g / 1 lb 12 oz new potatoes, halved
4 tbsp olive oil
300 g / 10 ½ oz green (string) beans
slices of cold roast beef to serve

FOR THE DRESSING:
1 tbsp balsamic vinegar
1 tbsp lemon juice
1 tsp runny honey
1 tsp Dijon mustard
4 tbsp olive oil

- Preheat the oven to 200°C (180° fan) / 400F / gas 6.
- Boil the potatoes in salted water for 10 minutes then drain well and leave to steam dry for 2 minutes.
- Put the oil in a large roasting tin in the oven to heat for 2 minutes.
- Add the potatoes to the roasting tin and stir to coat in the oil.
- Season well with salt and pepper then roast for 45 minutes.
- Meanwhile, cook the beans in boiling salted water for 4 minutes then drain well.
- Put all of the dressing ingredients in a jam jar with a pinch of salt and pepper then shake vigorously to emulsify.
- When the potatoes are ready, toss them with the beans and enough dressing to lightly coat.

Warm Potato and Broccoli Salad

 105

- Replace the green beans with 350 g of purple sprouting broccoli.

106
SERVES 4

Walnut and Cinnamon French Toast

Cinnamon Poached Pears

107

- Put 4 chopped pears in a saucepan with 2 cinnamon sticks and enough apple juice to just cover them. Simmer gently for 8 minutes then drain well.

Cinnamon Chocolate French Toast

108

- Drizzle the French toast with melted chocolate before sprinkling with cinnamon and sugar.

PREPARATION TIME 4 MINUTES

COOKING TIME 4 MINUTES

INGREDIENTS

2 large eggs
75 ml / 7 ½ fl. oz / ⅓ cup milk
2 tbsp butter
4 walnut rolls, sliced into 3 horizontally
2 tbsp icing (confectioners') sugar
1 tsp ground cinnamon
cinnamon poached pears to serve

- Lightly beat the eggs with the milk in a wide, shallow dish and heat the butter in a large frying pan until sizzling.
- Dip the bread roll slices in the egg mixture on both sides until evenly coated then fry them in the butter for 2 minutes on each side or until golden brown.
- Mix the sugar with the cinnamon and sprinkle liberally over the French toast then serve with the cinnamon poached pears.

109

SERVES 4

Homemade Crisps

Lemon and Mustard Mayonnaise

110

- Stir 2 tbsp lemon juice and 2 tsp Dijon mustard into 150 g of mayonnaise and serve with the crisps.

Smoked Paprika Crisps

111

- Sprinkle some smoked paprika over the crisps as soon as you remove them from the pan, then sprinkle some sea salt over before serving.

PREPARATION TIME 35 MINUTES

COOKING TIME 7 MINUTES

INGREDIENTS

600 g / 1 lb 5 ½ oz Maris Piper potatoes
2 - 3 litres / 3 ½ pints – 5 pints sunflower oil
lemon and mustard mayonnaise for dipping
sea salt for sprinkling

- Cut the potatoes into very thin slices with a mandolin or sharp knife.
- Put the slices in a bowl of cold water and leave them to soak for 25 minutes to remove some of the starch.
- Drain the potatoes and dry them completely with a clean tea towel.
- Heat the oil in a deep fat fryer, according to the manufacturer's instructions, to a temperature of 130°C.
- Lower the potatoes in the fryer basket and cook for 5 minutes so that they cook all the way through but don't brown. You may need to do this in batches so that the fryer isn't overcrowded.
- Pull up the fryer basket and increase the temperature to 190°C.
- Cook the crisps at the hotter temperature for 1 - 2 minutes or until crisp and golden brown.
- Line a large bowl with a thick layer of kitchen paper and when the crisps are ready, tip them into the bowl to remove any excess oil.
- Leave to cool then sprinkle with sea salt flakes and serve with lemon and mustard mayonnaise for dipping.

MAKES 12

Leek and Cheese Muffins

- Preheat the oven to 180°C (160° fan) / 350F / gas 4 and oil 12 ramekin dishes.
- Fry the leeks in the butter for 5 minutes or until soft.
- Beat the egg in a jug with the oil, yoghurt, Parmesan and fried leeks until well mixed.
- Mix the flour, raising agents and salt in a bowl, then pour in the egg mixture and stir just enough to combine.
- Divide the mixture between the dishes and sprinkle with Emmental, then bake in the oven for 20 – 25 minutes.
- Test with a wooden toothpick, if it comes out clean, the muffins are done.
- Serve warm.

PREPARATION TIME 10 MINUTES

COOKING TIME 20 – 25 MINUTES

INGREDIENTS

2 leeks, sliced
2 tbsp butter
2 large eggs
120 ml / 4 fl. oz / ½ cup sunflower oil
180 ml / 6 fl. oz / ¾ cup Greek yoghurt
110 g / 4 oz / 1 cup Parmesan, grated
225 g / 8 oz / 1 ½ cups plain (all purpose) flour
2 tsp baking powder
½ tsp bicarbonate of (baking) soda
½ tsp salt
50 g / 1 ¾ oz / ½ cup Emmental, grated

Cauliflower Cheese Muffins

113

- Replace the leeks with 100 g of diced cauliflower.

SERVES 4

Creamy Mushroom Soup

- Heat the oil and butter in a saucepan and fry the onion for 5 minutes or until softened.
- Add the garlic and mushrooms to the pan and cook for 5 more minutes, then stir in the vegetable stock and bring to the boil.
- Simmer for 15 minutes then stir in the double cream and nutmeg.
- Blend the soup until smooth with a liquidiser or emersion blender then try the soup and adjust the seasoning with salt and pepper.
- Ladle into warm bowls and sprinkle with parsley.

PREPARATION TIME 5 MINUTES

COOKING TIME 30 MINUTES

INGREDIENTS

2 tbsp olive oil
2 tbsp butter
1 onion, finely chopped
2 cloves of garlic, crushed
400 g / 14 oz portabella mushrooms, chopped
1 litre / 1 pint 15 fl. oz / 4 cups vegetable stock
100 ml / 3 ½ fl. oz / ½ cup double (heavy) cream
¼ tsp freshly ground nutmeg
shredded flat leaf parsley to garnish

Creamy Mushroom and Thyme Soup

115

- Add 1 tbsp of fresh thyme leaves to the onions when they're frying.

39

116

SERVES 6

Spicy Lamb Samosas

PREPARATION TIME 20 MINUTES

COOKING TIME 35 MINUTES

....

INGREDIENTS

2 tbsp olive oil
1 small onion, finely chopped
2 cloves of garlic, crushed
250 g / 9 oz / 1 cup minced lamb
¼ tsp chilli (chili) powder
½ tsp ground cumin
½ tsp ground coriander
¼ tsp ground cinnamon
50 g / 1 ¾ oz / ⅓ cup frozen peas, defrosted
225 g / 8 oz filo pastry
100 g / 3 ½ oz / ½ cup butter, melted

- Preheat the oven to 180°C (160° fan) / 350F / gas 4 and grease a large baking tray.
- Heat the oil in a frying pan and fry the onion for 5 minutes or until softened.
- Add the garlic and minced lamb and cook for 5 more minutes then add the spices and peas. Turn off the heat and leave to cool for a few minutes.
- Cut the pile of filo sheets in half then take one halved sheet and brush it with melted butter.
- Arrange a tablespoon of the filling at one end and fold the corner over, then triangle-fold it up.
- Transfer the samosa to the baking tray and repeat with the rest of the filo and filling, then brush with any leftover butter.
- Bake the samosas for 20 minutes, turning half way through, until the pastry is crisp and golden brown.

Spiced Potato Samosas 117

- For a vegetarian alternative, replace the minced lamb with 250 g of leftover mashed potato.

118

SERVES 6

Cheese and Ham Croquettes

PREPARATION TIME 20 MINUTES

COOKING TIME 4 - 5 MINUTES

....

INGREDIENTS

4 tbsp plain (all purpose) flour
1 egg, beaten
75 g / 2 ½ oz / ½ cup panko breadcrumbs
450 g / 1 lb / 2 cups leftover mashed potato
100 g / 3 ½ oz / 1 cup Cheddar, grated
100 g / 3 ½ oz cooked ham, finely chopped
sunflower oil for deep-frying
grated carrot salad to serve

- Put the flour, egg and panko breadcrumbs in 3 separate bowls.
- Mix the mashed potato with the cheese and ham then shape it into 12 parcels.
- Dip the croquettes alternately in the flour, egg and breadcrumbs and shake off any excess.
- Heat the oil in a deep fat fryer, according to the manufacturer's instructions, to a temperature of 180°C.
- Lower the croquettes in the fryer basket and cook for 4 – 5 minutes or until crisp and golden brown.
- Tip the croquettes into a kitchen paper lined bowl to remove any excess oil.
- Serve hot with the grated carrot salad on the side.

Grated Carrot Salad 119

- Mix 2 tbsp lemon juice with 2 tsp runny honey and a pinch of salt. Toss with 3 grated carrots and leave to marinate for 10 minutes.

120

MAKES 16

Carrot, Mint and Cumin Soup

- Heat the oil and butter in a saucepan and fry the onion for 8 minutes or until softened.
- Add the garlic, carrots and cumin to the pan and cook for 2 more minutes, then stir in the vegetable stock and bring to the boil.
- Simmer for 20 minutes or until the carrots are tender. Remove a large spoonful of carrots from the pan with a slotted spoon and reserve for garnish, then blend the rest until smooth with a liquidiser or emersion blender.
- Taste the soup and adjust the seasoning with salt and pepper, then stir in half of the mint and divide between 4 warm bowls.
- Top with the reserved carrots, the rest of the mint and a final sprinkle of cumin.

PREPARATION TIME 5 MINUTES

COOKING TIME 30 MINUTES

....

INGREDIENTS

2 tbsp olive oil
2 tbsp butter
1 onion, finely chopped
2 garlic cloves, crushed
4 carrots, julienned
½ tsp ground cumin, plus extra to sprinkle
1 litre / 1 pint 15 fl. oz / 4 cups vegetable stock
2 tbsp mint leaves, finely chopped

Parsnip, Sage and Cumin Soup

 121

- Replace the carrots with parsnips and increase the cooking time to 25 minutes. Use fresh sage leaves in place of the mint.

122

MAKES 8

Pepper, Pancetta and Tomato Flatbreads

- In a large bowl, mix together the flour, yeast, sugar, herbs and salt. Stir the oil into 280 ml of warm water.
- Stir the liquid into the dry ingredients then knead on a lightly oiled surface for 10 minutes or until smooth and elastic.
- Leave the dough to rest covered with oiled clingfilm for 1 – 2 hours or until doubled in size.
- Preheat the oven to 220⁰C (200 fan) / 425F/ gas 7 and grease 2 large non-stick baking trays.
- Knead the dough for 2 more minutes then divide into 8 pieces.
- Roll each piece of dough into a thin flatbread and transfer to the baking trays.
- Top the flatbreads with the peppers and pancetta and add a cherry tomato and rosemary sprig to each one.
- Transfer the tray to the oven and bake for 8 - 10 minutes or until each bread is cooked through underneath.

PREPARATION TIME 2 HOURS 30 MINUTES

COOKING TIME 8 – 10 MINUTES

....

INGREDIENTS

400 g / 14 oz / 2 ⅔ cups strong white bread flour, plus extra for dusting
½ tsp easy blend dried yeast
2 tsp caster (superfine) sugar
1 tsp dried herbs de Provence
½ tsp fine sea salt
1 tbsp olive oil
250 g / 9 oz roasted peppers in oil, drained
100 g / 3 ½ oz pancetta, finely chopped
8 cherry tomatoes
8 small sprigs of flowering rosemary

Artichoke and Pancetta Flatbreads

123

- Omit the peppers and tomatoes and add half a preserved baby artichoke in oil to each flatbread after topping with the pancetta.

124

SERVES 4

Tomato and Thyme Soup

PREPARATION TIME 5 MINUTES

COOKING TIME 30 MINUTES

INGREDIENTS

2 tbsp olive oil
1 onion, finely chopped
4 cloves of garlic, crushed
2 tbsp thyme leaves
450 g / 1 lb ripe tomatoes, diced
500 ml / 17 ½ fl. oz / 2 cups
vegetable stock

- Heat the oil in a saucepan and fry the onion for 8 minutes or until softened.
- Add the garlic and half of the thyme to the pan and cook for 2 more minutes, then stir in the tomatoes and vegetable stock and bring to the boil.
- Simmer for 20 minutes then blend until smooth with a liquidiser or emersion blender.
- Taste the soup and adjust the seasoning with salt and pepper, then ladle into bowls and sprinkle with the rest of the thyme.

Tomato and Bacon Soup

125

- Replace the vegetable stock with ham stock and fry 4 chopped rashers of streaky bacon until crisp to garnish.

126

SERVES 4

Creamy Pea Soup

PREPARATION TIME 5 MINUTES

COOKING TIME 15 MINUTES

INGREDIENTS

2 tbsp olive oil
2 tbsp butter
1 onion, finely chopped
2 garlic cloves, crushed
400 g / 14 oz peas, defrosted if frozen
1 litre / 1 pint 15 fl. oz / 4 cups
vegetable stock
100 ml / 3 ½ fl. oz / ½ cup
double (heavy) cream
1 tbsp mint leaves, finely chopped

- Heat the oil and butter in a saucepan and fry the onion for 5 minutes or until softened.
- Add the garlic and peas to the pan and cook for 2 more minutes, then stir in the vegetable stock and bring to the boil.
- Simmer for 5 minutes then stir in the double cream and mint.
- Blend the soup until smooth with a liquidiser or emersion blender then try the soup and adjust the seasoning with salt and pepper.
- Ladle into warm bowls and sprinkle with black pepper.

Pea and Ham Soup
127

- Use ham stock instead of vegetable stock and stir in 100 g of finely cubed cooked ham after blending.

MAKES 16

128

Leek and Parmesan Choux Buns

Chorizo and Parmesan Choux Buns

129

- Replace the leek with 75 g of very finely chopped chorizo.

Red Onion and Parmesan Choux Buns

130

- Replace the leek with a small red onion finely sliced and chopped.

PREPARATION TIME 20 MINUTES

COOKING TIME 25 MINUTES

INGREDIENTS

1 small leek, trimmed and chopped
2 tbsp olive oil
55 g / 2 oz / ¼ cup butter, cubed
75 g / 2 ½ oz / ½ cup strong white bread flour, sieved
2 large eggs, beaten
50 g / 1 ¾ oz / ½ cup Parmesan, finely grated

- Preheat the oven to 200°C (180° fan) / 400F / gas 6.
- Fry the leeks in the oil for 6 minutes to soften.
- Oil and line a large baking tray with greaseproof paper, then spray it with a little water.
- Put the butter in a saucepan with 150 ml water and heat until the butter melts and the water starts to boil.
- Turn off the heat and immediately beat in the flour with a wooden spoon until it forms a smooth ball of pastry.
- Stir in the egg a little at a time until you have a glossy paste then beat in the Parmesan and leeks.
- Spoon the pastry into a piping bag fitted with a large star nozzle and pipe 2.5 cm / 1" buns onto the baking tray.
- Bake for 10 minutes, then increase the heat to 220°C (200° fan) / 425F / gas 7 and bake for another 10 minutes.
- Transfer the choux buns to a wire rack and make a small hole in the underneath of each one with a skewer so the steam can escape.

131

MAKES 16

Crab Cakes

Coriander and Lime Crab Cakes

132

- Add 2 tbsp of chopped coriander and the juice of 1 lime to the mixture before making the patties.

Chilli Crab Cakes

133

- Add 1 finely chopped deseeded red chilli and 1 finely chopped and deseeded green chilli for a spicy alternative.

PREPARATION TIME 20 MINUTES

COOKING TIME 4 - 5 MINUTES

....

INGREDIENTS

4 tbsp plain (all purpose) flour
1 egg, beaten
75 g / 2 ½ oz / ½ cup panko breadcrumbs
450 g / 1 lb / 2 cups leftover mashed potato
200 g / 7 oz / 1 1/4 cup fresh crab meat
2 spring onions, finely chopped
2 tbsp fresh dill, finely chopped
sunflower oil for deep-frying

- Put the flour, egg and panko breadcrumbs in 3 separate bowls.
- Mix the mashed potato with the crab, spring onions and dill then shape it into 16 small patties.
- Dip the crab cakes alternately in the flour, egg and breadcrumbs and shake off any excess.
- Heat the oil in a deep fat fryer, according to the manufacturer's instructions, to a temperature of 180⁰C.
- Lower the crab cakes in the fryer basket and cook for 4 – 5 minutes or until crisp and golden brown.
- Tip the crab cakes into a kitchen paper lined bowl to remove any excess oil.

134

MAKES 6

Poppy Seed Sausage Rolls

- Preheat the oven to 230°C (210° fan) / 450F / gas 8.
- Mix the sausagemeat with the onion and apple and season with salt and pepper.
- Roll out the pastry on a lightly floured surface into a large rectangle and cut in half lengthways.
- Shape the sausagemeat into 2 long sausages the length of the pastry strips, then fold over the pastry to enclose.
- Seal the edge with beaten egg and score at 1 cm intervals with a sharp knife. Cut each roll into 3 pieces and transfer them to a baking tray.
- Brush the tops with beaten egg and sprinkle with poppy seeds, then bake for 25 minutes or until golden brown and cooked through.

PREPARATION TIME 15 MINUTES

COOKING TIME 25 MINUTES

INGREDIENTS

350 g / 12 oz / 2 cups sausagemeat
1 small onion, grated
1 small apple, grated
500 g / 1 lb 2 oz all-butter puff pastry
1 egg, beaten
1 tbsp poppy seeds

Sesame Seed Sausage Rolls

135

- Add 1 tbsp of sesame oil to the sausagemeat and sprinkle with sesame seeds instead of poppy seeds.

136

MAKES 4

Goats' Cheese and Sultana Toasts

- Preheat the grill to its highest setting.
- Use a pastry cutter to cut each slice of bread into a circle.
- Toast the bread under the grill on one side until golden brown.
- Turn the slices over and toast on the other side until they just start to colour.
- Top each piece with a slice of goats' cheese and sprinkle with thyme, then put them back under the grill until the bread is golden brown and the goats' cheese has just started to melt.
- Drizzle with honey at the table.

PREPARATION TIME 5 MINUTES

COOKING TIME 4 MINUTES

INGREDIENTS

4 slices sultana bread
4 slices white-rinded goat's cheese
2 tsp thyme leaves
1 tbsp runny honey

Goats' Cheese and Walnut Toasts

137

- Use walnut bread instead of the sultana bread and drizzle with balsamic vinegar instead of honey.

138

MAKES 4

Chocolate and Hazelnut Toasted Sandwich

PREPARATION TIME 5 MINUTES

COOKING TIME 8 MINUTES

INGREDIENTS

8 slices white bread
4 tbsp butter, softened
100 g / 3 ½ oz dark chocolate
(minimum 60% cocoa solids),
chopped
50 g / 1 ¾ oz / ½ cup hazelnuts (cob
nuts), chopped

- Heat a large griddle pan until smoking hot.
- Spread the bread with butter then top 4 of the slices with the chocolate and hazelnuts.
- Top with the remaining bread slices, then transfer to the griddle pan.
- Leave the sandwiches to toast for 4 minutes, pressing down with a spatula.
- Turn the sandwiches over and repeat on the other side, then cut in half on the diagonal and serve straight away.

139

SERVES 4

Moroccan Chicken Salad

PREPARATION TIME 10 MINUTES

COOKING TIME 1 HOUR 20 MINUTES

INGREDIENTS

3 tbsp olive oil
1 tbsp ras al hanout spice mix
1.5 kg / 3 lb 5 oz chicken
75 g / 2 ½ oz / ⅓ cup mixed nuts
50 g / 1 ¾ oz / ¼ cup raisins
75 g / 2 ½ oz rocket leaves
2 tbsp argan oil

- Preheat the oven to 200°C (180° fan) / 400F / gas 6.
- Mix the oil with the ras al hanout and rub it all over the chicken, then lay it breast side down in a large roasting tin.
- Transfer the tin to the oven and roast for 30 minutes.
- Turn the chicken breast side up then roast for a further 40 minutes, basting with the juices half way through.
- To test if the chicken is cooked, insert a skewer into the thickest part of the thigh. If the juices run clear with no trace of blood, it is ready.
- Leave the chicken to cool a little and rest for 20 minutes, then joint it and cut into large chunks with a sharp knife.
- Arrange the chicken on a serving plate with the nuts, raisins and rocket leaves, then drizzle over the argan oil.

140

SERVES 4

Croque Monsieur

- Preheat the grill to its highest setting.
- Butter the bread on one side and toast under the grill until golden.
- Spread the untoasted side with mustard then top 4 of the slices with half of the cheese, followed by the ham.
- Top with the other slices of bread, mustard side down, and sprinkle with the rest of the cheese.
- Return the croques to the grill and toast until the cheese inside has melted and the cheese on top is golden brown.
- Cut in half and sprinkle with parsley before serving.

PREPARATION TIME 5 MINUTES

COOKING TIME 3 MINUTES

....

INGREDIENTS

8 slices white bread
4 tbsp butter, softened
3 tbsp Dijon mustard
8 slices cooked ham
250 g / 9 oz / 2 ½ cups Gruyere, grated
1 tbsp parsley, finely chopped

141

MAKES 4

Mini Salmon Pies

PREPARATION TIME 5 MINUTES

COOKING TIME 35 MINUTES

....,....

INGREDIENTS

2 tbsp butter
1 tsp plain (all purpose) flour
250 ml / 9 fl. oz / 1 cup milk
200 g / 7 oz salmon fillet, cubed

2 tbsp chives, chopped
250 g / 9 oz all-butter puff pastry
1 egg, beaten

- Preheat the oven to 200°C (180° fan) / 400F / gas 6.
- Heat the butter in a saucepan then stir in the flour and cook for 30 seconds.
- Gradually incorporate the milk, stirring all the time, then bring to a gentle simmer.
- Stir in the salmon, then season with salt and pepper and divide the mixture between 4 mini casserole dishes.
- Roll out the pastry on a lightly floured surface and cut out 4 circles.
- Top each dish with a pastry lid and press round the edges to seal.
- Brush the tops with beaten egg then bake for 25 – 30 minutes or until the pastry is golden brown and puffy.

142

SERVES 4

Prosciutto Potato Cakes

PREPARATION TIME 40 MINUTES

COOKING TIME 8 MINUTES

....

INGREDIENTS

450 g / 1 lb / 2 cups leftover mashed potato
100 g / 3 ½ oz prosciutto, finely chopped

1 tbsp thyme leaves
4 tbsp olive oil

- Mix the potato with the prosciutto and thyme and season to taste with salt and pepper.
- Divide the mixture into golf ball sized pieces and shape them into patties. Chill for 30 minutes.
- Heat the oil in a frying pan and fry the potato cakes in batches for 4 minutes on each side or until golden brown and cooked through.

143

SERVES 4

Stuffed Onions with Camembert

PREPARATION TIME 10 MINUTES

COOKING TIME 45 MINUTES

INGREDIENTS

8 medium onions, peeled
½ Camembert, cubed
150 g / 5 ½ oz / ¾ cup sundried tomatoes in oil, drained & chopped
2 tbsp oregano leaves

- Preheat the oven to 200°C (180° fan) / 400F / gas 6.
- Simmer the onions in salted water for 10 minutes, then scoop out the centres with a teaspoon and arrange on a baking tray.
- Mix the Camembert with the sundried tomatoes and oregano leaves and pack the mixture into the cavities.
- Bake the onions for 35 minutes or until they are tender all the way through.

Stuffed Onions with Bacon and Brie

144

- Replace the Camembert with 200 g of cubed brie and use 3 chopped rashers of streaky bacon instead of the sundried tomatoes.

145

SERVES 4

Sweetcorn and Bacon Chowder

PREPARATION TIME 10 MINUTES

COOKING TIME 20 MINUTES

INGREDIENTS

2 tbsp butter
1 onion, finely chopped
6 thick slices smoked streaky bacon
3 sweetcorn cobs
1 large potato, peeled and diced
500 ml / 17 ½ fl. oz / 2 cups ham or chicken stock
500 ml / 17 ½ fl. oz / 2 cups milk
30 g / 1 oz / ½ cup popcorn

- Heat the butter in a saucepan and fry the onion and bacon for 5 minutes.
- Hold the corn cobs vertically on a chopping board and cut down with a sharp knife to release the sweetcorn kernels.
- Add them to the pan with the potato, stock and milk and simmer for 15 minutes.
- Ladle half of the soup into a liquidiser and blend until smooth, then stir it back into the pan.
- Ladle the chowder into warm bowls and top with the popcorn just before serving.

Clam Chowder

146

- Omit the bacon and add a 400 g can of minced clams 2 minutes before the end of the cooking time.

147

SERVES 4

Chunky Vegetable Soup

- Heat the oil in a saucepan and fry the leeks for 5 minutes or until softened.
- Add the garlic and vegetables to the pan and cook for 2 more minutes, then stir in the vegetable stock and bring to the boil.
- Simmer for 10 minutes then season to taste with salt and pepper.
- Ladle the soup into 4 warm bowls and garnish with parsley.

PREPARATION TIME 5 MINUTES

COOKING TIME 20 MINUTES

INGREDIENTS

2 tbsp olive oil
2 leeks, sliced
2 cloves of garlic, crushed
4 spring onions, chopped
2 courgettes, chopped
1 red pepper, sliced
1 orange pepper, chopped
150 g / 5 ½ oz / 1 cup broad beans, defrosted if frozen
1 litre / 1 pint 15 fl. oz / 4 cups vegetable stock
a few sprigs of flat leaf parsley to serve

Chunky Vegetable and Butter Bean Soup

148

- Add 400 g of canned butter beans to the soup when you add the vegetables.

149

SERVES 4

Vegetable Soup

- Heat the oil and butter in a saucepan and fry the leeks for 8 minutes or until softened.
- Add the garlic and the rest of the vegetables to the pan and cook for 2 more minutes, then stir in the vegetable stock and bring to the boil.
- Simmer for 20 minutes then blend in a food processor or liquidiser until smooth.
- Taste the soup for seasoning and add salt and pepper as necessary.
- Ladle the soup into warm bowls and drizzle a spoonful of cream on top of each one.

PREPARATION TIME 5 MINUTES

COOKING TIME 30 MINUTES

INGREDIENTS

2 tbsp olive oil
2 tbsp butter
1 leek, chopped
2 cloves of garlic, crushed
2 carrots, chopped
1 large potato, cubed
2 courgettes, chopped
1 litre / 1 pint 15 fl. oz / 4 cups vegetable stock
4 tbsp double (heavy) cream

Vegetable and Basil Soup

150

- Add a small bunch of chopped basil to the soup just before blending.

151

SERVES 1

Tofu and Parsley Omelette

PREPARATION TIME 1 MINUTES

COOKING TIME 4 MINUTES

INGREDIENTS

3 large eggs
2 tbsp flat leaf parsley
1 tbsp butter
50 g / 1 ¾ oz firm tofu, cubed
½ tsp pink peppercorns, crushed

- Break the eggs into a jug with a pinch of salt and pepper and beat them gently to break up the yolks.
- Stir in the parsley and tofu.
- Heat the butter in a non-stick frying pan until sizzling then pour in the eggs.
- Cook over a medium heat until the eggs start to set around the outside. Use a spatula to draw the sides of the omelette into the centre and tilt the pan to fill the gaps with more liquid egg.
- Repeat the process until the top of the omelette is just set then sprinkle over the pink peppercorns.

Halloumi and Dill Omelette

 152

- Replace the tofu with cubes of Halloumi and use fresh dill instead of the parsley.

153

SERVES 4

Tomato and Mozzarella Sandwiches

PREPARATION TIME 10 MINUTES

COOKING TIME 3 - 4 MINUTES

INGREDIENTS

4 tbsp plain (all purpose) flour
1 egg, beaten
75 g / 2 ½ oz / ½ cup panko
breadcrumbs
8 mozzarella slices
16 tomato slices
sunflower oil for deep-frying
rocket leaves to serve

- Put the flour, egg and panko breadcrumbs in 3 separate bowls.
- Sandwich each slice of mozzarella between 2 slices of tomato.
- Dip the tomato sandwiches alternately in the flour, egg and breadcrumbs and shake off any excess.
- Heat the oil in a deep fat fryer, according to the manufacturer's instructions, to a temperature of 180°C.
- Lower the tomato sandwiches in the fryer basket and cook for 3 – 4 minutes or until crisp and golden brown.
- Tip them into a kitchen paper lined bowl to remove any excess oil and serve immediately with some rocket on the side

Aubergine and Mozzarella Sandwiches

 154

- Sprinkle 16 aubergine slices with salt and leave in a colander for 10 minutes. Remove any excess liquid then use in place of the tomato.

155

MAKES 6

Scotch Eggs

Quick Tomato Sauce 156

- Fry a crushed garlic clove in 2 tbsp olive oil, then stir in 400 g chopped canned tomatoes and simmer for 5 minutes. Season with salt and pepper and stir in 2 tbsp chopped parsley.

Chive and Parmesan Scotch Eggs 157

- Add 2 tbsp of dried chives and 5 tbsp of finely grated parmesan to the breadcrumb mixture.

PREPARATION TIME 30 MINUTES

COOKING TIME 10 MINUTES

INGREDIENTS

7 small eggs
4 good quality pork sausages
4 tbsp plain (all purpose) flour
75 g / 2 ½ oz panko breadcrumbs
2 - 3 litres / 3 ½ pints – 5 pints sunflower oil
quick tomato sauce to serve

- Put 6 of the eggs in a pan of cold water then bring to a simmer and cook for 5 minutes.

- Plunge the eggs into cold water for 2 minutes then peel off the shells.

- Skin the sausages and divide the meat into 6. Flatten a portion of sausage meat onto your hand and put an egg in the centre, then squeeze the meat round the outside to coat. Repeat with the other 5 eggs.

- Put the flour, remaining egg and panko breadcrumbs in 3 separate bowls.

- Dip the scotch eggs first in the flour, then in egg, then in the breadcrumbs.

- Heat the oil in a deep fat fryer, according to the manufacturer's instructions, to a temperature of 180⁰C.

- Lower the scotch eggs in the fryer basket and cook for 4 – 5 minutes or until crisp and golden brown.

- Line a large bowl with a thick layer of kitchen paper and when they are ready, tip them into the bowl to remove any excess oil.

- Serve warm with the tomato sauce spooned over the top.

158

SERVES 4

Ham and Cheese Croissants

PREPARATION TIME 5 MINUTES

COOKING TIME 3 MINUTES

INGREDIENTS

4 croissants
8 slices cooked ham
200 g / 7 oz Emmental, sliced
celeriac and apple remoulade to serve
1 tbsp French tarragon, chopped

- Preheat the oven to 200°C (180° fan) / 400F / gas 6.
- Cut open the croissants and fill them with the ham and cheese.
- Transfer the croissants to a baking tray and bake in the oven for 5 minutes or until the cheese has melted.
- Spoon some celeriac and apple remoulade on top and sprinkle with tarragon.

159

SERVES 6

Homemade Granola with Yoghurt

PREPARATION TIME 5 MINUTES

COOKING TIME 1 HOUR

INGREDIENTS

75 ml / 2 ½ fl. oz / ⅓ cup maple syrup
75 ml / 2 ½ fl. oz / ⅓ cup apple juice
1 tbsp sunflower oil
175 g / 6 oz / 1 ¾ cups rolled porridge oats
50 g / 1 ¾ oz / ½ cup walnuts, chopped
75 g / 2 ½ oz / ⅔ cup pumpkin seeds
50 g / 1 ¾ oz / ½ cup sunflower seeds
2 tbsp golden linseeds
100 g / 3 ½ oz / ½ cup raisins
600 ml / 1 pint / 2 ½ cups live yoghurt

- Preheat the oven to 160°C (140° fan) / 325F / gas 3.
- Stir the maple syrup, apple juice and oil together in a bowl with a pinch of salt then toss it with the oats, walnuts and seeds.
- Spread the mixture out on a large baking tray and bake for 1 hour, stirring every 10 minutes to ensure it all toasts evenly.
- Leave the granola to cool completely, then stir in the raisins.
- Divide the yoghurt between 6 bowls or glasses and crumble over the granola.

160

MAKES 4

Bacon, Pear and Cambozola Rolls

- Preheat the grill to its highest setting then grill the bacon for 2 minutes on each side.
- Divide the Cambozola between the rolls and top with the bacon, followed by the pear slices.
- Arrange some sprouting seeds on top then close the rolls and serve immediately.

PREPARATION TIME 5 MINUTES

COOKING TIME 4 MINUTES

INGREDIENTS

4 seeded rolls, split open
8 rashers of smoked streaky bacon
250 g / 9 oz Cambozola, sliced
1 pear, cored and very thinly sliced
3 tbsp sprouting seeds

Lime and Vanilla Stewed Pineapple

161

MAKES 6

PREPARATION TIME 5 MINUTES

COOKING TIME 10 MINUTES

COOLING TIME 1 HOUR

INGREDIENTS

150 ml / 5 ½ fl. oz / ⅔ cup pineapple juice
1 lime, juiced and zest thinly pared

1 vanilla pod, split lengthways
1 pineapple, peeled, cored and cut into chunks
3 tbsp runny honey
coconut ice cream to serve

- Put all of the ingredients in a saucepan and bring to a gentle simmer.
- Stew the pineapple for 10 minutes, then leave to cool completely.
- Serve with scoops of coconut ice cream.

White Bean Toasts

162

SERVES 4

PREPARATION TIME 10 MINUTES

COOKING TIME 45 MINUTES

INGREDIENTS

8 slices baguette
4 tbsp olive oil
1 clove of garlic, crushed
½ tsp dried rosemary

300 g / 10 ½ oz / 2 cups canned haricot beans, drained
½ lemon, juiced

- Toast the baguette slices in a toaster or under a hot grill.
- Meanwhile, heat the oil in a saucepan and fry the garlic and rosemary for 1 minute.
- Add the beans and heat through for 2 minutes, then roughly crush with the back of a fork.
- Take the pan off the heat and stir in the lemon juice and season to taste with salt and pepper.
- Spread the bean mixture onto the toasts and serve immediately.

TRADITIONAL MAINS

163

SERVES 4

Rabbit Stew

PREPARATION TIME 5 MINUTES

COOKING TIME 1 HOUR
30 MINUTES

....

INGREDIENTS

1 rabbit, jointed
3 tbsp plain (all purpose) flour
1 tsp mustard powder
3 tbsp olive oil
2 tbsp butter
150 g / 5 ½ oz pancetta, cubed
200 g / 7 oz baby onions, peeled
a few sprigs of thyme
350 ml / 12 ½ fl. oz / 1 ½ cups dry
white wine
300 ml / 10 ½ fl. oz / 1 ¼ cups double
(heavy) cream
200 g / 7 oz / 2 ⅔ cups small
chanterelles, cleaned

- Season the rabbit well with salt and pepper, then toss with the flour and mustard powder to coat.
- Heat half of the oil and butter in a casserole dish or saucepan and sear the rabbit pieces on all sides.
- Remove the rabbit from the pan and add the rest of the oil and butter, followed by the pancetta, onions and thyme.
- Sauté for 5 minutes, then pour in the wine and cream and bring to a simmer. Transfer the rabbit back to the pan, then simmer very gently for 1 hour.
- Stir in the chanterelles, season to taste with salt and pepper and cook for a further 15 minutes or until the rabbit is tender.

Rabbit and Prune Stew

164

- Add 100 g of stoned prunes to the stew when you add the chanterelles.

165

SERVES 6

Beef Fillet with Green Peppercorns

PREPARATION TIME 5 MINUTES

COOKING TIME 30 MINUTES

....

INGREDIENTS

1 kg / 2 lb 3 oz fillet of beef
3 tbsp olive oil
300 ml / 10 ½ fl. oz / 1 ¼ cups
white wine
1 tsp Dijon mustard
2 tbsp green peppercorns in brine,
drained
mixed salad leaves and herbs to serve

- Preheat the oven to 230°C (210° fan) / 450F / gas 8 and season the beef well with salt and pepper.
- Heat a large oven-proof frying pan on the hob until smoking hot, then add the olive oil and sear the beef on all sides.
- Transfer the pan to the oven and roast for 20 minutes.
- Move the beef to a warm plate, wrap with a double layer of foil and leave to rest while you make the sauce.
- Put the frying pan back over a high heat and pour in the wine.
- Use a wooden spoon to scrape any meaty bits from the bottom of the pan and allow the sauce to bubble and reduce for 5 minutes.
- Stir in the mustard and green peppercorns and simmer for 2 more minutes, then season to taste with salt and pepper.
- Carve the beef into thick slices and serve with a mixture of salad leaves and herbs with the sauce drizzled over.

Fillet of Venison with
Green Peppercorns

166

- Replace the beef fillet with venison fillet and reduce the roasting time to 18 minutes.

167

SERVES 4

Roast Chicken with New Potatoes

- Preheat the oven to 200°C (180° fan) / 400F / gas 6.
- Boil the potatoes in salted water for 10 minutes then drain well.
- Mix the potatoes, onions and chestnuts together in a large roasting tin, then drizzle with olive oil and season with salt and pepper.
- Season the chicken all over with sea salt and lay it breast side down on top of the vegetables.
- Transfer the tin to the oven and roast for 1 hour 10 minutes, turning the chicken over and stirring the vegetables half way through.
- To test if the chicken is cooked, insert a skewer into the thickest part of the thigh. If the juices run clear with no trace of blood, it is ready.

PREPARATION TIME 10 MINUTES

COOKING TIME 1 HOUR
20 MINUTES

INGREDIENTS

800 g / 1 lb 12 oz baby new potatoes, halved if large
300 g / 10 ½ oz baby onions, peeled
200 g / 7 oz whole chestnuts, peeled
3 tbsp olive oil
1.5 kg / 3 lb 5 oz chicken

Roast Guinea Fowl with New Potatoes

168

- Replace the chicken with a 1 kg guinea fowl and reduce the roasting time to 50 minutes.

169

SERVES 4

Pot-Roasted Rabbit with Vegetables

- Preheat the oven to 180°C (160° fan) / 350F / gas 4 and season the rabbit pieces well with salt and pepper.
- Heat the butter in a casserole dish and sear the rabbit on all sides.
- Add the whole garlic cloves to the pan and fry for a few minutes until they start to colour, then add the carrots, pour in the cider and bring to a gentle simmer.
- Put a lid on the casserole, transfer it to the oven and pot-roast for 30 minutes.
- Stir the rest of the vegetables into the casserole, put the lid back on and return it to the oven for a further 15 minutes.

PREPARATION TIME 5 MINUTES

COOKING TIME 55 MINUTES

INGREDIENTS

1 rabbit, jointed
2 tbsp butter
6 cloves of garlic, peeled
2 carrots, julienned
350 ml / 12 ½ fl. oz / 1 ½ cups dry cider
200 g / 7 oz green (string) beans, halved
250 g / 9 oz / 1 ⅔ cups peas
½ romanesco cauliflower, broken into florets

Pot-Roasted Hare with Vegetables

170

- Replace the rabbit with a jointed hare and increase the initial pot-roasting time to 45 minutes.

171

MAKES 4

Lamb Shanks with Provençale Tomatoes

PREPARATION TIME 5 MINUTES

COOKING TIME 2 HOURS

....

INGREDIENTS

4 lamb shanks
2 slices stale bread, cubed
1 clove of garlic, crushed
1 tsp fresh rosemary, finely chopped
2 tbsp flat leaf parsley, chopped
4 medium tomatoes
8 small rosemary sprigs
4 tbsp olive oil

FOR THE SAUCE:
2 tsp Dijon Mustard
1 tsp wholegrain mustard
2 tbsp crème fraiche

- Preheat the oven to 180°C (160° fan) / 350F / gas 4.
- Season the lamb shanks with salt and pepper then wrap each one tightly in a double layer of foil.
- Bake the lamb shanks for 2 hours or until the meat is very tender.
- 30 minutes before the end of the cooking time, put the bread, garlic, chopped rosemary and parsley in a food processor and pulse until you're left with green breadcrumbs.
- Cut the tomatoes in half and spread them out on a baking tray. Sprinkle over the breadcrumb mixture, season with salt and pepper and top each one with a sprig of rosemary.
- Drizzle the tomatoes with olive oil then bake for 20 minutes.
- While the tomatoes are cooking, mix the two mustards with the crème fraiche to make a sauce.

Ham Hocks with Provençale Tomatoes

172

- Replace the lamb shanks with 4 small ham hocks. Simmer gently in a saucepan of water for 1 hour before baking.

173

MAKES 8

Mutton Stew

PREPARATION TIME 30 MINUTES

COOKING TIME 3 HOURS

15 MINUTES

....

INGREDIENTS

2 tbsp plain (all purpose) flour
1 tsp mustard powder
1 kg / 2 lb 3 oz mutton shoulder, cubed
4 tbsp olive oil
1 onion, finely chopped
1 celery stick, finely chopped
100 g / 3 ½ oz pancetta, cubed
1 bay leaf
1200 ml / 2 pints / 5 cups good quality mutton or lamb stock
2 tbsp chives, chopped

- Preheat the oven to 140°C (120° fan) / 275F / gas 1.
- Mix the flour with the mustard powder and a good pinch of salt and pepper and toss it with the mutton to coat.
- Heat half of the oil in a large cast iron casserole dish then sear the meat in batches until well browned.
- Remove the mutton from the pan, add the rest of the oil and cook the onions, celery and pancetta for 5 minutes.
- Add the bay leaf, pour in the stock and bring to a simmer.
- Return the mutton to the pan and cover it with a lid then cook the casserole in the oven for 3 hours.
- Taste the sauce for seasoning and adjust with salt and pepper as necessary then stir in the chives before serving.

Goat Stew

174

- Replace the mutton with cubed goat shoulder and reduce the cooking time to 2 hours 30 minutes.

175

SERVES 8 # Beef and Orange Casserole

Beef and Star Anise Casserole

176

- Omit the orange juice and zest and replace with 3 whole star anise.

Venison and Orange Casserole

177

- Replace the beef with diced venison steak for a more gamey flavour.

PREPARATION TIME 30 MINUTES

COOKING TIME 3 HOURS
20 MINUTES

....

INGREDIENTS

2 tbsp plain (all purpose) flour
1 tsp mustard powder
1 kg / 2 lb 3 oz braising steak, cubed
4 tbsp olive oil
1 onion, quartered and sliced
100 g / 3 ½ oz pancetta, cubed
4 sprigs fresh rosemary
2 bay leaves
1 large orange
1 cinnamon stick
600 ml / 1 pint / 2 ½ cups red wine
600 ml / 1 pint / 2 ½ cups good quality beef stock

- Preheat the oven to 140°C (120° fan) / 275F / gas 1.
- Mix the flour with the mustard powder and a good pinch of salt and pepper and toss it with the beef to coat.
- Heat half of the oil in a large cast iron casserole dish then sear the meat in batches until well browned.
- Remove the beef from the pan, add the rest of the oil and cook the onions, pancetta and herbs for 5 minutes.
- Use a vegetable peeler to peel off the orange zest in strips and add it to the pan with the cinnamon stick.
- Pour in the wine and boil for 5 minutes. Squeeze the orange and add the juice to the pan with the stock and seared beef.
- Bring the casserole to a gentle simmer then put on a lid, transfer it to the oven and cook for 3 hours.
- Taste the sauce for seasoning and adjust with salt and pepper as necessary.

178

SERVES 12

Glazed Ham

Mustard-glazed Ham

179

- Omit the cloves and stir 2 tbsp of grain mustard into the glaze mixture.

Glazed Ham
with Peaches

180

- Add 6 firm peaches halved to the roasting tin 15 minutes before the end of cooking and serve with ham slices.

PREPARATION TIME 10 MINUTES

COOKING TIME 2 HOURS 25 MINUTES

INGREDIENTS

5 kg / 11 lb whole leg of ham, on the bone
2 carrots, in large chunks
2 celery sticks, in large chunks
2 onions, in large chunks
1 tbsp black peppercorns
2 bay leaves

FOR THE GLAZE:
70 – 80 cloves
100 ml / 3 ½ fl. oz / ½ cup runny honey
1 orange, juiced and zest finely grated

- Put the ham in a saucepan of cold water. Bring to the boil then discard the water.
- Add the vegetables to the pan with enough cold water to cover the meat by 5 cm. Bring to a gentle simmer and skim any scum off the surface.
- Add the peppercorns and bay leaf, then put on a lid and simmer gently for 2 hours.
- Remove the ham from the saucepan and leave to steam dry for 5 minutes.
- Preheat the oven to 220°C (200° fan) / 425F / gas 7.
- Using a sharp knife, carefully cut away the skin of the ham, leaving the fat intact.
- Score the fat into a diamond pattern and insert a clove into the centre of each diamond.
- Mix the honey with the orange juice and zest and pour half of it over the ham.
- Transfer the ham to the oven and roast for 10 minutes. Pour the other half of the glaze over the meat and roast for a further 15 minutes.
- Serve hot or leave to cool completely before slicing and serving cold.

181

SERVES 4

Bacon chops

- If you have trouble finding bacon chops, ask your butcher to cut you 1 cm thick slices from a whole back bacon.
- Heat the oil in a large frying pan and fry the chops for 3 minutes on each side or until the fat is crisp and golden.
- Serve with salad leaves and accompany with baked potatoes and coleslaw.

PREPARATION TIME 2 MINUTES

COOKING TIME 6 MINUTES

INGREDIENTS

2 tbsp sunflower oil
4 smoked bacon chops
salad leaves to serve

Bacon Chops with Buttered Cabbage

182

- Cook half a shredded cabbage in boiling salted water for 5 minutes then drain well and toss with 25 g of melted butter. Serve with the bacon chops.

183

SERVES 6

Osso Bucco

- Preheat the oven to 140°C (120° fan) / 275F / gas 1.
- Heat half of the oil in a large cast iron casserole dish and sear the beef shin on all sides until well browned.
- Remove the beef from the pan, add the rest of the oil and fry the onions, celery and carrot for 5 minutes.
- Add the tomatoes and stock and bring to a simmer then return the beef to the pan.
- Cover the casserole with a lid, transfer it to the oven and cook for 3 hours.
- Taste the sauce for seasoning and adjust with salt and pepper as necessary.

PREPARATION TIME 5 MINUTES

COOKING TIME 3 HOURS 15 MINUTES

INGREDIENTS

4 tbsp olive oil
6 thick slices beef shin, bone-in
1 onion, finely chopped
1 celery stick, finely chopped
2 carrots, grated
400 g / 14 oz / 2 cups canned tomatoes, chopped
400 ml / 14 fl. oz / 1 ⅔ cups good quality beef stock

Veal Osso Bucco

184

- Replace the beef shin with veal shin and reduce the cooking time to 2 hours.

185

SERVES 6

Navarin of Spring Lamb

PREPARATION TIME 5 MINUTES

COOKING TIME 2 HOURS 30 MINUTES

....

INGREDIENTS

2 tbsp olive oil
6 Spring lamb neck steaks, on the bone
2 leeks, cut into large chunks
3 carrots, cut into large chunks
175 ml / 6 fl. oz / ⅔ cup dry white wine
1 litre / 1 pint 15 fl. oz / 4 cups good quality lamb stock
½ lemon, sliced
2 tbsp mint leaves, shredded

- Preheat the oven to 140°C (120° fan) / 275F / gas 1.
- Heat the oil in a large cast iron casserole dish and sear the lamb on all sides until well browned.
- Remove the lamb from the pan and fry the leeks and carrots for 5 minutes.
- Add the wine and bubble until reduced by half. Pour in the stock and bring to a simmer then return the lamb to the pan.
- Cover the casserole with a lid, transfer it to the oven and cook for 2 hours.
- Taste the sauce for seasoning and adjust with salt and pepper as necessary then stir in the lemon slices and mint and return to the oven for 5 more minutes.

Navarin Printanier

186

- Replace the carrot chunks with 300 g of baby carrots and add 200 g of baby turnips to the casserole with the rest of the vegetables.

187

SERVES 8

Roast Capon with Braised Chicory

PREPARATION TIME 10 MINUTES

COOKING TIME 2 HOURS 15 MINUTES

....

INGREDIENTS

3 kg / 6 lb 10 oz capon (mature chicken)
500 ml / 17 fl. oz / 2 cups dry white wine
2 tbsp butter
4 heads of chicory, quartered

- Preheat the oven to 180°C (160° fan) / 350F / gas 4.
- Put the capon in a deep roasting tin and rub it all over with sea salt and pepper.
- Put the wine in a saucepan and simmer for 5 minutes to boil off some of the alcohol then pour it into the bottom of the roasting tin.
- Transfer the tin to the oven and roast for 2 hours 15 minutes.
- 30 minutes before the end of the cooking time, heat the butter in a large frying pan and brown the chicory quarters on all sides.
- Transfer the chicory to the bottom of the roasting tin and let it braise in the wine while the capon finishes cooking.
- To test if the capon is cooked, insert a skewer into the thickest part of the thigh. If the juices run clear with no trace of blood, it is ready.

Cabbage and Truffle Rolls

188

- Blanch 6 cabbage leaves for 4 minutes then drain and refresh in cold water. Fill with prepared sushi rice, then roll up tightly and slice. Top with slivers of truffle.

189

SERVES 4

Cassoulet

- Put the beans in a large saucepan with the duck stock and simmer gently for 1 hour.
- Meanwhile, put the confit duck skin-side-down in a large frying pan. Put the pan over a medium heat to render the fat then fry the legs until browned all over.
- Remove duck and sear the pork belly strips and sausages.
- Preheat the oven to 150°C (130° fan) / 300F / gas 2.
- Drain the beans and reserve the stock then stir in the garlic and thyme.
- Spoon a third of the beans into a cassole or baking dish and arrange the duck and pork on top. Spoon over the rest of the beans then press the sausages into the top.
- Add enough stock to cover the surface by 1 cm, then sprinkle with black pepper and drizzle over a tablespoon of duck fat from the frying pan.
- Transfer the dish to the oven and cook for 2 hours 30 minutes, adding more stock if it starts to look dry.

PREPARATION TIME 10 MINUTES

COOKING TIME 3 HOURS 30 MINUTES

INGREDIENTS

400 g / 14 oz / 2 ⅔ cups dried haricot beans, soaked overnight
3 litres / 5 pints 6 fl. oz / 12 cups good quality duck stock
4 confit duck legs
4 slices demi-salé pork belly
4 Toulouse sausages
2 cloves of garlic, crushed
a few sprigs of thyme

Pork Cassoulet

190

- Omit the duck legs and double the quantity of Toulouse Sausages.

191

SERVES 4

Mediterranean Lamb Shanks

- Preheat the oven to 180°C (160° fan) / 350F / gas 4.
- Mix all of the ingredients together in a large roasting tin or baking dish and season well with salt and pepper.
- Wrap the dish in a double layer of foil, sealing the edges tightly, then transfer it to the oven and bake for 2 hours or until the lamb is very tender.
- Carefully remove the foil, position the lamb shanks on top of the vegetables and return the dish to the oven for 15 minutes to colour the meat.

PREPARATION TIME 5 MINUTES

COOKING TIME 2 HOURS 15 MINUTES

INGREDIENTS

4 lamb shanks
1 onion, finely chopped
1 red pepper, sliced
1 yellow pepper, sliced
2 heads of chicory, quartered
100 g / 3 ½ oz green (string) beans, trimmed
400 g / 14 oz / 2 cups canned tomatoes, chopped
100 ml / 3 ½ fl. oz / ½ cup dry white wine
4 cloves of garlic, sliced
1 tbsp fresh rosemary
1 lemon, zest pared into thin strips

Mediterranean Shoulder of Lamb

192

- Replace the lamb shanks with a whole shoulder of lamb and increase the cooking time to 3 hours.

SERVES 8

Venison Stew

193

PREPARATION TIME 10 MINUTES

COOKING TIME 2 HOURS 50 MINUTES

INGREDIENTS

2 tbsp plain (all purpose) flour
1 tsp mustard powder
1 kg / 2 lb 3 oz venison haunch, cubed
4 tbsp olive oil
100 g / 3 ½ oz pancetta, cubed
1 onion, quartered and sliced
16 small shallots, peeled
16 whole baby carrots
8 whole garlic cloves
4 sprigs fresh thyme
600 ml / 1 pint / 2 ½ cups dry white wine
600 ml / 1 pint / 2 ½ cups good quality beef stock
150 g / 5 ½ oz / 1 cup green olives, pitted

- Preheat the oven to 140°C (120° fan) / 275F / gas 1.
- Mix the flour with the mustard powder and a good pinch of salt and pepper and toss it with the venison to coat.
- Heat half of the oil in a large cast iron casserole dish then sear the meat in batches until well browned.
- Remove the venison from the pan, add the rest of the oil and cook the pancetta, vegetables and herbs for 5 minutes.
- Pour in the wine and boil for 5 minutes. Add the stock and seared venison and bring it back to a gentle simmer.
- Put a lid on the casserole, transfer it to the oven and cook for 2 hours.
- Taste the sauce for seasoning and adjust with salt and pepper as necessary, then stir in the olives and return to the oven for 30 minutes.

Venison and Butterbean Stew

194

- Add 400 g of canned butterbeans to the casserole when you add the olives.

SERVES 6

Provençale Veal Stew

195

PREPARATION TIME 5 MINUTES

COOKING TIME 3 HOURS 15 MINUTES

INGREDIENTS

4 tbsp olive oil
800 g / 1 lb 12 oz veal braising steak, diced
1 onion, finely chopped
4 cloves of garlic, finely chopped
1 celery stick, finely chopped
2 red peppers, diced
400 g / 14 oz / 2 cups canned tomatoes, chopped
400 ml / 14 fl. oz / 1 ⅔ cups good quality beef stock
150 g / 5 ½ oz / 1 cup black olives, pitted
4 tbsp capers, drained and rinsed
a few sprigs of basil

- Preheat the oven to 140°C (120° fan) / 275F / gas 1.
- Heat half of the oil in a large cast iron casserole dish and sear the veal pieces on all sides until well browned.
- Remove the veal from the pan, add the rest of the oil and fry the onions, garlic, celery and peppers for 5 minutes.
- Add the tomatoes and stock and bring to a simmer then return the veal to the pan.
- Cover the casserole with a lid, transfer it to the oven and cook for 3 hours.
- 30 minutes before the end of the cooking time, stir in the olives and capers and season the sauce with salt and pepper as necessary.

Spicy Veal Stew

196

- Add a finely chopped red chilli and 2 tsp of smoked paprika to the vegetables when they're frying.

197

SERVES 8

Pineapple-Glazed Gammon

Orange-Glazed Gammon

198

- Replace the pineapple juice in the cooking liquor and glaze with orange juice and stir 2 tbsp of marmalade into the glaze.

Honey Pineapple Glazed Gammon

199

- Replace the sugar in the glaze for 4 tbsp of Manuka honey.

PREPARATION TIME 15 MINUTES

COOKING TIME 2 HOUR 25 MINUTES

....

INGREDIENTS

3 kg / 6 lb 10 oz boneless
gammon joint
2 carrots, in large chunks
2 celery sticks, in large chunks
2 onions, in large chunks
1 litre / 1 pint 15 fl. oz / 4 cups
pineapple juice

FOR THE GLAZE:
100 ml / 3 ½ fl. oz / ½ cup
pineapple juice
4 tbsp light soft brown sugar
1 tsp Dijon mustard

- Put the ham in a saucepan of cold water. Bring to the boil then discard the water.
- Add the vegetables to the pan then add the pineapple juice and top up with enough cold water to cover the meat by 5 cm.
- Cover the pan and simmer gently for 2 hours.
- Remove the ham from the saucepan and leave to steam dry for 5 minutes.
- Preheat the oven to 220°C (200° fan) / 425F / gas 7.
- Using a sharp knife, carefully cut away the skin of the ham, then score the fat in a diamond pattern.
- To make the glaze, stir the pineapple juice into the sugar and mustard and spoon half of it over the ham.
- Transfer the ham to the oven and roast for 10 minutes. Pour the other half of the glaze over the meat and roast for a further 15 minutes.
- Serve hot or leave to cool completely before slicing and serving cold.

200

SERVES 10

Roast Beef

Mustard-Crusted Roast Beef

201

- Spread the outside of the beef with 4 tbsp of wholegrain mustard before roasting.

Horseradish-Crusted Roast Beef

202

- Spread the outside of the beef with 4 tbsp of horseradish sauce halfway through the cooking time.

PREPARATION TIME 10 MINUTES

COOKING TIME 2 HOURS 25 MINUTES

....

INGREDIENTS

4 carrots, cut into large chunks
4 leeks, cut into large chunks
4 celery sticks, cut into large chunks
2 onions, cut into wedges
1 small squash, cut into wedges
4 kg / 8 lb 13 oz boneless rib of beef
3 tbsp olive oil
2 tbsp flat leaf parsley, finely chopped

- Preheat the oven to 230°C (210° fan) / 450F / gas 8.
- Arrange the vegetables in a large roasting tin and sit the beef on top. Rub the meat with olive oil then season everything liberally with salt and pepper.
- Transfer the tin to the oven and roast for 15 minutes, then reduce the temperature to 160°C (140° fan) / 325F / gas 3 and roast for 1 hour 45 minutes.
- Cover the roasting tin with a double layer of foil and leave the beef to rest for 10 minutes before carving.
- Sprinkle the vegetables with parsley just before serving.

203

SERVES 6

Navarin of Mutton

- Preheat the oven to 140°C (120° fan) / 275F / gas 1.
- Heat the oil in a large cast iron casserole dish and sear the mutton on all sides until well browned.
- Remove the mutton from the pan and fry the baby vegetables for 5 minutes.
- Add the tomatoes and wine and bubble until reduced by half. Pour in the stock and bring to a simmer then return the mutton to the pan.
- Cover the casserole with a lid, transfer it to the oven and cook for 3 hours.
- Taste the sauce for seasoning and adjust with salt and pepper as necessary then stir in the beans and return to the oven for 20 minutes.

PREPARATION TIME 5 MINUTES

COOKING TIME 3 HOURS 45 MINUTES

INGREDIENTS

2 tbsp olive oil
800 g / 1 lb 12 oz boneless neck of mutton, in large chunks
200 g / 7 oz baby onions, peeled
200 g / 7 oz baby carrots, peeled
200 g / 7 oz baby turnips, peeled
100 g / 3 ½ oz tomato, cubed
175 ml / 6 fl. oz / ⅔ cup dry white wine
1 litre / 1 pint 15 fl. oz / 4 cups good quality lamb stock
200 g / 7 oz green (string) beans, trimmed

Navarin of Mutton with Pistou   204

- Blend a handful of basil with a crushed garlic clove, 2 tbsp grated Parmesan and 75 ml olive oil in a blender. Drizzle over the Navarin at the table.

205

SERVES 4

Andouillette with Crushed Potato

- Cook the potatoes in boiling salted water for 10 minutes.
- Tip the potatoes into a colander and leave to drain.
- Add the milk and butter to the saucepan.
- Heat until the milk starts to simmer then return the potatoes to the pan.
- Take the pan off the heat and crush the potatoes gently with a fork. Keep it warm in a low oven.
- Heat the oil in a frying pan and fry the onions and andouillette over a low heat for 20 minutes. Turn the sausages and stir the onions regularly.
- Remove the andouillette and keep warm in the oven, then increase the frying pan heat and stir in the vinegar.
- When the vinegar has almost all evaporated, stir in the double cream and chives.
- Serve the andouillette with the crushed potatoes on the side and spoon over the onion cream.

PREPARATION TIME 2 MINUTES

COOKING TIME 40 MINUTES

INGREDIENTS

900 g / 2 lb potatoes, peeled and cubed
250 ml / 9 fl. oz / 1 cup whole milk
150 g / 5 ½ oz / ⅔ cup butter, cubed
2 tbsp olive oil
4 andouillette sausages
1 onion, finely chopped
2 tbsp white wine vinegar
100 ml / 3 ½ fl. oz / ½ cup double (heavy) cream
2 tbsp chives, chopped

Andouillette with Crushed Swede   206

- Replace the potato with an equal weight of cubed swede. Increase the cooking time to 30 minutes and omit the milk. Season with plenty of black pepper.

SERVES 6

Moroccan Lamb with Prunes

PREPARATION TIME 5 MINUTES

COOKING TIME 2 HOURS 45 MINUTES

INGREDIENTS

2 tbsp olive oil
800 g / 1 lb 12 oz lamb neck in large chunks
1 onion, quartered and sliced
3 carrots, diced
3 cloves of garlic, finely chopped
2 tsp ras el hanout spice mix
1 litre / 1 pint 15 fl. oz / 4 cups good quality lamb stock
150 g / 5 ½ oz / 1 cup stoneless prunes

- Preheat the oven to 140°C (120° fan) / 275F / gas 1.
- Heat the oil in a large cast iron casserole dish and sear the lamb on all sides until well browned.
- Remove the lamb from the pan and fry the onion, carrots and garlic for 5 minutes.
- Stir in the spice mix then add the stock and bring to a simmer.
- Return the lamb to the pan, cover the casserole with a lid and cook in the oven for 2 hours.
- Add the prunes 30 minutes before the end of the cooking time.

Moroccan Lamb with Apricots 208

- Replace the prunes with dried apricots and stir in 2 tbsp of chopped coriander leaves at the end.

SERVES 6

Lamb with Bacon and Cabbage

PREPARATION TIME 5 MINUTES

COOKING TIME 15 MINUTES

INGREDIENTS

2 tbsp olive oil
6 lamb chops
6 rashers smoked bacon
½ savoy cabbage, sliced
175 ml / 6 fl. oz / ⅔ cup dry white wine
175 ml / 6 fl. oz / ⅔ cup good quality lamb stock

- Heat the oil in a large cast iron casserole dish and sear the lamb on all sides until well browned.
- Stir in the bacon and cabbage, then add the wine and stock and bring to a simmer.
- Cover the pan with a lid and simmer for 6 minutes or until the cabbage is cooked.

Lamb with Caraway and Cabbage 210

- Leave out the bacon and add 1 tsp caraway seeds when you fry the lamb.

211

SERVES 4

Spiced Pork and Apple Stew

- Toss the pork with the curry powder and leave to marinate for 30 minutes.
- Heat half of the oil and butter in a saucepan and sear the pork on all sides.
- Remove the pork from the pan and add the rest of the oil and butter, followed by the onion and apple.
- Sauté for 5 minutes, then pour in the stock and cream and bring to a simmer. Transfer the pork back to the pan then simmer very gently for 1 hour.
- Stir in the mustard and season to taste with salt and pepper.

PREPARATION TIME 35 MINUTES

COOKING TIME 1 HOUR 30 MINUTES

INGREDIENTS

800 g / 1 lb 12 oz pork shoulder, cubed
2 tbsp mild curry powder
3 tbsp olive oil
2 tbsp butter
1 onion, finely chopped
3 apples, peeled and cut into chunks
350 ml / 12 ½ fl. oz / 1 ½ cups chicken stock
300 ml / 10 ½ fl. oz / 1 ¼ cups double (heavy) cream
2 tsp Dijon mustard

Spiced Pork and Pineapple Stew

212

- Replace the apple with half a fresh pineapple, peeled and cut into chunks.

213

SERVES 4

Sticky Pork and Apricot Stew

- Heat the oil and butter in a saucepan and sear the pork on all sides.
- Remove the pork from the pan and add the onion, garlic, star anise and lime wedges.
- Sauté for 5 minutes, then pour in the stock and soy sauce and bring to a simmer. Transfer the pork back to the pan then simmer very gently for 1 hour.
- Stir in the dried apricots and cook with the lid off for a further 30 minutes or until the pork is tender and the sauce is reduced and sticky.

PREPARATION TIME 5 MINUTES

COOKING TIME 1 HOUR 45 MINUTES

INGREDIENTS

1 tbsp olive oil
2 tbsp butter
800 g / 1 lb 12 oz pork shoulder, cubed
1 onion, finely chopped
3 cloves of garlic, finely chopped
2 star anise
1 lime, cut into wedges
600 ml / 1 pint / 2 ½ cups chicken stock
2 tbsp dark soy sauce
150 g / 5 ½ oz / ¾ cup dried apricots

Sticky Pork and Date Stew

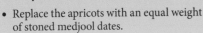

214

- Replace the apricots with an equal weight of stoned medjool dates.

215 SERVES 6

Sticky Pork with Mediterranean Vegetables

PREPARATION TIME 35 MINUTES

COOKING TIME 35 MINUTES

INGREDIENTS

2 tbsp runny honey
1 tbsp balsamic vinegar
½ orange, juice and zest finely grated
800 g / 1 lb 12 oz pork shoulder, cubed
2 tbsp olive oil
1 aubergine (eggplant), cut into chunks
2 red peppers, cut into chunks
350 ml / 12 ½ fl. oz / 1 ½ cups chicken stock
1 courgette (zucchini), thinly sliced lengthways
a few sprigs of thyme

- Mix the honey, balsamic vinegar and orange juice and zest together and massage it into the pork. Leave to marinate for 30 minutes.
- Heat the oil in a large sauté pan and sauté the pork until golden brown.
- Add the aubergine and peppers to the pan and stir-fry for 5 more minutes, then pour in the chicken stock.
- Let the mixture simmer until only a small amount of liquid remains, then stir in the courgette and thyme.
- Sauté for 3 more minutes, then taste for seasoning and add salt and pepper as necessary.

Sticky Pork with Pasta   216

- While the pork is simmering, cook 600 g of penne in boiling salted water according to the manufacturer's instructions. Drain well and stir into the sauce with the courgette.

217 SERVES 4

Thai Spiced Roast Chicken

PREPARATION TIME 10 MINUTES

COOKING TIME 1 HOUR 20 MINUTES

INGREDIENTS

100 g / 3 ½ oz / ½ cup butter, softened
2 cloves of garlic, crushed
2 tsp root ginger, finely grated
2 kaffir lime leaves, very finely chopped
1 red chilli (chili), very finely chopped
1 stem lemongrass, very finely chopped
1.5 kg / 3 lb 5 oz chicken

TO GARNISH:
1 tbsp lime zest, in thin shreds
1 stem lemongrass, thinly sliced
a few kaffir lime leaves

- Preheat the oven to 200°C (180° fan) / 400F / gas 6.
- Beat the butter with the spices and a pinch of salt until well combined.
- Use your fingers to make a cavity between the skin and the breast of the chicken and pack it with the butter.
- Season the chicken all over with sea salt and sit it in a roasting tin.
- Transfer the tin to the oven and roast for 1 hour 10 minutes, basting with the buttery juices every 20 minutes.
- To test if the chicken is cooked, insert a skewer into the thickest part of the thigh. If the juices run clear with no trace of blood, it is ready.
- Sprinkle over the lime zest and lemongrass just before serving with the lime leaves tucked around.

Thai Spiced Chicken Quarters   218

- Use the spiced butter between the skin and flesh of 4 chicken leg quarters and reduce the cooking time to 40 minutes.

219

SERVES 6

Lamb and Fresh Apricot Tagine

Chicken and Fresh Apricot Tagine

220

- Replace the lamb with 800 g of boneless chicken thigh, cut into large chunks, and use chicken stock in place of the lamb stock.

Lamb and Peach Tagine

221

- Replace the apricots with 6 sliced, stoned peaches.

PREPARATION TIME 5 MINUTES

COOKING TIME 1 HOUR 30 MINUTES

INGREDIENTS

800 g / 1 lb 12 oz lamb shoulder, cubed
2 tsp ras el hanout spice mix
2 tbsp olive oil
2 tbsp honey
4 spring onions (scallions), sliced
3 cloves of garlic, finely chopped
50 g / 1 ¾ oz / ¼ cup sultanas
500 ml / 17 ½ fl. oz / 2 cups good quality lamb stock
12 fresh apricots, halved and stoned
75 g / 2 ½ oz / ½ cup blanched almonds

- Preheat the oven to 160°C (140° fan) / 325F / gas 3.
- Put the lamb, spices, oil, honey, onions, garlic and sultanas in a large tagine with a big pinch of salt and stir well to mix.
- Pour over the stock then put on the lid and transfer the tagine to the oven.
- Cook the tagine for 1 hour 15 minutes, then stir in the apricots and almonds and return to the oven for 15 minutes.

222

SERVES 6

Mushroom-Stuffed Fillet of Beef

Mozzarella-Stuffed Fillet of Beef

223

- Replace the mushrooms in the stuffing with 2 balls of mozzarella, cut into chunks.

Almond and Mushroom Fillet of Beef

224

- Add 2 tbsp of chopped almonds to the stuffing mixture.

PREPARATION TIME 15 MINUTES

COOKING TIME 35 MINUTES

INGREDIENTS

2 tbsp butter
225 g / 8 oz chestnut mushrooms, cleaned
2 tbsp olive oil
1 kg / 2 lb 3 oz fillet of beef

FOR THE STUFFING:
2 tbsp olive oil
1 small onion, finely chopped
4 rashers streaky bacon, finely chopped
1 clove of garlic, crushed
50 g / 1 ¾ oz / ⅔ cup fresh breadcrumbs
2 tsp Dijon mustard

- Preheat the oven to 230°C (210° fan) / 450F / gas 8.
- First make the stuffing. Heat the oil in a frying pan and fry the onion, bacon and garlic for 5 minutes, stirring occasionally.
- Stir in the breadcrumbs and mustard and season with black pepper.
- Heat the butter in a large ovenproof frying pan and cook the mushrooms with a sprinkle of salt for 5 minutes. Remove them from the pan and reserve.
- Make 2 long cavities in the beef and pack them alternately with the stuffing and some of the whole mushrooms.
- Heat the oil in the mushroom pan. Season the beef well with salt and pepper then sear it on all sides.
- Arrange the rest of the mushrooms round the outside of the beef, then transfer the pan to the oven and roast for 20 minutes.
- Leave the beef to rest somewhere warm for 10 minutes before carving into thick slices.

225

SERVES 4

Veal Blanquette

- Heat the butter in a saucepan and cook the veal until very lightly coloured on all sides.
- Remove the veal from the pan and add the onion, carrot and celery then cook gently, without colouring, for 5 minutes.
- Pour in the stock and return the veal to the pan then simmer very gently for 1 hour.
- Add the peas and cream and simmer for a further 5 minutes then taste for seasoning and add salt and white pepper as necessary.

PREPARATION TIME 5 MINUTES

COOKING TIME 1 HOUR 15 MINUTES

....

INGREDIENTS

2 tbsp butter
800 g / 1 lb 12 oz veal shoulder, cubed
1 onion, finely chopped
1 carrot, finely chopped
1 celery stick, finely chopped
600 ml / 1 pint / 2 ½ cups light veal or chicken stock
100 g / 3 ½ oz / ⅔ cup peas, defrosted if frozen
300 ml / 10 ½ fl. oz / 1 ¼ cups double (heavy) cream

Turkey Blanquette

226

- Replace the veal with turkey and use chicken stock in place of the veal stock.

227

MAKES 4

Mini Chicken Pies

- Preheat the oven to 200°C (180° fan) / 400F / gas 6.
- Heat the butter in a saucepan and fry the leek and carrot for 5 minutes without colouring.
- Sprinkle in the flour and stir well, then stir in the milk and bubble until it thickens slightly.
- Add the chicken and peas to the pan and heat through, then season to taste with salt and white pepper.
- Roll out the pastry on a lightly floured surface and cut out 4 circles.
- Divide the filling between 4 individual pie dishes and brush the rims with water.
- Top each pie with a pastry lid and press the edges to seal.
- Lightly score the pastry into a diamond pattern then brush the tops with beaten egg.
- Bake the pies for 25 – 30 minutes or until the pastry is golden brown and puffy.

PREPARATION TIME 15 MINUTES

COOKING TIME 45 MINUTES

....

INGREDIENTS

2 tbsp butter
1 leek, chopped
1 carrot, chopped
1 tsp plain (all purpose) flour
250 ml / 9 fl. oz / 1 cup milk
200 g / 7 oz cooked chicken breast, cubed
75 g / 2 ½ oz / ½ cup peas, defrosted if frozen
800 g / 1 lb 12 oz all-butter puff pastry
1 egg, beaten

Mini Chicken and Ham Pies

228

- Add 100 g of ham in small cubes when you add the chicken and peas.

229

SERVES 4

Sausages with Champ Potatoes

PREPARATION TIME 5 MINUTES

COOKING TIME 20 MINUTES

INGREDIENTS

2 tbsp olive oil
12 sausages
900 g / 2 lb potatoes, peeled and cubed
250 ml / 9 fl. oz / 1 cup whole milk
150 g / 5 ½ oz / ⅔ cup butter, cubed
4 spring onions (scallions), chopped

- Heat the oil in a frying pan and fry the sausages very gently for 20 minutes, turning regularly.
- Meanwhile, cook the potatoes in boiling salted water for 10 minutes or until tender all the way through.
- Tip the potatoes into a colander and leave to drain.
- Put the saucepan back on the heat and add the milk and butter.
- Heat until the milk starts to simmer then return the potatoes to the pan.
- Mash the potatoes until smooth then stir in the spring onions and season well with salt and pepper.

230

SERVES 4

Citrus Roasted Chicken

PREPARATION TIME 10 MINUTES

COOKING TIME 1 HOUR 20 MINUTES

INGREDIENTS

1.5 kg / 3 lb 5 oz chicken
1 lemon, thinly sliced
1 lime, thinly sliced
4 kumquats, thinly sliced
3 tbsp olive oil

TO SERVE:
4 lemons, halved
4 figs, quartered
2 tbsp whole almonds

- Preheat the oven to 200°C (180° fan) / 400F / gas 6.
- Season the chicken all over with sea salt and sit it in a roasting tin.
- Cover the crown of the chicken with the lemon, lime and kumquat slices and drizzle with olive oil.
- Transfer the tin to the oven and roast for 1 hour 10 minutes, basting with the juices every 20 minutes.
- To test if the chicken is cooked, insert a skewer into the thickest part of the thigh. If the juices run clear with no trace of blood, it is ready.
- Leave the chicken to rest for 10 minutes while you prepare the garnish.
- Heat a griddle pan until smoking hot then griddle the cut face of the lemons and figs for 5 minutes or until well coloured.
- Mix with the almonds and spoon around the chicken before serving.

231

SERVES 4

Glazed Pork Belly Chops

- Mix the honey, lemon juice and soy together and drizzle it over the belly chops. Leave to marinate for 30 minutes.
- Preheat the grill to its highest setting.
- Grill the pork for 15 – 20 minutes, turning regularly, until cooked through and golden brown.

PREPARATION TIME 35 MINUTES

COOKING TIME 20 MINUTES

....

INGREDIENTS

2 tbsp runny honey
2 tbsp lemon juice
1 tbsp dark soy sauce
4 pork belly chops

Rotisserie Chicken

232

SERVES 4

PREPARATION TIME 10 MINUTES

COOKING TIME 1 HOUR 30 MINUTES

....

INGREDIENTS

1 tsp paprika
1 tsp caster sugar
1 tsp garlic powder
1.5 kg / 3 lb 5 oz chicken

- Prepare a rotisserie oven according to the manufacturer's instructions.
- Mix the paprika, sugar and garlic powder with 1 tsp of salt and rub it all over the chicken.
- Skewer the chicken onto the spit so that it is evenly balanced and transfer it to the rotisserie oven.
- Cook the chicken for 1 hour 30 minutes, or until the chicken is bronzed and cooked through.
- To test if the chicken is cooked, insert a skewer into the thickest part of the thigh. If the juices run clear with no trace of blood, it is ready.

Stewed Oxtail with Prunes

233

SERVES 4

PREPARATION TIME 10 MINUTES

COOKING TIME 2 HOURS 30 MINUTES

....

INGREDIENTS

3 tbsp olive oil
4 portions of oxtail
2 red onions, sliced

2 carrots, julienned
1 bay leaf
1 tsp dried chilli (chili) flakes
2 juniper berries
350 ml / 12 ½ fl. oz / 1 ½ cups red wine
200 g / 7 oz / 1 cup prunes, stoned
300 ml / 10 ½ fl. oz / 1 ¼ cups beef stock

- Heat the oil in a frying pan then season the oxtail with salt and pepper and brown it well all over.
- Transfer the oxtail to a large bowl and combine with the rest of the ingredients, apart from the stock.
- Leave the oxtail to marinate for a minimum of 3 hours or preferably overnight.
- Strain the marinade into a cast iron casserole dish and add the stock. Bring to a gentle simmer, then add the oxtail, put on a lid and stew very gently for 2 hours.
- Add the vegetables and prunes from the marinade and continue to cook for 30 minutes or until the meat is very tender.

234

SERVES 4

Braised Chicken with Peas

PREPARATION TIME 5 MINUTES

COOKING TIME 1 HOUR 15 MINUTES

....

INGREDIENTS

1 chicken, jointed
3 tbsp olive oil
2 tbsp butter
150 g / 5 ½ oz pancetta, diced
4 shallots, peeled and quartered
2 leeks, thickly sliced
350 ml / 12 ½ fl. oz / 1 ½ cups dry cider
300 ml / 10 ½ fl. oz / 1 ¼ cups double (heavy) cream
100 g / 3 ½ oz / ⅔ cup peas, defrosted if frozen
1 tbsp flat leaf parsley, finely chopped

- Preheat the oven to 140°C (120° fan) / 275F / gas 1 and season the chicken well with salt and pepper.
- Heat half of the oil and butter in a casserole dish and sear the chicken on all sides.
- Remove the chicken from the pan and add the rest of the oil and butter, followed by the pancetta, shallots and leeks.
- Sauté for 5 minutes, then pour in the cider and cream and bring to a simmer. Transfer the chicken back to the dish then braise in the oven for 45 minutes.
- Stir in the peas, season to taste with salt and pepper and cook for a further 15 minutes.
- Sprinkle with parsley before serving.

Braised Chicken with Mushrooms

235

- Replace the peas with sliced button mushrooms.

236

MAKES 4

Mini Chicken and Vegetable Pies

PREPARATION TIME 45 MINUTES

COOKING TIME 45 MINUTES

....

INGREDIENTS

2 tbsp butter
1 onion, chopped
1 potato, chopped
1 tsp plain (all purpose) flour
250 ml / 9 fl. oz / 1 cup milk
200 g / 7 oz cooked chicken breast, cubed
75 g / 2 ½ oz / ½ cup peas, defrosted if frozen
75 g / 2 ½ oz / 1 cup button mushrooms, quartered
6 cherry tomatoes, quartered

FOR THE PASTRY:
100 g / 3 ½ oz / ½ cup butter, cubed and chilled
200 g / 7 oz / 1 ⅓ cups plain (all purpose) flour

- First make the pastry. Rub the butter into the flour until the mixture resembles fine breadcrumbs.
- Stir in just enough cold water to bring the pastry together into a pliable dough then chill for 30 minutes.
- Preheat the oven to 200°C (180° fan) / 400F / gas 6.
- Heat the butter in a saucepan and fry the onion and potato for 5 minutes without colouring.
- Sprinkle in the flour and stir well, then stir in the milk and bubble until it thickens slightly.
- Add the chicken, peas, mushrooms and tomatoes to the pan and heat through, then season to taste.
- Roll out the pastry on a floured surface and cut out 4 circles.
- Divide the filling between 4 individual pie dishes and brush the rims with water.
- Top each pie with a pastry lid and crimp the edges to seal.
- Bake the pies for 25 – 30 minutes.

Curried Chicken and Vegetable Pies

237

- Add 2 crushed cloves of garlic and 2 tsp of mild curry powder after frying the onion and potatoes. Fry for 2 minutes before adding the flour and milk.

238

SERVES 4

Lamb Leg Steaks with Vegetables

- Preheat the oven to 200°C (180° fan) / 400F / gas 6.
- Heat half of the oil in a roasting tin then stir in the vegetables and season with salt and pepper.
- Transfer the tin to the oven and roast for 30 minutes, turning half way through.
- Meanwhile, heat the rest of the oil in a cast iron casserole dish and sear the lamb steaks on both sides until well browned.
- Remove from the pan and fry the shallots and garlic for 2 minutes without colouring.
- Pour in the wine and bring to a simmer then stir in the tomato puree and return the lamb.
- Put a lid on the casserole and transfer to the oven for 15 minutes.
- Turn the lamb over and add the roasted vegetables to the pot, then return the dish to the oven uncovered for 10 minutes.

PREPARATION TIME 5 MINUTES

COOKING TIME 45 MINUTES

....

INGREDIENTS

4 tbsp olive oil
2 medium potatoes, peeled and cut into chunks
2 carrots, peeled and cut into chunks
2 parsnips, peeled and cut into chunks
3 tbsp olive oil
4 thick lamb leg steaks, boned
2 shallots, finely chopped
2 cloves of garlic, finely chopped
150 ml / 5 ½ fl. oz / 1 cup red wine
1 tbsp tomato puree

Lamb Steaks with Roast Turnips

239

- Replace the potatoes, carrots and parsnips with 500 g of baby turnips.

240

SERVES 4

Salmon, Leek and Chorizo Gratin

- Preheat the oven to 200°C (180° fan) / 400F / gas 6.
- Put the milk and bay leaf in a small saucepan and heat until simmering.
- Meanwhile, heat the butter in a small saucepan and fry the leek for 5 minutes.
- Stir in the flour then strain in the milk, stirring constantly. Cook until the sauce is thick and smooth.
- Arrange the salmon in an even layer in a baking dish, then pour over the sauce.
- Sprinkle the sauce with breadcrumbs and parsley and arrange the chorizo on top, then bake for 30 minutes

PREPARATION TIME 10 MINUTES

COOKING TIME 45 MINUTES

....

INGREDIENTS

450 g / 1 lb salmon fillet, skinned and cubed
500 ml / 17 ½ fl. oz / 2 cups milk
1 bay leaf
4 tbsp butter
1 leek, chopped
2 tbsp plain flour
3 tbsp breadcrumbs
1 tbsp flat leaf parsley, finely chopped
12 thin slices chorizo

Cod, Leek and Chorizo Gratin

241

- Replace the salmon with an equal weight of fresh cod fillet.

242

SERVES 4

Braised Duck with Mushroom Sauce

PREPARATION TIME 10 MINUTES

COOKING TIME 1 HOUR 15 MINUTES

INGREDIENTS

1 duck, jointed
2 shallots, finely chopped
200 g / 7 oz / 2 ⅔ cups button mushrooms, sliced
3 bay leaves
a few sprig of thyme
350 ml / 12 ½ fl. oz / 1 ½ cups dry white wine
350 ml / 12 ½ fl. oz / 1 ½ cups good quality duck stock
100 ml / 3 ½ fl. oz / ½ cup double (heavy) cream

- Preheat the oven to 140°C (120° fan) / 275F / gas 1 and season the duck well with salt and pepper.
- Put the duck skin side down into a cold cast iron casserole dish and put it over a medium high heat.
- Cook until some of the fat renders out and the skin browns, then turn the pieces over and brown the other side.
- Remove the duck from the pan and add the shallots, mushrooms, bay leaves and thyme.
- Sauté for 5 minutes, then pour in the cider and stock and bring to a simmer. Transfer the duck back to the dish then braise it in the oven for 45 minutes.
- Stir in the cream, season to taste with salt and pepper and cook for a further 15 minutes.

Braised Duck with Mushrooms and Pancetta

243

- Add 200 g of pancetta in small cubes when you fry the mushrooms.

244

SERVES 4

Penne with Fennel Seed Ragu

PREPARATION TIME 2 MINUTES

COOKING TIME 25 MINUTES

INGREDIENTS

4 tbsp olive oil
2 cloves of garlic, crushed
1 tsp fennel seeds
4 pork sausages, skinned
400 g / 14 oz / 1 ¾ cups canned plum tomatoes
400 g / 14 oz penne

- Heat the oil in a frying pan and fry the garlic and fennel seeds for 2 minutes.
- Add the sausagemeat, breaking it up with a spatula as it browns.
- Stir in the canned tomatoes and simmer for 20 minutes.
- Meanwhile, cook the penne in boiling salted water according to the packet instructions or until al dente.
- Taste the sauce for seasoning, adding plenty of freshly ground black pepper.
- Drain the pasta and stir it into the sauce before serving.

Penne with Fennel Sausage Cream

245

- Replace the canned tomatoes with 400 ml double cream and 1 tsp of Dijon mustard and reduce the simmering time to 5 minutes.

246

SERVES 4

Sweet Potato Cottage Pie

Sweet Potato
Baked Chilli

247

- Add 200 g of canned kidney beans and 1 tsp of Cayenne pepper to the mince when you add the tomatoes and stock.

Sweet Potato
Shepherd's Pie

248

- Replace the beef with lamb and replace the beef stock with lamb stock to create a Shepherd's pie.

PREPARATION TIME 2 MINUTES

COOKING TIME 1 HOUR 30 MINUTES

INGREDIENTS

2 tbsp olive oil
1 small onion, finely chopped
2 cloves of garlic, crushed
450 g / 1 lb / 2 cups minced beef
400 g / 14 oz / 1 ¾ cups canned tomatoes, chopped
400 ml / 14 fl. oz / 1 ⅔ cups beef stock

FOR THE TOPPING:
2 large sweet potatoes
50 g / 1 ¾ oz / ¼ cup butter
2 tsp fresh thyme leaves

- Preheat the oven to 200°C (180° fan) / 400F / gas 6.
- Bake the sweet potatoes in their skins for 45 or until a skewer inserted slides in easily.
- Meanwhile, heat the oil in a large saucepan and fry the onion for 3 minutes, stirring occasionally.
- Add the garlic and cook for 2 minutes, then add the mince.
- Fry the mince until it starts to brown then add the chopped tomatoes and stock and bring to a gentle simmer.
- Cook for 1 hour, stirring occasionally, until the mince is tender and the sauce has thickened a little.
- When the sweet potatoes are ready, peel off and discard the skins and mash the flesh with the butter and thyme leaves.
- Spoon the mince mixture into a large baking dish then top with the mashed sweet potatoes.
- Use a fork to level the surface and make stripes in the potato then bake in the oven for 20 minutes or until golden brown.

249

MAKES 6

Lamb, Sage and Coriander Pies

Lamb and Mint Potato Pies

250

- Replace the coriander seeds and sage with a small bunch of mint leaves, tied with string and garnish with more fresh mint.

Lamb, Sage and Tarragon Pies

251

- Replace the coriander seeds with 2 tbsp of finely chopped tarragon.

PREPARATION TIME 2 MINUTES

COOKING TIME 1 HOUR 30 MINUTES

INGREDIENTS

2 tbsp olive oil
1 small onion, finely chopped
2 cloves of garlic, crushed
½ tsp coriander (cilantro) seeds
a few sprigs of sage, tied with string
450 g/ 1 lb lamb shoulder, cubed
600 ml / 1 pint / 2 ½ cups lamb stock

FOR THE TOPPING:

450 g / 1 lb floury potatoes, peeled and cubed
100 ml / 3 ½ fl. oz / ½ cup milk
50 g / 1 ¾ oz / ¼ cup butter
50 g / 1 ¾ oz / ⅓ cup panko breadcrumbs
a few sprig of sage to garnish

- Heat the oil in a saucepan and fry the onion, garlic, coriander seeds and sage for 3 minutes. Add the lamb shoulder and fry for 2 minutes then add the stock and bring to a gentle simmer.
- Lay a crumpled sheet of greaseproof paper on top of the meat and cover the pan with a lid then simmer very gently for 2 hours.
- Preheat the oven to 200°C (180° fan) / 400F / gas 6.
- Cook the potatoes in salted water for 10 minutes, or until they are tender, then drain well. Return the potatoes to the saucepan and add the milk and butter, then mash until smooth.
- Remove the sage from the lamb then shed the meat with 2 forks and season to taste with salt and pepper. Arrange 6 metal ring moulds on a baking tray and half-fill each one with the lamb.
- Top the lamb with the mashed potato and sprinkle with breadcrumbs, then bake in the oven for 15 minutes or until the tops are golden brown.
- Unmould the pies onto warm plates and garnish with sage.

Pot-Roasted Brisket with Carrots

252

SERVES 8

- Preheat the oven to 140°C (120° fan) / 275F / gas 1 and season the brisket well with salt and pepper.
- Heat the oil in a cast iron casserole dish and sear the brisket on all sides.
- Remove the brisket from the pan then fry the onion, garlic, caraway and lardons for 5 minutes.
- Tie the savoury and bay leaf together with string and add to the pan with the carrots, then pour in the stock and bring to a simmer.
- Return the beef to the pot, then put on a lid, transfer it to the oven and pot-roast for 3 hours.
- Remove the herbs and transfer the brisket with the carrots and cooking liquor to a warm serving dish.

PREPARATION TIME 5 MINUTES

COOKING TIME 3 HOURS 20 MINUTES

INGREDIENTS

1.5 kg / 3 lb 3 oz rolled beef brisket
3 tbsp olive oil
1 onion, sliced
3 cloves of garlic, chopped
2 tsp caraway seeds
100 g / 3 ½ oz smoked lardons
a few sprigs of summer savoury
1 bay leaf
5 carrots, sliced
600 ml / 1 pint / 2 ½ cups good quality beef stock

Pot-Roasted Brisket with Mushrooms

253

- Leave out the carrots and add 250 g of button mushrooms to the pot 30 minutes before the end of the cooking time.

Sausages and Baked Onion Gravy

254

SERVES 4

- Preheat the oven to 180°C (160° fan) / 350F / gas 4.
- Arrange the sausages and onion wedges in a baking dish and season with salt and pepper.
- Mix the honey with the mustard then slowly incorporate the chicken stock.
- Pour the mixture over the sausages and onions then transfer the dish to the oven.
- Bake for 30 minutes, turning the sausages and stirring the onions half way through.

PREPARATION TIME 5 MINUTES

COOKING TIME 20 MINUTES

INGREDIENTS

8 sausages
2 red onions, cut into wedges
2 tbsp runny honey
1 tbsp Dijon mustard
250 ml / 9 fl. oz / 1 cup chicken stock

Spring Onion and Mustard Mash

255

- Mash 800 g of boiled potatoes with 100 ml double cream, 4 chopped spring onions and a tablespoon of wholegrain mustard. Season to taste with salt and pepper.

256

SERVES 4

Braised Mushroom Potato-Topped Pie

PREPARATION TIME 2 MINUTES

COOKING TIME 1 HOUR 30 MINUTES

INGREDIENTS

2 tbsp olive oil
1 small onion, finely chopped
2 tbsp fresh thyme leaves
2 cloves of garlic, crushed
450 g / 1 lb / 6 cups chestnut mushrooms, sliced
200 g / 7 oz / 2 ⅔ cups shitake mushrooms, sliced
1 tbsp tomato puree
200 ml / 7 fl. oz / ¾ cup good quality vegetable stock

FOR THE TOPPING:
450 g / 1 lb floury potatoes, peeled and cubed
100 ml / 3 ½ fl. oz / ½ cup milk
50 g / 1 ¾ oz / ¼ cup butter
50 g / 1 ¾ oz / ½ cup Cheddar, grated

- Heat the oil in a large saucepan and fry the onion and thyme for 3 minutes, stirring occasionally.
- Add the garlic and cook for 2 minutes, then add the mushrooms and fry, stirring occasionally, for 15 minutes.
- Stir in the tomato puree then pour in the stock and simmer gently for 10 minutes
- Taste for seasoning and add salt and freshly ground black pepper as necessary.
- Meanwhile, cook the potatoes in salted water for 10 minutes, or until they are tender, then drain well.
- Return the potatoes to the saucepan and add the milk, butter and cheese. Mash the potatoes until smooth.
- Preheat the oven to 200°C (180° fan) / 400F / gas 6.
- Spoon the mushroom mixture into a baking dish then top with the mashed potatoes.
- Bake the pie for 20 minutes or until golden brown on top.

Braised Mushroom Puff Pie

257

- Top the mushrooms with a puff pastry lid, brush with beaten egg and bake at 220°C for 30 minutes or until puffy and golden.

258

SERVES 4

Beer-Battered Fish and Chips

PREPARATION TIME 1 HOUR 45 MINUTES

COOKING TIME 25 MINUTES

INGREDIENTS

FOR THE FISH:
200 g / 7 oz / 1 ⅓ cups plain (all purpose)
2 tbsp olive oil
250 ml / 9 fl. oz / 1 cup pale ale
4 portions pollock fillet

FOR THE CHIPS:
4 large Maris Piper potatoes, peeled and cut into chips
sunflower oil for deep-frying

- Soak the potatoes in cold water for 1 hour.
- Drain the chips and dry completely with a clean tea towel, then air-dry on a wire rack for 30 minutes.
- Meanwhile, make the batter. Sieve the flour into a bowl then whisk in the oil and ale until smoothly combined.
- Heat the oil in a deep fat fryer, according to the manufacturer's instructions, to a temperature of 130°C.
- Par-cook the chips for 10 minutes.
- Drain the chips on kitchen paper to absorb excess oil.
- Increase the fryer temperature to 180°C. Dip the fish in the batter and fry for 6 minutes or until golden brown.
- Transfer the fish to a kitchen paper lined bowl and increase the fryer temperature to 190°C.
- Return the chips to the fryer and cook for 4 – 5 minutes.
- Drain the chips of excess oil and serve with the fish.

Beer-Battered Sausage and Chips

259

- Replace the pollock with 8 good quality pork sausages.

260

SERVES 4

Chilli Con Carne

- Heat the oil in a large saucepan and fry the onion and chilli for 3 minutes, stirring occasionally.
- Add the garlic and Cayenne and cook for 2 minutes, then add the mince.
- Fry the mince until it starts to brown then add the chopped tomatoes, stock and kidney beans and bring to a gentle simmer.
- Cook the chilli con carne for 1 hour, stirring occasionally, until the mince is tender and the sauce has thickened a little.
- Taste for seasoning and add salt and freshly ground black pepper as necessary.
- Serve with boiled rice and coriander soured cream.

PREPARATION TIME 5 MINUTES

COOKING TIME 1 HOUR 10 MINUTES

INGREDIENTS

2 tbsp olive oil
1 onion, finely chopped
1 red chilli (chili), finely chopped
2 cloves of garlic, crushed
½ tsp Cayenne pepper
450 g / 1 lb / 2 cups minced beef
400 g / 14 oz / 1 ¾ cups canned tomatoes, chopped
200 ml / 7 fl. oz / ¾ cup beef stock
400 g / 14 oz / 1 ¾ cups canned kidney beans, drained
boiled rice and coriander (cilantro) soured cream to serve

Coriander Soured Cream   261

- Mix 2 tbsp chopped coriander leaves with ½ crushed clove of garlic and 200 ml soured cream. Add a squeeze of lime and season to taste with salt and pepper.

262

SERVES 6

Lamb Hotpot

- Preheat the oven to 160°C (140° fan) / 325F / gas 3 and season the lamb liberally with salt and pepper.
- Melt half the butter with the oil in a frying pan over a high heat then sear the lamb and kidneys in batches.
- Remove the meat from the pan, lower the heat and add the onions. Cook for 5 minutes, stirring occasionally.
- Add the garlic and thyme and cook for 2 more minutes.
- Increase the heat and stir in the flour then add the stock.
- Arrange the lamb and kidneys in a casserole dish and pour over the onion liquor.
- Slice the potatoes 3mm thick with a sharp knife or mandolin and arrange them on top of the lamb.
- Cut the remaining butter into small pieces and dot it over the top of the potatoes then cover the dish tightly with foil or a lid.
- Bake the hotpot for 1 hour 30 minutes then remove the lid and cook for a further hour.

PREPARATION TIME 5 MINUTES

COOKING TIME 3 HOURS

INGREDIENTS

900 g / 2 lb boneless lamb neck, cubed
2 lamb kidneys, trimmed and quartered
50 g / 1 ¾ oz / ¼ cup butter
2 tbsp olive oil
2 onions, sliced
a few sprigs of thyme
1 tbsp plain (all purpose) flour
800 ml / 1 pint 8 oz / 3 ¼ cups lamb stock
900 g / 2 lb potatoes, cut into 3mm slices

Lamb and Mint Hotpot   263

- Replace the thyme with 2 tbsp of finely chopped mint leaves.

SERVES 4

Braised Spring Vegetables

PREPARATION TIME 5 MINUTES

COOKING TIME 25 MINUTES

······································

INGREDIENTS

2 tbsp olive oil
4 baby artichokes, halved
175 ml / 6 fl. oz / ⅔ cup dry white
wine
2 leeks, cut into large chunks
8 shallots, peeled
12 small chantenay carrots, scrubbed
500 ml / 17 ½ fl. oz / 2 cups good
quality vegetable stock
12 asparagus spears, trimmed
150 g / 5 ½ oz / 1 cup fresh peas
1 tbsp lemon juice
2 tbsp flat leaf parsley, finely
chopped

- Heat the oil in a large cast iron casserole dish and sear the cut sides of the artichokes until well browned.
- Pour in the wine and bring to the boil, then add the leeks, shallots, carrots and stock and bring back to the boil.
- Reduce the heat and simmer gently for 10 minutes, then add the asparagus and peas and simmer for a further 8 minutes.
- Add a squeeze of lemon then season to taste with salt and pepper and sprinkle with parsley.

Spring Vegetable Broth
265

- Cut the vegetables into bite-sized pieces and double the quantity of stock then serve the dish as a soup.

266

SERVES 4

Quick Bouillabaisse

PREPARATION TIME 5 MINUTES

COOKING TIME 15 MINUTES

······································

INGREDIENTS

2 tbsp olive oil
1 small onion, finely chopped
½ celery stick, finely chopped
3 cloves of garlic, crushed
3 tbsp Pernod
1 tomato, diced
a pinch of saffron
600 ml / 1 pint / 2 ½ cups good
quality fish stock
2 sea bass fillets, cut into large
chunks
2 gurnard fillets, cut into large
chunks
450 g / 1 lb live mussels, scrubbed
300 g / 10 ½ oz raw king prawns,
heads removed
2 tbsp flat leaf parsley, chopped

- Heat the oil in a large sauté pan and fry the onion and celery for 5 minutes without colouring.
- Add the garlic and fry for 2 more minutes, then pour in the Pernod and bubble until almost evaporated.
- Add the tomato, saffron and stock and bring to a simmer, then add the sea bass, gurnard and mussels, put on the lid and simmer very gently for 3 minutes.
- Add the prawns to the bouillabaisse, put the lid back on and simmer for 3 more minutes then sprinkle with parsley and serve.

Quick Fish Soup
267

- Pick out the mussel meat and discard the shells, then transfer everything to a liquidiser and blend until smooth.

268

MAKES 12

Greek Easter Rolls

Tsoureki

269

- Shape the bread dough into a plaited ring and stud the top with 3 hen's eggs that have been dyed red with food colouring. Increase the baking time to 40 minutes.

Sun-Dried Tomato Easter Rolls

270

- Exclude the ground cardamom and add 3 tbsp of chopped sun-dried tomatoes to the dough before kneading.

PREPARATION TIME 3 HOURS 30 MINUTES

COOKING TIME 10-12 MINUTES

INGREDIENTS

400 g / 14 oz / 2 ⅔ cups strong white bread flour
½ tsp easy blend dried yeast
4 tbsp caster (superfine) sugar
1 tsp fine sea salt
¼ tsp ground cardamom
4 tbsp melted butter
1 tsp vanilla extract
250 ml / 9 fl. oz / 1 cup milk, warmed
12 quail's eggs

- In a large bowl, mix together the flour, yeast, caster sugar, salt and ground cardamom. Stir the butter and vanilla into the milk then stir it into the dry ingredients.
- Knead the mixture on a lightly oiled surface with your hands for 10 minutes or until the dough is smooth and elastic.
- Leave the dough to rest in a lightly oiled bowl, covered with oiled clingfilm, for 2 - 3 hours or until doubled in size. Punch the dough with your fist to knock out the air then knead it for 2 more minutes.
- Shape the dough into 12 rolls and spread them out on a greased baking tray then cover with oiled clingfilm and leave to prove for 1 hour or until doubled in size.
- Preheat the oven to 220°C (200° fan) / 425F / gas 7.
- When the rolls have risen, press a quail's egg into the top of each one then bake for 10 - 12 minutes or until the bases sound hollow when tapped.
- Transfer the rolls to a wire rack and leave to cool before serving.

271

SERVES 4

Roast Chicken with Shallots

Chicken with
40 Cloves of Garlic

272

- Omit the shallots and use 40 cloves of garlic (3 – 4 bulbs). The roasted garlic can be squeezed from the skins at the table as a sauce for the chicken.

Roast Chicken with
Lemon and Garlic

273

- Add 3 lemons cut into wedges amongst the garlic and shallots, and squeeze the juice of ½ a lemon over the chicken when turning.

PREPARATION TIME 10 MINUTES

COOKING TIME 1 HOUR 20 MINUTES

INGREDIENTS

1.5 kg / 3 lb 5 oz chicken
3 tbsp olive oil
300 g / 10 ½ oz shallots, peeled and halved
1 bulb of garlic, broken into cloves
a few sprigs of rosemary

- Preheat the oven to 200°C (180° fan) / 400F / gas 6.
- Season the chicken all over with sea salt and black pepper, then drizzle with olive oil and lay it breast side down in a large roasting tin.
- Transfer the tin to the oven and roast for 30 minutes.
- Turn the chicken breast side up and surround it with the shallots, garlic and rosemary. Turn the vegetables to coat them in the juices then roast for a further 40 minutes.
- To test if the chicken is cooked, insert a skewer into the thickest part of the thigh. If the juices run clear with no trace of blood, it is ready.

274
SERVES 4
Moroccan Lamb Shanks

- Preheat the oven to 180°C (160° fan) / 350F / gas 4.
- Mix all of the ingredients together in a large roasting tin or baking dish and season well with salt and pepper.
- Wrap the dish in a double layer of foil, sealing the edges tightly, then transfer it to the oven and bake for 2 hours or until the lamb is very tender.
- Carefully remove the foil and return the dish to the oven for 15 minutes to colour the meat.

PREPARATION TIME 5 MINUTES

COOKING TIME 2 HOURS 15 MINUTES

INGREDIENTS

4 lamb shanks
1 tbsp ras el hanout spice mix
1 onion, finely chopped
1 red pepper, finely chopped
4 cloves of garlic, finely chopped
½ preserved lemon, finely chopped
400 ml / 14 fl. oz / 1 ⅔ cups lamb stock

Roasted Vegetable Couscous
275

- Put 300 g of couscous in a bowl with 300 ml boiling stock and 200 g of leftover roasted vegetables. Cover with clingfilm and leave to stand for 5 minutes.

276
SERVES 8
Pepper-Stuffed Topside of Beef

- Preheat the oven to 200°C (180° fan) / 400F / gas 6.
- Make a long cavity through the centre of the joint with a sharp knife.
- Mix the peppers with the basil and plenty of black pepper, then stuff the mixture into the cavity.
- Heat the oil in a large oven-proof frying pan. Season the beef well with salt and pepper then sear it on all sides.
- Transfer the pan to the oven and roast for 45 minutes.
- Leave the beef to rest somewhere warm for 10 minutes before carving into thick slices.

PREPARATION TIME 15 MINUTES

COOKING TIME 35 MINUTES

INGREDIENTS

1 kg / 2 lb 3 oz topside of beef
450 g / 1 lb jar roasted peppers in oil, drained
a small bunch of basil, chopped
2 tbsp olive oil

Mascarpone Tomatoes
277

- Cut 12 tomatoes in half and top with 150 g of mascarpone mixed with 2 tbsp chopped basil leaves and ½ a crushed clove of garlic.

278

SERVES 4

Andouillette with Horseradish Mash

PREPARATION TIME 2 MINUTES

COOKING TIME 40 MINUTES

....

INGREDIENTS

900 g / 2 lb potatoes, peeled and
cubed
250 ml / 9 fl. oz / 1 cup whole milk
150 g / 5 ½ oz / ⅔ cup butter, cubed
2 tbsp horseradish sauce
2 tbsp olive oil
4 andouillette sausages
1 onion, finely chopped
2 tbsp balsamic vinegar
100 ml / 3 ½ fl. oz / ½ cup Madeira
200 ml / 7 fl. oz / 1 cup beef stock
mixed leaves to serve

- Cook the potatoes in boiling salted water for 10 minutes.
- Tip the potatoes into a colander and leave to drain.
- Put the saucepan back on the heat and add the milk, butter and horseradish sauce.
- Heat until the milk starts to simmer then return the potatoes to the pan and mash until smooth. Keep warm.
- Heat the oil in a frying pan and fry the onions and andouillette over a low heat for 20 minutes. Turn the sausages and stir the onions regularly.
- Remove the andouillette from the pan and keep warm in the oven, then increase the heat under the frying pan and stir in the vinegar and Madeira
- When the liquid has almost all evaporated, stir in the stock and reduce by half.
- Strain the gravy through a sieve and serve with the andouillette, mash and some mixed salad leaves.

Andouillette with Parsnip Purée **279**

- Replace the potato with an equal weight of cubed parsnip. Increase the cooking time to 30 minutes and puree in a food processor instead of mashing.

280

SERVES 6

Mince and Cauliflower Pie

PREPARATION TIME 5 MINUTES

COOKING TIME 1 HOUR 30 MINUTES

....

INGREDIENTS

2 tbsp olive oil
1 small onion, finely chopped
2 cloves of garlic, crushed
450 g / 1 lb / 2 cups minced beef
600 ml / 1 pint / 2 ½ cups beef stock

FOR THE TOPPING:

300 g / 10 ½ oz floury potatoes,
peeled and cubed
1 romanesco cauliflower, broken into
florets
3 tbsp milk
2 tbsp butter
50 g / 1 ¾ oz / ½ cup Cheddar, grated

- Heat the oil in a saucepan and fry the onion for 3 minutes.
- Add the garlic, cook for 2 minutes, then add the mince.
- Fry the mince until it starts to brown then add the stock and bring to a gentle simmer.
- Cook for 1 hour, until the mince is tender and the sauce has thickened.
- Add salt and freshly ground black pepper to taste.
- Meanwhile, boil the potatoes in salted water for 8 minutes, then add the cauliflower florets and cook for a further 5 minutes.
- Drain well and reserve some cauliflower for decoration then mash the rest with the milk, butter and cheese.
- Preheat the oven to 200°C (180° fan) / 400F / gas 6.
- Spoon the mince mixture into a large baking dish then top with the mash.
- Stud the top with the reserved cauliflower then bake in the oven for 20 minutes or until golden brown.

Mushroom and Cauliflower Pie **281**

- Put 450 g of button mushrooms in a food processor and pulse until finely chopped. Use in place of the beef mince and replace the beef stock with vegetable stock.

282
SERVES 6

Braised Oxtail

- Preheat the oven to 140°C (120° fan) / 275F / gas 1.
- Tie the oxtail pieces together with string and season well with salt and pepper.
- Heat half of the oil in a large cast iron casserole dish and sear the oxtail on both sides until well browned.
- Remove it from the pan, add the rest of the oil and fry the carrots and celery for 5 minutes.
- Tie the bay leaves, thyme and parsley stalks into a bouquet garni with string and add it to the pot with the oxtail, marrowbone and stock and bring to a simmer.
- Cover the casserole with a lid, transfer it to the oven and cook for 3 hours.
- Stir in the reserved celery leaves, taste the sauce for seasoning and adjust with salt and pepper as necessary.

PREPARATION TIME 5 MINUTES

COOKING TIME 3 HOURS 15 MINUTES

INGREDIENTS

6 thick slices oxtail, on the bone
4 tbsp olive oil
3 carrots, cut into large chunks
3 celery sticks, cut into large chunks, leaves reserved
2 bay leaves
a few brigs of thyme
a few parsley stalks
1 litre / 1 pint 15 fl. oz / 4 cups good quality beef stock
2 large pieces of marrowbone

Oxtail Soup   283

- Remove the oxtail, marrowbone and bouquet garni from the pan and blend the vegetables and stock until smooth. Pick the meat from the bones and stir it into the soup.

284
SERVES 4

Chunky Beef Chilli

- Heat the oil in a large saucepan and fry the onion, carrot, celery and chilli for 3 minutes, stirring occasionally.
- Add the garlic and Cayenne and cook for 2 minutes, then add the beef.
- Fry the beef until it starts to brown then add the stock and bring to a gentle simmer.
- Cook for 1 hour, stirring occasionally, then add the kidney beans, sweetcorn and courgette and cook for a further 30 minutes.
- Taste for seasoning and add salt and freshly ground black pepper as necessary.

PREPARATION TIME 5 MINUTES

COOKING TIME 1 HOUR 45 MINUTES

INGREDIENTS

2 tbsp olive oil
1 onion, finely chopped
1 carrot, finely chopped
1 celery stick, finely chopped
1 red chilli (chili), finely chopped
2 cloves of garlic, crushed
½ tsp Cayenne pepper
450 g / 1 lb / 2 cups braising steak, cubed
400 g / 14 oz / 1 ⅔ cups beef stock
400 g / 14 oz / 1 ¾ cups canned kidney beans, drained
400 g / 14 oz / 1 ¾ cups canned sweetcorn, drained
2 courgettes (zucchini), sliced

Chunky Vegetable Chilli   285

- Replace the beef with 300 g of button mushrooms and reduce the initial simmering time to 20 minutes. Replace the beef stock with vegetable stock.

286

SERVES 4

Lamb and Summer Vegetable Stew

PREPARATION TIME 5 MINUTES

COOKING TIME 1 HOUR
15 MINUTES

....

INGREDIENTS

4 tbsp olive oil
450 g / 1 lb lamb leg, cubed
1 onion, diced
3 cloves of garlic, finely chopped
200 g / 7 oz / 1 cup canned tomatoes,
chopped
600 ml / 1 pint / 2 ½ cups good
quality lamb stock
½ Japanese aubergine (eggplant),
sliced
2 courgettes (zucchini), cubed
150 g / 5 ½ oz green (string) beans
a few sprigs of flat leaf parsley to
serve

- Heat half of the oil in a large saucepan and sear the lamb on all sides until well browned.
- Remove the lamb from the pan, add the rest of the oil and fry the onions and garlic for 5 minutes.
- Add the tomatoes and stock and bring to a simmer then return the lamb to the pan.
- Cover the pan with a lid and simmer gently for 45 minutes.
- Add the aubergine, courgette and beans and simmer for a further 15 minutes then taste the sauce for seasoning and adjust with salt and pepper.
- Garnish with parsley just before serving.

Pork and Summer Vegetable Stew   287

- Replace the lamb leg with cubes of pork shoulder and increase the initial simmering time to 1 hour 30 minutes.

288

SERVES 6

Duck Cottage Pie

PREPARATION TIME 30 MINUTES

COOKING TIME 2 HOURS
20 MINUTES

....

INGREDIENTS

6 duck legs
600 ml / 1 pint / 2 ½ cups duck stock
4 spring onions, finely chopped
2 cloves of garlic, crushed

FOR THE TOPPING:
600 g / 1 lb 5 oz floury potatoes,
peeled and cubed
100 ml / 3 ½ fl. oz / ½ cup milk
50 g / 1 ¾ oz / ¼ cup butter
4 spring onions, chopped
50 g / 1 ¾ oz / ½ cup Cheddar, grated

- Put the duck legs in a large saucepan and pour over the stock. Bring to the boil, then cover the pan, turn down the heat and simmer gently for 2 hours.
- Meanwhile, cook the potatoes in salted water for 10 minutes, or until they are tender, then drain well.
- Return the potatoes to the saucepan and add the milk, butter and spring onions. Mash the potatoes.
- Remove the duck legs from the stock and discard the skin. Shred the meat off the bones with a fork and transfer it to a mixing bowl. Add the spring onions and garlic and enough cooking liquor to moisten, then season to taste with salt and pepper.
- Preheat the oven to 200°C (180° fan) / 400F / gas 6.
- Spoon the duck mixture into a large baking dish then top with the mashed potatoes.
- Sprinkle over the grated cheese and bake in the oven for 20 minutes or until golden brown.

Chicken Cottage Pie   289

- Replace the duck legs with chicken leg quarters and reduce the cooking time to 1 hour.

290

SERVES 6

Veal and Artichoke Stew

Aubergine and Artichoke Stew
291

- Replace the veal with 2 aubergines, cut into large chunks and use vegetable stock instead of veal stock. Cook at 180°C for 45 minutes.

Chicken and Artichoke Stew
292

- Replace the veal with the same weight of chicken thighs.

PREPARATION TIME 5 MINUTES

COOKING TIME 2 HOURS 15 MINUTES

INGREDIENTS

4 tbsp olive oil
800 g / 1 lb 12 oz veal braising steak, in large chunks
1 onion, finely chopped
1 bulb of garlic, broken into cloves
a few sprigs of thyme
6 baby artichokes, halved
12 small chantenay carrots, peeled
600 ml / 1 pints / 2 ½ cups good quality veal stock
1 green chilli (chili), deseeded and very thinly sliced

- Preheat the oven to 140°C (120° fan) / 275F / gas 1.
- Heat half of the oil in a large cast iron casserole dish and sear the veal pieces on all sides until well browned.
- Remove the veal from the pan, add the rest of the oil and fry the onions, garlic and thyme for 5 minutes.
- Add the artichokes, carrots and stock and bring to a simmer then return the veal to the pan.
- Cover the casserole with a lid, transfer it to the oven and cook for 2 hours.
- Taste the sauce for seasoning and adjust with salt and pepper as necessary.

293

MAKES 6

Mini Sausage Cassoulet

Mini Veggie Cassoulet

294

- Use vegetable stock instead of the chicken stock and replace the meat with cubes of carrot, celery, parsnip and mushroom.

Spicy Merguez Cassoulet

295

- Replace half the sausages with Merguez sausages and add a finely chopped red chilli.

PREPARATION TIME 10 MINUTES

COOKING TIME 1 HOUR 45 MINUTES

INGREDIENTS

400 g / 14 oz / 2 ⅔ cups dried haricot beans, soaked overnight
3 litres / 5 pints 6 fl. oz / 12 cups good quality chicken stock
2 tbsp olive oil
6 good quality pork sausages
1 morteau sausage, sliced
100 g / 3 ½ oz chorizo, cubed
2 cloves of garlic, crushed
50 g / 1 ¾ oz / ⅔ cup breadcrumbs
a few sprigs of parsley to garnish

- Put the beans in a large saucepan with the stock and simmer gently for 1 hour.
- Meanwhile, heat the oil in a frying pan and brown the sausages all over, then cut them in half.
- Preheat the oven to 150°C (130° fan) / 300F / gas 2.
- Drain the beans and reserve the stock then stir in the sausages, morteau, chorizo and garlic.
- Divide the mixture between 6 mini casserole dishes, then sprinkle with breadcrumbs.
- Bake the cassoulets for 45 minutes, topping up with extra stock if necessary.

296

SERVES 4

Wild Mushrooms with Soured Cream

- Pick over the mushrooms and brush away any soil with a pastry brush.
- Heat the olive oil and butter in a large sauté pan until sizzling.
- Add the mushrooms and shallot, season with salt and pepper and cook for 10 minutes, stirring occasionally.
- When all of the liquid that comes out of the mushrooms has evaporated and they start to colour, add the garlic and cook for 2 more minutes.
- Divide between 4 mini casserole dishes and top with the soured cream and a sprinkle of parsley.

PREPARATION TIME 1 MINUTES

COOKING TIME 12 MINUTES

INGREDIENTS

300 g / 10 ½ oz mixed wild mushrooms (to include chanterelles and morels)
1 tbsp olive oil
2 tbsp butter
1 shallot, finely chopped
1 clove of garlic, crushed
2 tbsp soured cream
2 tbsp parsley, chopped

Wild Mushrooms with Bacon   297

- Chop 3 rashers of streaky bacon and add them to the mushrooms when you add the garlic.

298

SERVES 6

Mini Chilli Con Carne

- Preheat the oven to 140°C (120° fan) / 275F / gas 1.
- Heat the oil in a large saucepan and fry the onion, pepper and chilli for 3 minutes, stirring occasionally.
- Add the garlic and Cayenne and cook for 2 minutes, then add the mince.
- Fry the mince until it starts to brown then add the stock and kidney beans and bring to a gentle simmer.
- Divide the mixture between 6 mini casserole dishes and transfer them to the oven, then bake for 1 hour.
- Garnish the dishes with a slice of orange and an extra sprinkle of Cayenne.

PREPARATION TIME 5 MINUTES

COOKING TIME 1 HOUR 10 MINUTES

INGREDIENTS

2 tbsp olive oil
1 onion, finely chopped
1 red pepper, diced
1 red chilli (chili), finely chopped
2 cloves of garlic, crushed
½ tsp Cayenne pepper, plus extra for sprinkling
450 g / 1 lb / 2 cups minced beef
200 ml / 7 fl. oz / ¾ cup beef stock
400 g / 14 oz / 1 ¾ cups canned kidney beans, drained
1 orange, peeled, halved and sliced

Chilli Tacos   299

- Serve the individual dishes at the table with 2 corn taco shells per person and a bowl of soured cream for spooning.

300

SERVES 6

Pork Tenderloin with Apples

PREPARATION TIME 10 MINUTES

COOKING TIME 1 HOUR 20 MINUTES

....

INGREDIENTS

800 g / 1 lb 12 oz baby new potatoes, halved if large
3 tbsp olive oil
1 large pork tenderloin
2 apples, cored and sliced
1 tsp mustard seeds
300 ml / 10 ½ fl. oz / 1 ¼ cups dry cider
a few sprigs of parsley to garnish

- Preheat the oven to 200°C (180° fan) / 400F / gas 6.
- Boil the potatoes in salted water for 10 minutes then drain well.
- Heat the oil in a large roasting tin and sear the pork all over.
- Add the potatoes and apple slices to the pan and sprinkle with mustard seeds, salt and pepper, then roast for 15 minutes.
- Pour over the cider and return to the oven for 20 minutes.
- Cut the pork into slices and divide between 6 warm mini casserole dishes with the apple and potatoes. Garnish with parsley before serving.

301

SERVES 4

Tagliatelle with Pancetta and Mushrooms

PREPARATION TIME 5 MINUTES

COOKING TIME 12 MINUTES

....

INGREDIENTS

400 g / 14 oz tagliatelle
2 tbsp olive oil
150 g / 5 ½ oz pancetta, cubed
150 g / 5 ½ oz / 2 cups button mushrooms, sliced
2 cloves of garlic, crushed
2 tbsp flat leaf parsley, finely chopped
250 ml / 9 fl. oz / 1 cup double (heavy) cream
1 tsp Dijon mustard

- Boil the pasta in salted water according to the packet instructions or until al dente.
- Meanwhile, heat the olive oil in a large sauté pan and sauté the pancetta and mushrooms for 8 minutes. Stir in the garlic and half the parsley and fry for 2 more minutes, then pour in the cream and mustard and bubble briefly.
- Drain the pasta and stir it into the pancetta pan, coating it well with the sauce.
- Divide the pasta between 4 warm bowls and serve immediately.

Sticky Pork with Bamboo Shoots

- Heat the oil in a wok and sear the pork on all sides.
- Add the onion, garlic and bamboo shoots and stir-fry for 4 minutes.
- Pour in the honey, soy and rice wine and cook for 3 more minutes stirring occasionally.
- Sprinkle in the sesame seeds then divide the mixture between 4 warm mini casserole dishes.

PREPARATION TIME 5 MINUTES

COOKING TIME 15 MINUTES

INGREDIENTS

2 tbsp sunflower oil

800 g / 1 lb 12 oz pork shoulder, cubed

1 onion, sliced

3 cloves of garlic, finely chopped

400 g / 14 oz canned bamboo shoots, drained

2 tbsp runny honey

2 tbsp dark soy sauce

2 tbsp rice wine or dry sherry

2 tsp sesame seeds

Moroccan Lamb with Dried Fruit

303

SERVES 6

PREPARATION TIME 1 HOUR

COOKING TIME 2 HOURS 15 MINUTES

INGREDIENTS

800 g / 1 lb 12 oz lamb shoulder, cubed

2 tsp ras el hanout spice mix

2 tbsp olive oil

1 onion, finely chopped

3 cloves of garlic, finely chopped

1 cinnamon stick, halved

1 litre / 1 pint 15 fl. oz / 4 cups good quality lamb stock

1 preserved lemon

150 g / 5 ½ oz / 1 cup stoneless prunes

150 g / 5 ½ oz / 1 cup dried apricots

150 g / 5 ½ oz / 1 cup dried figs, quartered

- Toss the lamb with the spice mix and leave to marinate for 1 hour.
- Preheat the oven to 140°C (120° fan) / 275F / gas 1.
- Heat the oil in a large cast iron casserole dish and sear the lamb on all sides until well browned.
- Remove the lamb from the pan and fry the onion, garlic and cinnamon for 5 minutes.
- Stir in the stock and bring to a simmer, then return the lamb, cover the casserole with a lid and cook in the oven for 1 hour 30 minutes.
- Cut the preserved lemon into quarters then scrape out and discard the centre. Cut the rind into strips and stir it into the casserole with the dried fruit.
- Return the casserole to the oven for 30 minutes then portion into mini casserole dishes to serve.

Braised Beef with Mustard

304

SERVES 6

PREPARATION TIME 5 MINUTES

COOKING TIME 1 HOUR 45 MINUTES

INGREDIENTS

3 tbsp olive oil

2 tbsp butter

800 g / 1 lb 12 oz braising steak, sliced

1 onion, sliced

1 tbsp thyme leaves

300 g / 10 ½ oz baby new potatoes, scrubbed

350 ml / 12 ½ fl. oz / 1 ½ cups beef stock

300 ml / 10 ½ fl. oz / 1 ¼ cups double (heavy) cream

2 tsp Dijon mustard

- Heat half of the oil and butter in a saucepan and sear the beef on all sides.
- Remove the beef from the pan and add the rest of the oil and butter, followed by the onion and thyme.
- Sauté for 5 minutes, then add the potatoes, pour in the stock and cream and bring to a simmer. Transfer the beef back to the pan then simmer very gently for 1 hour 30 minutes.
- Stir in the mustard and season to taste with salt and pepper, then divide between 6 mini casserole dishes to serve.

305

SERVES 4

Rabbit with Mustard and Carrots

PREPARATION TIME 5 MINUTES

COOKING TIME 1 HOUR 30 MINUTES

....

INGREDIENTS

1 tbsp olive oil
2 tbsp butter
1 rabbit, jointed
1 onion, finely chopped
2 cloves of garlic, crushed
2 carrots, sliced
a few sprigs of thyme
350 ml / 12 ½ fl. oz / 1 ½ cups dry white wine
300 ml / 10 ½ fl. oz / 1 ¼ cups chicken stock
300 ml / 10 ½ fl. oz / 1 ¼ cups double (heavy) cream
1 tbsp wholegrain mustard

- Heat the oil and butter in a saucepan then sear the rabbit pieces on all sides.
- Remove the rabbit from the pan and add the onion, garlic, carrots and thyme.
- Sauté for 5 minutes, then pour in the wine and boil until reduced by half.
- Add the stock and transfer the rabbit back to the pan, then simmer very gently for 1 hour.
- Remove the rabbit pieces from the pan and add the cream and mustard.
- Boil rapidly for 10 minutes until slightly thickened.
- Meanwhile, strip the meat from the carcass and discard the bones.
- Stir the rabbit back into the sauce and taste for seasoning, then portion into mini casserole dishes to serve.

Rabbit with Mustard and Butterbeans

306

- Replace the carrots with 150 g of butterbeans that have been soaked in cold water overnight.

307

SERVES 4

Sticky Lamb Shanks with Shallots

PREPARATION TIME 5 MINUTES

COOKING TIME 2 HOURS

....

INGREDIENTS

3 tbsp redcurrant jelly
1 tbsp tomato puree
1 tbsp balsamic vinegar
2 tbsp white wine
4 lamb shanks
4 banana shallots, peeled and halved

FOR THE SAUCE:
2 tsp Dijon Mustard
1 tsp wholegrain mustard
2 tbsp crème fraiche

- Preheat the oven to 180°C (160° fan) / 350F / gas 4.
- Put the redcurrant jelly, tomato puree, vinegar and wine in a small pan and stir over a low heat until runny.
- Season the lamb shanks with salt and pepper and sit each one in a large square of tin foil with 2 shallot halves. Drizzle over the redcurrant mixture, then fold up the foil and crimp the edges tightly to seal.
- Bake the lamb shanks for 2 hours then carefully unwrap them and decant into individual casserole dishes to serve.

Sticky Lamb Shanks with Squash

308

- Replace the shallots with large chunks of butternut squash.

309
SERVES 6 Meatballs with Parsnips and Gravy

- Preheat the oven to 190°C (170° fan) / 375F / gas 5.
- Roast the parsnips in 2 tbsp of the oil for 25 minutes.
- Heat 2 tbsp of the oil in a frying pan and fry the onion for 5 minutes.
- Add the garlic and cook for 2 more minutes, stirring constantly, then transfer to a large mixing bowl.
- Add the mince, sausagemeat, breadcrumbs, thyme and egg yolk and mix it all together.
- Portion into meatballs and roll them with your hands.
- Sear the meatballs on all sides in the sauté pan.
- Transfer the meatballs to the roasting tin with the parsnips and roast for a further 15 minutes.
- Cook the peas in boiling water for 5 minutes.
- Drain the peas and whisk 300 ml of the cooking water with gravy granules until smooth.
- Transfer to a serving dish and mix with the gravy.

PREPARATION TIME 5 MINUTES

COOKING TIME 45 MINUTES

....

INGREDIENTS

4 parsnips, cut into large chunks
6 tbsp olive oil
1 onion, finely chopped
1 clove of garlic, crushed
250 g / 9 oz / 1 cup minced beef
250 g / 9 oz / 1 cup pork sausagemeat
50 g / 1 ¾ oz / ⅔ cup fresh white breadcrumbs
1 tbsp fresh thyme leaves
1 egg yolk
200 g / 7 oz / 1 ⅓ cups peas, defrosted if frozen
2 tbsp gravy granules

Meatballs with Jerusalem Artichokes
310

- Replace the parsnips with peeled Jerusalem artichokes and reduce the initial roasting time to 20 minutes.

311
SERVES 8 Stuffed Breast of Veal

- Preheat the oven to 190°C (170° fan) / 375F / gas 5.
- Heat 2 tablespoons of the oil in a frying pan and fry the onion for 5 minutes or until softened.
- Add the garlic and cook for 2 more minutes, stirring constantly, then transfer to a large mixing bowl.
- Add the mince, sausagemeat, breadcrumbs, sage and egg yolk and mix it all together.
- Use the mixture to stuff the veal, then roll it up and tie with butchers twine.
- Heat the rest of the oil in a large roasting tin and sear the veal on all sides.
- Transfer the tin to the oven and roast for 1 hour 30 minutes.
- Add the potatoes to the pan and pour in the stock, then return to the oven for a further 45 minutes.

PREPARATION TIME 5 MINUTES

COOKING TIME 45 MINUTES

....

INGREDIENTS

4 tbsp olive oil
1 onion, finely chopped
1 clove of garlic, crushed
250 g / 9 oz / 1 cup minced veal
250 g / 9 oz / 1 cup pork sausagemeat
50 g / 1 ¾ oz / ⅔ cup fresh white breadcrumbs
1 tbsp sage leaves, finely chopped
1 egg yolk
1.4 kg / 3 lb breast of veal, boned
600 g / 1 lb 4 oz jersey royal potatoes
250 ml / 9 fl. oz / 1 cup veal stock

Stuffed Breast of Lamb
312

- Use the stuffing to stuff 3 boneless breasts of lamb, replacing the veal mince with lamb mince.

313

SERVES 8

Venison with Chocolate and Orange

PREPARATION TIME 10 MINUTES

COOKING TIME 2 HOURS 20 MINUTES

INGREDIENTS

2 tbsp plain (all purpose) flour
1 tsp mustard powder
1 kg / 2 lb 3 oz venison haunch, cubed
4 tbsp olive oil
1 onion, finely chopped
3 cloves of garlic, finely chopped
1 tsp smoked paprika
1 cinnamon stick, halved
600 ml / 1 pint / 2 ½ cups dry white wine
1 orange, juiced and zest cut into thin strips
600 ml / 1 pint / 2 ½ cups good quality beef stock
50 g / 1 ¾ oz dark chocolate, grated

- Preheat the oven to 140°C (120° fan) / 275F / gas 1.
- Mix the flour with the mustard powder and a good pinch of salt and pepper and toss it with the venison to coat.
- Heat half of the oil in a large cast iron casserole dish then sear the meat in batches until well browned.
- Remove the venison from the pan, add the rest of the oil and cook the onion, garlic, paprika and cinnamon for 5 minutes.
- Pour in the wine and boil for 5 minutes. Add the orange juice and zest, stock and seared venison and bring it back to a gentle simmer.
- Put a lid on the casserole, transfer it to the oven and cook for 2 hours.
- Stir in the chocolate then taste for seasoning and adjust with salt and black pepper.

Venison Mole

314

- Add 400 g of canned tomatoes instead of the white wine and omit the orange.

315

SERVES 8

Pot-Roasted Topside with Chicory

PREPARATION TIME 10 MINUTES

COOKING TIME 1 HOUR 45 MINUTES

INGREDIENTS

3 kg / 6 lb 10 oz topside of beef
2 tbsp beef dripping
500 ml / 17 fl. oz / 2 cups dry white wine
4 heads of chicory (endive), quartered
4 cloves of garlic, sliced

- Preheat the oven to 180°C (160° fan) / 350F / gas 4 and season the beef well with salt and pepper.
- Heat the beef dripping in a large roasting tin then sear the beef until well browned all over.
- Pour in the wine and let it simmer for 2 minutes, then add the chicory and garlic to the pan and cover it tightly with a double layer of foil.
- Transfer the tin to the oven and roast for 1 hour 30 minutes.
- Remove the foil 30 minutes before the end of the cooking time to colour the beef and chicory.

Pot-Roasted Topside with Fennel

316

- Replace the chicory with 3 sliced fennel bulbs.

317

SERVES 6

Capon Stuffed with Boudin Blanc

Quail Stuffed with Boudin Blanc

318

- Use the stuffing to fill 12 quail and reduce the roasting time to 35 minutes.

Capon Stuffed with Boudin Noir

319

- Replace the boudin blanc with boudin noir for a richer meatier flavour.

PREPARATION TIME 10 MINUTES

COOKING TIME 2 HOURS 15 MINUTES

....

INGREDIENTS

3 kg / 6 lb 10 oz capon (mature chicken)
6 boudin blanc, skinned
100 g / 3 ½ oz button mushrooms, chopped
2 tbsp flat leaf parsley, finely chopped
250 ml / 9 fl. oz / 1 cup dry white wine

- Preheat the oven to 180°C (160° fan) / 350F / gas 4.
- Put the capon in a deep roasting tin and rub it all over with sea salt and pepper.
- Crumble the boudin blanc and mix with the mushrooms and parsley then stuff the mixture into the capon.
- Transfer the tin to the oven and roast for 2 hours 15 minutes, adding the wine to the bottom of the roasting tin half way through.
- To test if the capon is cooked, insert a skewer into the thickest part of the thigh. If the juices run clear with no trace of blood, it is ready.

320

SERVES 6

Confit Rabbit with Capers

Barbequed Confit Rabbit

321

- Barbeque the confit rabbit for 2 minutes on each side then squeeze over some lemon and serve with salad leaves.

Confit Rabbit with Green Olives

322

- Replace the capers with 50g pitted green olives chopped.

PREPARATION TIME 10 HOURS

COOKING TIME 2 HOURS 30 MINUTES

....

INGREDIENTS

1 large rabbit, jointed
2 tbsp coarse sea salt
1 tbsp brown sugar
1 bulb of garlic, halved
4 sprigs of rosemary
200 g / 7 oz cherry tomatoes
600 ml / 1 pint / 2 ½ cups olive oil
50 g / 1 ¾ oz / ⅓ cup baby capers, rinsed

- Rub the rabbit pieces all over with the salt and sugar then refrigerate for 10 hours.
- Preheat the oven to 150°C (130° fan) / 300F / gas 2.
- Rinse the marinade off the rabbit and dry well with kitchen paper.
- Put the rabbit in a snugly fitting casserole dish with the garlic, rosemary and cherry tomatoes.
- Pour over the olive oil then weigh the rabbit down with an ovenproof saucer to keep it all submerged.
- Put a lid on the casserole and transfer it to the oven to cook for 2 hours 30 minutes.
- Carefully tip the contents of the casserole into a colander set over a mixing bowl.
- Wait a few minutes for the oil to separate out, then ladle all but a few tablespoons of the oil off the top and reserve for using in salad dressings. Stir the capers into the remaining juices to make a dressing.
- Divide the rabbit and tomatoes between 6 warm bowls, then spoon over the dressing.

323

SERVES 6 Beef in Beer with Mushrooms

- Preheat the oven to 140°C (120° fan) / 275F / gas 1.
- Mix the flour with the mustard powder and a good pinch of salt and pepper and toss it with the beef to coat.
- Heat half of the oil in a large cast iron casserole dish then sear the meat in batches until well browned.
- Remove the beef from the pan, add the rest of the oil and cook the onions, garlic and herbs for 5 minutes.
- Pour in the beer and boil for 5 minutes then add the stock to the pan and return the beef.
- Bring the casserole to a gentle simmer then put on a lid, transfer it to the oven and cook for 3 hours.
- 30 minutes before the end of the cooking time, season to taste with salt and pepper and stir in the mushrooms.

PREPARATION TIME 10 MINUTES

COOKING TIME 3 HOURS 20 MINUTES

INGREDIENTS

2 tbsp plain (all purpose) flour
1 tsp mustard powder
1 kg / 2 lb 3 oz braising steak, cubed
4 tbsp olive oil
1 onion, finely chopped
3 cloves of garlic, finely chopped
4 sprigs thyme
2 bay leaves
600 ml / 1 pint / 2 ½ cups real ale
600 ml / 1 pint / 2 ½ cups good quality beef stock
250 g / 9 oz mixed wild mushrooms

Beef and Stout Stew

324

- Replace the ale with stout and use 250 g of cherry tomatoes in place of the mushrooms.

325

SERVES 4 Pot-Roasted Pheasant with Squash

- Preheat the oven to 180°C (160° fan) / 350F / gas 4 and season the pheasants well with salt and pepper.
- Heat the oil in a large cast iron casserole dish and sear the pheasants on all sides.
- Add the garlic, thyme and squash to the pan then pour in the cider and bring to a gentle simmer.
- Put a lid on the casserole, transfer it to the oven and pot-roast for 30 minutes.
- Remove the lid from the dish and return to the oven for a further 15 minutes.
- Joint the pheasants and divide between 4 warm plates with the squash.
- Stir the raspberries and redcurrants into the cooking juices, then spoon over the meat.

PREPARATION TIME 5 MINUTES

COOKING TIME 55 MINUTES

INGREDIENTS

2 pheasants
2 tbsp olive oil
3 cloves of garlic, bruised
a few sprigs of thyme
1 butternut squash, peeled and cut into wedges
350 ml / 12 ½ fl. oz / 1 ½ cups dry cider
75 g / 2 ½ oz / ½ cup raspberries
75 g / 2 ½ oz / ½ cup redcurrants

Pot-Roasted Pheasant with Root Vegetables

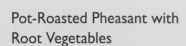

326

- Replace the squash with 2 carrots and 2 parsnips, cut into chunks. Leave out the fruit and add a squeeze of lemon to the cooking juices before spooning over the meat.

327

SERVES 4

Honey and Balsamic Lamb Neck

PREPARATION TIME 4 HOURS

COOKING TIME 8 MINUTES

INGREDIENTS

2 tbsp runny honey
2 tbsp balsamic glaze
½ lemon, juiced and zest finely grated
a few sprigs rosemary
2 lamb neck fillets, cut into chunks
2 tbsp olive oil
braised leeks and mushrooms to serve

- Mix the honey, balsamic glaze, lemon juice and zest and rosemary together and massage it into the lamb. Leave to marinate for 4 hours.
- Drain the lamb well, reserving the juices.
- Heat the oil in a large sauté pan and sauté the lamb until golden brown.
- Pour over the drained marinade and bubble for 1 minute then serve with braised leeks and mushrooms.

Braised Leeks with Mushrooms 328

- Sauté 2 leeks, cut into long slices, with 100 g sliced kabanos sausage and 200 g of mushrooms for 5 minutes. Add 100 ml stock and braise for 15 minutes.

329

SERVES 4

Monkfish and Red Snapper Soup

PREPARATION TIME 15 MINUTES

COOKING TIME 30 MINUTES

INGREDIENTS

2 tbsp olive oil
1 small onion, finely chopped
½ celery stick, finely chopped
3 cloves of garlic, crushed
3 tbsp Pernod
4 tomatoes
1 litre / 1 pint 15 fl. oz / 4 cups good quality fish stock
4 baby leeks
a few sprigs of thyme
4 monkfish cutlets
4 red snapper, heads removed

- Heat the oil in a large sauté pan and fry the onion and celery for 5 minutes without colouring.
- Add the garlic and fry for 2 more minutes, then pour in the Pernod and bubble until almost evaporated.
- Dice 2 of the tomatoes and add them to the pan with the stock then simmer for 10 minutes.
- Transfer the soup to a liquidiser and blend until smooth, then pass it through a sieve back into the pan.
- Bring the soup back to a simmer, then add the leeks and thyme and simmer for 5 minutes.
- Cut the remaining tomatoes into wedges and add them to the pan with the monkfish and snapper. Simmer for a further 5 minutes then season to taste with salt and pepper.

Conger and Bream Soup 330

- Replace the monkfish with conger eel steaks and use sea bream fillets in place of the snapper.

331

SERVES 4 Herb-Crusted Rack of Lamb

- Preheat the oven to 160°C (140° fan) / 325F / gas 3.
- Mix the breadcrumbs with the thyme and savoury and season with salt and pepper.
- Rub the lamb racks with half of the oil, then roll them in the breadcrumb mixture to coat.
- Heat the rest of the oil in a large frying pan and sear the lamb on all sides.
- Transfer the racks to a roasting tin and roast in the oven for 8 minutes.
- Leave the lamb to rest for 4 minutes before serving with chunky ratatouille.

PREPARATION TIME 10 MINUTES

COOKING TIME 15 MINUTES

INGREDIENTS

50 g / 1 ¾ oz / ⅓ cup dry breadcrumbs
1 tbsp thyme leaves
1 tbsp summer savoury leaves
4 x 3-bone racks of lamb
4 tbsp olive oil
chunky ratatouille to serve

Chunky Ratatouille   332

- Roast a cubed aubergine, 2 sliced courgettes, 2 sliced red onions and 150 g cherry tomatoes with plenty of olive oil, salt and pepper for 30 minutes at 180°C.

333

SERVES 4 Coq au Vin

- Season the chicken well with salt and pepper, then toss with the flour and mustard powder to coat.
- Heat half of the oil and butter in a sauté pan and sear the chicken pieces on all sides.
- Remove the chicken from the pan and add the rest of the oil and butter, followed by the pancetta, onions and thyme.
- Sauté for 5 minutes, then pour in the wine and bring to a simmer. Transfer the chicken back to the pan, then simmer very gently for 1 hour.
- Season to taste with salt and black pepper.

PREPARATION TIME 10 MINUTES

COOKING TIME 1 HOUR 15 MINUTES

INGREDIENTS

1 chicken, jointed
3 tbsp plain (all purpose) flour
1 tsp mustard powder
3 tbsp olive oil
2 tbsp butter
150 g / 5 ½ oz pancetta, cubed
200 g / 7 oz baby onions, peeled
a few sprigs of thyme
600 ml / 1 pint / 2 ½ cups red wine

Chicken and Mushrooms in Red Wine   334

- Replace the pancetta with 150 g of baby button mushrooms, adding them half way through the cooking time.

335

SERVES 4

Baked Rabbit with Potatoes

PREPARATION TIME 10 MINUTES

COOKING TIME 1 HOUR 20 MINUTES

....

INGREDIENTS

800 g / 1 lb 12 oz baby new potatoes, halved if large
300 g / 10 ½ oz baby onions, peeled
3 tbsp olive oil
1 large rabbit, jointed
200 g / 7 oz / 1 ⅓ cups red and yellow cherry tomatoes
a few sprigs of thyme

- Preheat the oven to 200°C (180° fan) / 400F / gas 6.
- Boil the potatoes in salted water for 10 minutes then drain well.
- Arrange the potatoes with the onions and rabbit pieces in a large baking dish, then drizzle with olive oil and season with salt and pepper.
- Transfer the dish to the oven and bake for 30 minutes.
- Add the tomatoes to the dish with the thyme and return to the oven for 15 minutes.

Baked Rabbit with Squash

336

- Replace the potatoes with cubes of butternut squash, added raw to the baking dish without boiling first.

337

SERVES 4

Saddle of Rabbit with Tapenade

PREPARATION TIME 10 MINUTES

COOKING TIME 25 MINUTES

....

INGREDIENTS

2 boned rabbit saddles
4 tbsp black olive tapenade
4 tbsp olive oil
1 large onion, halved and sliced
1 tbsp capers, drained
8 kalamata olives
mashed potato to serve

- Preheat the oven to 160°C (140° fan) / 325F / gas 3.
- Spread the rabbit saddles with tapenade then roll up and secure with string. Season with salt and pepper.
- Heat the olive oil in a frying pan then sear the rabbit all over until golden brown.
- Transfer the rabbit to a roasting tin and roast in the oven for 20 minutes.
- Meanwhile, add the onions to the frying pan and fry over a low heat for 18 minutes, stirring occasionally.
- Stir the capers and olives into the onions and spoon onto 4 warm plates.
- Cut each saddle into 4 medallions and serve 2 pieces per person with mashed potato on the side.

Saddle of Rabbit with Pesto

338

- Replace the tapenade with pesto and stir 2 tbsp of shredded basil leaves into the onions at the end.

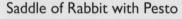

SERVES 6

Lamb and Onion Potato-Topped Pie

Lamb and Onion Pasties | 340

- Use the lamb and onion mixture to fill 300 g of shortcrust pastry, cut into 4 large circles. Crimp the edges, brush with egg and bake for 35 minutes.

Lamb and Onion Sweet Potato Pie | 341

- Replace the potatoes with sweet potatoes for a sweeter topping.

PREPARATION TIME 15 MINUTES

COOKING TIME 3 HOUR 15 MINUTES

INGREDIENTS

300 ml / 10 ½ fl. oz / 1 ¼ cups lamb stock
600 g/ 1 lb 5 oz lamb shoulder, in large chunks
3 onions, sliced

FOR THE TOPPING:
450 g / 1 lb floury potatoes, peeled and cubed
100 ml / 3 ½ fl. oz / ½ cup milk
50 g / 1 ¾ oz / ¼ cup butter
3 tbsp flat leaf parsley, leaves only
25 g / 1 oz / ⅓ cup breadcrumbs

- Preheat the oven to 150°C (130° fan) / 300F / gas 2 and bring the stock to the boil.
- Mix the lamb and onions together in a cast iron casserole dish and season well with salt and pepper. Pour over the hot stock then cover the dish and transfer to the oven for 3 hours.
- 30 minutes before the end of the cooking time, remove the lid so that the onions take on some colour.
- Boil the potatoes in salted water for 12 minutes, or until they are tender, then drain well. Return the potatoes to the saucepan and add the milk, butter and parsley, then mash until smooth.
- Remove the lamb from the oven and increase the temperature to 200°C (180° fan) / 400F / gas 6.
- Shred the lamb into smaller chunks with 2 forks and stir it back into the onions.
- Top the lamb with the mashed potato and sprinkle with breadcrumbs, then bake in the oven for 15 minutes or until the top is golden brown.

342

MAKES 18

Steak, Potato and Tomato Pie

Sausage and Potato Pie

343

- Replace the steak with 4 good quality pork sausages, skinned and broken into small chunks.

Gammon, Potato and Tomato Pie

344

- Replace the beef steak with thick gammon steak.

PREPARATION TIME 1 HOUR

COOKING TIME 45 MINUTES

....

INGREDIENTS

450 g / 1 lb potatoes, peeled and sliced
2 tbsp wholegrain mustard
1 large rump steak, diced
4 large ripe tomatoes, peeled, deseeded and chopped
1 egg, beaten

FOR THE PASTRY:
300 g / 10 ½ oz / 2 cups plain (all purpose) flour
150 g / 5 ½ oz / ⅔ cup butter, chilled

- Sieve the flour into a bowl then grate in the butter and mix well.
- Mix in enough cold water to form a pliable dough then wrap it in clingfilm and chill for 30 minutes.
- Boil the potatoes in salted water for 5 minutes then drain well.
- Preheat the oven to 190°C (170° fan) / 375F / gas 5 and butter a 23 cm round pie tin.
- Roll out half of the pastry and use it to line the prepared pie tin.
- Spread the base with mustard then layer up the potatoes with the steak and top with the tomatoes.
- Roll out the rest of the pastry, lay it over the pie and press down round the outside to seal.
- Cut away the excess pastry and crimp the edges with your fingers.
- Cut 2 holes in the lid for the steam to escape then brush the top of the pie with beaten egg.
- Bake the pie for 45 minutes – the pastry should be crisp and golden brown on top and starting to shrink away from the edge of the tin.

345

SERVES 6

Lamb and Mint Potato-Topped Pie

- Heat the oil in a saucepan and fry the onion and garlic for 3 minutes. Add the mince and fry for 2 minutes then add the stock and bring to a gentle simmer.
- Cover the pan with a lid and simmer very gently for 1 hour.
- Preheat the oven to 200°C (180° fan) / 400F / gas 6.
- Cook the potatoes in salted water for 10 minutes, or until they are tender, then drain well. Return the potatoes to the saucepan and add the milk and butter, then mash until smooth.
- Spoon half of the mash into a baking dish and spread it out in an even layer.
- Top with the lamb, then arrange the mint leaves on top before spooning over the rest of the mash.
- Sprinkle the top of the pie with breadcrumbs, then bake in the oven for 25 minutes or until the top is golden brown.

Lamb and Basil Potato-Topped Pie   346

- Stir 2 tbsp of pesto into the mince mixture before layering and replace the mint leaves with fresh basil leaves.

PREPARATION TIME 1 HOUR

COOKING TIME 1 HOUR 35 MINUTES

....

INGREDIENTS

2 tbsp olive oil
1 small onion, finely chopped
2 cloves of garlic, crushed
450 g / 1 lb / 2 cups minced lamb
300 ml / 10 fl. oz / 1 ¼ cups lamb stock
a small bunch of mint, leaves only

FOR THE TOPPING:
800 g / 1 lb 12 oz floury potatoes, peeled and cubed
100 ml / 3 ½ fl. oz / ½ cup milk
100 g / 3 ½ oz / ½ cup butter
50 g / 1 ¾ oz / ⅓ cup panko breadcrumbs

347

SERVES 4

Beef, Mushroom and Ale Pie

- Mix the flour with the mustard powder then season and toss with the beef to coat.
- Heat half of the oil in an oven-proof saucepan and sear the meat in batches until well browned.
- Remove the beef from the pan, add the rest of the oil and cook the onions, carrots, garlic and thyme for 5 minutes.
- Pour in the beer and boil for 5 minutes then add the stock and return the beef.
- 30 minutes before end, stir in the mushrooms and season.
- Bring the casserole to a simmer, cover and cook for 2 hours.
- Preheat the oven to 220°C (200° fan) / 425F / gas 7.
- Roll out the pastry on a floured surface and cut out a circle a little larger than the saucepan.
- Brush the top with egg then make the off-cuts into a lattice pattern on top.
- Transfer the pastry to the top of the saucepan, brush with egg, then bake in the oven for 15 minutes.

Beef, Stilton and Ale Pie   348

- Omit the mushrooms and stir 150 g of cubed Stilton into the beef before topping with the pastry lid.

PREPARATION TIME 25 MINUTES

COOKING TIME 2 HOURS 40 MINUTES

....

INGREDIENTS

2 tbsp plain (all purpose) flour
1 tsp mustard powder
1 kg / 2 lb 3 oz braising steak, cubed
4 tbsp olive oil
1 onion, finely chopped
1 carrot, cubed
3 cloves of garlic, finely chopped
4 sprigs of thyme
600 ml / 1 pint / 2 ½ cups real ale
600 ml / 1 pint / 2 ½ cups good quality beef stock
250 g / 9 oz / 3 cups mushrooms, quartered
250 g / 9 oz all-butter puff pastry
1 egg, beaten

SERVES 4

Steak and Kidney Pie

PREPARATION TIME 25 MINUTES

COOKING TIME 2 HOURS 40 MINUTES

INGREDIENTS

4 tbsp olive oil
1 kg / 2 lb 3 oz braising steak, cubed
4 lamb's kidneys, trimmed and cubed
1 onion, finely chopped
3 cloves of garlic, finely chopped
2 bay leaves
600 ml / 1 pint / 2 ½ cups good quality beef stock
250 g / 9 oz / 3 cups mushrooms, quartered
450 g / 1 lb all-butter puff pastry
1 egg, beaten

- Heat the oil in an oven-proof saucepan and sear the steak and kidney in batches until well browned.
- Remove the meat from the pan, add the onions, garlic and bay and cook for 5 minutes.
- Pour in the stock, return the beef then simmer for 2 hours.
- 30 minutes before the end of the cooking time, season to taste with salt and pepper and stir in the mushrooms.
- Preheat the oven to 220°C (200° fan) / 425F / gas 7.
- Roll out half of the pastry and use it to line a large pie dish.
- Ladle the pie filling into the pastry case and brush round the edge with beaten egg.
- Roll out the rest of the pastry and lay it over the pie.
- Scallop the edges and decorate the top with shapes from the off-cuts, then brush with beaten egg and make a hole.
- Bake the pie for 45 minutes or until the pastry is golden.

Steak and Oyster Pie

 350

- Omit the kidney and stir 8 freshly-shucked oysters into the pie filling before ladling it into the pastry case.

SERVES 4

Leek and Chilli Mashed Potato

PREPARATION TIME 5 MINUTES

COOKING TIME 20 MINUTES

INGREDIENTS

900 g / 2 lb potatoes, peeled and cubed
150 g / 5 ½ oz / ⅔ cup butter, cubed
1 leek, trimmed and sliced
2 mild red chillies (chilies), deseeded and sliced
2 tbsp flat leaf parsley, chopped
250 ml / 9 fl. oz / 1 cup milk

- Cook the potatoes in boiling salted water for 12 minutes or until tender all the way through.
- Tip the potatoes into a colander and leave to drain.
- Put the saucepan back on the heat and add the butter. Fry the leeks, chilli and parsley in the butter for 5 minutes, then pour in the milk and bring to a simmer.
- Take the pan off the heat and add the potatoes, then mash until smooth.

Garlic and Chilli Mashed Potato

352

- Omit the leek and fry 3 sliced cloves of garlic with the chilli and parsley until it just starts to turn pale gold in colour.

353

SERVES 4

Gammon with Honey Gravy

- Snip the fat of the gammon with scissors at 2 cm intervals to prevent the steaks from curling up in the pan.
- Heat the oil in a large frying pan and fry the steaks for 3 minutes on each side or until the fat is crisp and golden.
- Transfer the gammon to a warm plate and add the honey, chicken stock and Worcester sauce to the pan.
- Boil rapidly for 2 minutes, stirring all the time, to make a thin gravy.
- Serve the gammon steaks with the gravy spooned over and some leek and mustard mash on the side.

PREPARATION TIME 5 MINUTES

COOKING TIME 8 MINUTES

....

INGREDIENTS

4 smoked gammon steaks
2 tbsp sunflower oil
2 tbsp runny honey
150 ml / 5 ½ fl. oz / ⅔ cup chicken stock
1 tsp Worcester sauce
leek and mustard mash to serve

Leek and Mustard Mash

354

- Boil 900 g of potatoes until tender then drain well and mash with 3 chopped fried leeks, 100 g butter, 150 ml warm milk and 2 tsp Dijon mustard.

355

SERVES 4

Roasted Chicken and Peaches

- Preheat the oven to 200°C (180° fan) / 400F / gas 6.
- Mix the honey, mustard and lemon juice together and season with salt and pepper.
- Rub the mixture all over the chicken and peaches then arrange them in a roasting tin.
- Transfer the tin to the oven and roast for 40 minutes, basting with the juices halfway through.
- To test if the chicken is cooked, insert a skewer into the thickest part of the thigh. If the juices run clear with no trace of blood, it is ready.
- Peel off and discard the skin of the peaches, then serve with the chicken, same plain boiled rice and some rosemary roasted peppers.

PREPARATION TIME 10 MINUTES

COOKING TIME 40 MINUTES

....

INGREDIENTS

3 tbsp runny honey
3 tbsp wholegrain mustard
2 tbsp lemon juice
4 chicken leg quarters
4 fresh peaches
boiled rice and rosemary roasted peppers to serve

Rosemary Roasted Peppers

356

- Slice 4 red peppers and toss them with 2 tsp dried rosemary and 2 tbsp olive oil. Roast on the shelf below the chicken for 30 minutes, stirring halfway through.

357

SERVES 4

Ox Cheek and Pepper Stew

PREPARATION TIME 10 MINUTES

COOKING TIME 3 HOURS

INGREDIENTS

3 tbsp olive oil
800 g / 1 lb 12 oz ox cheek, cut into
large chunks
1 onion, chopped
1 carrot, chopped
3 red peppers, sliced
2 bay leaves
1 tbsp tomato puree
350 ml / 12 ½ fl. oz / 1 ½ cups
red wine
300 ml / 10 ½ fl. oz / 1 ¼ cups
beef stock

- Heat the oil in a saucepan then season the ox cheek with salt and pepper and brown it well all over.
- Remove the ox cheek from the pan and add the onion, carrot and peppers. Sauté for 5 minutes, then stir in the bay leaves and tomato puree.
- Pour in the wine and stock and bring to a gentle simmer, then return the ox cheek to the pan, put on a lid and stew very gently for 3 hours.
- Taste the sauce for seasoning and add salt and pepper as necessary before serving.

Ox Cheek and Cherry Stew

358

- Omit the red peppers and add 150 g of stoned cherries 30 minutes before the end of the cooking time.

359

SERVES 10

Mediterranean Roast Pork

PREPARATION TIME 3 HOURS 30
MINUTES

COOKING TIME 3 HOURS 15
MINUTES

INGREDIENTS

1 tsp fennel seeds
1 tsp white peppercorns
½ tsp dried chilli (chili) flakes
3 cloves of garlic, peeled
2 tbsp tomato puree
3 tbsp olive oil
4 kg / 8 lb 13 oz pork shoulder, on
the bone
3 leeks, cut into chunks
1 branch of bay leaves
200 ml / 7 fl. oz / ¾ cup dry
white wine

- Crush the fennel seeds, peppercorns and chilli flakes with a pestle and mortar. Add the garlic and a big pinch of salt and pound to a paste.
- Stir in the tomato puree and olive oil then rub the mixture all over the pork and leave to marinate for 3 hours or overnight.
- Preheat the oven to 230°C (210° fan) / 450F / gas 8.
- Arrange the leeks in a large roasting tin and sit the pork and bay on top.
- Transfer the tin to the oven and roast for 15 minutes, then pour over the wine.
- Reduce the temperature to 160°C (140° fan) / 325F / gas 3 and roast for 3 hours, basting every half an hour.
- Cover the roasting tin with a double layer of foil and leave the pork to rest for 10 minutes before carving.

Mediterranean Pork Chops

360

- Use the marinade for pork chops and grill them for 4 minutes on each side instead of roasting.

361

SERVES 4

Lamb Shank and Vegetable Tagines

Oxtail and Vegetable Tagines   362

- Replace the lamb shanks with oxtail cutlets.

Pork Knuckle Tagine   363

- Replace the lamb shanks with 2 pork knuckles and regularly baste. The pork knuckle may take a little longer to cook, so ensure its cooked through before serving.

PREPARATION TIME 5 MINUTES

COOKING TIME 2 HOURS

INGREDIENTS

4 lamb shanks
12 baby carrots, peeled
8 spring onions, trimmed
4 small turnips, peeled
6 new potatoes, peeled and halved
400 ml / 14 fl. oz / 1 ⅔ cups lamb stock
2 cloves of garlic, crushed
1 lemon, juiced
1 tbsp flat leaf parsley, chopped

- Preheat the oven to 180°C (160° fan) / 350F / gas 4.
- Put each lamb shank in an individual tagine and divide the vegetables between them.
- Mix the lamb stock with the garlic and lemon juice and season well with salt and pepper, then pour it over the lamb and put on the lids.
- Transfer the tagines to the oven and bake for 2 hours.
- Remove the lids and sprinkle with parsley before serving.

364

MAKES 18

Veal with Creamy Mustard Sauce

Veal with Green Peppercorn sauce

365

- Stir 2 tbsp of brined green peppercorns into the sauce before seasoning.

Beef with Creamy Mustard Sauce

366

- Replace the veal with good quality beef sirloin.

PREPARATION TIME 2 MINUTES

COOKING TIME 15 MINUTES

INGREDIENTS

800 g / 1 lb 12 oz veal sirloin steak
2 tbsp butter
1 clove of garlic, crushed
1 tbsp Dijon mustard
300 ml / 10 ½ fl. oz / 1 ¼ cups double
(heavy) cream
lemon juice to taste
sprigs of flowering thyme to garnish

- Cut the veal steaks into large chunks, discarding any fat or sinew, and season well with salt and pepper.
- Melt the butter in a frying pan over a high heat, then fry the veal for 10 minutes, turning regularly, so that the pieces brown evenly.
- Remove the veal from the pan and keep warm while you make the sauce.
- Add the garlic to the pan and fry for 1 minute, then stir in the mustard and cream and simmer for 3 minutes or until thickened. Add lemon juice, salt and pepper to taste.
- Divide the veal between 4 warm plates, spoon over the sauce and garnish with flowering thyme.

367

MAKES 1 LITRE

Homemade Vegetable Stock

- Put all of the ingredients into a large saucepan and cover with 2 litres of cold water.
- Bring the mixture to the boil and skim off any scum that rises to the surface.
- Reduce the heat to a simmer and cook for 1 hour or until the liquid has reduced by half.
- Strain the stock through a sieve and store in the fridge until needed.

PREPARATION TIME 5 MINUTES

COOKING TIME 1 HOUR

INGREDIENTS

2 carrots, cut into chunks
1 parsnip, cut into chunks
2 leeks, cut into chunks
4 small turnips
1 thick slice root ginger
4 bay leaves
a small bunch of parsley stalks
1 lemongrass stalk, quartered
1 tsp black peppercorns

Homemade Chicken Stock   368

- Roast 500 g of chicken wings at 200⁰C for 30 minutes, then add them to the stock pan with the vegetables. Increase the simmering time to 2 hours.

369

SERVES 4

Stewed Oxtail

- Season the oxtail well with salt and pepper.
- Heat half of the oil in a large saucepan and sear the oxtail on both sides until well browned.
- Remove it from the pan, add the rest of the oil and fry the carrots and onions for 5 minutes.
- Add the bay leaves and stock to the pan and bring to a simmer, then return the oxtail pieces.
- Cover the pan with a lid and simmer very gently for 3 hours.
- Taste the sauce for seasoning and adjust with salt and pepper as necessary, then ladle into warm bowls and garnish with parsley.

PREPARATION TIME 5 MINUTES

COOKING TIME 3 HOURS 15 MINUTES

INGREDIENTS

8 pieces of oxtail, on the bone
4 tbsp olive oil
2 carrots, thickly sliced
250 g / 9 oz baby onions, peeled
2 bay leaves
1 litre / 1 pint 15 fl. oz / 4 cups good quality beef stock
a few parsley sprigs to serve

Stewed Oxtail with Parsnip   370

- Replace the carrots with 2 sliced parsnips and use 2 sprigs of rosemary instead of the bay.

(371) SERVES 6

Stewed Veal with Olives

PREPARATION TIME 5 MINUTES

COOKING TIME 2 HOURS 45 MINUTES

INGREDIENTS

4 tbsp olive oil
800 g / 1 lb 12 oz veal braising steak, cut into chunks
1 onion, chopped
3 cloves of garlic, crushed
1 tsp dried herbs de Provence
1 red pepper, diced
1 green pepper, diced
400 g / 14 oz / 2 cups canned tomatoes, chopped
200 ml / 7 fl. oz / ¾ cup veal stock
150 g / 5 ½ oz / 1 cup green olives
bay-infused boiled potatoes to serve

- Heat half of the oil in a large cast iron casserole dish and sear the veal pieces on all sides until well browned.
- Remove the veal from the pan, add the rest of the oil and fry the onions, garlic, herbs and peppers for 5 minutes.
- Add the tomatoes and stock and bring to a simmer then return the veal to the pan.
- Cover the casserole with a lid and simmer gently for 2 hours.
- Season the sauce to taste with salt and pepper, then stir in the olives and simmer for a further 30 minutes.

(372) SERVES 4

Mediterranean Duck Stew

PREPARATION TIME 5 MINUTES

COOKING TIME 2 HOURS 15 MINUTES

INGREDIENTS

4 tbsp olive oil
1 duck, jointed
8 small pork sausages
1 onion, chopped
3 cloves of garlic, crushed
a few sprigs of thyme
1 red pepper, diced
1 yellow pepper, diced
400 g / 14 oz / 2 cups canned tomatoes, chopped
400 g / 14 oz / 2 cups canned butterbeans, drained
200 ml / 7 fl. oz / ¾ cup white wine

- Heat half of the oil in a large cast iron casserole dish and sear the duck pieces and sausages on all sides until well browned.
- Remove the meat from the pan, add the rest of the oil and fry the onions, garlic, thyme and peppers for 5 minutes.
- Add the tomatoes, beans and stock and bring to a simmer then return the meat to the pan.
- Cover the casserole with a lid and simmer gently for 2 hours.
- Season the sauce to taste with salt and pepper before serving.

Duck and Sweet Potato Gratin

- Preheat the oven to 200°C (180° fan) / 400F / gas 6.
- Bake the sweet potatoes in their skins for 45 or until a skewer inserted slides in easily.
- Peel off and discard the skins and mash the flesh with the butter and garlic, seasoning with salt and pepper.
- Shred the duck with a fork and discard the bones. Stir the duck into the sweet potato mixture and spoon it into a baking dish.
- Sprinkle the top with breadcrumbs then bake for 20 minutes or until the top is golden brown.

PREPARATION TIME 10 MINUTES

COOKING TIME 1 HOUR 5 MINUTES

....

INGREDIENTS

3 sweet potatoes
50 g / 1 ¾ oz / ¼ cup butter
1 clove of garlic, crushed
2 confit duck legs
25 g / 1 oz / ⅓ cup fine breadcrumbs

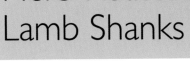

374

SERVES 8

Roast Fillet of Beef

PREPARATION TIME 5 MINUTES

COOKING TIME 45 MINUTES

....

INGREDIENTS

1 kg / 2 lb 3 oz fillet of beef
3 tbsp olive oil

- Preheat the oven to 230°C (210° fan) / 450F / gas 8 and season the beef well with salt and pepper.
- Heat a large oven-proof frying pan on the hob until smoking hot, then add the olive oil and sear the beef on all sides.
- Transfer the pan to the oven and roast for 35 minutes.
- Move the beef to a warm plate, wrap with a double layer of foil and leave to rest for 10 minutes before carving.

375

SERVES 4

Herb Roasted Lamb Shanks

PREPARATION TIME 10 MINUTES

COOKING TIME 2 HOURS 15 MINUTES

....

INGREDIENTS

4 lamb shanks
1 onion, cut into wedges
3 carrots, cut into chunks

1 bulb of garlic, broken into cloves
1 bunch mint
1 bunch basil
1 bunch thyme
4 tbsp olive oil

- Preheat the oven to 180°C (160° fan) / 350F / gas 4.
- Mix all of the ingredients together in a large roasting tin or baking dish and season well with salt and pepper.
- Wrap the dish in a double layer of foil, sealing the edges tightly, then transfer it to the oven and bake for 2 hours or until the lamb is very tender.
- Carefully remove the foil then return the dish to the oven for 15 minutes to colour the meat.

376

SERVES 4

Thai Red Pork Curry

PREPARATION TIME 2 MINUTES

COOKING TIME 12 MINUTES

....

INGREDIENTS

2 tbsp vegetable oil
2 tbsp Thai red curry paste
600 g / 1 lb 5 ½ oz pork tenderloin,
cubed
1 green pepper, sliced
400 ml / 14 fl. oz / 1 ⅔ cups
coconut milk
1 tsp caster (superfine) sugar
1 tbsp Thai fish sauce
1 large mild red chilli (chili), sliced
3 kaffir lime leaves, finely shredded

- Heat the oil in a wok and fry the curry paste for 2 minutes.
- Add the pork and green pepper to the wok and stir-fry for 4 minutes then add the coconut milk and bring to a simmer.
- Simmer for 3 minutes then season to taste with the caster sugar and fish sauce.
- Spoon the curry onto a serving plate and garnish with chilli and lime leaves.

Thai Red Prawn Curry

 377

- Omit the pork and add 300 g of raw peeled prawns when the coconut milk starts to simmer.

378

SERVES 4

Homemade Baked Beans with Sausages

PREPARATION TIME 10 MINUTES

COOKING TIME 3 HOURS 30 MINUTES

....

INGREDIENTS

400 g / 14 oz / 2 ⅔ cups dried haricot
beans, soaked overnight
1 large ham hock
400 g / 14 oz / 2 ⅔ cups canned
tomatoes, chopped
2 tbsp vegetable oil
8 pork sausages
2 tbsp flat leaf parsley,
finely chopped

- Preheat the oven to 150°C (130° fan) / 300F / gas 2.
- Drain the beans and put them in a large cast iron casserole dish with the ham hock and canned tomatoes, then add enough cold water to cover it all by 5 cm.
- Bring the pan to the boil on the stove, then cover with a lid and transfer to the oven for 4 hours, topping up with water if it starts to get too dry.
- Heat the oil in a frying pan and brown the sausage all over. Stir the baked beans and taste for seasoning, then add the sausages and return to the oven for a further 30 minutes.
- Slice the ham off the bone and divide between 4 warm bowls with the sausages and beans, then sprinkle with parsley.

Vegetarian Baked Beans

379

- Omit the ham and sausages and use a good quality vegetable stock instead of the water.

MAKES 4

Sausage and Cauliflower Cheese Pots

- Preheat the oven to 180°C (160° fan) / 350 F, gas 4.
- Cook the cauliflower in boiling, salted water for 6 minutes or until almost cooked, then drain well.
- Meanwhile, heat the oil in a frying pan and brown the sausages all over.
- Melt the butter in a saucepan then stir in the flour.
- Gradually whisk in the milk a little at a time until it is all incorporated.
- Cook the sauce over a low heat, stirring, until the mixture thickens. Beat vigorously to remove any lumps.
- Take the pan off the heat and stir in the cauliflower and half of the cheese. Season to taste with salt and pepper.
- Divide the mixture between 4 gratin dishes, press 2 sausages into the top. Sprinkle with the remaining cheese.
- Sprinkle with nutmeg and bake for 25 minutes or until the tops are golden brown and the sausages are cooked.

PREPARATION TIME 20 MINUTES

COOKING TIME 25 MINUTES

....

INGREDIENTS

400 g / 14 oz cauliflower, cubed
2 tbsp olive oil
8 chipolata sausages
2 tbsp butter
2 tbsp plain (all-purpose) flour
600 ml / 1 pint / 2 ½ cups milk
150 g / 5 ½ oz Cheddar cheese, grated
freshly grated nutmeg for sprinkling

Sausage and Macaroni Cheese Pots

381

- Boil 400 g of dried macaroni for 10 minutes and use in place of the cauliflower.

382

SERVES 4

Chicken, Mustard and Potato Hotpot

- Coat the chicken with mustard and leave to marinate for 1 hour.
- Boil the potatoes in salted water for 8 minutes then drain well.
- Preheat the oven to 160°C (140° fan) / 325F / gas 3.
- Melt the butter with the oil in a frying pan over a high heat then sear the chicken in batches until browned all over.
- Remove the meat from the pan, lower the heat and add the onions. Cook for 5 minutes, stirring occasionally until softened.
- Add the garlic and herbs and cook for 2 more minutes, then incorporate the stock and bring to a simmer.
- Layer up the chicken and potatoes with the stock in a casserole dish, then cover tightly with foil or a lid.
- Bake the hotpot for 1 hour 30 minutes then remove the lid and cook for a further 30 minutes.

PREPARATION TIME 1 HOUR

COOKING TIME 2 HOURS 15 MINUTES

....

INGREDIENTS

4 chicken breasts, halved horizontally
3 tbsp wholegrain mustard
900 g / 2 lb potatoes, cut into 3mm slices
1 tbsp butter
2 tbsp olive oil
2 onions, finely chopped
2 cloves of garlic, finely chopped
a few sprigs of thyme
1 bay leaf
800 ml / 1 pint 8 oz / 3 ¼ cups chicken stock

Beef, Mustard and Potato Hotpot

383

- Replace the chicken breast with 600 g of beef braising steak, cut into thick slices.

384

SERVES 6

Chorizo and Parsley Potato-Topped Pie

PREPARATION TIME 15 MINUTES

COOKING TIME 3 HOUR 15 MINUTES

INGREDIENTS

450 g / 1 lb floury potatoes, peeled and cubed
100 ml / 3 ½ fl. oz / ½ cup milk
50 g / 1 ¾ oz / ¼ cup butter
2 tbsp olive oil
1 onion, finely chopped
2 cloves of garlic, crushed
3 medium tomatoes, diced
250 g / 9 oz chorizo, thinly sliced
a large bunch of parsley, chopped

- Preheat the oven to 200°C (180° fan) / 400F / gas 6.
- Boil the potatoes in salted water for 12 minutes, or until they are tender, then drain well. Return the potatoes to the saucepan and add the milk and butter, then mash until smooth.
- While the potatoes are cooking, heat the oil in a frying pan and fry the onion and garlic for 5 minutes. Add the tomatoes and cook for 2 more minutes, then combine with the chorizo and parsley.
- Spoon the mixture into a baking dish and top with the mashed potato.
- Level the top with a spatula, then bake in the oven for 15 minutes or until the potato is golden brown.

Bacon and Parsley Potato-Topped Pie

385

- Use 250 g of bacon, cut into bite-sized pieces, instead of the chorizo.

386

SERVES 6

Beef and Turnip Stew

PREPARATION TIME 10 MINUTES

COOKING TIME 3 HOURS 20 MINUTES

INGREDIENTS

2 tbsp plain (all purpose) flour
1 tsp mustard powder
1 kg / 2 lb 3 oz braising steak, cubed
4 tbsp olive oil
1 onion, finely chopped
100 g / 3 ½ oz pancetta, cubed
300 g / 10 ½ oz young turnips, halved
3 cloves of garlic, finely chopped
2 bay leaves
600 ml / 1 pint / 2 ½ cups red wine
1 orange, juiced and zest pared
600 ml / 1 pint / 2 ½ cups good quality beef stock

- Preheat the oven to 140°C (120° fan) / 275F / gas 1.
- Mix the flour with the mustard powder and a good pinch of salt and pepper and toss it with the beef to coat.
- Heat half of the oil in a large cast iron casserole dish then sear the meat in batches until well browned.
- Remove the beef from the pan, add the rest of the oil and cook the onions and pancetta for 5 minutes.
- Add the turnips, garlic and bay and stir-fry for 2 minutes.
- Pour in the wine and boil for 5 minutes then add the stock to the pan with the orange juice and zest and return the beef.
- Bring the casserole to a gentle simmer then put on a lid, transfer it to the oven and cook for 3 hours.
- Season to taste with salt and pepper before serving.

Beef and Fennel Stew

387

- Replace the turnips with a sliced bulb of fennel and add 1 tsp of fennel seeds when you fry the onion.

MAKES 18

388

Beef and Carrot Meatloaf

Beef and Mushroom Meatloaf

389

- Replace the carrots with 200 g of finely chopped mushrooms.

Veal and Carrot Meatloaf

390

- Replace the minced beef with minced rose veal for a more subtle flavour.

PREPARATION TIME 15 MINUTES

COOKING TIME 45 MINUTES

INGREDIENTS

2 tbsp olive oil
1 onion, finely chopped
2 carrots, finely chopped
1 clove of garlic, crushed
¼ tsp chilli (chili) flakes
250 g / 9 oz / 1 cup minced beef
250 g / 9 oz / 1 cup sausagemeat
50 g / 1 ¾ oz / ⅔ cup fresh white breadcrumbs
3 tbsp flat leaf parsley, finely chopped
1 egg yolk

- Preheat the oven to 190°C (170° fan) / 375F / gas 5.
- Heat the oil in a frying pan and fry the onion and carrots for 10 minutes or until softened.
- Add the garlic and chilli flakes and cook for 2 more minutes, stirring constantly, then transfer to a large mixing bowl.
- Add the mince, sausagemeat, breadcrumbs, parsley and egg yolk and mix it all together.
- Season with salt and pepper then pack the mixture into a loaf tin or baking dish.
- Transfer the dish to the oven and bake for 45 minutes or until cooked through and golden brown.

391

SERVES 6

Lamb and Turnip Tagine

Chicken and Turnip Tagine

392

- Replace the lamb with 800 g of boneless chicken thigh, cut into large chunks, and use chicken stock in place of the lamb stock.

Beef and Turnip Tagine

393

- Instead of lamb, use 800g of diced beef steak and use beef stock instead of lamb stock.

PREPARATION TIME 5 MINUTES

COOKING TIME 1 HOUR 30 MINUTES

INGREDIENTS

800 g / 1 lb 12 oz lamb shoulder, cubed
450 g / 1 lb young turnips, cut into wedges
2 tsp ras el hanout spice mix
2 tbsp olive oil
2 tbsp honey
4 spring onions (scallions), sliced
3 cloves of garlic, finely chopped
50 g / 1 ¾ oz / ¼ cup sultanas
2 tbsp mint leaves, finely chopped, plus extra for garnish
500 ml / 17 ½ fl. oz / 2 cups good quality lamb stock

- Preheat the oven to 160°C (140° fan) / 325F / gas 3.
- Put the lamb, turnips, spices, oil, honey, onions, garlic, sultanas and mint in a large tagine with a big pinch of salt and stir well to mix.
- Pour over the stock then put on the lid and transfer the tagine to the oven.
- Cook the tagine for 1 hour 30 minutes, then garnish with a little more mint.

394

SERVES 4

Poussin with Apple and Parsnip

- Preheat the oven to 200°C (180° fan) / 400F / gas 6.
- Put the poussin in a roasting tin and season well with salt and pepper.
- Transfer the tin to the oven and roast for 40 minutes, basting with the juices halfway through.
- To test if the poussin are cooked, insert a skewer into the thickest part of the thigh. If the juices run clear with no trace of blood, they are ready.
- While the poussin are roasting, cook the parsnip in boiling salted water for 10 minutes or until tender, then drain well.
- Heat the butter in a sauté pan and add the parsnips, apple and chilli (chili) flakes. Sauté for 10 minutes then drizzle with honey and season to taste with salt and pepper.

PREPARATION TIME 10 MINUTES

COOKING TIME 40 MINUTES

....

INGREDIENTS

4 whole poussin
4 parsnips, peeled and diced
2 tbsp butter
3 eating apples, peeled and diced
¼ tsp chilli (chili) flakes
1 tbsp runny honey

Poussin with Apple and Parsnip Mash
395

- Transfer the sautéed apple and parsnip to a food processor and blend to a smooth puree.

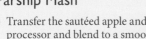
396

SERVES 4

Smoked Haddock and Sweet Potato Gratin

- Preheat the oven to 200°C (180° fan) / 400F / gas 6.
- Bake the sweet potatoes in their skins for 45 or until a skewer inserted slides in easily.
- Peel off and discard the skins and mash the flesh with the butter and garlic, seasoning with salt and pepper.
- While the potatoes are cooking, put the milk and bay leaf in a small saucepan and bring to a simmer.
- Lay the haddock in a snugly-fitting dish and pour the hot milk over the top. Cover the dish with clingfilm and leave to stand for 10 minutes.
- Remove any skin and bones from the haddock then flake the flesh into the mashed sweet potato, adding enough of the milk to make a soft consistency.
- Spoon the mixture into a baking dish and scatter with the cheese and chives then bake for 20 minutes or until the top is golden brown.

PREPARATION TIME 10 MINUTES

COOKING TIME 1 HOUR 5 MINUTES

....

INGREDIENTS

3 large sweet potatoes
50 g / 1 ¾ oz / ¼ cup butter
1 clove of garlic, crushed
500 ml / 17 ½ fl. oz / 2 cups milk
1 bay leaf
400 g / 14 oz smoked haddock fillet
50 g / 1 ¾ oz / ½ cup Red Leicester, grated
1 tbsp chives

Salmon and Sweet Potato Gratin
397

- Use 400 g of salmon fillet in place of the haddock and use fish stock instead of the milk.

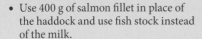

121

398

SERVES 4

Duck Breast with Balsamic Gravy

PREPARATION TIME 5 MINUTES

COOKING TIME 15 MINUTES

....

INGREDIENTS

2 tbsp sunflower oil
3 small duck breasts
2 tbsp balsamic glaze
50 ml / 1 ¾ fl. oz / ¼ cup port
150 ml / 5 ½ fl. oz / ⅔ cup duck stock
1 tbsp chives, finely chopped
sautéed peppers and mushrooms
to serve

- Preheat the oven to 200°C (180° fan) / 400F / gas 6 and put a roasting tin in to heat.
- Heat the oil in a large frying pan and fry the duck, skin side down, for 10 minutes or until the fat is crisp and golden.
- Transfer the duck breasts to the roasting tin in the oven, with the skin facing up and roast for 5 minutes.
- Meanwhile, add the balsamic and port to the frying pan and bubble for 1 minute then add the stock and boil until reduced to a syrupy gravy.
- Transfer the duck to a warm plate to rest for 5 minutes, then slice and divide between 4 warm plates.
- Spoon over the gravy and serve with the sautéed peppers and mushrooms.

Sautéed Peppers and Mushrooms | 399

- Heat 2 tbsp olive oil in a pan and sauté a sliced red and yellow pepper with 200 g of wild mushrooms for 6 minutes. Season well with salt and pepper.

400

SERVES 6

Spaghetti with Veal Meatballs

PREPARATION TIME 20 MINUTES

COOKING TIME 35 MINUTES

....

INGREDIENTS

4 tbsp olive oil
1 onion, finely chopped
1 clove of garlic, crushed
250 g / 9 oz minced veal
250 g / 9 oz sausagemeat
50 g fresh white breadcrumbs
1 tsp dried oregano
1 egg yolk
400 ml / 7 fl. oz / 1 ⅔ cups tomato
passata
600 g / 1 lb 4 oz spaghetti
2 tbsp flat leaf parsley, finely
chopped
50 g / 1 ¾ oz / ½ cup Parmesan,
finely grated

- Heat half of the oil in a large sauté pan and fry the onion for 5 minutes or until softened.
- Add the garlic and cook for 2 more minutes, stirring constantly, then scrape the mixture into a mixing bowl and leave to cool.
- Add the mince, sausagemeat, breadcrumbs, oregano and egg yolk and mix well then shape into cherry-sized meatballs.
- Heat the rest of the oil in the sauté pan and sear the meatballs on all sides.
- Pour over the tomato passata and 200 ml of water and simmer gently for 20 minutes. Season well.
- While the sauce is cooking, boil the pasta in salted water according to the packet instructions or until al dente.
- Drain the pasta and stir it into the pan, divide between 6 bowls then sprinkle with parsley and Parmesan.

Meatball Pasta Bake | 401

- Use penne instead of spaghetti. Transfer everything to a baking dish after cooking and top with 150 g sliced mozzarella and the Parmesan, then bake at 200°C for 25 minutes.

402

SERVES 6 Beef and Butterbean Stew

- Preheat the oven to 140°C (120° fan) / 275F / gas 1.
- Heat half of the oil in a large cast iron casserole dish and sear the beef on all sides until well browned.
- Remove the meat from the pan, add the rest of the oil and fry the onions and garlic for 5 minutes.
- Add the tomatoes and stock and bring to a simmer then return the beef to the pan.
- Cover the casserole with a lid, transfer it to the oven and cook for 3 hours.
- 30 minutes before the end of the cooking time, stir in the butterbeans and broccoli and season the sauce with salt and pepper as necessary.
- Ladle into bowls and top with a spoonful of fresh tomato and chilli relish.

PREPARATION TIME 5 MINUTES

COOKING TIME 3 HOURS 15 MINUTES

....

INGREDIENTS

4 tbsp olive oil
800 g / 1 lb 12 oz braising steak, diced
1 onion, finely chopped
4 cloves of garlic, finely chopped
400 g / 14 oz / 2 cups canned tomatoes, chopped
400 ml / 14 fl. oz / 1 ⅔ cups good quality beef stock
400 g / 14 oz / 2 cups canned butterbeans, drained
1 head of broccoli, broken into florets
fresh tomato and chilli (chili) relish to serve

Fresh Tomato and Chilli Relish   403

- Put 3 skinned, deseeded tomatoes in a food processor with 3 peeled garlic cloves, 2 deseeded red chillies (chilies), ½ tsp salt and 4 tbsp olive oil. Pulse until finely chopped.

404

MAKES 6 Lamb and Hazelnut Potato-Topped Pies

- Heat the oil in a saucepan and fry the onion, garlic, carrot and cumin for 3 minutes. Add the lamb shoulder and fry for 2 minutes then add the stock.
- Lay greaseproof paper on top of the meat and cover the pan with a lid then simmer gently for 2 hours.
- Preheat the oven to 200°C (180° fan) / 400F / gas 6.
- Cook the potatoes in salted water for 10 minutes, then drain well. Return the potatoes to the saucepan and add the milk and butter, then mash.
- Shred the lamb with 2 forks and season to taste with salt and pepper. Arrange 6 metal ring moulds on a baking tray and half-fill each one with the lamb.
- Top the lamb with the mashed potato and sprinkle with hazelnuts, then bake in the oven for 15 minutes or until the tops are golden brown.
- Unmould the pies onto warm plates and garnish with salad leaves.

PREPARATION TIME 10 MINUTES

COOKING TIME 2 HOURS 30 MINUTES

....

INGREDIENTS

2 tbsp olive oil
1 small onion, finely chopped
1 carrot, grated
2 cloves of garlic, crushed
1 tsp ground cumin
450 g/ 1 lb lamb shoulder, cubed
600 ml / 1 pint / 2 ½ cups lamb stock
salad leaves to garnish

FOR THE TOPPING:
450 g / 1 lb floury potatoes, peeled and cubed
100 ml / 3 ½ fl. oz / ½ cup milk
50 g / 1 ¾ oz / ¼ cup butter
50 g / 1 ¾ oz / ⅓ cup hazelnuts (cob nuts), chopped

Lamb and Walnut Potato-Topped Pies   405

- Add a tbsp of pomegranate molasses to the lamb after shredding and replace the hazelnuts with walnuts.

406

MAKES 1

Hawaiian Pizza

PREPARATION TIME 2 HOURS 30 MINUTES

COOKING TIME 10 – 12 MINUTES

INGREDIENTS

200 g / 7 oz / 1 ⅓ cups strong white bread flour, plus extra for dusting
½ tsp easy blend dried yeast
1 tsp caster (superfine) sugar
½ tsp fine sea salt
1 tbsp olive oil
3 tbsp tomato pizza sauce
100 g / 3 ½ oz canned pineapple chunks, drained
100 g / 3 ½ oz cooked ham, sliced
4 button mushrooms, sliced
100 g / 3 ½ oz mozzarella, sliced
basil leaves to garnish

- Mix together the flour, yeast, sugar and salt and stir the oil into 140 ml of warm water.
- Stir the liquid into the dry ingredients then knead on a lightly oiled surface for 10 minutes.
- Leave the dough to rest covered with oiled clingfilm for 1 – 2 hours until doubled in size.
- Preheat the oven to 220°C (200° fan) / 425F/ gas 7 and grease a non-stick baking tray.
- Knead the dough for 2 more minutes then roll out thinly into a circle and transfer to the baking tray.
- Spread the dough with the pizza sauce and top with the pineapple, ham, mushrooms and mozzarella.
- Transfer the tray to the oven and bake for 10 – 12 minutes or until the pizza dough is cooked through underneath.
- Sprinkle with black pepper and basil leaves.

Bacon and Mushroom Pizza   407

- Omit the pineapple and use chopped streaky bacon instead of the ham.

408

SERVES 4

Sedanini with Pork Ragu

PREPARATION TIME 10 MINUTES

COOKING TIME 45 MINUTES

INGREDIENTS

4 tbsp olive oil
2 cloves of garlic, crushed
1 red chilli (chili), finely chopped
200 g / 7 oz pork shoulder, cubed
400 g / 14 oz / 1 ¾ cups canned tomatoes, chopped
400 g / 14 oz sedanini pasta
a few basil leaves to garnish

- Heat the oil in a frying pan and fry the garlic and chilli for 2 minutes.
- Add the pork and sauté until lightly browned.
- Stir in the canned tomatoes and simmer gently for 1 hour 30 minutes, adding a little water if the mixture gets too dry.
- Cook the pasta in boiling salted water according to the packet instructions or until al dente.
- Taste the sauce and season with salt and black pepper.
- Drain the pasta and stir it into the sauce then garnish with basil leaves.

Sedanini with Wild Boar Ragu   409

- Replace the pork with wild boar and add 150 ml of red wine when you add the tomatoes. Increase the simmering time to 2 hours 30 minutes.

410

SERVES 2

Steak Tagliata with Rocket

Steak Tagliata with Parmesan Salad

411

- Shave some Parmesan over the rocket with a vegetable peeler and dress with lemon juice and olive oil.

Steak Tagliata with Baby Spinach

412

- Replace the rocket with fresh baby leaf spinach and sprinkle with freshly ground black pepper.

PREPARATION TIME 5 MINUTES

COOKING TIME 30 MINUTES

INGREDIENTS

225 g / 8 oz rump steak
1 tbsp butter
50 g / 1 ¾ oz rocket (arugula) leaves
balsamic vinegar to dress

- Preheat the oven to 200°C (180° fan) / 400F / gas 6 and put a frying pan on to heat for 5 minutes or until smoking hot.
- Trim the beef of any fat and dry it really well with kitchen paper.
- Season the steak liberally with sea salt and black pepper, then transfer it to the frying pan.
- Allow it to cook, without disturbing, for 3 minutes, then turn it over, add the knob of butter and transfer the pan to the oven for 4 minutes.
- Move the beef to a warm plate, wrap with a double layer of foil and leave to rest for 5 minutes.
- Arrange the rocket on a wooden board. When the steak has rested, cut it into thick slices and arrange on top of the rocket.
- Serve with balsamic vinegar on the side for drizzling over.

(413)

SERVES 4

Ham and Leek Potato-Topped Pie

Ham, Leek and Mushroom Pie

(414)

- Add 150 g of sliced button mushrooms to the leeks before frying.

Ham, Leek and Sweet Potato Pie

(415)

- Use sweet potatoes instead of potatoes for the topping for a richer flavour.

PREPARATION TIME 10 MINUTES

COOKING TIME 30 MINUTES

INGREDIENTS

450 g / 1 lb potatoes, peeled and cubed
4 tbsp butter
2 tbsp plain (all purpose) flour
500 ml / 17 ½ fl. oz / 2 cups milk
2 tbsp olive oil
2 leeks, chopped
200 g / 7 oz cooked ham, sliced
75 g / 2 ½ oz / ¾ cup Cheddar, grated
1 tbsp flat leaf parsley, chopped

- Preheat the oven to 200°C (180° fan) / 400F / gas 6.
- Cook the potatoes in boiling salted water for 12 minutes or until tender then drain well.
- Heat half of the butter in a small saucepan and stir in the flour.
- Reserve 100 ml of the milk for the potatoes and slowly incorporate the rest into the butter and flour mixture, stirring constantly. Cook until the sauce is thick and smooth.
- Heat the oil in a frying pan and fry the leeks for 5 minutes or until soft, then stir them into the sauce with the ham.
- Season to taste with salt and pepper then scrape the mixture into a baking dish.
- Mash the potatoes with the reserved milk and remaining butter and spoon it on top of the leek and ham mixture.
- Sprinkle with cheese and parsley then bake for 30 minutes or until the topping is golden brown.

416

SERVES 4

Spaghetti with Ragu

- Heat the oil in a large saucepan and fry the onion, carrot and celery for 5 minutes, stirring occasionally.
- Add the garlic and cook for 2 minutes, then add the mince.
- Fry the mince until it starts to brown then add the chopped tomatoes and stock and bring to a gentle simmer.
- Cook for 1 hour, stirring occasionally, until the mince is tender and the sauce has thickened a little.
- Boil the pasta in salted water according to the packet instructions or until al dente.
- Drain the pasta and stir it into the ragu, then divide between 4 warm bowls.
- Use a vegetable peeler to shave over some Parmesan and garnish with basil leaves.

Tagliatelle with Ragu   417

- Use 500 g freshly made tagliatelle instead of the dried spaghetti to capture more of the sauce.

PREPARATION TIME 2 MINUTES

COOKING TIME 1 HOUR 30 MINUTES

INGREDIENTS

2 tbsp olive oil
½ onion, finely chopped
½ carrot, finely chopped
½ celery stick, finely chopped
2 cloves of garlic, crushed
250 g / 9 oz / 1 ¼ cups minced beef
400 g / 14 oz / 1 ¾ cups canned tomatoes, chopped
150 ml / 5 ½ fl. oz / ⅔ cup beef stock
400 g / 14 oz dried spaghetti
50 g / 1 ¾ oz Parmesan
basil leaves to garnish

418

SERVES 4

Chicken and Bucatini Pasta Bake

- Preheat the oven to 180⁰C (160⁰ fan), gas 4.
- Cook the bucatini in boiling, salted water for 10 minutes or until almost cooked. Drain well.
- Meanwhile, heat the oil in a sauté pan and fry the garlic and chilli for 2 minutes. Add the chicken and sauté for 3 minutes or until lightly coloured, then pour in the passata.
- Simmer for 5 minutes, then stir in the pasta and basil.
- Scrape the mixture into a baking dish and sprinkle with cheese.
- Transfer the dish to the oven and bake for 30 minutes or until the top is golden brown and the pasta is cooked.

Chicken and Bacon Pasta Bake   419

- Add 6 chopped rashers of smoked streaky bacon when you fry the chicken.

PREPARATION TIME 5 MINUTES

COOKING TIME 45 MINUTES

INGREDIENTS

400 g / 14 oz bucatini pasta
2 tbsp olive oil
2 cloves of garlic, crushed
1 red chilli (chili), finely chopped
2 chicken breasts, cubed
400 ml / 7 fl. oz / 1 ⅔ cups tomato passata
150 g / 5 ½ oz Cheddar cheese, grated
2 tbsp basil leaves, chopped

420

SERVES 4

Veal Blanquette with Mushrooms

PREPARATION TIME 5 MINUTES

COOKING TIME I HOUR 15 MINUTES

....

INGREDIENTS

2 tbsp butter
800 g / 1 lb 12 oz veal shoulder, cubed
1 leek, sliced
1 carrot, chopped
1 celery stick, chopped
200 g / 7 oz baby onions, peeled
150 g 5 ½ oz baby button mushrooms
600 ml / 1 pint / 2 ½ cups light veal or chicken stock
300 ml / 10 ½ fl. oz / 1 ¼ cups double (heavy) cream

- Heat the butter in a saucepan and cook the veal until very lightly coloured on all sides.
- Remove the veal from the pan and add the leek, carrot and celery then cook gently, without colouring, for 5 minutes.
- Return the veal to the pan with the baby onions and mushrooms, then add the stock and simmer very gently for 1 hour.
- Add the cream and simmer for a further 5 minutes then taste for seasoning and add salt and black pepper as necessary.

Chicken and Mushroom Blanquette

421

- Replace the veal with chicken breast and use chicken stock in place of the veal stock.

422

SERVES 4

Creamy Fish Stew

PREPARATION TIME 5 MINUTES

COOKING TIME 20 MINUTES

....

INGREDIENTS

2 tbsp butter
1 onion, finely chopped
1 carrot, julienned
1 courgette (zucchini), julienned
4 tbsp dry white wine
300 ml / 10 ½ oz / 1 ¼ cups fish stock
300 ml / 10 ½ fl. oz / 1 ¼ cups double (heavy) cream
200 g / 7 oz salmon fillet, cut into 4 pieces
200 g / 7 oz turbot fillet, cut into 4 pieces
8 raw king prawns, peeled
1 tbsp dill, roughly chopped

- Heat the butter in a saucepan and cook the onion, carrot and courgette without colouring, for 5 minutes.
- Add the wine and bubble until almost all evaporated then pour in the stock and cream and simmer for 5 minutes.
- Add salmon and turbot to the pan and simmer for 5 minutes then add the prawns and cook for 2 more minutes.
- Taste the sauce for seasoning and add salt and white pepper as necessary, then garnish with dill.

Creamy Fish and Mushroom Stew

423

- Add 150 g of sliced button mushrooms to the pan when you fry the vegetables.

424

SERVES 6

Beef and Courgette Potato-Topped Pie

- Heat the oil in a saucepan and fry the onion, courgette and garlic for 3 minutes. Add the mince and fry for 2 minutes then stir in the tomato puree.
- Add the stock and bring to a simmer then cover the pan with a lid and simmer very gently for 1 hour.
- Preheat the oven to 200°C (180° fan) / 400F / gas 6.
- Cook the potatoes in salted water for 10 minutes, or until they are tender, then drain well. Return the potatoes to the saucepan and add the milk and butter, then mash until smooth.
- Spoon the mince into a baking dish and spread it out in an even layer.
- Top with the mashed potato and smooth it over.
- Sprinkle the top of the pie with Parmesan and breadcrumbs, then bake in the oven for 25 minutes or until the top is golden brown.

PREPARATION TIME 10 MINUTES

COOKING TIME 1 HOUR 35 MINUTES

INGREDIENTS

2 tbsp olive oil
1 small onion, finely chopped
2 courgettes (zucchini), halved and sliced
2 cloves of garlic, crushed
1 tbsp tomato puree
450 g / 1 lb / 2 cups minced beef
300 ml / 10 fl. oz / 1 ¼ cups beef stock

FOR THE TOPPING:
800 g / 1 lb 12 oz floury potatoes, peeled and cubed
100 ml / 3 ½ fl. oz / ½ cup milk
100 g / 3 ½ oz / ½ cup butter
2 tbsp Parmesan, finely grated
50 g / 1 ¾ oz / ⅓ cup panko breadcrumbs

Beef, Courgette and Aubergine Pie

425

- Add half a chopped aubergine to the saucepan when you fry the courgettes.

426

SERVES 4

Lamb with Apricot Sauce

- Heat the oil in a sauté pan and season the lamb with salt and pepper.
- Fry the lamb pieces for 3 minutes on each side or until cooked to your liking, then remove from the pan and keep warm.
- Add the onions and thyme to the pan and sauté for 4 minutes.
- Drain the apricots and reserve the juice, then chop the apricots and add them to the pan.
- Pour in the juice and bring to a simmer, then return the pieces of lamb to the pan and turn in the sauce.
- Serve with buttered beans and peas.

PREPARATION TIME 5 MINUTES

COOKING TIME 15 MINUTES

INGREDIENTS

2 tbsp olive oil
4 thick lamb leg steaks, cut into large chunks
1 onion, thickly sliced
a few sprigs of thyme
400 g / 14 oz canned apricots in juice
buttered beans and peas to serve

Buttered Beans and Peas

 427

- Boil 150 g green beans, 150 g podded broad beans and 100 g of peas in salted water for 5 minutes then drain well and toss with 1 tbsp butter.

428

SERVES 4

Pork Belly Slices with Rosemary

PREPARATION TIME 35 MINUTES

COOKING TIME 8 MINUTES

....

INGREDIENTS

1 tbsp fresh rosemary
1 lemon, zest finely grated
2 tsp pink peppercorns, crushed
4 tbsp olive oil
4 pork belly slices
apple and onion relish to serve

- Mix the rosemary, lemon zest and peppercorns with the oil and rub it all over the pork, then leave to marinate for 30 minutes.
- Heat a griddle pan until smoking hot.
- Season the pork with salt then fry on the griddle for 4 minutes on each side or until cooked through and nicely marked.
- Serve with the apple and onion relish.

Apple and Onion Relish

429

- Fry 1 sliced onion with one diced bramley apple in 2 tbsp butter for 10 minutes or until the onion has softened and the apple breaks down into a puree.

430

SERVES 6

Couscous and Vegetable Gratin

PREPARATION TIME 30 MINUTES

COOKING TIME 50 MINUTES

....

INGREDIENTS

300 g / 10 ½ oz / 1 ¾ cups couscous
2 tbsp olive oil
1 carrot, diced
100 g / 3 ½ oz green (string) beans, chopped
100 g / 3 ½ oz / ⅔ cup podded baby broad beans
2 tbsp pine nuts
2 tbsp flat leaf parsley, finely chopped

FOR THE TOPPING:
450 g / 1 lb carrots, peeled and chopped
450 g / 1 lb broccoli, broken into florets
100 g / 3 ½ oz / ½ cup butter
50 g / 1 ¾ oz / ½ cup Emmental, grated

- Preheat the oven to 200°C (180° fan) / 400F / gas 6.
- To make the topping, cook the carrots and broccoli in separate pans of salted water for 10 minutes, or until they are tender, then drain well. Add half of the butter to each pan, then blend each one to a puree with an emersion blender.
- Pour 300 ml of boiling water over the couscous then cover and leave to steam for 5 minutes.
- Meanwhile, heat the oil in a frying pan and fry the vegetables and pine nuts for 5 minutes.
- Fluff up the couscous grains with a fork and stir in the vegetables and parsley and transfer the mixture to a baking dish.
- Spread the broccoli puree on top, followed by the carrot puree, then sprinkle with cheese.
- Bake the gratin for 30 minutes or until golden brown.

Couscous, Mozzarella and Vegetable Gratin

431

- Add 200 g of sliced mozzarella between the couscous layer and the broccoli puree.

MAKES 2

Vegetable Pizza

Anchovy and Vegetable Pizza

433

- Arrange 8 halved anchovy fillets on top of the pizzas before topping with the vegetables.

King Prawn and Vegetable Pizza

434

- Add 12 shelled King prawns to the pizza toppings before cooking.

PREPARATION TIME 2 HOURS 30 MINUTES

COOKING TIME 10 – 12 MINUTES

INGREDIENTS

400 g / 14 oz / 2 ⅔ cups strong white bread flour, plus extra for dusting
½ tsp easy blend dried yeast
2 tsp caster (superfine) sugar
1 tsp fine sea salt
1 tbsp olive oil
4 tbsp tomato pizza sauce
½ aubergine (eggplant), chopped
1 courgette (zucchini), chopped
1 red pepper, chopped
1 yellow pepper, chopped
100 g / 3 ½ oz preserved artichokes in oil, drained and chopped
150 g / 5 ½ oz mozzarella, grated
2 tsp dried oregano

- Mix together the flour, yeast, sugar and salt and stir the oil into 140 ml of warm water.
- Stir the liquid into the dry ingredients then knead on a lightly oiled surface for 10 minutes or until smooth and elastic.
- Leave the dough to rest covered with oiled clingfilm for 1 – 2 hours until doubled in size.
- Preheat the oven to 220°C (200° fan) / 425F/ gas 7 and grease 2 non-stick baking trays.
- Knead the dough for 2 more minutes then divide in half and roll out into 2 circles.
- Transfer the bases to the baking trays, spread with pizza sauce and sprinkle with cheese.
- Arrange the vegetables on top and sprinkle with oregano then bake for 10 – 12 minutes or until the base is cooked through underneath.

SERVES 4

Lamb Chops with Tomato Sauce

Lamb Chops with Cream Sauce

436

- Replace the passata with double (heavy) cream and add a squeeze of lemon at the end.

Lamb Chops with Tomato and Thyme

437

- Replace the rosemary with 1 tbsp chopped fresh thyme.

PREPARATION TIME 5 MINUTES

COOKING TIME 25 MINUTES

....

INGREDIENTS

2 bulbs of fennel, thickly sliced
4 tbsp olive oil
8 lamb chops
4 rashers back bacon
1 onion, sliced
1 tbsp rosemary leaves
150 g / 5 ½ oz / 2 cups button mushrooms, sliced
100 ml / 3 ½ fl. oz / ½ cup dry white wine
400 ml / 7 fl. oz / 1 ⅔ cups tomato passata
a few sprigs of basil

- Cook the fennel in boiling salted water for 5 minutes or until tender then drain and keep warm.
- Heat the oil in a large sauté pan and fry the lamb chops for 3 minutes on each side, or until cooked to your liking, then leave to rest somewhere warm.
- Fry the bacon for 2 minutes on each side, then reserve with the chops.
- Add the onion and rosemary to the pan and sauté for 2 minutes, then add the mushrooms and cook for 4 minutes.
- Divide the mixture between 4 warm plates and top with the fennel, lamb chops and bacon.
- Put the sauté pan back on the heat and add the wine, then bubble until almost evaporated.
- Stir in the passata, season to taste with salt and pepper, then bring to a simmer.
- Spoon the sauce over the lamb and vegetables and garnish with basil.

438

SERVES 4

Penne with Egg and Basil Sauce

- Cook the penne in boiling salted water according to the packet instructions or until al dente.
- While the pasta is cooking, beat the eggs with the basil and Parmesan and season with salt and pepper.
- Drain the pasta, reserving a few tablespoons of the cooking water, then return it to the pan and stir in the egg mixture.
- If the sauce looks too thick, add a little of the pasta water to thin it.
- Divide between 4 warm bowls and serve immediately, garnished with basil sprigs.

PREPARATION TIME 5 MINUTES

COOKING TIME 12 MINUTES

INGREDIENTS

400 g / 14 oz penne
2 large eggs
3 tbsp basil leaves, finely chopped
50 g / 1 ¾ oz / ½ cup Parmesan, finely grated
a few sprigs of basil to serve

Penne with Basil and Walnut Sauce

439

- Add 75 g of chopped walnuts to the egg mixture.

440

SERVES 4

Rabbit with Pears and Red Wine

- Season the rabbit well with salt and pepper, then toss with the flour and mustard powder to coat.
- Heat the oil in a casserole dish or saucepan and sear the rabbit pieces on all sides.
- Remove the rabbit from the pan and add the pancetta, onions, carrot and celery.
- Sauté for 5 minutes, then pour in the wine and bring to a simmer. Transfer the rabbit back to the pan, then simmer very gently for 1 hour.
- Stir in the pears, season to taste with salt and pepper and cook for a further 15 minutes or until the rabbit is tender.

PREPARATION TIME 5 MINUTES

COOKING TIME 1 HOUR 30 MINUTES

INGREDIENTS

1 rabbit, jointed
3 tbsp plain (all purpose) flour
1 tsp mustard powder
3 tbsp olive oil
150 g / 5 ½ oz pancetta, cubed
200 g / 7 oz baby onions, peeled
2 carrots, finely chopped
1 celery stick, finely chopped
600 ml / 1 pint / 2 ½ cups red wine
2 pears, peeled, cored and quartered

Rabbit with Quince and Red Wine

441

- Replace the pears with 2 quinces, cut into wedges, but add them when you return the rabbit to the pan.

133

442

SERVES 4 # Lamb and Sweet Potato Gratin

PREPARATION TIME 15 MINUTES

COOKING TIME 2 HOURS 30 MINUTES

....

INGREDIENTS

2 tbsp olive oil
1 red onion, sliced
2 cloves of garlic, crushed
450 g / 1 lb lamb shoulder, cubed
500 ml / 17 ½ fl. oz / 2 cups red wine
3 sweet potatoes
50 g / 1 ¾ oz / ¼ cup butter
25 g / 1 oz / ⅓ cup fine breadcrumbs

- Heat the oil in a saucepan and fry the onion, garlic and lamb shoulder until it starts to colour.
- Pour in the wine and simmer for 2 hours or until the meat is tender.
- Preheat the oven to 200°C (180° fan) / 400F / gas 6.
- While the lamb is cooking, bake the sweet potatoes in their skins for 45 or until a skewer inserted slides in easily.
- Peel off and discard the skins and mash the flesh with the butter, seasoning with salt and pepper.
- Shred the lamb with a fork and tip the mixture into a baking dish, then top with the sweet potato mash.
- Sprinkle the top with breadcrumbs then bake for 20 minutes or until the top is golden brown.

443

MAKES 1 # Margherita Pizza

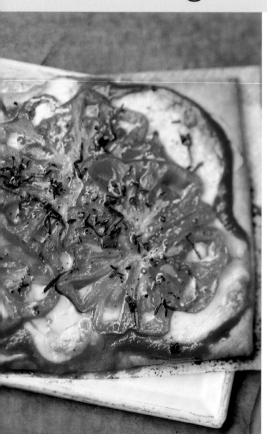

PREPARATION TIME 2 HOURS 30 MINUTES

COOKING TIME 10 – 12 MINUTES

....

INGREDIENTS

200 g / 7 oz / 1 ⅓ cups strong white bread flour, plus extra for dusting
½ tsp easy blend dried yeast
1 tsp caster (superfine) sugar
½ tsp fine sea salt
1 tbsp olive oil, plus extra for drizzling
3 tbsp tomato pizza sauce
150 g / 5 ½ oz mozzarella, sliced
4 large slices marmande tomato
2 tbsp basil leaves, shredded

- Mix together the flour, yeast, sugar and salt and stir the oil into 140 ml of warm water.
- Stir the liquid into the dry ingredients then knead on a lightly oiled surface for 10 minutes or until smooth and elastic.
- Leave the dough to rest covered with oiled clingfilm for 1 – 2 hours until doubled in size.
- Preheat the oven to 220°C (200° fan) / 425F / gas 7 and grease a non-stick baking tray.
- Knead the dough for 2 more minutes then roll out thinly into a rectangle, trim the edges and transfer to the baking tray.
- Spread the dough with the pizza sauce and top with the mozzarella, followed by the tomato and basil. Drizzle with olive oil and sprinkle with salt and pepper.
- Transfer the tray to the oven and bake for 10 – 12 minutes or until the pizza dough is cooked through underneath.

Beef and Palm Heart Stew

444

SERVES 6

- Preheat the oven to 140°C (120° fan) / 275F / gas 1.
- Mix the flour with the mustard powder and a good pinch of salt and pepper and toss it with the beef to coat.
- Heat half of the oil in a large cast iron casserole dish then sear the meat in batches until well browned.
- Remove the beef from the pan, add the rest of the oil and cook the onions and garlic for 5 minutes.
- Pour in the beer and boil for 5 minutes then add the stock to the pan and return the beef.
- Bring the casserole to a gentle simmer then put on a lid, transfer it to the oven and cook for 2 hours.
- Season to taste with salt and pepper then stir in the drained palm hearts and return to the oven for 15 minutes.
- Scatter over the croutons just before serving.

PREPARATION TIME 10 MINUTES

COOKING TIME 2 HOURS 30 MINUTES

....

INGREDIENTS

2 tbsp plain (all purpose) flour
1 tsp mustard powder
1 kg / 2 lb 3 oz braising steak, cubed
4 tbsp olive oil
1 onion, finely chopped
3 cloves of garlic, finely chopped
600 ml / 1 pint / 2 ½ cups real ale
600 ml / 1 pint / 2 ½ cups good quality beef stock
400 g / 14 oz canned palm hearts
50 g / 1 ¾ oz croutons

Confit Duck Dauphinoise

445

SERVES 4

PREPARATION TIME 10 MINUTES

COOKING TIME 35 MINUTES

....

INGREDIENTS

450 g / 1 lb potatoes, cut into thick slices
3 confit duck legs
1 small onion, sliced
50 g / 1 ¾ oz / ½ cup Gruyere, grated

- Preheat the oven to 200°C (180° fan) / 400F / gas 6.
- Cook the potatoes in boiling, salted water for 10 minutes or until just tender. Drain well.
- Peel off and discard the skin of the duck and shred the meat with a fork. Discard the bones and arrange the duck in a baking dish.
- Arrange the potato and sliced onions on top, then sprinkle with the cheese and bake for 25 minutes or until the cheese is just starting to turn golden.

Braised Chicken with Vegetables

446

SERVES 4

PREPARATION TIME 5 MINUTES

COOKING TIME 2 HOURS 15 MINUTES

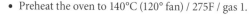

INGREDIENTS

2 tbsp olive oil
1 chicken, jointed
12 baby onions, peeled
12 baby carrots, peeled
3 celery sticks, cut into large chunks
a few sprigs of thyme
1 litre / 1 pint 15 fl. oz / 4 cups good quality chicken stock

- Preheat the oven to 140°C (120° fan) / 275F / gas 1.
- Heat the oil in a large cast iron casserole dish and sear the chicken on all sides until well browned.
- Add the rest of the ingredients to the pot and bring to a gentle simmer.
- Cover the casserole with a lid, transfer it to the oven and cook for 2 hours.
- Taste the sauce for seasoning and adjust with salt and pepper as necessary.

447

SERVES 4

Braised Chicken with Carrots

PREPARATION TIME 5 MINUTES

COOKING TIME 2 HOURS 15 MINUTES

....

INGREDIENTS

2 tbsp olive oil
1 chicken, jointed
1 onion, finely chopped
2 carrots, cut into chunks
2 yellow carrots, cut into chunks
½ tsp black peppercorns
1 bay leaf
1 tbsp tomato puree
1 litre / 1 pint 15 fl. oz / 4 cups good quality chicken stock

- Preheat the oven to 140°C (120° fan) / 275F / gas 1.
- Heat the oil in a large cast iron casserole dish and sear the chicken on all sides until well browned.
- Add the rest of the ingredients to the pot and bring to a gentle simmer.
- Cover the casserole with a lid, transfer it to the oven and cook for 2 hours.
- Taste the sauce for seasoning and adjust with salt and pepper as necessary.

Braised Chicken with Celeriac

 448

- Replace 3 of the carrots with 400 g of celeriac, cut into large chunks.

449

SERVES 4

Spaghetti with Pancetta and Gorgonzola

PREPARATION TIME 5 MINUTES

COOKING TIME 15 MINUTES

....

INGREDIENTS

400 g / 14 oz dried spaghetti
200 g / 7 oz Gorgonzola
2 tbsp flat leaf parsley, finely chopped
4 tbsp olive oil
2 cloves of garlic, crushed
200 g / 7 oz pancetta, cubed

- Boil the pasta in salted water according to the packet instructions or until al dente.
- Meanwhile, beat the Gorgonzola with the parsley and set aside.
- Heat the olive oil in a large sauté pan and fry the garlic and pancetta for 5 minutes or until browned.
- Drain the pasta, reserving a few tablespoons of the cooking liquor, and stir it into pancetta pan. Add the reserved cooking liquor if it looks a little dry.
- Toss the spaghetti with the gorgonzola mixture and sprinkle with black pepper before serving.

Spaghetti with Mushrooms and Gorgonzola

450

- Use 150 g of sliced button mushrooms instead of the pancetta for a vegetarian alternative.

451

SERVES 6

Lamb Stew with Winter Vegetables

- Preheat the oven to 140°C (120° fan) / 275F / gas 1.
- Heat half of the oil in a large cast iron casserole dish and sear the lamb shanks on all sides until well browned.
- Remove the lamb from the pan, add the rest of the oil and fry the onions, carrots, celery and swede for 5 minutes.
- Add the tomatoes and stock and bring to a simmer then return the shanks to the pan.
- Cover the casserole with a lid, transfer it to the oven and cook for 3 hours.
- Taste the sauce for seasoning and adjust with salt and pepper as necessary then stir in the parsley just before serving.

PREPARATION TIME 5 MINUTES

COOKING TIME 3 HOURS 15 MINUTES

INGREDIENTS

4 tbsp olive oil
6 small lamb shanks
1 onion, cubed
2 carrots, cubed
1 celery stick, cubed
½ swede, cubed
200 g / 7 oz / 1 cup canned tomatoes, chopped
1 litre / 1 pint 15 fl. oz / 4 cups good quality lamb stock
3 tbsp flat leaf parsley, chopped

Lamb Stew with Pearl Barley

452

- Add 150 g dried pearl barley to the stew when you add the stock.

453

SERVES 8

Stuffed Salmon with Mustard and Mint

- Preheat the oven to 180°C (160° fan) / 350F / gas 4.
- Sandwich the 2 salmon fillets together with the mustard and mint leaves and lay it in a large roasting tin.
- Season the skin with salt and pepper, then cover the tin with foil and bake in the oven for 40 minutes.
- Slice the salmon across into 8 cutlets to serve.

PREPARATION TIME 15 MINUTES

COOKING TIME 40 MINUTES

INGREDIENTS

1 salmon, filleted and pin-boned
4 tbsp wholegrain mustard
2 tbsp mint leaves
minted asparagus and mange tout to serve

Minted Asparagus and Mange Tout

454

- Toss 300 g of boiled asparagus spears and 300 g of boiled mange tout in the juices from the roasting tin, then stir in 1 tbsp of mint leaves.

455

SERVES 4

Baked Cod with Crushed Potatoes

PREPARATION TIME 10 MINUTES

COOKING TIME 20 MINUTES

....

INGREDIENTS

4 portions of cod fillet
2 tbsp olive oil

FOR THE POTATOES:

600 g / 1 lb 4 oz new potatoes, peeled and halved
100 ml / 3 ½ fl. oz / ½ cup olive oil
a small bunch of dill, roughly chopped
3 tbsp mint leaves, roughly chopped

- Preheat the oven to 180°C (160° fan) / 350F / gas 4.
- Put the cod in a roasting tin and drizzle with oil then season with salt and pepper.
- Cover the tin with foil and bake in the oven for 20 minutes.
- Meanwhile, boil the potatoes in salted water for 12 minutes or until tender, then drain well.
- Return the potatoes to the pan and add the oil, dill and mint and season well with salt and pepper.
- Roughly crush the potatoes with a fork, then divide them between 4 warm plates.
- Flake the cod and discard the skin, then arrange it on top of the potatoes.

Baked Salmon with Crushed Potatoes

456

- Replace the cod with 4 portions of salmon fillet.

457

MAKES 18

Pan-Fried Sea Bass with Chinese Artichokes

PREPARATION TIME 25 MINUTES

COOKING TIME 40 – 50 MINUTES

....

INGREDIENTS

½ butternut squash, cut into chunks
200 g / 7 oz Chinese artichokes, scrubbed
2 tbsp olive oil
4 portions of sea bass fillet
2 tbsp butter
2 courgettes (zucchini), cut into chunks
100 g / 3 ½ oz chestnut mushrooms, halved
50 g / 1 ¾ oz / ⅓ cup walnuts

- Preheat the oven to 180°C (160° fan) / 350F / gas 4 and put a roasting tin in to heat.
- Boil the butternut squash in salted water for 3 minutes, then add the Chinese artichokes and cook for a further 4 minutes. Drain well.
- Heat the oil in a frying pan and fry the sea bass skin side down for 3 minutes. Transfer the fillets, skin side up to the roasting tin in the oven and cook for 5 minutes.
- Meanwhile, put the frying pan back on the hob and add the butter.
- Fry the drained squash and artichokes with the courgette and mushrooms for 5 minutes, then stir in the walnuts and season with salt and pepper.
- Divide the vegetables between 4 warm plates and top each one with a portion of sea bass.

Pan-Fried Duck with Chinese Artichokes

458

- Replace the sea bass fillets with 4 small duck breasts. Fry for 8 minutes, skin side down, then transfer to the oven for 8 minutes.

459

SERVES 4

Braised Pork with Carrots and Lime

Braised Pork with Sweet Potatoes

460

- Omit the carrots and honey and add a cubed sweet potato to the casserole for the final 45 minutes of cooking.

Braised Pork with Butternut Squash

461

- Replace the carrots with a peeled and diced butternut squash and add to the casserole for the final 45 minutes of cooking.

PREPARATION TIME 5 MINUTES

COOKING TIME 2 HOURS 15 MINUTES

INGREDIENTS

2 tbsp olive oil
4 pork cheeks, cut into chunks
1 onion, finely chopped
3 carrots, cut into chunks
1 litre / 1 pint 15 fl. oz / 4 cups good quality chicken stock
2 tbsp soy sauce
1 tbsp runny honey
2 limes, quartered
1 tbsp French tarragon leaves, chopped

- Preheat the oven to 140°C (120° fan) / 275F / gas 1.
- Heat the oil in a large cast iron casserole dish and sear the pork on all sides until well browned.
- Add the onion and carrots to the pot and fry until lightly browned then pour in the stock and bring to a simmer.
- Cover the casserole with a lid, transfer it to the oven and cook for 2 hours.
- Stir in the soy, honey and limes then return the dish to the oven, uncovered, for 15 minutes.
- Sprinkle over the tarragon before serving.

462

SERVES 8

Gluten-Free Boeuf en Croute

Gluten-Free Venison en Croute

463

- Replace the beef with venison fillet and reduce the cooking time to 25 minutes to allow for the smaller girth.

Herbed Boeuf en Croute

464

- Add 2 tbsp of dried herbs de Provence to the pastry.

PREPARATION TIME 5 MINUTES

COOKING TIME 45 MINUTES

INGREDIENTS

100 g / 3 ½ oz / ½ cup butter, cubed
200 g / 7 oz / 1 ⅓ cups gluten free flour
1 tsp cracked black pepper
1 kg / 2 lb 3 oz fillet of beef
3 tbsp olive oil

- Rub the butter into the flour and pepper until the mixture resembles fine breadcrumbs. Add just enough cold water to bring the mixture together into a pliable dough, then wrap in clingfilm and chill for 30 minutes.
- Preheat the oven to 230°C (210° fan) / 450F / gas 8 and season the beef well with salt and pepper.
- Heat a large oven-proof frying pan on the hob until smoking hot, then add the olive oil and sear the beef on all sides.
- Roll the pastry out thinly on a lightly floured work surface. Position the beef in the centre of the pastry, then roll up and secure the edges with a little water.
- Transfer the beef to a baking tray and bake in the oven for 35 minutes.
- Carve into thick slices to serve.

465

SERVES 4 # Baked Monkfish with Crushed Potatoes

- Preheat the oven to 180°C (160° fan) / 350F / gas 4.
- Put the monkfish in a roasting tin and drizzle with oil then season with salt and pepper.
- Cover the tin with foil and bake in the oven for 20 minutes.
- Meanwhile, boil the potatoes in salted water for 12 minutes or until tender, then drain well.
- Return the potatoes to the pan and add the oil and mustard then season well with salt and pepper.
- Roughly crush the potatoes with a fork, then use a ring mould to portion them onto 4 warm plates.
- Top the potatoes with the monkfish, garnish with chervil and serve with some cider vinegar vinaigrette drizzled round.

PREPARATION TIME 10 MINUTES

COOKING TIME 20 MINUTES

INGREDIENTS

4 portions of monkfish tail
2 tbsp olive oil

FOR THE POTATOES:
600 g / 1 lb 4 oz new potatoes, peeled and halved
100 ml / 3 ½ fl. oz / ½ cup olive oil
2 tsp Dijon mustard
a few sprigs of chervil to garnish
cider vinegar vinaigrette to serve

Cider Vinegar Vinaigrette 466

- Put 2 tsp of honey in a jam jar with 3 tbsp of cider vinegar, a crushed garlic clove and a large pinch of salt, then shake to dissolve the salt. Add 4 tbsp of olive oil then shake to emulsify.

467

SERVES 4 # Barbecue Baby Back Ribs

- Heat the oil in a saucepan and fry the onion, garlic and ginger for 3 minutes without colouring.
- Stir in the mixed spice then add the rest of the ingredients with a large pinch of salt and bring to the boil.
- Turn down the heat and simmer for 10 minutes or until the sauce is thick and smooth.
- Leave the sauce to cool, then brush half of it over the ribs and leave to marinate in the fridge for 4 hours or overnight.
- Preheat the oven to 110°C (90° fan) / 225F / gas ¼.
- Transfer the ribs to a roasting tin and slow-roast for 3 hours, turning occasionally and basting with the rest of the sauce.
- The ribs can either be served straight away or cooked over a hot charcoal barbecue for a few minutes to give a smoky taste.

PREPARATION TIME 4 HOURS 30 MINUTES

COOKING TIME 3 HOURS 15 MINUTES

INGREDIENTS

2 tbsp olive oil
1 small onion, grated
3 cloves of garlic, crushed
1 tbsp ginger, finely grated
1 tsp mixed spice
200 ml / 7 fl. oz / ¾ cup tomato passata
200 ml / 7 fl. oz / ¾ cup apple juice
3 tbsp dark brown sugar
1 ½ lemons, juiced
1 tbsp Worcester sauce
1 tbsp Dijon mustard
2 racks of baby back pork ribs, membrane removed

Barbecue Spare Ribs 468

- Use spare ribs instead of the baby back ribs and increase the cooking time by 30 minutes.

469

SERVES 2

Mushroom Risotto with Crispy Bacon

PREPARATION TIME 5 MINUTES

COOKING TIME 25 MINUTES

INGREDIENTS

1 litre / 1 pint 15 fl. oz good quality chicken stock
2 tbsp olive oil
1 onion, finely chopped
2 cloves of garlic, crushed
150 g / 5 ½ oz / ¾ cup risotto rice
150 g / 5 ½ oz / 2 cups mushrooms, sliced
50 g / 1 ¾ oz Parmesan, finely grated
2 tbsp butter
3 tbsp flat leaf parsley, chopped
4 rashers of smoked streaky bacon

- Heat the stock in a saucepan, keeping it just below simmering point.
- Heat the olive oil in a sauté pan and gently fry the onion for 5 minutes without colouring.
- Add the garlic and cook for 2 more minutes then stir in the rice and mushrooms.
- When they are well coated with the oil, add 2 ladles of the hot stock.
- Cook, stirring occasionally, until most of the stock has been absorbed before adding the next 2 ladles.
- Continue in this way for around 15 minutes.
- Preheat the grill to its highest setting.
- Stir the Parmesan, butter and parsley into the risotto and season. Cover the pan and rest for 4 minutes.
- Meanwhile, grill the bacon for 2 minutes on each side.
- Serve the risotto and garnish with the bacon.

Mushroom and Blue Cheese Risotto

470

- Stir 100 g of cubed blue cheese through the risotto just before serving and omit the bacon.

471

SERVES 4

Baked Salmon with Honeyed Onions

PREPARATION TIME 25 MINUTES

COOKING TIME 40 – 50 MINUTES

INGREDIENTS

4 tbsp olive oil
4 portions of salmon fillet
2 red onions, halved and sliced
2 tbsp runny honey
2 tbsp white wine vinegar

- Preheat the oven to 180°C (160° fan) / 350F / gas 4.
- Put the salmon in a roasting tin and drizzle with half of the oil then season with salt and pepper.
- Cover the tin with foil and bake in the oven for 30 minutes.
- Meanwhile, heat the oil in a large sauté pan and fry the onions over a gentle heat for 20 minutes, stirring occasionally.
- Stir in the honey and vinegar and season with salt and pepper, then cook for 2 more minutes.
- Serve the salmon with the onions and any liquid from the onion pan spooned around.

Baked Cod with Honeyed Onions

472

- Replace the salmon with 4 portions of cod fillet.

473

SERVES 4

Chicken Korma

- Mix the chicken breast pieces with the curry powder and leave to marinate for 30 minutes.
- Heat the oil in a large saucepan and fry the onion and chilli for 3 minutes, stirring occasionally.
- Add the garlic and cook for 2 minutes or until the mustard seeds start to pop.
- Add the chicken and cook for 4 minutes, stirring occasionally, until it starts to colour on the outside.
- Add the chopped tomatoes, coconut milk, ground almonds and mango chutney and bring to a gentle simmer.
- Cook the curry for 35 minutes, stirring occasionally, until the chicken is tender and the sauce has thickened.

PREPARATION TIME 30 MINUTES

COOKING TIME 50 MINUTES

INGREDIENTS

450 g / 1 lb skinless chicken breast, cubed
2 tbsp korma curry powder
2 tbsp olive oil
1 onion, finely chopped
1 red chilli (chili), finely chopped
2 cloves of garlic, crushed
200 g / 7 oz / 1 cup canned tomatoes, chopped
400 ml/ 14 fl. oz / 1 ⅔ cups coconut milk
4 tbsp ground almonds
2 tbsp mango chutney

King Prawn Korma   474

- Omit the chicken and add 300 g of raw, peeled king prawns 5 minutes before the end of the cooking time.

475

SERVES 4

Sausagemeat Pie

- Fry the onion for 3 minutes, stirring occasionally.
- Add the garlic and cook for 2 minutes, then add the sausagemeat, breaking it up with the spoon.
- Fry the sausagemeat until it starts to brown then add the stock and bring to a gentle simmer.
- Cook for 30 minutes, until the meat is tender.
- Add salt and ground black pepper to taste.
- Meanwhile, cook the potatoes in salted water for 10 minutes, or until they are tender, then drain well.
- Return the potatoes to the saucepan and add the milk and butter. Mash the potatoes until smooth.
- Preheat the oven to 200°C (180° fan) / 400F / gas 6.
- Spoon the mince mixture into a large baking dish then top with the mashed potatoes.
- Level the top then bake in the oven for 20 minutes or until golden brown. Garnish with parsley.

PREPARATION TIME 2 MINUTES

COOKING TIME 1 HOUR 30 MINUTES

INGREDIENTS

2 tbsp olive oil
1 small onion, finely chopped
2 cloves of garlic, crushed
450 g / 1 lb / 2 cups pork sausagemeat
400 ml / 14 fl. oz / 1 ⅔ cups beef stock

FOR THE TOPPING:
450 g / 1 lb floury potatoes, peeled and cubed
100 ml / 3 ½ fl. oz / ½ cup milk
50 g / 1 ¾ oz / 1/4 cup butter
flat leaf parsley to garnish

Faggot Pie ——   476

- Remove the caul fat from the outside of 6 faggots and crumble them into the saucepan in place of the sausagemeat.

477

SERVES 4

Vegetable Lasagne

PREPARATION TIME 5 MINUTES

COOKING TIME 20 MINUTES

INGREDIENTS

2 tbsp olive oil
1 red onion, finely chopped
1 red pepper, diced
2 cloves of garlic, crushed
200 g / 7 oz green (string) beans, chopped
100 g / 3 ½ oz spinach
400 g / 14 oz / 2 ⅔ cups canned tomatoes, chopped
300 g / 10 ½ oz fresh lasagne sheets
2 tbsp Parmesan, finely grated

- Heat the oil in a large saucepan and fry the onion and red pepper for 3 minutes, stirring occasionally.
- Add the garlic and cook for 2 minutes, then add the green beans, spinach and tomatoes.
- Bring the mixture to the boil and simmer for 10 minutes.
- Preheat the oven to 190°C (170° fan) / 375F / gas 5.
- Oil a large baking dish and line it with lasagne sheets.
- Add half of the vegetable mixture, then top with another layer of pasta.
- Spoon the rest of the vegetables on top, followed by the rest of the lasagne then sprinkle with parmesan.
- Transfer the dish to the oven and bake for 30 minutes or until cooked through and golden brown.

Vegetable and Pesto Lasagne

478

- Spread 4 tbsp of pesto on top of each layer of lasagne sheets before topping with the vegetables. Top with more pesto and 150 g sliced mozzarella before baking.

479

SERVES 4

Traditional Stuffed Tomatoes

PREPARATION TIME 10-15 MINUTES

COOKING TIME 15-20 MINUTES

INGREDIENTS

FOR THE TOMATOES
6 large vine tomatoes
600 g / 1 lb 5 oz / 4 cups beef mince
30 ml / 1 fl. oz / 2 tbsp sunflower oil
2 cloves of garlic, minced
1 tsp dried oregano
1 tsp dried basil
salt and pepper

TO GARNISH
250 g / 9 oz / 1 1/2 cups cooked white long grain rice
a few sprigs of oregano

- Preheat the oven to 190°C (170° fan) / 375F / gas 5.
- Heat the sunflower oil in a large sauté pan set over a moderate heat.
- Sauté the garlic for 30 seconds before adding the beef mince.
- Cook until browned all over before adding the dried herbs and seasoning to taste.
- Remove to one side to cool as you prepare the tomatoes.
- Remove their tops and reserve to one side before scooping out the seeds and flesh.
- Fill with the beef mince and replace their tops.
- Spoon the rice into an oval baking dish and sprinkle with cold water.
- Sit the stuffed tomatoes on top and bake for 10-12 minutes until warmed through.
- Remove from the oven and garnish with oregano before serving.

Lamb Stuffed Tomatoes

480

- Substitute the beef mince for the same amount of lamb mince, adding a small handful of pine nuts to the mixture before spooning into the tomatoes.

SERVES 8

Pot-Roasted Beef with Vegetables

Pot-Roasted Beef with Mushrooms

 482

- Replace the tomato with 150 g of quartered button mushrooms.

Pot-Roasted Beef with Sweet Potatoes

483

- Replace the carrots with 2 diced sweet potatoes.

PREPARATION TIME 5 MINUTES

COOKING TIME 1 HOUR

INGREDIENTS

1.5 kg / 3 lb 3 oz roti de boeuf joint
3 tbsp olive oil
4 cloves of garlic, roughly chopped
3 carrots, diced
1 celery stick, cut into short lengths
300 ml / 10 ½ fl. oz / 1 ¼ cups good quality beef stock
1 tomato, quartered

- Preheat the oven to 180°C (160° fan) / 350F / gas 4 and season the beef well with salt and pepper.
- Heat the oil in a cast iron casserole dish and sear the beef on all sides.
- Remove the beef from the pan then fry the garlic, carrot and celery for 5 minutes.
- Return the beef to the pot, then pour in the stock and bring to a simmer.
- Put on a lid, transfer it to the oven and pot-roast for 45 minutes.
- Remove the lid and add the tomato then return to the oven for 15 minutes.
- Leave to rest for 10 minutes before carving.

484

SERVES 6

Stewed Pork with Olives

Stewed Pork with Capers

485

- Replace the olives with capers.

Stewed Pork with Chilli

486

- Add a chopped red chilli when you add the stock for a spicy kick.

PREPARATION TIME 5 MINUTES

COOKING TIME 2 HOURS 45 MINUTES

....

INGREDIENTS

4 tbsp olive oil
800 g / 1 lb 12 oz pork shoulder, cut into chunks
1 onion, chopped
3 cloves of garlic, crushed
1 tsp black peppercorns
1 yellow pepper, diced
400 g / 14 oz / 2 cups canned tomatoes, chopped
400 ml / 14 fl. oz / 1 ⅔ cups chicken stock
150 g / 5 ½ oz / 1 cup green olives

- Heat half of the oil in a large cast iron casserole dish and sear the pork on all sides until well browned.
- Remove the pork from the pan, add the rest of the oil and fry the onions, garlic, peppercorns and peppers for 5 minutes.
- Add the tomatoes and stock and bring to a simmer then return the pork to the pan.
- Cover the casserole with a lid and simmer gently for 2 hours.
- Season the sauce to taste with salt and pepper, then stir in the olives and simmer for a further 30 minutes.

487

SERVES 4

Sausage, Bean and Carrot Stew

- Heat the oil in a large cast iron casserole dish and brown the sausages all over. Remove from the pan and add the onion, carrots and thyme and fry for 5 minutes.
- Drain the beans and add them to the pan with the stock and bring to the boil.
- Turn down the heat and simmer with the lid on for 2 hours or until the beans are tender.

PREPARATION TIME 10 MINUTES

COOKING TIME 2 HOURS 15 MINUTES

INGREDIENTS

2 tbsp olive oil
450 g / 1 lb chipolata sausages
1 onion, finely chopped
2 carrots, sliced
a few sprigs of thyme
400 g / 14 oz / 2 ⅔ cups dried haricot beans, soaked overnight
1 litre / 1 pint 15 fl. oz vegetable stock

Chicken, Bean and Carrot Stew

488

- Omit the sausages and use 8 chicken thighs instead.

489

SERVES 4

Lentil Stew

- Fry the onion in the oil for 5 minutes then add the carrot, pepper and garlic and cook for 2 more minutes.
- Stir in the tomatoes, stock and lentils then simmer for 45 minutes - 1 hour or until the lentils are tender.
- Taste for seasoning and add salt and black pepper as necessary then garnish with parsley.

PREPARATION TIME 2 MINUTES

COOKING TIME 1 HOUR

INGREDIENTS

1 red onion, finely chopped
4 tbsp olive oil
1 carrot, finely chopped
1 red pepper, finely chopped
2 cloves of garlic, crushed
400 g / 14 oz / 2 ⅔ cups canned tomatoes, chopped
600 ml / 1 pint / 2 ½ cups vegetable stock
400 g / 14 oz / 3 1/4 cups green lentils
flat leaf parsley to garnish

Lentil and Chickpea Stew

490

- Soak 200 g of chickpeas (garbanzo beans) overnight and add to the saucepan to replace half of the lentils.

DESSERTS

491

SERVES 4

Peach and Almond Crumble

PREPARATION TIME 5 MINUTES

COOKING TIME 40 MINUTES

....

INGREDIENTS

2 yellow peaches, peeled, stoned
and cubed
2 white peaches, peeled, stoned and
cubed
75 g / 2 ½ oz / ⅓ cup butter
50 g / 1 ¾ oz / ⅓ cup plain (all
purpose) flour
25 g / 1 oz / ¼ cup ground almonds
40 g / 1 ½ oz / ¼ cup light
brown sugar

FOR THE HOT CHOCOLATE
SAUCE:
100 ml / 3 ½ fl. oz / ½ cup double
(heavy) cream
1 tbsp brandy
75 g / 2 ½ oz dark chocolate
(minimum 60 % cocoa solids),
chopped

- Preheat the oven to 180°C (160° fan) / 350F / gas 4.
- Arrange the cubed peaches in a baking dish.
- Rub the butter into the flour and stir in the ground almonds and sugar.
- Take a handful of the topping and squeeze it into a clump, then crumble it over the fruit.
- Repeat with the rest of the crumble mixture then bake for 40 minutes or until the topping is golden brown.
- Just before you're ready to serve, heat the cream and brandy to simmering point then pour it over the chocolate and stir to emulsify.

Apricot and Almond Crumble   492

- Replace the peaches with 8 apricots that have been stoned and quartered.

493

SERVES 4

Waffles

PREPARATION TIME 10 MINUTES

COOKING TIME 25 MINUTES

....

INGREDIENTS

250 g / 9 oz / 1 ⅔ cups plain (all
purpose)flour
2 tsp baking powder
2 large eggs
300 ml / 10 ½ fl. oz / 1 ¼ cups milk
2 tbsp melted butter
sunflower oil for oiling the waffle
maker
icing (confectioners') sugar to serve

- Put the oven on a low setting and put an electric waffle maker on to heat.
- Mix the flour and baking powder in a bowl and make a well in the centre.
- Break in the eggs and pour in the milk then use a whisk to gradually incorporate all of the flour from round the outside, followed by the melted butter.
- Spoon some of the batter into the waffle maker and close the lid. Cook for 4 minutes or according to the manufacturer's instructions until golden brown.
- Repeat until all the batter has been used, keeping the finished batches warm in the oven.
- Dust the waffles liberally with icing sugar before serving.

Lemon Waffles   494

- Add the grated zest of a lemon to the waffle batter and serve the waffles topped with lemon curd.

MAKES 4

495

MAKES 4 # Chocolate and Banana Meringue Pies

- Preheat the oven to 200°C (180° fan) / 400F / gas 6.
- Rub butter into the flour and add cold water to bind.
- Chill for 30 minutes then roll out on a floured surface.
- Line 4 tart cases with pastry and prick the bases.
- Line the pastry with clingfilm and fill with baking beans or rice then bake for 10 minutes.
- Remove the clingfilm and beans and cook for 8 minutes.
- Mash the bananas with the lime juice until smooth then stir in half of the chocolate chips.
- Divide the mixture between the pastry cases.
- Whisk the egg whites until stiff, then gradually add the sugar and whisk until the mixture is thick and shiny.
- Spoon into a piping bag and pipe onto the tarts.
- Return the tarts to the oven to bake for 10 minutes.
- Sprinkle over the remaining chocolate chips and serve.

PREPARATION TIME 55 MINUTES

COOKING TIME 28 MINUTES

INGREDIENTS

100 g / 3 ½ oz / ½ cup butter, cubed
200 g / 7 oz / 1 ⅓ cups plain
(all purpose) flour
4 large ripe bananas
1 lime, juiced
75 g / 2 ½ oz / ½ cup dark
chocolate chips

FOR THE MERINGUE:
4 large egg whites
110g / 4 oz / ½ cup caster
(superfine) sugar

Banana and Coconut Meringue Pie

496

- Replace the chocolate chips with an equal weight of coconut flakes.

497

SERVES 4 # Apricot and Almond French Toast

- Put the oven on a low heat.
- Lightly beat the eggs with the milk in a wide, shallow dish and heat the butter in a large frying pan until sizzling.
- Dip the bread in the egg mixture on both sides until evenly coated, then fry in batches for 2 minutes on each side or until golden brown. Keep the first batches warm in the oven while you cook the rest.
- Meanwhile, put the apricot slices and honey in a small saucepan and warm through gently.
- When the toast is ready, spoon over the honeyed apricots and sprinkle with flaked almonds.

PREPARATION TIME 5 MINUTES

COOKING TIME 12 MINUTES

INGREDIENTS

2 large eggs
100 ml / 3 ½ fl. oz / ½ cup milk
2 tbsp butter
8 slices white bread
400 g / 14 oz / 2 cups canned apricot
slices, drained
4 tbsp runny honey
2 tbsp flaked (slivered) almonds

Pear and Almond French Toast

498

- Replaced the canned apricots with canned pears.

499

SREVES 6

Raspberry Upside-Down Cake

PREPARATION TIME 15 MINUTES

COOKING TIME 25 MINUTES

INGREDIENTS

100 g / 3 ½ oz / ⅔ cup self-raising
flour
1 tsp baking powder
100 g / 3 ½ oz / ½ cup caster
(superfine) sugar
100 g / 3 ½ oz / ½ cup butter,
softened
2 large eggs
250 g / 9 oz / 2 cups fresh raspberries
icing (confectioners') sugar for
dusting

- Preheat the oven to 180°C (160° fan) / 350F / gas 4 and butter a 20 cm round cake tin.
- Sieve the flour and baking powder into a mixing bowl and add sugar, butter and eggs.
- Beat the mixture with an electric whisk for 4 minutes or until smooth and well whipped.
- Arrange half of the raspberries in the cake tin and spoon the cake mixture on top.
- Level the cake mixture with a palette knife and bake for 25 minutes or until a skewer inserted comes out clean.
- Leave the cake to cool for 20 minutes before turning out onto a serving plate.
- Top with the rest of the raspberries and sprinkle with icing sugar just before serving.

Raspberry and Orange Upside-Down Cake

500

- Add the grated zest of an orange to the raspberries in the cake tin and add 1 tbsp of orange juice to the cake mixture.

501

MAKES 6

Small Summer Berry Crumbles

PREPARATION TIME 10 MINUTES

COOKING TIME 25 MINUTES

INGREDIENTS

200 g / 7 oz / 1 ⅓ cups raspberries
200 g / 7 oz / 1 ⅓ cups strawberries,
halved
4 tbsp caster (superfine) sugar
75 g / 2 ½ oz / ⅓ cup butter
50 g / 1 ¾ oz / ⅓ cup plain (all
purpose) flour
25 g / 1 oz / ¼ cup ground almonds
40 g / 1 ½ oz / ¼ cup light
brown sugar

- Preheat the oven to 180°C (160° fan) / 350F / gas 4.
- Mix the raspberries and strawberries with the sugar and divide them between 6 ramekin dishes.
- Rub the butter into the flour and stir in the ground almonds and brown sugar.
- Crumble the mixture over the fruit then bake for 25 minutes or until the topping is golden brown.

Strawberry and Rose Crumbles

502

- Omit the raspberries and double the quantity of strawberries. Sprinkle the strawberries with 1 tbsp of rose water before adding the crumble topping.

503

MAKES 4

Mini Pear Quinoa Crumbles

Mini Apple Quinoa Crumbles

504

- Replace the pears with 3 bramley apples in cubes and add 2 tbsp of sultanas.

Pear and Blackberry Crumbles

505

- Add 100g blackberries when you toss the pears with the sugar.

PREPARATION TIME 15 MINUTES

COOKING TIME 40 MINUTES

INGREDIENTS

200 g / 7 oz / 1 cup quinoa
1 cinnamon stick
4 pears, peeled and cubed
2 tbsp caster (superfine) sugar
50 g / 1 ¾ oz / ¼ cup butter, melted
50 g / 1 ¾ oz / ½ cup ground almonds
75 g / 2 ½ oz / ½ cup dark brown sugar

- Preheat the oven to 200°C (180° fan) / 400F / gas 6.
- Put the quinoa and cinnamon in a saucepan with 450 ml water and bring to the boil. Cover the pan, then reduce the heat and simmer gently for 15 minutes or until all the water has been absorbed.
- Spread the quinoa out onto a tray and leave to steam dry for a few minutes.
- Toss the pears with the caster sugar and divide them between 4 individual baking dishes.
- Stir the melted butter, ground almonds and brown sugar into the quinoa, then sprinkle the mixture on top of the pears.
- Bake the crumbles in the oven for 25 minutes or until the tops are golden brown.

506

SERVES 8

Pear, Chocolate and Coconut Tart

Pear, Chocolate and Hazelnut Tart

507

- Replace the coconut with 2 tbsp of chopped hazelnuts (cob nuts).

Apple, Chocolate and Coconut Tart

508

- Replace the pears with slices of eating apples and sprinkle with 2 tbsp of golden caster sugar before cooking.

PREPARATION TIME 40 MINUTES

COOKING TIME 35 MINUTES

INGREDIENTS

110 g / 4 oz / ½ cup butter, cubed and chilled
225 g / 8 oz / 1 ½ cups plain (all purpose) flour
200 g / 7 oz dark chocolate (minimum 60% cocoa solids), chopped
4 pears, cored and sliced
2 tbsp desiccated coconut

- Rub the butter into the flour then add just enough cold water to bind the mixture into a pliable dough.
- Roll out the pastry on a floured surface and use it to line a 23 cm / 9" round tart case.
- Leave the pastry to chill the fridge for 30 minutes.
- Preheat the oven to 200°C (180° fan) / 400F / gas 6.
- Line the pastry case with clingfilm and fill it with baking beans, then bake for 15 minutes.
- Remove the clingfilm and baking beans and fill the case with chopped chocolate then arrange the pear slices on top.
- Bake for 15 – 20 minutes or until the pears are soft and golden.
- Sprinkle the tart with desiccated coconut just before serving.

Chocolate and Banana Granola Pots

509

MAKES 6

- Heat the cream until it starts to simmer, then pour it over the chopped chocolate and stir until the mixture has cooled and thickened.
- Layer the chocolate ganache with the sliced banana inside 6 glasses and top with a sprinkle of granola.

PREPARATION TIME 5 MINUTES

COOKING TIME 5 MINUTES

INGREDIENTS

200 ml / 7 fl. oz / ¾ cup double (heavy) cream
200 g / 7 oz dark chocolate, minimum 60% cocoa solids, chopped
4 bananas, sliced
4 tbsp granola

Chocolate and Banana Crunch Sundae

510

- Layer up the glasses with scoops of vanilla ice cream.

Cinnamon Brioche French Toast

511

SERVES 2

- Lightly beat the eggs with the milk in a wide, shallow dish and heat the butter in a large frying pan until sizzling.
- Dip the brioche slices in the egg mixture on both sides until evenly coated then fry them in the butter for 2 minutes on each side or until golden brown.
- Mix the sugar with the cinnamon and sprinkle liberally over the French toast at the table.

PREPARATION TIME 4 MINUTES

COOKING TIME 4 MINUTES

INGREDIENTS

2 large eggs
75 ml / 7 ½ fl. oz / ⅓ cup milk
2 tbsp butter
6 thick slices brioche
2 tbsp caster (superfine) sugar
1 tsp ground cinnamon

Cinnamon Banana Brioche French Toast

512

- Add a sliced banana to each portion of French Toast.

513

SERVES 4

Buttered Pancakes

PREPARATION TIME 10 MINUTES

COOKING TIME 30 MINUTES

INGREDIENTS

250 g / 9 oz / 1 ⅔ cups plain (all purpose) flour
2 tsp baking powder
2 large eggs
300 ml / 10 ½ fl. oz / 1 ¼ cups milk
2 tbsp melted butter
4 small knobs butter
jam (jelly) and maple syrup to serve

- Mix the flour and baking powder in a bowl and make a well in the centre.
- Break in the eggs and pour in the milk then use a whisk to incorporate all of the flour from round the outside.
- Melt the butter in a frying pan then whisk into the batter.
- Put the buttered frying pan back over a low heat. You will need a tablespoon of batter for each pancake and you should be able to cook 4 pancakes at a time.
- Spoon the batter into the pan and cook for 2 minutes.
- Turn the pancakes over with a spatula and cook the other side until golden brown and cooked through.
- Repeat until all the batter has been used.
- Pile the pancakes onto warm plates and top each one with a knob of butter. Serve with your choice of jam or maple syrup.

Nutella Pancakes

514

- Omit the knobs of butter and add a heaped teaspoon of Nutella to the top of each stack of pancakes.

515

SERVES 6

Prune Clafoutis

PREPARATION TIME 10 MINUTES

COOKING TIME 35-45 MINUTES

INGREDIENTS

75 g / 2 ½ oz / ⅓ cup caster (superfine) sugar
75 g / 2 ½ oz / ⅓ cup butter
300 ml / 10 ½ fl. oz / 1 ¼ cups whole milk
2 large eggs
50 g / 1 ¾ oz / ⅓ cup plain (all purpose) flour
2 tbsp ground almonds
300 g / 10 ½ oz / 2 cups stoneless prunes
freshly grated nutmeg for sprinkling

- Preheat the oven to 190°C (170° fan) / 375F / gas 5.
- Melt the butter in a saucepan and cook over a low heat until it starts to smell nutty.
- Brush a little of the butter around the inside of a baking dish then add a spoonful of caster sugar and shake to coat.
- Whisk together the milk and eggs with the rest of the butter.
- Sift the flour into a mixing bowl with a pinch of salt, then stir in the ground almonds and the rest of the sugar.
- Make a well in the middle of the dry ingredients and gradually whisk in the liquid, incorporating all the flour from round the outside until you have a lump-free batter.
- Arrange the prunes in the prepared baking dish, pour over the batter and grate over a little nutmeg.
- Bake the clafoutis for 35 – 45 minutes or until a skewer inserted in the centre comes out clean.

Dried Apricot Clafoutis

516

- Replace the prunes with 250 g of dried apricots.

Pear and Plum Tarte Tatin

517

SERVES 8

- Preheat the oven to 220°C (200° fan) / 425F / gas 7.
- Dot the butter over the base of a large ovenproof frying pan and sprinkle with sugar.
- Arrange the pears round the outside of the pan, followed by a ring of plums and the mirabelles in the centre.
- Roll out the pastry on a floured surface and cut out a circle the same size as the frying pan.
- Lay the pastry over the fruit and tuck in the edges, then transfer the pan to the oven and bake for 25 minutes or until the pastry is golden brown and cooked through.
- Using oven gloves, put a large plate on top of the frying pan and turn them both over in one smooth movement to unmold the tart.

PREPARATION TIME 10 MINUTES

COOKING TIME 25 MINUTES

INGREDIENTS

3 tbsp butter, softened and cubed
4 tbsp soft light brown sugar
4 pears, peeled, cored and quartered
12 small plums, stoned
6 mirabelles, stoned
250 g / 9 oz all-butter puff pastry

Three Plum Tarte Tatin

518

- Replace the pears with 24 stoned greengages.

Fruits of the Forest Crumble

519

SERVES 6

- Preheat the oven to 180°C (160° fan) / 350F / gas 4.
- Mix the forest fruits with the sugar and arrange in an even layer in the bottom of a baking dish.
- Rub the butter into the flour and stir in the ground almonds and brown sugar.
- Squeeze a handful of the mixture into a clump and then crumble it over the fruit. Use up the rest of the topping in the same way, then shake the dish to level the top.
- Bake the crumble for 40 minutes or until the topping is golden brown and the fruit is bubbling.

PREPARATION TIME 10 MINUTES

COOKING TIME 40 MINUTES

INGREDIENTS

450 g / 1 lb / 3 cups mixed forest fruits (defrosted if frozen)
4 tbsp caster (superfine) sugar
75 g / 2 ½ oz / ⅓ cup butter
50 g / 1 ¾ oz / ⅓ cup plain (all purpose) flour
25 g / 1 oz / ¼ cup ground almonds
40 g / 1 ½ oz / ¼ cup light brown sugar

Winter Fruit Crumble

520

- Soak 250 g of mixed dried fruit in 400 ml of hot tea for 1 hour then drain well and use instead of the forest fruits.

SERVES 4

Pancakes with Honey and Blueberries

PREPARATION TIME 10 MINUTES

COOKING TIME 30 MINUTES

INGREDIENTS

250 g / 9 oz / 1 ⅔ cups plain (all purpose) flour
2 tsp baking powder
2 large eggs
300 ml / 10 ½ fl. oz / 1 ¼ cups milk
2 tbsp butter
150 g / 5 ½ oz / 1 cup blueberries
4 tbsp runny honey

- Mix the flour and baking powder in a bowl and make a well in the centre.
- Break in the eggs and pour in the milk then use a whisk to gradually incorporate all of the flour from round the outside.
- Melt the butter in a small frying pan then whisk it into the batter.
- Put the buttered frying pan back over a low heat. You will need a tablespoon of batter for each pancake and you should be able to cook 4 pancakes at a time in the frying pan.
- Spoon the batter into the pan and cook for 2 minutes or until small bubbles start to appear on the surface.
- Turn the pancakes over with a spatula and cook the other side until golden brown and cooked through.
- Repeat until all the batter has been used, keeping the finished batches warm in a low oven.
- Layer up the pancakes with the blueberries and drizzle the stack with runny honey.

Pancakes with Honey and Pears
522

- Replace the blueberries with canned sliced pears.

SERVES 6

Redcurrant Sponge Pudding

PREPARATION TIME 10 MINUTES

COOKING TIME 30-35 MINUTES

INGREDIENTS

110 g / 4 oz / ⅔ cup self-raising flour, sifted
110 g / 4 oz / ½ cup caster (superfine) sugar
110 g / 4 oz / ½ cup butter, softened
2 large eggs
1 tsp vanilla extract
125 g / 4 ½ oz / ⅓ cup redcurrant jelly
75 g / 2 ½ oz / ½ cup redcurrant sprigs
icing (confectioners') sugar to dust

- Preheat the oven to 190°C (170° fan) / 375F / gas 5 and butter a baking dish.
- Combine the flour, sugar, butter, eggs and vanilla extract in a bowl and whisk together for 2 minutes or until smooth.
- Spread the redcurrant jelly over the bottom of the baking dish and spoon in the cake mixture.
- Transfer the dish to the oven and bake for 30 – 35 minutes.
- Test with a wooden toothpick, if it comes out clean, the cake is done.
- Arrange the redcurrant sprigs on top of the pudding and dust the top with icing sugar before serving.

Blueberry Sponge Pudding
524

- Replace the redcurrant jelly with blueberry jam and decorate the top with fresh blueberries.

525

MAKES 6

Summer Fruit and Mint Crumbles

Summer Fruit and Orange Crumbles

526

- Replace the mint with the zest and juice of an orange.

Summer Fruit and Chocolate Crumble

527

- Mix 5 tbsp of fine chocolate chips into the crumble mixture before topping the fruit filling.

PREPARATION TIME 15 MINUTES

COOKING TIME 25 MINUTES

INGREDIENTS

200 g / 7 oz / 1 ⅓ cups raspberries
200 g / 7 oz / 1 ⅓ cups blueberries
4 tbsp caster (superfine) sugar
3 sprigs of mint
75 g / 2 ½ oz / ⅓ cup butter
50 g / 1 ¾ oz / ⅓ cup plain (all purpose) flour
25 g / 1 oz / ¼ cup ground almonds
40 g / 1 ½ oz / ¼ cup light brown sugar

- Preheat the oven to 180°C (160° fan) / 350F / gas 4.
- Put the raspberries, blueberries, caster sugar and mint in a saucepan and cover it with a lid.
- Heat gently for 5 minutes to soften the fruit and infuse it with mint, then discard the mint and divide the fruit between 6 individual baking dishes.
- Rub the butter into the flour and stir in the ground almonds and brown sugar.
- Crumble the mixture over the fruit then bake for 25 minutes or until the topping is golden brown.

SERVES 4

528

Raspberry and Vanilla Clafoutis

Strawberry and Vanilla Clafoutis
529

- Replace the raspberries with an equal weight of halved strawberries.

Blackberry and Vanilla Clafoutis
530

- Swap the raspberries for blackberries for a more tart flavour.

PREPARATION TIME 10 MINUTES

COOKING TIME 20-25 MINUTES

....

INGREDIENTS

75 g / 2 ½ oz / ⅓ cup caster (superfine) sugar
75 g / 2 ½ oz / ⅓ cup butter
300 ml / 10 ½ fl. oz / 1 ¼ cups milk
1 tsp vanilla extract
2 large eggs
50 g / 1 ¾ oz / ⅓ cup plain (all purpose) flour
300 g / 10 ½ oz / 2 cups raspberries

- Preheat the oven to 190°C (170° fan) / 375F / gas 5.
- Melt the butter in a saucepan and cook over a low heat until it starts to smell nutty.
- Brush a little of the butter around the inside of 4 individual baking dishes then sprinkle with caster sugar and shake to coat.
- Whisk together the milk, vanilla and eggs with the rest of the butter.
- Sift the flour into a mixing bowl with a pinch of salt, then stir in the rest of the sugar.
- Make a well in the middle of the dry ingredients and gradually whisk in the liquid, incorporating all the flour from round the outside until you have a lump-free batter.
- Arrange the raspberries in the prepared baking dishes and pour over the batter.
- Bake the clafoutis for 20 – 25 minutes or until a skewer inserted in the centre comes out clean.

531

MAKES 8

Mini Cherry and Almond Clafoutis

- Preheat the oven to 190°C (170° fan) / 375F / gas 5.
- Melt the butter in a saucepan and cook over a low heat until it starts to smell nutty.
- Brush a little of the butter around the inside of 8 ramekins then sprinkle with caster sugar and shake to coat.
- Whisk together the milk and eggs with the rest of the butter.
- Sift the flour into a mixing bowl with a pinch of salt, then stir in the ground almonds and the rest of the sugar.
- Make a well in the middle of the dry ingredients and gradually whisk in the liquid, incorporating all the flour from round the outside until you have a lump-free batter.
- Arrange the prunes in the prepared ramekins, then pour in the batter and scatter with flaked almonds.
- Bake the clafoutis for 15 – 20 minutes or until a skewer inserted in the centre comes out clean.

PREPARATION TIME 10 MINUTES

COOKING TIME 45 MINUTES

INGREDIENTS

75 g / 2 ½ oz / ⅓ cup caster (superfine) sugar
75 g / 2 ½ oz / ⅓ cup butter
300 ml / 10 ½ fl. oz / 1 ¼ cups whole milk
2 large eggs
50 g / 1 ¾ oz / ⅓ cup plain (all purpose) flour
2 tbsp ground almonds
300 g / 10 ½ oz / 2 cups cherries, stoned
4 tbsp flaked (slivered) almonds
icing (confectioners') sugar
for dusting

Mini Blackberry and Orange Clafoutis

532

- Replace the cherries with fresh blackberries and add the grated zest of an orange to the batter.

533

SERVES 4

Mango and Almond Crumble

- Preheat the oven to 180°C (160° fan) / 350F / gas 4.
- Arrange the mango in a baking dish.
- Rub the butter into the flour and stir in the ground almonds, sugar and flaked almonds.
- Take a handful of the topping and squeeze it into a clump, then crumble it over the fruit.
- Repeat with the rest of the crumble mixture then bake for 40 minutes or until the topping is golden brown.

PREPARATION TIME 5 MINUTES

COOKING TIME 40 MINUTES

INGREDIENTS

2 ripe mangos, peeled, stoned and sliced
75 g / 2 ½ oz / ⅓ cup butter
50 g / 1 ¾ oz / ⅓ cup plain (all purpose) flour
25 g / 1 oz / ¼ cup ground almonds
40 g / 1 ½ oz / ¼ cup light brown sugar
50 g / 1 ¾ oz / ⅔ cup flaked (slivered) almonds

Mango and Lime Crumble

534

- Squeeze the juice of a lime over the mango when it goes into the baking dish and add 1 tsp of finely grated lime zest to the crumble topping instead of the flaked almonds.

535

SERVES 6

Wholemeal Cherry and Raspberry Crumbl

PREPARATION TIME 10 MINUTES

COOKING TIME 40 MINUTES

....

INGREDIENTS

225 g / 8 oz / 1 ½ cups red cherries, stoned
225 g / 8 oz / 1 ½ cups raspberries
4 tbsp caster (superfine) sugar
75 g / 2 ½ oz / ⅓ cup butter
50 g / 1 ¾ oz / ⅓ cup wholemeal flour
25 g / 1 oz / ¼ cup ground almonds
40 g / 1 ½ oz / ¼ cup light
brown sugar
1 orange, zest finely grated

• Preheat the oven to 180°C (160° fan) / 350F / gas 4.
• Mix the cherries and raspberries with the sugar and arrange in an even layer in the bottom of a baking dish.
• Rub the butter into the flour and stir in the ground almonds, brown sugar and orange zest.
• Squeeze a handful of the mixture into a clump and then crumble it over the fruit. Use up the rest of the topping in the same way, then shake the dish to level the top.
• Bake the crumble for 40 minutes or until the topping is golden brown and the fruit is bubbling.

Wholemeal Cranberry Crumble   **536**

• Replace the cherries and raspberries with 450 g of cranberries and increase the amount of caster sugar to 75 g.

537

SERVES 4

Raspberry and Almond Crumble

PREPARATION TIME 5 MINUTES

COOKING TIME 40 MINUTES

....

INGREDIENTS

450 g / 1 lb / 3 cups raspberries
2 tbsp caster (superfine) sugar
75 g / 2 ½ oz / ⅓ cup butter
50 g / 1 ¾ oz / ⅓ cup plain (all purpose) flour
25 g / 1 oz / ¼ cup ground almonds
40 g / 1 ½ oz / ¼ cup light
brown sugar
50 g / 1 ¾ oz / ⅔ cup flaked (slivered) almonds

• Preheat the oven to 180°C (160° fan) / 350F / gas 4.
• Arrange the raspberries in a baking dish and sprinkle over the caster sugar.
• Rub the butter into the flour and stir in the ground almonds, sugar and flaked almonds.
• Take a handful of the topping and squeeze it into a clump, then crumble it over the fruit.
• Repeat with the rest of the crumble mixture then bake for 40 minutes or until the topping is golden brown.

Raspberry and Oat Crumble   **538**

• Replace the ground and flaked almonds in the crumble with 50 g of rolled porridge oats.

539

SERVES 8 Mango Tarte Tatin

- Preheat the oven to 220°C (200° fan) / 425F / gas 7.
- Dot the butter over the base of a large ovenproof frying pan and sprinkle with sugar, then arrange the mango on top.
- Roll out the pastry on a floured surface and cut out a circle the same size as the frying pan.
- Lay the pastry over the fruit and tuck in the edges, then transfer the pan to the oven and bake for 25 minutes or until the pastry is golden brown and cooked through.
- Using oven gloves, put a large plate on top of the frying pan and turn them both over in one smooth movement to unmold the tart.

PREPARATION TIME 10 MINUTES

COOKING TIME 25 MINUTES

INGREDIENTS

3 tbsp butter, softened and cubed
4 tbsp soft light brown sugar
2 mangos, peeled, stoned and sliced
250 g / 9 oz all-butter puff pastry

Pineapple Tarte Tatin   540

- Replace the mango with a whole pineapple that has been peeled, quartered and sliced.

541

MAKES 6 Banana, Mango and Coconut Pots

- Preheat the oven to 180°C (160° fan) / 350F / gas 4.
- Layer the mango and banana pieces inside 6 ovenproof glasses.
- Put the biscuits in a food processor and pulse to make them into crumbs.
- Mix the desiccated coconut with the biscuit crumbs and sprinkle it over the fruit.
- Transfer the glasses to the oven and bake for 15 - 20 minutes or until the topping is lightly toasted.

PREPARATION TIME 10 MINUTES

COOKING TIME 20 MINUTES

INGREDIENTS

1 large ripe mango, peeled, stoned and cubed
3 bananas, sliced
4 coconut biscuits
2 tbsp desiccated coconut

Banana, Mango and Ginger Pots   542

- Replace the coconut topping with 6 crushed ginger nut biscuits and serve with a scoop of stem ginger ice cream.

543

SERVES 4

Speedy Plum Tart

PREPARATION TIME 10 MINUTES

COOKING TIME 25 MINUTES

INGREDIENTS

250 g / 9 oz all-butter puff pastry
1 egg, beaten
6 plums, stoned and thinly sliced
2 tbsp caster (superfine) sugar

- Preheat the oven to 220°C (200° fan) / 425F / gas 7.
- Roll out the pastry on a floured surface into a rectangle.
- Transfer the pastry to a baking sheet and brush with beaten egg then arrange the sliced plums on top.
- Sprinkle with sugar, then transfer the tray to the oven and bake for 25 minutes or until the pastry is golden brown and cooked through.

Speedy Plum and Almond Tart
544

- Roll out 200 g of marzipan into a rectangle and lay it on top of the pastry before topping with the plums and sugar.

545

MAKES 6

Chocolate and Pear Crumble Pots

PREPARATION TIME 2 MINUTES

COOKING TIME 10 MINUTES

INGREDIENTS

4 large ripe pears, peeled and diced
2 tbsp caster (superfine) °sugar
100 g / 3 ½ oz milk chocolate, chopped
6 digestive biscuits, crushed
2 tbsp desiccated coconut

- Preheat the oven to 220°C (200° fan) / 425F / gas 7.
- Put the pears and sugar in a saucepan with 3 tablespoons of cold water.
- Put a lid on the pan then cook over a gentle heat for 10 minutes, stirring occasionally.
- Take the pan off the heat and stir in the chocolate to melt.
- Divide the mixture between 6 ovenproof tea cups and sprinkle with the crushed biscuits and coconut.
- Bake the crumbles for 5 minutes to toast the tops.

Chocolate and Pear Turnovers
546

- Leave the filling to cool then add a tablespoon to the centre of 6 pastry discs. Fold in half and seal with beaten egg then bake at 220°C for 20 minutes.

547

MAKES 12

Scones with Cream and Jam

Thunder and Lightning Scones

548

- Replace the strawberry jam with a drizzle of black treacle.

Date and Raisin Scones

549

- Add 50g of raisins and 50g chopped dates for a fruity alternative.

PREPARATION TIME 25 MINUTES

COOKING TIME 10-15 MINUTES

INGREDIENTS

225 g / 8 oz / 1 ½ cups self-raising flour
55 g / 2 oz / ¼ cup butter
150 ml / 5 fl. oz / ⅔ cup milk
200 g / 7 oz / ¾ cup clotted cream
200 g / 7 oz / ¾ cup strawberry jam (jelly)

- Preheat the oven to 220°C (200° fan) / 425F / gas 7 and oil a large baking sheet.
- Sieve the flour into a bowl and rub in the butter until the mixture resembles fine breadcrumbs.
- Stir in enough milk to bring the mixture together into a soft dough.
- Flatten the dough with your hands on a floured work surface until 2.5 cm / 1" thick.
- Use a pastry cutter to cut out 12 circles and transfer them to the prepared baking sheet.
- Bake in the oven for 10 – 15 minutes or until golden brown and cooked through.
- Transfer the scones to a wire rack to cool a little.
- Split open the scones then sandwich them back together with clotted cream and jam.

550

SERVES 6

Apple and Bramble Crumble

Apple and Blackcurrant Crumble

551

- Double the amount of apples and use 300 g of blackcurrants instead of the blackberries and raspberries.

Pear and Bramble Crumble

552

- Swap the apples for pears for a sweeter taste.

PREPARATION TIME 10 MINUTES

COOKING TIME 40 MINUTES

INGREDIENTS

2 apples, peeled, cored and sliced
225 g / 8 oz / 1 ½ cups blackberries
225 g / 8 oz / 1 ½ cups raspberries
4 tbsp caster (superfine) sugar
75 g / 2 ½ oz / ⅓ cup butter
50 g / 1 ¾ oz / ⅓ cup plain (all purpose) flour
25 g / 1 oz / ¼ cup ground almonds
40 g / 1 ½ oz / ¼ cup light brown sugar

- Preheat the oven to 180°C (160° fan) / 350F / gas 4.
- Mix the apples, blackberries and raspberries with the sugar and arrange in the bottom of a baking dish.
- Rub the butter into the flour and stir in the ground almonds and brown sugar.
- Squeeze a handful of the mixture into a clump and then crumble it over the fruit. Use up the rest of the topping in the same way, then shake the dish to level the top.
- Bake the crumble for 40 minutes or until the topping is golden brown and the fruit is bubbling.

553
SERVES 4
Crème Brûlée

- Pour the milk into a saucepan and bring to simmering point.
- Meanwhile, whisk the egg yolks with the caster sugar, cornflour and vanilla extract until thick.
- Gradually incorporate the hot milk, whisking all the time, then scrape the mixture back into the saucepan.
- Stir the custard over a low heat until it thickens then divide it between 4 ramekins.
- Chill in the fridge for 25 minutes.
- Sprinkle the tops with Demerara sugar then caramelise with a blow torch or under a hot grill.

PREPARATION TIME 35 MINUTES

COOKING TIME 10 MINUTES

INGREDIENTS

450 ml / 12 ½ fl. oz / 1 ¾ cups whole milk
4 large egg yolks
75 g / 2 ½ oz / ⅓ cup caster (superfine) sugar
2 tsp cornflour (cornstarch)
1 tsp vanilla extract
4 tsp Demerara sugar

Lemon Crème Brûlée
554
- Replace the vanilla extract with the finely grated zest of 1 lemon.

555
MAKES 6
Trifle Pots

- Layer the Swizz roll and fruit inside 6 glasses and drizzle over the sherry.
- Combine the milk and vanilla pod in a saucepan and bring to simmering point.
- Meanwhile, whisk the egg yolks with the caster sugar and cornflour until thick.
- Gradually incorporate the hot milk, whisking all the time, then scrape the mixture back into the saucepan.
- Stir the custard over a low heat until it thickens then spoon it into the glasses.
- Leave the custard to cool to room temperature then whip the cream until it forms soft peaks and spoon it on top of the trifles.

PREPARATION TIME 35 MINUTES

COOKING TIME 10 MINUTES

INGREDIENTS

300 g / 10 ½ oz raspberry Swiss roll, sliced
100 g / 3 ½ oz / ⅔ cup strawberries, sliced
100 g / 3 ½ oz / ⅔ cup blueberries
100 g / 3 ½ oz / ⅔ cup raspberries
4 tbsp sherry
300 ml / 10 ½ fl. oz / 1 ¼ cups double (heavy) cream

FOR THE CUSTARD:
450 ml / 12 ½ fl. oz / 1 ¾ cups whole milk
1 vanilla pod, split lengthways
4 large egg yolks
75 g / 2 ½ oz / ⅓ cup caster (superfine) sugar
1 tsp cornflour (cornstarch)

Cherry Trifle Pots
556
- Replace the berries with 300 g of stoned black cherries and top each trifle with a maraschino cherry.

557

SERVES 4

Crêpes with Poached Dried Fruit

PREPARATION TIME 5 MINUTES

COOKING TIME 25 MINUTES

INGREDIENTS

150 g / 5 ½ oz / 1 cup plain (all purpose) flour
325 ml / 11 ½ fl. oz / 1 ⅓ cups whole milk
1 large egg, beaten
2 tbsp butter

FOR THE POACHED FRUIT:
125 g / 4 ½ oz / ⅔ cup dried apricots
125 g / 4 ½ oz / ⅔ cup prunes, stoned
2 pears, cored and sliced
1 cinnamon stick
600 ml / 1 pint / 2 ½ cups apple juice

- Put the fruit and cinnamon in a saucepan and pour over the apple juice. Simmer for 5 minutes then turn off the heat.
- Put the oven on a low setting.
- Sieve the flour into a bowl and make a well in the centre. Pour in the milk and egg then use a whisk to gradually incorporate all of the flour from round the outside.
- Melt the butter in a small non-stick frying pan then whisk it into the batter.
- Put the buttered frying pan back over a low heat. Add a small ladle of batter and swirl the pan to coat the bottom.
- When it starts to dry and curl up at the edges, turn the crêpe over with a spatula and cook the other side until golden brown and cooked through.
- Transfer the crêpe to a plate, cover with a clean tea towel and keep warm in the oven.
- Repeat the process until all the batter has been used, then fold up the crêpes, divide between 4 warm plates and spoon over the stewed fruit.

558

MAKES 18

Banana, Pear and Chocolate Pots

PREPARATION TIME 5 MINUTES

COOKING TIME 5 MINUTES

INGREDIENTS

200 ml / 7 fl. oz / ¾ cup double (heavy) cream
200 g / 7 oz dark chocolate, minimum 60% cocoa solids, chopped
3 bananas, sliced
2 pears, cored and diced
100 g / 3 ½ oz amaretti biscuits, crushed

- Heat the cream until it starts to simmer, then pour it over the chopped chocolate and stir until the mixture has cooled and thickened.
- Layer the chocolate ganache with the banana and pear inside 6 glass mugs and top with a sprinkle of crushed amaretti.

Little Apple Crumbles

- Preheat the oven to 180°C (160° fan) / 350F / gas 4.
- Put the apples in a saucepan with the sugar and a splash of water and cook with the lid on for 5 minutes or until softened.
- Meanwhile, rub the butter into the flour and stir in the ground almonds and brown sugar.
- Divide the cooked apple between 4 small baking dishes.
- Squeeze a handful of the crumble mixture into a clump and then crumble it over the apples. Use up the rest of the topping in the same way, then shake the dishes to level the tops.
- Bake the crumbles for 25 minutes or until the tops are golden brown.

PREPARATION TIME 10 MINUTES

COOKING TIME 30 MINUTES

INGREDIENTS

2 cooking apples, peeled, cored and diced
4 tbsp caster (superfine) sugar
75 g / 2 ½ oz / ⅓ cup butter
50 g / 1 ¾ oz / ⅓ cup plain (all purpose) flour
25 g / 1 oz / ¼ cup ground almonds
40 g / 1 ½ oz / ¼ cup light brown sugar

Mirabelle Clafoutis

PREPARATION TIME 15 MINUTES

COOKING TIME 35-45 MINUTES

INGREDIENTS

75 g / 2 ½ oz / ⅓ cup caster (superfine) sugar
75 g / 2 ½ oz / ⅓ cup butter
300 ml / 10 ½ fl. oz / 1 ¼ cups whole milk
2 large eggs
50 g / 1 ¾ oz / ⅓ cup plain (all purpose) flour
2 tbsp ground almonds
300 g / 10 ½ oz / 2 cups mirabelle plums
demerara sugar for sprinkling

- Preheat the oven to 190°C (170° fan) / 375F / gas 5.
- Melt the butter in a saucepan and cook over a low heat until it starts to smell nutty.
- Brush a little of the butter around the inside of a baking dish then add a spoonful of the caster sugar and shake to coat.
- Whisk together the milk and eggs with the rest of the butter.
- Sift the flour into a mixing bowl with a pinch of salt, then stir in the ground almonds and the rest of the sugar.
- Make a well in the middle of the dry ingredients and gradually whisk in the liquid, incorporating all the flour from round the outside until you have a lump-free batter.
- Arrange the mirabelles in the prepared baking dish, pour over the batter and sprinkle with demerara sugar.
- Bake the clafoutis for 35 – 45 minutes or until a skewer inserted in the centre comes out clean.

Individual Grape Crumbles

PREPARATION TIME 10 MINUTES

COOKING TIME 25 MINUTES

INGREDIENTS

200 g / 7 oz / 1 ⅓ cups red grapes
200 g / 7 oz / 1 ⅓ cups green grapes
75 g / 2 ½ oz / ⅓ cup butter
50 g / 1 ¾ oz / ⅓ cup plain (all purpose) flour
25 g / 1 oz / ¼ cup ground almonds
40 g / 1 ½ oz / ¼ cup light brown sugar

- Preheat the oven to 180°C (160° fan) / 350F / gas 4.
- Mix the grapes together and divide them between 6 ramekin dishes.
- Rub the butter into the flour and stir in the ground almonds and brown sugar.
- Crumble the mixture over the fruit then bake for 25 minutes or until the topping is golden brown.

SERVES 6

Peach and Pistachio Clafoutis

PREPARATION TIME 10 MINUTES

COOKING TIME 35-45 MINUTES

INGREDIENTS

75 g / 2 ½ oz / ⅓ cup caster (superfine) sugar
75 g / 2 ½ oz / ⅓ cup butter
300 ml / 10 ½ fl. oz / 1 ¼ cups whole milk
2 large eggs
50 g / 1 ¾ oz / ⅓ cup plain (all purpose) flour
2 peaches, stoned and sliced
3 tbsp pistachio nuts, chopped

- Preheat the oven to 190°C (170° fan) / 375F / gas 5.
- Melt the butter in a saucepan and cook over a low heat until it starts to smell nutty.
- Brush a little of the butter around the inside of a baking dish then add a spoonful of caster sugar and shake to coat.
- Whisk together the milk and eggs with the rest of the butter.
- Sift the flour into a mixing bowl with a pinch of salt, then stir in the rest of the sugar.
- Make a well in the middle of the dry ingredients and gradually whisk in the liquid, incorporating all the flour from round the outside until you have a lump-free batter.
- Arrange the peaches in the prepared baking dish, pour over the batter and sprinkle with chopped pistachios.
- Bake the clafoutis for 35 – 45 minutes or until a skewer inserted in the centre comes out clean.

Apricot and Pistachio Clafoutis   563

- Replace the peach slices with 6 halved apricots.

564

MAKES 8

Chocolate Steamed Puddings

PREPARATION TIME 10 MINUTES

COOKING TIME 35-40 MINUTES

INGREDIENTS

200 g / 7 oz / 1 ⅓ cups self-raising flour
200 g / 7 oz / ¾ cup dark brown sugar
200 g / 7 oz / ¾ cup butter
4 large eggs
1 tsp baking powder
3 tbsp unsweetened cocoa powder

FOR THE SAUCE:
200 ml / 7 fl. oz / ¾ cup double (heavy) cream
200 g / 7 oz dark chocolate, minimum 60% cocoa solids, chopped

- Butter 8 individual pudding basins and put a steamer on to heat.
- Put all of the cake ingredients in a large mixing bowl and whisk with an electric whisk for 4 minutes.
- Divide the mixture between the pudding basins then transfer them to the steamer and steam for 1 hour.
- Heat the cream until it starts to simmer, then pour it over the chopped chocolate and stir until smooth.
- Carefully unmould the puddings onto warm plates and pour over the sauce.

Chocolate Orange   565
Steamed Puddings

- Add the grated zest of an orange to the cake mixture and use orange-flavoured chocolate instead of dark chocolate in the sauce.

566

SERVES 4

Fig Jam Bread and Butter Pudding

- Spread the bread with butter and cut it into triangles.
- Arrange the triangles in a baking dish, adding spoonsful of the jam as you go.
- Whisk the milk, cream, eggs and caster sugar together and pour it over the top, then leave to soak for 30 minutes.
- Preheat the oven to 180°C (160° fan) / 350F / gas 4.
- Bake the pudding for 40 minutes or until the top is golden brown.

PREPARATION TIME 35 MINUTES

COOKING TIME 40 MINUTES

INGREDIENTS

1 loaf white bread, cut into thick slices
3 tbsp butter, softened
200 g / 7 oz / ¾ cup fig jam
250 ml / 9 fl. oz / 1 cup whole milk
200 ml / 7 fl. oz / ¾ cup double (heavy) cream
4 large egg yolks
75 g / 2 ½ oz / ⅓ cup caster (superfine) sugar

Marmalade Bread and Butter Pudding

567

- Replace the fig jam with marmalade.

568

SERVES 8

Speedy Summer Fruit Trifle

- Whip the cream with the icing sugar and vanilla extract until it forms soft peaks.
- Arrange half of the cake in a glass bowl and top with half of the cream, then scatter over half of the fruit.
- Repeat with the rest of the cake, cream and fruit, then refrigerate until ready to serve.

PREPARATION TIME 35 MINUTES

COOKING TIME 10 MINUTES

INGREDIENTS

450 ml / 16 fl. oz / 1 ¾ cups double (heavy) cream
4 tbsp icing (confectioners') sugar
1 tsp vanilla extract
300 g / 10 ½ oz Madeira cake, sliced
150 g / 5 ½ oz / 1 cup blueberries
150 g / 5 ½ oz / 1 cup raspberries

Speedy Tropical Fruit Trifle

569

- Replace the berries with 1 chopped mango, ½ a chopped pineapple, 2 chopped bananas and the pulp from 4 passion fruit.

570

MAKES 8

Guava Upside-Down Cakes

PREPARATION TIME 15 MINUTES

COOKING TIME 20 MINUTES

INGREDIENTS

300 g / 10 ½ oz / 2 cups self-raising flour
2 tsp baking powder
250 g / 9 oz / 1 ¼ cups caster (superfine) sugar
250 g / 9 oz / 1 ¼ cups butter, softened
5 large eggs
4 guavas, peeled and halved

- Preheat the oven to 180°C (160° fan) / 350F / gas 4 and butter a 8 individual cake tins.
- Sieve the flour and baking powder into a mixing bowl and add sugar, butter and eggs.
- Beat the mixture with an electric whisk for 4 minutes or until smooth and well whipped.
- Put a guava half, cut side down inside each tin.
- Spoon in the cake mixture and bake for 20 minutes or until a skewer inserted comes out clean.
- Leave the cakes to cool for 10 minutes then turn out onto serving plates.

Guava and Ginger Upside-Down Cakes
571

- Add 1 tsp ground ginger and 2 chopped pieces of stem ginger to the cake mixture.

572

SERVES 6

Plum Upside-Down Cake

PREPARATION TIME 15 MINUTES

COOKING TIME 25 MINUTES

INGREDIENTS

100 g / 3 ½ oz / ⅔ cup self-raising flour
1 tsp baking powder
100 g / 3 ½ oz / ½ cup caster (superfine) sugar
100 g / 3 ½ oz / ½ cup butter, softened
2 large eggs
250 g / 9 oz plums, stoned and halved
spiced plum sauce to serve

- Preheat the oven to 180°C (160° fan) / 350F / gas 4 and butter a 20 cm square cake tin.
- Sieve the flour and baking powder into a mixing bowl and add sugar, butter and eggs.
- Beat the mixture with an electric whisk for 4 minutes or until smooth and well whipped.
- Arrange the plums cut side down in the cake tin and spoon the cake mixture on top.
- Level the cake mixture with a palette knife and bake for 25 minutes or until a skewer inserted comes out clean.
- Leave the cake to cool for 20 minutes before turning out onto a serving plate.
- Cut into slices and serve with spiced plum sauce

Spiced Plum Sauce
573

- Simmer 250 g stoned chopped plums, 1 tsp mixed spice and 50 g caster sugar in 400 ml orange juice for 10 minutes. Blend until smooth in a liquidiser.

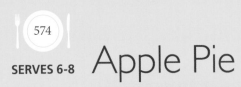

SERVES 6-8 574

Apple Pie

Apple and Sultana Pie 575

- Add 100 g of sultanas and the finely grated zest of a lemon to the apples.

Pear and Cinnamon Pie 576

- Swap the apples for pears and increase the cinnamon to 1 tsp.

PREPARATION TIME 45 MINUTES

COOKING TIME 35-45 MINUTES

INGREDIENTS

125 g / 4 ½ oz / ½ cup caster (superfine) sugar
2 tbsp plain (all purpose) flour
½ tsp ground cinnamon
800 g / 12 oz bramley apples, peeled, cored and cut into chunks
1 egg, beaten

FOR THE PASTRY:
300 g / 10 ½ oz / 2 cups plain (all purpose) flour
150 g / 5 ½ oz / ⅔ cup butter, chilled

- Sieve the flour into a bowl then grate in the butter and mix well.
- Mix in enough cold water to form a pliable dough then wrap it in clingfilm and chill for 30 minutes.
- Preheat the oven to 190°C (170° fan) / 375F / gas 5 and butter a 23 cm round pie tin.
- Mix the sugar, flour and cinnamon together in a bowl then toss with the apples.
- Roll out half of the pastry and use it to line the prepared pie tin.
- Pack the apples into the pastry case and brush around the rim with beaten egg.
- Roll out the rest of the pastry, lay it over the apples and press down round the outside to seal.
- Cut away the excess pastry and crimp the edges with your fingers.
- Cut 2 holes in the lid for the steam to escape then brush the top of the pie with beaten egg.
- Bake the pie for 35 – 45 minutes – the pastry should be crisp and golden brown on top and starting to shrink away from the edge of the tin.

577

SERVES 6

Peach and Marsala Tiramisu

Apricot and Amaretto Tiramisu

578

- Use fresh apricots in place of the peaches and use amaretto instead of the Marsala.

Pineapple and Coconut Tiramisu

579

- Swap the peaches for pineapple, replace the Marsala with coconut liqueur and mix 3 tbsp of desiccated coconut into the mascarpone.

PREPARATION TIME 30 MINUTES

....

INGREDIENTS

600 ml / 1 pint / 2 ½ cups double (heavy) cream
300 g / 10 ½ oz / 1 ⅓ cups mascarpone
4 tbsp icing (confectioners') sugar
100 ml / 3 ½ fl. oz / ½ cup Marsala
300 g / 10 ½ oz sponge fingers
4 ripe peaches, peeled, stoned and cubed
unsweetened cocoa powder for dusting

- Put the cream, mascarpone and sugar in a bowl with half of the Marsala and whip with an electric whisk until it holds its shape.
- Spoon a quarter of the mixture into a rectangular serving dish and top with half of the sponge fingers.
- Sprinkle the cake with half of the remaining Marsala, then spread with another quarter of the mascarpone mixture and scatter over the peaches.
- Lay the rest of the sponge fingers on top and press down lightly.
- Drizzle over the rest of the Marsala and spread with another quarter of the mascarpone.
- Spoon the rest of the mascarpone into a piping bag fitted with a large plain nozzle and pipe the mixture in lines across the top of the pudding.
- Dust the tiramisu with cocoa and chill in the fridge for 2 – 4 hours for the flavours to develop.

Poached Apples with Cranberry Compote

580

SERVES 4

- Put the apples, cut side down in a single layer in a wide sauté pan. Pour over the grape juice and sprinkle with lemon zest.
- Bring the pan to a gently simmer, then put on a lid and poach for 15 minutes.
- Meanwhile, put the cranberries in a small saucepan with the sugar and orange zest. Cover and cook gently for 5 minutes then remove the lid, give it a stir and cook for a further 10 minutes or until the cranberries start to burst and the juices thicken.
- Leave the apples and cranberry compote to cool completely.
- Turn the apples cut side up in a serving dish and spoon the compote on top.

PREPARATION TIME 5 MINUTES

COOKING TIME 15 MINUTES

INGREDIENTS

4 eating apples, peeled, halved and cored
600 ml / 1 pint / 2 ½ cups white grape juice
1 lemon, zest finely pared

FOR THE COMPOTE:
100 g / 3 ½ oz / ⅔ cup cranberries
75 g / 2 ½ oz / ⅓ cup brown sugar
1 orange, zest finely grated

Poached Apples with Redcurrant Compote

581

- Replace the cranberries with redcurrants and reduce the simmering time to 5 minutes.

Pannacotta with Blackberries and Blueberries

582

SERVES 6

- Heat half of the cream with the honey until small bubbles appear at the edges of the pan. Take off the heat.
- Pour the milk over the gelatine leaves and leave to soften for 10 minutes, then whisk into the warm cream.
- When the gelatine has fully dissolved, strain the cream into a jug. Put the base of the jug in a bowl of iced water.
- When the gelatine mixture starts to gel, whip the rest of the cream and fold it in.
- Pour into 6 moulds and refrigerate for 4 hours.
- Meanwhile, put the berries and sugar in a small saucepan with a splash of water and cook with the lid on for 5 minutes. Stir in the lemon juice then leave to cool.
- When you're ready to serve, dip the outside of the moulds in hot water, give them a shake then turn out the pannacottas onto serving plates. Spoon over the compote and garnish with mint.

PREPARATION TIME 30 MINUTES

COOKING TIME: 5 MINUTES

INGREDIENTS

600ml / 1 pint / 2 ½ cups double (heavy) cream
4 tbsp honey
50 ml / 1 ¾ fl. oz / ¼ cup milk
3 sheets leaf gelatine, chopped
mint sprigs to garnish

FOR THE COMPOTE:
150 g / 5 ½ oz / 1 cup blackberries
150 g / 5 ½ oz / 1 cup blueberries
100 g / 3 ½ oz / ½ cup caster (superfine) sugar
1 tbsp lemon juice

Lavender Pannacotta with Raspberry Compote

583

- Add a few stems of lavender to the cream as it infuses with the honey and replace the blackberries and blueberries with 300 g of raspberries.

584

SERVES 4

Maple and Spice Rice Pudding

PREPARATION TIME 25 MINUTES

COOKING TIME I HOUR 30 MINUTES

INGREDIENTS

1.2 litres / 2 pints / 4 ½ cups whole milk
2 star anise
4 cardamom pods
6 cloves
50 g / 1 ¾ oz / ¼ cup butter
110 g / 4 oz / ½ cup short grain rice
75 g / 2 ½ oz / ⅓ cup caster (superfine) sugar
4 tbsp maple syrup

- Preheat the oven to 140°C (120° fan) / 275F / gas 1.
- Warm the milk in a saucepan with the spices then leave to infuse for 20 minutes.
- Melt the butter in a cast iron casserole dish and add the rice and sugar.
- Stir over a low heat for 2 minutes then gradually incorporate the hot milk and spices.
- Cover the dish and bake in the oven for 1 hour 30 minutes then spoon into bowls and drizzle with maple syrup.

Maple and Pecan Rice Pudding   585

- Omit the spices and stir in 75 g of chopped pecan nuts before serving and topping with the syrup.

586

SERVES 4

Mint Chocolate Rice Pudding

PREPARATION TIME 5 MINUTES

COOKING TIME I HOUR 30 MINUTES

INGREDIENTS

50 g / 1 ¾ oz / ¼ cup butter
110 g / 4 oz / ½ cup short grain rice
75 g / 2 ½ oz / ⅓ cup caster (superfine) sugar
25 g / 1 oz / ¼ cup unsweetened cocoa powder
1.2 litres / 2 pints / 4 ½ cups whole milk
a few drops of peppermint extract
mint sprigs to garnish

- Preheat the oven to 140°C (120° fan) / 275F / gas 1.
- Melt the butter in a cast iron casserole dish and add the rice, sugar and cocoa powder.
- Stir over a low heat for 2 minutes then gradually incorporate the milk and peppermint extract and bring to a simmer.
- Cover the casserole dish and bake in the oven for 1 hour 30 minutes.
- Spoon the rice pudding into mugs and garnish with mint.

Mint Choc Chip Rice Pudding   587

- Leave the rice pudding to cool to room temperature then stir in 100 g of chocolate chips.

588

SERVES 4

Vanilla and Cinnamon Rice Pudding

- Preheat the oven to 140°C (120° fan) / 275F / gas 1.
- Warm the milk in a saucepan with the cinnamon and vanilla then leave to infuse for 20 minutes.
- Melt the butter in a cast iron casserole dish and add the rice and sugar.
- Stir over a low heat for 2 minutes then gradually incorporate the hot milk and reserve the spices.
- Cover the dish and bake in the oven for 1 hour 30 minutes.
- Rinse the vanilla pods and cinnamon sticks and leave them to dry somewhere warm while the pudding bakes.
- Spoon the rice pudding into glass mugs and decorate with the vanilla and cinnamon sticks.

PREPARATION TIME 25 MINUTES

COOKING TIME 1 HOUR 30 MINUTES

INGREDIENTS

1.2 litres / 2 pints / 4 ½ cups whole milk
4 small cinnamon sticks
2 vanilla pods, halved
50 g / 1 ¾ oz / ¼ cup butter
110 g / 4 oz / ½ cup short grain rice
75 g / 2 ½ oz / ⅓ cup caster (superfine) sugar

Liquorice Rice Pudding 589

- Replace the cinnamon and vanilla with 4 pieces of liquorice root.

590

SERVES 8

Custard Tart

- Preheat the oven to 200°C (180° fan) / 390F/ gas 6.
- Rub the butter into the flour and add just enough cold water to bind.
- Chill for 30 minutes then roll out on a floured surface. Use the pastry to line a 23 cm round tart case.
- Prick the pastry with a fork, line with clingfilm and fill with baking beans or rice.
- Bake for 10 minutes then remove the clingfilm and baking beans and cook for a further 8 minutes to crisp.
- Reduce the oven temperature to 160°C (140° fan) / 325F / gas 3.
- Whisk together the egg yolks, sugar, vanilla, cornflour and milk and strain it through a sieve into the pastry case.
- Bake the tart for 35 minutes or until the custard is just set in the centre.
- Leave to cool completely before slicing.

PREPARATION TIME 40 MINUTES

COOKING TIME 55 MINUTES

INGREDIENTS

100 g / 3 ½ oz / ½ cup butter, cubed
200 g / 7 oz / 1 ⅓ cups plain (all purpose) flour
4 large egg yolks
75 g / 2 ½ oz / ⅓ cup caster (superfine) sugar
1 tsp vanilla extract
2 tsp cornflour (cornstarch)
450 ml / 16 fl. oz / 1 ¾ cups milk

Apricot Custard Tart 591

- Halve and stone 4 apricots and arrange them in the pastry case before pouring in the custard.

592

MAKES 4

Mini Kiwi Clafoutis

PREPARATION TIME 10 MINUTES

COOKING TIME 25 MINUTES

INGREDIENTS

75 g / 2 ½ oz / ⅓ cup caster (superfine) sugar
75 g / 2 ½ oz / ⅓ cup butter
300 ml / 10 ½ fl. oz / 1 ¼ cups whole milk
2 large eggs
50 g / 1 ¾ oz / ⅓ cup plain (all purpose) flour
2 tbsp ground almonds
4 kiwis, cut into 4 slices

- Preheat the oven to 190°C (170° fan) / 375F / gas 5.
- Melt the butter in a saucepan and cook over a low heat until it starts to smell nutty.
- Brush a little of the butter around the inside of 4 gratin dishes then sprinkle with caster sugar and shake to coat.
- Whisk together the milk and eggs with the rest of the butter.
- Sift the flour into a mixing bowl with a pinch of salt, then stir in the ground almonds and the rest of the sugar.
- Make a well in the middle of the dry ingredients and gradually whisk in the liquid, incorporating all the flour from round the outside until you have a lump-free batter.
- Arrange the kiwi slices in the prepared dishes, then pour in the batter.
- Bake the clafoutis for 25 minutes or until a skewer inserted in the centre comes out clean.

Mini Kiwi and Lime Clafoutis   593

- Add the finely grated zest of 2 limes to the batter.

594

SERVES 6

Hazelnut and Coffee Pavlova

PREPARATION TIME 30 MINUTES

COOKING TIME 1 HOUR

INGREDIENTS

225 ml / 8 fl. oz / 1 cup double (heavy) cream
2 tbsp icing (confectioners') sugar
1 tbsp Frangelico liqueur
50 g / 1 ¾ oz dark chocolate (minimum 60% cocoa solids), chopped
50 g / 1 ¾ oz / ½ cup toasted hazelnuts (cob nuts), roughly chopped

FOR THE MERINGUE:
4 large egg whites
110g / 4 oz / 1 cup caster (superfine) sugar
1 tsp cornflour (cornstarch)
2 tsp instant espresso powder
50 g / 1 ¾ oz / ½ cup ground hazelnuts (cob nuts)

- Preheat the oven to 140°C (120° fan) / 275F / gas 1 and oil and line a baking tray with greaseproof paper.
- Whisk the egg whites until stiff, then gradually whisk in half the sugar until the mixture is very shiny.
- Fold in the remaining sugar, cornflour, espresso powder and hazelnuts then spoon the mixture onto the baking tray.
- Bake the meringue for 1 hour or until crisp on the outside, but still a bit chewy in the middle.
- Leave to cool completely.
- Whip the cream with the icing sugar and Frangelico until it just holds its shape, then spoon it on top of the meringue.
- Melt the chocolate in a microwave or bain marie then drizzle it over the top and sprinkle with the chopped hazelnuts.

Cappuccino Pavlova   595

- Omit the ground and chopped hazelnuts and use Tia Maria instead of Frangelico in the cream. Sprinkle the pavlova with a little cocoa powder to finish.

MAKES 6 # Tasty Lemon Tarts

Grapefruit Tarts 597

- Replace the lemon juice with the juice of a large grapefruit.

Lime Tarts 598

- Replace the lemon juice with the juice of 5 limes.

PREPARATION TIME 1 HOUR

COOKING TIME 25 – 30 MINUTES

INGREDIENTS

3 lemons, juiced
175 g / 6 oz / ¾ cup caster (superfine) sugar
2 tsp cornflour (cornstarch)
4 large eggs, beaten
225 ml / 8 fl. oz / ¾ cup double (heavy) cream

FOR THE PASTRY:
150 g / 5 ½ oz / ⅔ cup butter, cubed and chilled
300 g / 10 ½ oz / 1 ½ / 2 cups plain (all-purpose) flour

- Rub the butter into the flour until the mixture resembles fine breadcrumbs. Stir in just enough cold water to bring the pastry together into a pliable dough.
- Leave the pastry to chill the fridge for 30 minutes.
- Preheat the oven to 200°C (180° fan) / 400F / gas 6.
- Roll out the pastry on a floured surface and use it to line 6 individual tart cases. Line them with clingfilm and fill with baking beans then bake for 10 minutes.
- Remove the pastry cases from the oven and reduce the heat to 160°C (140° fan) / 325F / gas 3.
- Stir the lemon juice into the caster sugar and cornflour to dissolve, then whisk in the eggs and cream.
- Strain the mixture into the pastry cases and bake for 15 - 20 minutes or until just set in the centre.

SERVES 6

Apple Charlotte with Toffee Sauce

Pear Charlotte with Toffee Sauce

600

- Replace the apples with 4 large chopped pears.

Apple Charlotte with Cinnamon Toffee Sauce

601

- Add ½ tsp ground cinnamon to the toffee for a more spicy flavour.

PREPARATION TIME 40 MINUTES

COOKING TIME 45 MINUTES

....

INGREDIENTS

3 bramley apples, peeled, cored and cubed
100 g / 3 ½ oz / ½ cup brown sugar
½ tsp mixed spice
1 lemon, zest finely grated
1 loaf white bread, sliced and crusts removed
75 g / 2 ½ oz / ⅓ cup butter, softened

FOR THE TOFFEE SAUCE:
100 g / 3 ½ oz / ½ cup butter
100 g / 3 ½ oz / ½ cup muscovado sugar
100 g / 3 ½ oz / ⅓ cup golden syrup
100 ml / 3 ½ fl. oz / ½ cup double (heavy) cream

- First make the toffee sauce. Put all of the sauce ingredients in a small saucepan and stir over a low heat until the sugar dissolves.
- Bring to the boil then take off the heat and leave to cool to room temperature. Chill the sauce for 1 hour to thicken.
- Preheat the oven to 180°C (160° fan) / 350F / gas 4.
- Mix the apples with the sugar, spice and lemon zest in a saucepan then cook, covered, over a medium heat for 8 minutes, stirring occasionally.
- Butter the bread and cut each slice into quarters.
- Line a deep 20 cm round spring-form cake tin with some of the bread and fill with half of the apple.
- Top with more bread slices and spoon in the rest of the apple before adding a final layer of bread.
- Bake the charlotte for 30 minutes or until the top is golden brown. Unmould the cake and cut into wedges, then spoon over the chilled toffee sauce.

602

SERVES 4 # Strawberry Crumble

- Preheat the oven to 180°C (160° fan) / 350F / gas 4.
- Arrange the strawberries in a baking dish and drizzle with lime juice.
- Rub the butter into the flour and stir in the ground almonds, sugar and lime zest.
- Take a handful of the topping and squeeze it into a clump, then crumble it over the fruit.
- Repeat with the rest of the crumble mixture then bake for 20 minutes or until the topping is golden brown.
- Spoon into bowls and top with lime cream.

PREPARATION TIME 5 MINUTES

COOKING TIME 20 MINUTES

INGREDIENTS

250 g / 9 oz / 1 ⅔ cups strawberries, sliced
1 lime, juice and zest finely pared
75 g / 2 ½ oz / ⅓ cup butter
50 g / 1 ¾ oz / ⅓ cup plain (all purpose) flour
25 g / 1 oz / ¼ cup ground almonds
40 g / 1 ½ oz / ¼ cup caster (superfine) sugar
lime cream to serve

Crumble with Lime Cream   603

- Whip 300 ml double cream with 2 tbsp icing sugar and the juice of a lime. Serve on the crumble.

604

SERVES 4 # Plum Pudding

- Mix all of the ingredients together and spoon the mixture into the centre of a large double layer square of muslin.
- Gather up the edges and twist together so that the pudding forms a tight ball.
- Tie securely with string, then place in the top of a steamer and steam for 3 ½ hours.
- Carefully unwrap the pudding and transfer to a serving plate then spoon over the brandy sauce.

PREPARATION TIME 10 MINUTES

COOKING TIME 30 MINUTES

INGREDIENTS

225 g / 8 oz / 1 ½ cups suet
225 g / 8 oz / 1 cup dark brown sugar
2 large eggs, beaten
225 g / 8 oz / 3 cups white breadcrumbs
450 g / 1 lb / 2 ¼ cups raisins
100 g / 3 ½ oz / ⅔ cup plain (all purpose) flour
300 ml / 10 ½ fl. oz / 1 ¼ cups milk
1 tsp nutmeg, freshly grated
brandy sauce for serving

Brandy Pudding Sauce   605

- Put 50 g each of plain flour, butter and caster sugar in a pan with 600 ml milk. Stir over a low heat until bubbling and thickened. Stir in 75 ml brandy.

606

SERVES 6

Fig Crème Brûlée

PREPARATION TIME 35 MINUTES

COOKING TIME 10 MINUTES

....

INGREDIENTS

450 ml / 12 ½ fl. oz / 1 ¾ cups whole milk
4 large egg yolks
75 g / 2 ½ oz / ⅓ cup caster (superfine) sugar, plus extra for sprinkling
2 tsp cornflour (cornstarch)
1 tsp vanilla extract
3 fresh figs, quartered
3 tbsp granulated sugar

- Pour the milk into a saucepan and bring to simmering point.
- Meanwhile, whisk the egg yolks with the caster sugar, cornflour and vanilla extract until thick.
- Gradually incorporate the hot milk, whisking all the time, then scrape the mixture back into the saucepan.
- Stir the custard over a low heat until it thickens.
- Put 2 fig quarters in each of 6 small ramekins then pour over the custard.
- Chill in the fridge for 25 minutes.
- Sprinkle the tops with sugar then caramelise with a blow torch or under a hot grill.

Fig and Orange Crème Brûlée   607

- Replace the vanilla extract with the finely grated zest of an orange.

608

SERVES 8

Moist Pear Loaf Cake

PREPARATION TIME 15 MINUTES

COOKING TIME 55 MINUTES

....

INGREDIENTS

300 g / 10 ½ oz / 2 cups self-raising flour
2 tsp baking powder
250 g / 9 oz / 1 ¼ cups caster (superfine) sugar
250 g / 9 oz / 1 ¼ cups butter, softened
6 large eggs
3 ripe pears, peeled and chopped

- Preheat the oven to 160°C (140° fan) / 325F / gas 3 and line a large loaf tin with greaseproof paper.
- Sieve the flour and baking powder into a mixing bowl and add the sugar, butter and eggs.
- Beat the mixture with an electric whisk for 4 minutes or until smooth then fold in the pears.
- Spoon the mixture into the tin and level the top with a spatula.
- Bake the cake for 55 minutes or until a skewer inserted comes out clean.
- Transfer the cake to a wire rack and leave to cool completely before slicing.

Moist Raspberry Loaf Cake   609

- Add 150 g of raspberries to the cake mixture instead of the pear.

610

MAKES 4

Orange and Gingerbread Yoghurt Pots

- Cut the top and bottom off the oranges then slice away the peel in long strips.
- Carefully cut out the individual segments, leaving the membrane behind like the pages of a book.
- Divide ⅓ of the cake crumbs between 4 glasses and top with half of the yoghurt.
- Add a few orange segments to each and drizzle with a little honey then add another third of the crumbs and the rest of the yoghurt.
- Sprinkle over the remaining crumbs and garnish with more orange segments and a final drizzle of honey.

PREPARATION TIME 10 MINUTES

INGREDIENTS

2 oranges
200 g / 7 oz gingerbread, crumbled
400 g / 14 oz / 2 ½ cups Greek yoghurt
4 tbsp runny honey

Pear and Gingerbread Yoghurt Pots

611

- Poach 2 chopped pears in apple juice for 8 minutes then drain well and use in place of the orange.

612

MAKES 4

Mini Pear and Hazelnut Tatin

- Preheat the oven to 220°C (200° fan) / 425F / gas 7.
- Melt the butter in a frying pan then fry the pears, cut side down in a single layer, for 5 minutes or until they start to colour.
- Stir the sugar into the apple juice, pour it over the pears then cook until the liquid has reduced to a syrupy glaze.
- Arrange 2 pears in each hole of a 4-hole Yorkshire pudding tin, then stir the hazelnuts into the glaze and spoon them over and around the pears.
- Roll out the pastry on a floured surface and cut out 4 circles the same diameter as the holes.
- Lay the pastry over the pears and tuck in the edges, then transfer the tin to the oven and bake for 25 minutes or until the pastry is golden brown and cooked through.
- Using oven gloves, put a large plate or chopping board on top of the tin and turn them both over in one smooth movement to unmold the tarts.

PREPARATION TIME 10 MINUTES

COOKING TIME 40 MINUTES

INGREDIENTS

3 tbsp butter, softened and cubed
4 small pears, peeled, halved and cored
4 tbsp soft light brown sugar
100 ml / 3 ½ fl. oz / ½ cup apple juice
100 g / 3 ½ oz / ½ cup hazelnuts (cob nuts)
300 g / 10 ½ oz all-butter puff pastry

Mini Crab Apple Tatin

613

- Replace the pears with 400 g of crab apples that have been halved and cored.

SERVES 8

Pear Tarte Tatin

614

PREPARATION TIME 10 MINUTES

COOKING TIME 40 MINUTES

....

INGREDIENTS

3 tbsp butter, softened and cubed
5 small pears, peeled, quartered
and cored
4 tbsp soft light brown sugar
100 ml / 3 ½ fl. oz / ½ cup apple juice
300 g / 10 ½ oz all-butter puff pastry

- Preheat the oven to 220°C (200° fan) / 425F / gas 7.
- Melt the butter in a large frying pan then fry the pears, in a single layer, for 5 minutes or until they start to colour.
- Stir the sugar into the apple juice and pour it over the pears then cook until the liquid has reduced to a syrupy glaze.
- Arrange the pears in a small oven-proof prying pan and spoon over the cooking liquor.
- Roll out the pastry on a floured surface and cut out a circle the same diameter as the pan.
- Lay the pastry over the pears and tuck in the edges, then transfer the tin to the oven and bake for 25 minutes or until the pastry is golden brown and cooked through.
- Using oven gloves, put a large plate on top of the pan and turn them both over in one smooth movement to unmould the tart.

Pear and Lemon Tarte Tatin   615

- Replace the apple juice with lemon juice and add the finely grated zest of a lemon to the cooking liquor before spooning it over the pears.

616

MAKES 6

Chocolate and Brazil Nut Lumpy Cakes

PREPARATION TIME 15 MINUTES

COOKING TIME 15 MINUTES

....

INGREDIENTS

100 g / 3 ½ oz / ½ cup butter
200 g / 7 oz / 1 ⅓ cups self-raising
flour
100 g / 3 ½ oz / ½ cup caster
(superfine) sugar
100 g / 3 ½ oz / ½ cup milk
chocolate chunks
75 g / 2 ½ oz / ½ cup Brazil nuts,
roughly chopped
1 large egg
2 tbsp milk

- Preheat the oven to 200°C (180° fan) / 400F / gas 6 and grease a large baking tray.
- Rub the butter into the flour until the mixture resembles fine breadcrumbs then stir in the sugar, raisins and apple.
- Beat the egg with the milk and stir it into the dry ingredients to make a sticky dough.
- Divide the mixture between 6 buttered gratin dishes, then bake for 15 minutes or until just cooked in the centre.
- Serve hot from the oven.

Double Chocolate Lumpy Cakes   617

- Omit the Brazil nuts and replace with 100 g of white chocolate chunks.

MAKES 18

Floating Islands

618

Caramel Floating Islands

619

- To make the traditional topping, put 75 g of caster (superfine) sugar in a heavy-based saucepan and warm over a low heat until it dissolves into caramel. Drizzle over the meringues.

Spicy Floating Islands

620

- Add ½ a teaspoon of ground cinnamon and 2 pinches of nutmeg to the crème anglaise for a more spicy taste.

PREPARATION TIME 40 MINUTES

COOKING TIME 20 MINUTES

INGREDIENTS

600 ml / 1 pint / 2 ½ cups milk
1 vanilla pod, split lengthways
4 large egg yolks
75 g / 2 ½ oz / ⅓ cup caster (superfine) sugar

FOR THE POACHED MERINGUE:
600 ml / 1 pint / 2 ½ cups milk
4 large egg whites
1 vanilla pod, seeds only
110 g / 4 oz / ½ cup caster (superfine) sugar

- First make the crème anglaise. Combine the milk and vanilla pod in a saucepan and bring to simmering point, then turn off the heat and leave to infuse for 20 minutes.
- Whisk the egg yolks with the caster sugar until thick.
- Gradually incorporate the hot milk, whisking all the time, then scrape the mixture back into the saucepan.
- Stir the custard over a low heat until it just starts to thicken, then pour it into a chilled jug, cover the surface with clingfilm and chill for 2 hours.
- Put the milk in a saucepan with 500 ml of boiling water and bring to a gentle simmer.
- Whisk the egg whites with the vanilla seeds until stiff, then gradually add the sugar and whisk until the mixture is thick and shiny.
- Transfer heaped tablespoons of the mixture to the simmering milk and poach the meringues for 10 minutes, turning halfway through.
- Transfer the meringues to a wire rack and leave to steam dry for a few minutes.
- Divide the crème anglaise between 6 glasses and top each one with a meringue.

621

SERVES 4

Semolina Pudding with Dried Fruit

Lebanese Semolina Pudding

622

- Omit the raisins, cherries and nutmeg and flavour the pudding with 1 tsp each of rose water and orange flower water. Chill the mixture in small bowls instead of baking.

Apricot Semolina Pudding

623

- Replace the glace cherries for the same weight of dried apricots.

PREPARATION TIME 5 MINUTES

COOKING TIME 30 MINUTES

INGREDIENTS

600 ml / 1 pint / 2 ½ cups whole milk
75 g / 2 ½ oz / ½ cup semolina (cream of wheat)
50 g / 1 ¾ oz / ¼ cup butter
75 g / 2 ½ oz / ⅓ cup caster (superfine) sugar
50 g / 1 ¾ oz / ¼ cup raisins
50 g / 1 ¾ oz / ¼ cup glace cherries, halved
1 lemon, zest finely grated
freshly grated nutmeg for sprinkling

- Preheat the oven to 200°C (180° fan) / 400F / gas 6 and butter a baking dish.
- Heat the milk until the surface starts to shimmer, then take it off the heat and whisk in the semolina.
- Put the pan back over the heat and stir until the mixture bubbles and thickens.
- Beat in the butter, sugar, raisins, cherries and lemon zest, then scrape the mixture into the prepared baking dish.
- Grate over a little nutmeg then bake the pudding for 20 minutes or until the top is golden brown.

624
MAKES 18

Chocolate and Summer Fruit Pavlovas

- Preheat the oven to 140°C (120° fan) / 275F / gas 1 and oil and line a baking tray with greaseproof paper.
- Whisk the egg whites until stiff, then gradually whisk in half the sugar until the mixture is very shiny.
- Fold in the remaining sugar and cornflour then spoon the mixture into a piping bag. Pipe the meringue into 6 spirals on the prepared baking tray.
- Bake the meringues for 45 minutes or until they are crisp on the outside, but still a bit chewy in the middle, then leave to cool completely.
- While the meringues are cooking, heat the cream to simmering point then pour it over the chocolate and stir until smooth. Chill for 1 hour.
- Whip the chocolate cream until thick then spoon it into a piping bag, fitted with a plain nozzle.
- Pipe a spiral of chocolate cream on top of each meringue and decorate with the berries and cherries.

Chocolate and Mandarin Pavlovas | 625
- Replace the berries with a drained 400 g can of mandarin segments.

PREPARATION TIME 30 MINUTES

COOKING TIME 45 MINUTES

INGREDIENTS

225 ml / 8 fl. oz / 1 cup double (heavy) cream
50 g / 1 ¾ oz milk chocolate, chopped
½ tsp vanilla extract
100 g / 3 ½ oz / ⅔ cup small strawberries
100 g / 3 ½ oz / ⅔ cup raspberries
100 g / 3 ½ oz / ⅔ cup redcurrants
6 cherries

FOR THE MERINGUE:
4 large egg whites
110 g / 4 oz / 1 cup caster (superfine) sugar
1 tsp cornflour (cornstarch)

626
MAKES 6

Spiced Pineapple and Lime Crumbles

- Preheat the oven to 180°C (160° fan) / 350F / gas 4.
- Put the pineapple juice and lime juice in a small saucepan with the cinnamon and vanilla and simmer for 5 minutes or until syrupy.
- Divide the pineapple between 6 disposable baking dishes and spoon over the spiced pineapple juice, discarding the spices.
- Rub the butter into the flour and stir in the ground almonds, sugar and lime zest.
- Take a handful of the topping and squeeze it into a clump, then crumble it over the fruit.
- Repeat with the rest of the crumble mixture then bake for 25 minutes or until the topping is golden brown.

Spiced Mango and Lime Crumbles | 627
- Replace the pineapple with 3 peeled, diced mangos.

PREPARATION TIME 10 MINUTES

COOKING TIME 25 MINUTES

INGREDIENTS

150 ml / 5 ½ fl. oz / ⅔ cup pineapple juice
1 lime, juiced and zest thinly pared
1 cinnamon stick, halved
1 vanilla pod, split lengthways
1 pineapple, peeled, cored and cubed
75 g / 2 ½ oz / ⅓ cup butter
50 g / 1 ¾ oz / ⅓ cup plain (all purpose) flour
25 g / 1 oz / ¼ cup ground almonds
40 g / 1 ½ oz / ¼ cup caster (superfine) sugar

628

SERVES 4

Coconut Pancakes

PREPARATION TIME 10 MINUTES

COOKING TIME 30 MINUTES

··

INGREDIENTS

250 g / 9 oz / 1 ⅔ cups plain (all purpose) flour
2 tsp baking powder
2 large eggs
300 ml / 10 ½ fl. oz / 1 ¼ cups coconut milk
2 tbsp melted butter
2 tbsp shredded coconut, plus extra to serve

- Mix the flour and baking powder in a bowl and make a well in the centre.
- Break in the eggs and pour in the coconut milk then use a whisk to gradually incorporate all of the flour from round the outside.
- Melt the butter in a small frying pan then whisk it into the batter with the shredded coconut.
- Put the buttered frying pan back over a low heat. You will need a tablespoon of batter for each pancake and you should be able to cook 4 pancakes at a time in the frying pan.
- Spoon the batter into the pan and cook for 2 minutes or until small bubbles start to appear on the surface.
- Turn the pancakes over with a spatula and cook the other side until golden brown and cooked through.
- Repeat until all the batter has been used, keeping the finished batches warm in a low oven.
- Pile the pancakes onto warm plates and sprinkle with some more shredded coconut.

629

MAKES 6

Apple and Hazelnut Pastries

PREPARATION TIME 10 MINUTES

COOKING TIME 10 MINUTES

··

INGREDIENTS

3 large cooking apples, peeled and diced
3 tbsp caster (superfine) sugar
1 tsp mixed spice
800 g / 1 lb 12 oz all-butter puff pastry
1 egg, beaten
50 g / 1 ¾ oz / ½ cup hazelnuts (cob nuts), chopped
2 tbsp light brown sugar

- Preheat the oven to 220°C (200° fan) / 425F / gas 7.
- Put the apples, sugar and spice in a saucepan with 4 tablespoons of cold water.
- Put a lid on the pan then cook over a gentle heat for 10 minutes, stirring occasionally. Leave to cool.
- Roll out the pastry on a lightly floured surface and cut into 6 squares.
- Add a heaped tablespoon of apple compote to the centre of each one. Fold in the corners, seal in the centre and brush the tops with beaten egg.
- Mix the hazelnuts with the brown sugar then sprinkle over the top of the pastries.
- Transfer to a baking tray and bake for 18 minutes or until golden brown and cooked through.

630

MAKES 4

Individual Apple and Camembert Tatin

- Preheat the oven to 220°C (200° fan) / 425F / gas 7.
- Melt the butter in a large frying pan then fry the apple slices for 5 minutes or until they start to colour.
- Pour over the apple juice then cook until the liquid has almost all evaporated.
- Arrange the apple slices in 4-hole Yorkshire pudding tin and top with the sliced camembert.
- Roll out the pastry on a floured surface and cut out 4 circles the same diameter as the holes.
- Lay the pastry over the apples, then transfer the tin to the oven and bake for 25 minutes or until the pastry is golden brown and cooked through.
- Using oven gloves, put a large plate or chopping board on top of the tin and turn them both over in one smooth movement to unmold the tarts.

PREPARATION TIME 10 MINUTES

COOKING TIME 40 MINUTES

INGREDIENTS

3 tbsp butter, softened and cubed
4 eating apples, peeled and sliced
100 ml / 3 ½ fl. oz / ½ cup apple juice
½ camembert, sliced
300 g / 10 ½ oz all-butter puff pastry

Strawberry and Mint Yoghurt Pots

631

MAKES 4

PREPARATION TIME 10 MINUTES

INGREDIENTS

400 g / 14 oz / 2 ½ cups Greek yoghurt
4 tbsp runny honey
200 g / 7 oz / 1 ⅓ cups strawberries, sliced
2 tbsp mint leaves, shredded

- Mix the yoghurt with the honey and divide between 4 glasses.
- Top with the strawberries and sprinkle with shredded mint.

Apple Bread and Butter Puddings

632

MAKES 6

PREPARATION TIME 15 MINUTES

COOKING TIME 20 MINUTES

INGREDIENTS

1 brioche loaf, sliced
3 tbsp butter, softened
3 apples, cored and sliced
4 tbsp walnuts, chopped

250 ml / 9 fl. oz / 1 cup milk
200 ml / 7 fl. oz / ¾ cup double (heavy) cream
4 large egg yolks
75 g / 2 ½ oz / ¼ cup caster (superfine) sugar
1 orange, zest finely pared

- Spread the brioche slices with butter and cut into triangles. Arrange the brioche with the apple slices inside 6 individual casserole dishes and sprinkle with walnuts.
- Whisk the milk, cream, eggs, sugar and orange zest together and divide it between the dishes, then leave to soak for 10 minutes.
- Preheat the oven to 180°C (160° fan) / 350F / gas 4.
- Bake the puddings for 20 minutes or until the tops are golden brown.

633

MAKES 4

Cherry and Ginger Sponge Puddings

PREPARATION TIME 10 MINUTES

COOKING TIME 20 MINUTES

INGREDIENTS

110 g / 4 oz / ⅔ cup self-raising flour, sifted

110 g / 4 oz / ½ cup caster (superfine) sugar

110 g / 4 oz / ½ cup butter, softened

2 large eggs

1 tsp ground ginger

150 g / 5 ½ oz / 1 cup cherries, stoned

- Preheat the oven to 190°C (170° fan) / 375F / gas 5 and butter 4 individual baking dishes.
- Combine the flour, sugar, butter, eggs and ground ginger in a bowl and whisk together for 2 minutes or until smooth.
- Stir in the cherries then divide the mixture between the baking dishes.
- Transfer the dishes to the oven and bake for 20 minutes.
- Test with a wooden toothpick, if it comes out clean, the cakes are done.
- Serve hot from the oven.

Cherry and Orange Sponge Puddings

 634

- Replace the ground ginger with the zest and juice of an orange.

635

MAKES 6

Creamy Cranberry Crumbles

PREPARATION TIME 10 MINUTES

COOKING TIME 25 MINUTES

INGREDIENTS

200 g / 7 oz / 1 ⅓ cups cranberries

200 ml / 7 fl. oz / ¾ cup double (heavy) cream

4 tbsp caster (superfine) sugar

75 g / 2 ½ oz / ⅓ cup butter

50 g / 1 ¾ oz / ⅓ cup plain (all purpose) flour

25 g / 1 oz / ¼ cup ground almonds

40 g / 1 ½ oz / ¼ cup light brown sugar

- Preheat the oven to 180°C (160° fan) / 350F / gas 4.
- Mix the cranberries with the cream and sugar and divide the mixture between 6 ramekin dishes.
- Rub the butter into the flour and stir in the ground almonds and brown sugar.
- Crumble the mixture over the fruit then bake for 25 minutes or until the topping is golden brown.

Creamy Raspberry Crumbles

636

- Replace the cranberries with raspberries and reduce the sugar in the filling to 3 tbsp.

637

SERVES 8-10 Chocolate and Peanut Butter Cheesecake

- Preheat the oven to 180°C (160° fan) / 350F / gas 4 and grease a 20 cm round spring-form cake tin.
- Mix the biscuit crumbs with the peanut butter and press into an even layer in the bottom of the tin.
- Bake the biscuit layer for 5 minutes or until firm.
- Whisk together the filling ingredients until smooth.
- Spoon the cheesecake mixture on top of the biscuit base, levelling the top with a palette knife, then sprinkle with the peanuts.
- Bake the cheesecake for 40 – 50 minutes or until the centre is only just set.
- Leave to cool completely in the tin then chill for at least 3 hours before serving.

PREPARATION TIME 25 MINUTES

COOKING TIME 40-50 MINUTES

INGREDIENTS

600 g / 1 lb 5 oz / 2 ¾ cups cream cheese
150 ml / 5 fl. oz. / ⅔ cup double cream
175 g / 6 oz / ¾ cup caster (superfine) sugar
2 large eggs, plus 1 egg yolk
2 tbsp plain (all purpose) flour
100 g / 3 ½ oz milk chocolate, melted
150 g / 5 ½ oz salted peanuts, roughly chopped

FOR THE BASE:
200 g / 7 oz digestive biscuits, crushed
50 g / 1 ¾ oz / ¼ cup smooth peanut butter

Chocolate, Peanut and Caramel Cheesecake

638

- Swirl the cheesecake mixture with 250 g of dulce de leche before baking.

639

SERVES 8-10 Tropical Fruit Cheesecake

- Preheat the oven to 180°C (160° fan) / 350F / gas 4 and grease a 20 cm round spring-form cake tin.
- Mix the biscuit crumbs with the coconut and butter and press into an even layer in the bottom of the tin.
- Bake the biscuit layer for 5 minutes or until firm then arrange the pineapple chunks round the sides of the tin.
- Whisk together the filling ingredients until smooth.
- Spoon the cheesecake mixture on top of the biscuit base, levelling the top with a palette knife.
- Bake the cheesecake for 40 – 50 minutes or until the centre is only just set.
- Leave to cool completely in the tin then chill for 3 hours.
- When you're ready to serve, arrange the mango slices on top, spoon over the lemon curd and sprinkle with coconut.

PREPARATION TIME 25 MINUTES

COOKING TIME 40-50 MINUTES

INGREDIENTS

200 g / 7 oz digestive biscuits, crushed
2 tbsp desiccated coconut
3 tbsp butter, melted

FOR THE FILLING:
½ pineapple, peeled and cut into chunks
600 g / 1 lb 5 oz / 2 ¾ cups cream cheese
150 ml / 5 fl. oz. / ⅔ cup coconut milk
175 g / 6 oz / ¾ cup caster (superfine) sugar
2 large eggs, plus 1 egg yolk
2 tbsp plain (all purpose) flour
4 tbsp desiccated coconut
4 passion fruit, pulp sieved to remove the seeds

FOR THE TOPPING:
1 large mango, peeled and sliced
250 g / 9 oz / ¾ cup lemon curd
1 tbsp desiccated coconut, toasted

Tropical Fruit Cheesecake Pots

640

- To make the mixture into 6 individual cheesecakes, divide between 6 ramekin dishes and reduce the cooking time to 25 minutes.

641

SERVES 8

Deep Dish Cherry Clafoutis

PREPARATION TIME 15 MINUTES

COOKING TIME 50 MINUTES

....

INGREDIENTS

150 g / 5 ½ oz / ⅔ cup butter
4 tbsp granulated sugar
600 ml / 1 pint / 2 ½ cups whole milk
4 large eggs
100 g / 3 ½ oz / ⅔ cup plain (all purpose) flour
4 tbsp ground almonds
125 g / 4 ½ oz / ½ cup caster (superfine) sugar
300 g / 10 ½ oz / 2 cups cherries, stoned
demerara sugar for sprinkling

- Preheat the oven to 190°C (170° fan) / 375F / gas 5 and line a 23 cm deep spring-form cake tin with greaseproof paper.
- Melt the butter in a saucepan and cook over a low heat until it starts to smell nutty.
- Brush a little of the butter around the inside of the cake tin then add 3 tbsp of the granulated sugar and shake to coat.
- Whisk together the milk and eggs with the rest of the butter.
- Sift the flour into a mixing bowl with a pinch of salt, then stir in the ground almonds and the caster sugar.
- Make a well in the middle of the dry ingredients and gradually whisk in the liquid, incorporating all the flour from round the outside until you have a lump-free batter.
- Arrange the cherries in the prepared cake tin, pour over the batter and sprinkle with the rest of the granulated sugar.
- Bake the clafoutis for 50 minutes or until the centre is just set. Leave to cool completely before unmoulding and slicing.

Deep Dish Pear Clafoutis   642

- Poach 4 chopped pears in apple juice for 5 minutes then drain well and use in place of the cherries.

643

MAKES 4

Small Rhubarb Crumbles

PREPARATION TIME 10 MINUTES

COOKING TIME 30 MINUTES

....

INGREDIENTS

300 g / 9 oz rhubarb, cut into short lengths
4 tbsp caster (superfine) sugar
75 g / 2 ½ oz / ⅓ cup butter
50 g / 1 ¾ oz / ⅓ cup plain (all purpose) flour
25 g / 1 oz / ¼ cup ground almonds
40 g / 1 ½ oz / ¼ cup light brown sugar

- Preheat the oven to 180°C (160° fan) / 350F / gas 4.
- Put the rhubarb in a saucepan with the sugar and a splash of water and cook with the lid on for 5 minutes or until softened.
- Meanwhile, rub the butter into the flour and stir in the ground almonds and brown sugar.
- Divide the cooked rhubarb between 4 gratin dishes.
- Squeeze a handful of the crumble mixture into a clump and then crumble it over the rhubarb. Use up the rest of the topping in the same way, then shake the dishes to level the tops.
- Bake the crumbles for 25 minutes or until the tops are golden brown.

Rhubarb and Ginger Crumbles   644

- Finely chop 2 pieces of stem ginger and add to the rhubarb with the sugar and add 1 tsp of ground ginger to the crumble topping.

645

MAKES 6

Strawberry and Vanilla Pots

Strawberry and Orange Pots

646

- Omit the vanilla sugar and sprinkle 3 tbsp of Cointreau over the sliced strawberries. Replace the vanilla extract with the finely grated zest of an orange.

Raspberry Vanilla Pots

647

- Replace the strawberries with raspberries reserving a few for decoration.

PREPARATION TIME 10 MINUTES

COOKING TIME 10 MINUTES

....

INGREDIENTS

150 g / 5 ½ oz / 1 cup strawberries, sliced
1 tbsp vanilla sugar

FOR THE CUSTARD:
450 ml / 12 ½ fl. oz / 1 ¾ cups whole milk
4 large egg yolks
75 g / 2 ½ oz / ⅓ cup caster (superfine) sugar
1 tsp cornflour (cornstarch)
1 tsp vanilla extract

- Reserve 12 strawberry slices for decoration then toss the rest with the vanilla sugar and divide between 6 shallow dishes.
- Put the milk in a saucepan and bring to simmering point.
- Whisk the egg yolks with the caster sugar and cornflour until thick.
- Gradually incorporate the hot milk, whisking all the time, then scrape the mixture back into the saucepan.
- Stir the custard over a low heat until it thickens then spoon it on top of the strawberries.
- Lay 2 strawberry slices on top of each dish and serve warm or chilled.

SERVES 8 Apricot Jam Tart

Greengage Jam Tart   649

• Replace the apricot jam with greengage jam.

Strawberry Jam Tart   650

• Replace the apricot jam with strawberry jam and decorate with a fresh strawberry after cooking.

PREPARATION TIME 40 MINUTES

COOKING TIME 35 MINUTES

....

INGREDIENTS

100 g / 3 ½ oz / ½ cup butter, cubed and chilled
200 g / 7 oz / 1 ⅓ cups plain (all purpose) flour
450 g / 1 lb / 1 ¼ cups apricot jam
1 egg, beaten
physalis to garnish

• Preheat the oven to 200°C (180° fan) / 400F / gas 6.
• Rub the butter into the flour until the mixture resembles fine breadcrumbs.
• Stir in just enough cold water to bring the pastry together into a pliable dough then chill for 30 minutes.
• Roll out the pastry on a floured surface and use it to line a 23 cm round tart case, then trim off and reserve the excess pastry.
• Spoon the jam into the pastry case and level the top. Roll out the pastry trimmings and cut into 1 cm slices. Arrange them in a lattice pattern on top of the tart then seal the edges and brush the top with beaten egg.
• Bake for 25 – 30 minutes or until the pastry is cooked through underneath then garnish with physalis.

651

MAKES 4 Baked Berries with Amaretti Biscuits

- Preheat the oven to 180°C (160° fan) / 350F / gas 4 and line 4 ovenproof bowls with greaseproof paper.
- Mix the berries with the amaretti biscuits and divide between the lined bowls.
- Transfer the bowls to the oven and bake for 15 - 20 minutes or until the berries just start to soften and burst.

PREPARATION TIME 5 MINUTES

COOKING TIME 15 - 20 MINUTES

INGREDIENTS

100 g / 3 ½ oz / ⅔ cup blackberries
100 g / 3 ½ oz / ⅔ cup raspberries
100 g / 3 ½ oz / ⅔ cup redcurrants
200 g / 7 oz amaretti biscuits, crushed

Baked Berries with Ginger Cake 652

- Replace the amaretti biscuits with crumbled ginger cake.

653

SERVES 8 Lime Meringue Pie

- Preheat the oven to 200°C (180° fan), 390 F, gas 6.
- Mix the biscuit crumbs with the butter and press into an even layer in the bottom of a 23cm round tart case.
- Bake the biscuit layer for 5 minutes or until firm.
- Meanwhile, dissolve the cornflour in the lime juice and put it in a saucepan with the rest of the ingredients.
- Stir constantly over a medium heat to melt the butter and dissolve the sugar. Bring to a gentle simmer then pour it onto the biscuit base.
- Whisk the egg whites until stiff, then gradually add the sugar and whisk until the mixture is thick and shiny.
- Spoon the meringue on top of the lime curd, then bake for 10 minutes or until golden brown on top.
- Cut the pie into slices and garnish with lime.

PREPARATION TIME 10 MINUTES

COOKING TIME 25 MINUTES

INGREDIENTS

2 tsp cornflour (cornstarch)
8 limes, juiced and zest finely grated
4 large eggs, beaten
225 g / 8 oz / 1 cup butter
175 g / 6 oz / ¾ cup caster (superfine) sugar

FOR THE BASE:
200 g / 7 oz ginger nut biscuits, crushed
3 tbsp butter, melted

FOR THE MERINGUE:
4 large egg whites
100g / 3 ½ oz / ½ cup caster (superfine) sugar
slices of lime to garnish

Lime and Chilli Meringue Pie 654

- Stir a finely chopped red chilli into the lime curd before pouring it onto the biscuit base.

655

SERVES 8

Orange Meringue Pie

PREPARATION TIME 55 MINUTES

COOKING TIME 25-30 MINUTES

....

INGREDIENTS

2 tsp cornflour (cornstarch)
2 oranges, juiced and zest finely grated
2 lemons, juiced and zest finely grated
4 large eggs, beaten
225 g / 8 oz / 1 cup butter
175 g / 6 oz / ¾ cup caster (superfine) sugar

FOR THE PASTRY:
100 g / 3 ½ oz / ½ cup butter, cubed
200 g / 7 oz / 1 ⅓ cups plain (all purpose) flour

FOR THE MERINGUE:
4 large egg whites
100g / 3 ½ oz / ½ cup caster (superfine) sugar

- Preheat the oven to 200°C (180° fan) / 390F/ gas 6.
- Rub butter into the flour and add cold water to bind.
- Chill for 30 minutes then roll out on a floured surface.
- Use the pastry to line a 24 cm loose-bottomed tart tin and prick it with a fork.
- Line the pastry with clingfilm and fill with baking beans or rice then bake for 10 minutes.
- Remove the clingfilm and beans and cook for 8 minutes.
- Dissolve the cornflour in the orange and lemon juice and put it in a pan with the rest of the ingredients.
- Stir constantly over a medium heat to melt the butter and dissolve the sugar. Pour it into the pastry case.
- Whisk the egg whites until stiff, then gradually add the sugar and whisk until the mixture is thick and shiny.
- Spoon the meringue on top of the orange mixture, leaving a border round the edge and make peaks. Bake for 10 minutes.

Orange and Cinnamon Meringue Pie

656

- Add 1 tsp of ground cinnamon to the filling before pouring it into the pastry case.

657

MAKES 6

Individual Blueberry Pies

PREPARATION TIME I HOUR

COOKING TIME 25 – 30 MINUTES

....

INGREDIENTS

200 g / 7 oz / 1 cup butter, cubed and chilled
400 g / 14 oz / 2 ⅔ cups plain (all purpose) flour
400 g / 14 oz / 2 ⅔ cups blueberries
4 tbsp caster (superfine) sugar
½ tsp cornflour (cornstarch)
1 egg, beaten

- Rub the butter into the flour then stir in just enough cold water to make the pastry into a pliable dough.
- Wrap the dough in clingfilm and chill for 30 minutes.
- Preheat the oven to 200°C (180° fan) / 400F / gas 6.
- Roll out half the pastry on a floured surface and cut out 6 circles to line 6 tartlet tins.
- Toss the blueberries with the sugar and cornflour and divide between the 6 pastry cases.
- Roll out the rest of the pastry and cut out 6 circles.
- Brush the rim of the pastry cases with egg before laying the lids on top then press down firmly round the outside.
- Cut excess pastry into strips and attach them to the top of the pies in a lattice pattern with a little beaten egg.
- Brush the top of the pies with more beaten egg then bake in the oven for 25 – 30 minutes.
- Transfer the pies to a wire rack to cool.

Individual Blackcurrant Pies

658

- Replace the blueberries with blackcurrants and double the amount of caster sugar.

659

SERVES 4

Blueberry Pancakes

- Mix the flour and baking powder in a bowl and make a well in the centre.
- Break in the eggs and pour in the milk then use a whisk to incorporate all of the flour from round the outside.
- Melt butter in a frying pan then whisk it into the batter.
- Put the buttered frying pan back over a low heat. You will need a tablespoon of batter for each pancake and you should be able to cook 4 pancakes at a time.
- Spoon the batter into the pan and stud the tops with blueberries. Cook for 2 minutes or until small bubbles start to appear on the surface.
- Turn the pancakes over with a spatula and cook the other side until golden brown and cooked through.
- Repeat until all the batter has been used, keeping the finished batches warm in a low oven.
- Pile the pancakes onto plates. Drizzle with maple syrup.

PREPARATION TIME 10 MINUTES

COOKING TIME 30 MINUTES

INGREDIENTS

250 g / 9 oz / 1 ⅔ cups plain (all purpose) flour
2 tsp baking powder
2 large eggs
300 ml / 10 ½ fl. oz / 1 ¼ cups milk
2 tbsp melted butter
100 g / 3 ½ oz / ⅔ cup blueberries
maple syrup to serve

Redcurrant Pancakes

660

- Replace the blueberries with redcurrants and add the finely grated zest of an orange to the pancake batter.

661

MAKES 6

Orange Crème Caramel

- Preheat the oven to 150°C (130° fan) / 300F / gas 2.
- Put 150 g of the sugar in a heavy-based saucepan and heat gently until it starts to turn liquid at the edges. Continue to heat and swirl the pan until the sugar has all melted and turned golden brown.
- Divide the caramel between 6 ramekin dishes and leave to set, then butter the sides of the ramekins.
- Whisk the rest of the ingredients with the remaining 25g of sugar and divide between the ramekins.
- Sit the ramekins in a roasting tin and pour boiling water around them to come halfway up the sides.
- Transfer the tin to the oven and bake for 25 minutes or until only just set in the centres.
- Remove the ramekins from the tray and chill for 4 hours or overnight.
- Give the ramekins a vigorous shake to loosen the crème caramels, then turn each one out onto a plate.

PREPARATION TIME 15 MINUTES

COOKING TIME 35 MINUTES

CHILLING TIME 4 HOURS

INGREDIENTS

175 g / 6 oz / ¾ cup caster (superfine) sugar
1 tbsp butter, softened
500 ml / 17 ½ fl. oz / 2 cups whole milk
100 ml / 3 ½ fl. oz / ½ cup orange juice, sieved
4 large eggs
1 tsp orange zest, finely grated
1 tbsp Cointreau

Orange and Rose Crème Caramel

662

- Omit the orange zest. Replace the Cointreau with rose water and add a few drops of orange flower water.

663

MAKES 6

Grape Baked Custards

PREPARATION TIME 5 MINUTES

COOKING TIME 25 MINUTES

INGREDIENTS

4 large egg yolks
75 g / 2 ½ oz / ⅓ cup caster
(superfine) sugar
1 tsp vanilla extract
2 tsp cornflour (cornstarch)
450 ml / 16 fl. oz / 1 ¾ cups milk
150 g / 5 ½ oz / 1 cup grapes, halved
and deseeded

- Preheat the oven to 160°C (140° fan) / 325F / gas 3 and butter 6 ramekin dishes.
- Whisk together the egg yolks, sugar, vanilla, cornflour and milk until smooth.
- Divide the grapes between the ramekins, then pour in the custard mixture.
- Sit the ramekins in a roasting tin and pour enough boiling water around them to come halfway up the sides.
- Transfer the tin to the oven and bake for 25 minutes or until only just set in the centre.
- Serve warm or chilled.

Raspberry Baked Custards   664

- Replace the grapes with fresh raspberries.

665

SERVES 4

Stewed Cherries with Fromage Frais

PREPARATION TIME 5 MINUTES

COOKING TIME 15 MINUTES

INGREDIENTS

100 ml / 3 ½ fl. oz / ½ cup rosé wine
100 g / 3 ½ oz / ½ cup caster
(superfine) sugar
450 g / 1 lb / 2 ½ cups cherries,
stoned
3 tbsp kirsch
½ tsp almond essence
450 g / 1 lb / 2 cups fromage frais
75 g / 2 ½ oz / ¾ cup icing
(confectioners') sugar

- Pour the wine into a saucepan and add the sugar then stir over a low heat until the sugar has dissolved.
- Turn up the heat and bring to a simmer then add the cherries, put on a lid and stew gently for 10 minutes.
- Stir in the kirsch and almond essence and leave to cool.
- Beat the fromage frais with the sugar until smooth then divide between 4 serving bowls or glasses.
- Spoon the stewed cherries over the top and serve immediately.

Stewed Mirabelles with   666
Fromage Frais

- Replace the cherries with stoned mirabelles and use eau de vie instead of kirsch.

667

SERVES 6

Milk Chocolate Fondants

Chocolate Orange Fondants

668

- Add the finely grated zest of an orange to the mixture along with 2 tbsp Cointreau.

Chocolate Mint Fondant

669

- Add a ½ tsp of peppermint essence to the mixture and garnish with fresh mint.

PREPARATION TIME 50 MINUTES

COOKING TIME 8 MINUTES

INGREDIENTS

2 tbsp unsweetened cocoa powder
150 g / 6 oz good quality milk chocolate, chopped
150 g / 6 oz / ⅔ cup butter, chopped
85 g / 3 oz / ½ cup caster (superfine) sugar
3 large eggs, plus 3 egg yolks
1 tbsp plain (all purpose) flour
icing (confectioners') sugar for dusting

- Oil 6 mini pudding basins and dust the insides with cocoa.
- Melt the chocolate, butter and sugar together in a saucepan, stirring to dissolve the sugar.
- Leave to cool a little then beat in the eggs and egg yolks and fold in the flour.
- Divide the mixture between the pudding basins and chill them for 30 minutes.
- Preheat the oven to 180°C (160° fan) / 350F / gas 4 and put a baking tray in to heat.
- Transfer the fondants to the heated baking tray and bake in the oven for 8 minutes.
- Leave the fondants to cool for 2 minutes then sprinkle with icing sugar and serve immediately.

670

MAKES 18

Pear Sponge Pudding

Pear and Ginger Sponge Pudding   671

- Add 1 tsp ground ginger to the cake mixture and stir in 3 chopped pieces of stem ginger with the pears.

Apple Sponge Pudding   672

- Replace the pears with the same weight of Bramley apples.

PREPARATION TIME 10 MINUTES

COOKING TIME 30 – 35 MINUTES

INGREDIENTS

110 g / 4 oz / ⅔ cup self-raising flour, sifted
110 g / 4 oz / ½ cup caster (superfine) sugar
110 g / 4 oz / ½ cup butter, softened
2 large eggs
1 tsp vanilla extract
3 pears, cored and sliced
1 tbsp granulated sugar

- Preheat the oven to 190°C (170° fan) / 375F / gas 5 and butter a baking dish.
- Combine the flour, caster sugar, butter, eggs and vanilla extract in a bowl and whisk together for 2 minutes or until smooth.
- Fold in the sliced pears then scrape the mixture into the baking dish and sprinkle the top with granulated sugar.
- Transfer the dish to the oven and bake for 30 – 35 minutes.
- Test with a wooden toothpick, if it comes out clean, the cake is done.
- Serve the pudding hot from the oven with cream or custard.

673

SERVES 4 Stewed Mango with Meringue

- Preheat the oven to 200°C (180° fan) / 400F / gas 6.
- Put the mango and sugar in a saucepan with 4 tablespoons of cold water.
- Put a lid on the pan and cook over a gentle heat for 10 minutes, stirring occasionally, until it breaks down into a compote.
- Spoon the mixture into 4 oven-proof glass bowls.
- Whisk the egg whites until stiff, then gradually add the sugar and whisk until the mixture is thick and shiny.
- Spoon the meringue on top of the mango then bake for 10 minutes or until the meringue is toasted.

PREPARATION TIME 5 MINUTES

COOKING TIME 20 MINUTES

INGREDIENTS

3 mangos, peeled, stoned and diced
2 tbsp light brown sugar

FOR THE MERINGUE:
4 large egg whites
110 g / 4 oz / ½ cup caster
(superfine) sugar

Stewed Plums with Meringue   674

- Replace the mango with 300 g of stoned, halved plums.

675

SERVES 6 Clotted Cream Pannacotta

- Heat half of the cream with the sugar until small bubbles appear at the edges of the pan. Take off the heat and leave to cool a little.
- Pour the milk over the gelatine leaves and leave to soften for 10 minutes, then whisk the mixture into the warm cream.
- When the gelatine has fully dissolved, strain the cream into a jug. Put the base of the jug in a bowl of iced water to speed the cooling process.
- When the gelatine mixture starts to gel, fold in the clotted cream.
- Pour the mixture into 6 pannacotta moulds and refrigerate for 4 hours or until set.
- When you're ready to serve, dip the outside of the moulds in hot water, give them a shake then turn out the pannacottas onto serving plates. Spoon over the poached figs and serve straight away.

PREPARATION TIME 30 MINUTES

COOKING TIME 5 MINUTES

INGREDIENTS

300 ml / 10 ½ fl. oz / 1 ¼ cups double (heavy) cream
4 tbsp caster (superfine) sugar
50 ml / 1 ¾ fl. oz / ¼ cup milk
3 sheets leaf gelatine, chopped
300 ml / 10 ½ fl. oz / 1 ¼ cups clotted cream
figs poached in port to serve

Figs Poached in Port   676

- Simmer 6 halved figs with 300 ml of port, the juice of an orange and a cinnamon stick for 10 minutes. Remove and reserve the figs then boil the liquid until syrupy.

677

SERVES 6

Spicy Toffee Bananas

PREPARATION TIME 5 MINUTES

COOKING TIME 10 MINUTES

....

INGREDIENTS

100 g / 3 ½ oz / ½ cup butter
100 g / 3 ½ oz / ½ cup muscovado
sugar
100 g / 3 ½ oz / ⅓ cup golden syrup
2 star anise
1 vanilla pod, seeds only
3 cardamom pods
50 g / 1 ¾ oz / ⅓ cup dates, stoned
and chopped
9 bananas, halved
vanilla ice cream to serve

- Put the butter, sugar and golden syrup in a saucepan with the spices and dates and stir over a low heat to melt the butter and dissolve the sugar.
- Increase the heat to a gentle simmer, then add the bananas to the pan and let them poach for 2 minutes.
- Divide between 6 small bowls and top each one with a scoop of vanilla ice cream.

Spicy Toffee Pears

678

- Replace the bananas with 9 peeled, halved pears and increase the poaching time to 8 minutes.

679

SERVES 4

Chocolate Crumble Pots

PREPARATION TIME 15 MINUTES

COOKING TIME 30 MINUTES

....

INGREDIENTS

200 g / 7 oz double (heavy) cream
200 g / 7 oz dark chocolate
(minimum 60 % cocoa solids),
chopped

FOR THE CRUMBLE:
75 g / 2 ½ oz butter
50 g / 1 ¾ oz plain (all purpose) flour
30 g / 1 oz ground almonds
30 g / 1 oz blanched
almonds, chopped
40 g / 1 ½ oz light brown sugar

- Preheat the oven to 180°C (160° fan) / 350F / gas 4.
- Heat the cream to simmering point then pour it over the chocolate and stir until smooth.
- Divide the mixture between 4 ramekins and chill for 1 hour.
- Rub the butter into the flour and stir in the ground almonds, chopped almonds and brown sugar.
- Crumble the mixture onto a baking tray and bake for 25 minutes or until golden and crisp.
- Leave the crumble to cool for 15 minutes then sprinkle it over the chocolate pots.

Mint Chocolate Crumble Pots

680

- Add 4 sprigs of mint to the cream while it is warming, then strain out before combining with the chocolate.

681
MAKES 8

Mini Cherry and Pistachio Clafoutis

- Preheat the oven to 190°C (170° fan) / 375F / gas 5.
- Put the cherries and kirsch in a small saucepan then cover and poach for 8 minutes.
- Melt the butter in a saucepan and cook over a low heat.
- Brush a little of the butter around the inside of 8 individual baking dishes then sprinkle with caster sugar and shake to coat.
- Whisk the milk and eggs with the rest of the butter.
- Sift the flour into a mixing bowl, then stir in the ground almonds, pistachio nuts and the rest of the sugar.
- Make a well in the middle of the dry ingredients and gradually whisk in the liquid, incorporating all the flour from round the outside.
- Spoon the poached cherries into the baking dishes and pour in the batter.
- Bake the clafoutis for 15 – 20 minutes.

PREPARATION TIME 10 MINUTES

COOKING TIME 15 - 20 MINUTES

INGREDIENTS

300 g / 10 ½ oz / 2 cups cherries, stoned
3 tbsp kirsch
75 g / 2 ½ oz / ⅓ cup butter
75 g / 2 ½ oz / ⅓ cup caster (superfine) sugar
300 ml / 10 ½ fl. oz / 1 ¼ cups whole milk
2 large eggs
50 g / 1 ¾ oz / ⅓ cup plain (all purpose) flour
2 tbsp ground almonds
50 g / 1 ¾ oz / ½ cup pistachio nuts, halved
icing (confectioners') sugar for dusting

Mini Gooseberry and Pistachio Clafoutis
682

- Replace the cherries with gooseberries and reduce the poaching time to 5 minutes.

683
SERVES 8

Raspberry and Violet Custard Tart

- Preheat the oven to 200°C (180° fan), 390 F, gas 6.
- Rub butter into the flour and add cold water to bind.
- Chill for 30 minutes then roll out on a floured surface. Use the pastry to line a 23 cm round tart case.
- Prick the pastry with a fork, line with clingfilm and fill with baking beans or rice.
- Bake for 10 minutes then remove the clingfilm and baking beans and cook for a further 8 minutes to crisp.
- Reduce oven temperature to 160°C (140° fan) / 325F / gas 3.
- Whisk together the egg yolks, sugar, vanilla, cornflour and milk and strain it through a sieve. Stir in the crystallised violets and pour it into the pastry case.
- Bake the tart for 35 minutes or until the custard is just set in the centre.
- Leave to cool completely then arrange the raspberries on top and sprinkle with a few more crystallised violets.

PREPARATION TIME 40 MINUTES

COOKING TIME 55 MINUTES

INGREDIENTS

100 g / 3 ½ oz / ½ cup butter, cubed
200 g / 7 oz / 1 ⅓ cups plain (all purpose) flour
4 large egg yolks
75 g / 2 ½ oz / ⅓ cup caster (superfine) sugar
1 tsp vanilla extract
2 tsp cornflour (cornstarch)
450 ml / 16 fl. oz / 1 ¾ cups milk
50 g / 1 ¾ oz / ⅔ cup crystallised violets, plus extra for sprinkling
250 g / 9 oz / 1 ⅔ cups raspberries

Raspberry and Rose Custard Tart
684

- Use crystallised rose petals instead of the violets and add 1 tbsp of rose water to the custard mixture.

SERVES 6

Pistachio, Apricot and Lemon Clafoutis

PREPARATION TIME 10 MINUTES

COOKING TIME 35 – 45 MINUTES

··

INGREDIENTS

75 g / 2 ½ oz / ⅓ cup caster
(superfine) sugar
75 g / 2 ½ oz / ⅓ cup butter
300 ml / 10 ½ fl. oz / 1 ¼ cups whole
milk
2 large eggs
1 lemon, zest finely grated
50 g / 1 ¾ oz / ⅓ cup plain
(all purpose) flour
400 g / 14 oz canned apricot
halves, drained
3 tbsp pistachio nuts, chopped

- Preheat the oven to 190°C (170° fan) / 375F / gas 5.
- Melt the butter in a saucepan and cook over a low heat until it starts to smell nutty.
- Brush a little of the butter around the inside of a baking dish then add a spoonful of caster sugar and shake to coat.
- Whisk together the milk and eggs with the lemon zest and the rest of the butter.
- Sift the flour into a mixing bowl with a pinch of salt, then stir in the rest of the sugar.
- Make a well in the middle of the dry ingredients and gradually whisk in the liquid, incorporating all the flour from round the outside until you have a lump-free batter.
- Pour the batter into the baking dish and top with the apricot halves and pistachios.
- Bake the clafoutis for 35 – 45 minutes or until a skewer inserted in the centre comes out clean.

Pistachio, Pear and Lemon Clafoutis

686

- Replace the apricots with a 400g can of pear halves.

687

MAKES 6

Grape and Maple Syrup Cakes

PREPARATION TIME 10 MINUTES

COOKING TIME 15 – 20 MINUTES

··

INGREDIENTS

110 g / 4 oz / 1 cup self-raising flour,
sifted
110 g / 4 oz / ½ cup caster
(superfine) sugar
110 g / 4 oz / ½ cup butter, softened
2 large eggs
1 tsp vanilla extract
150 g / 5 ½ oz / 1 cup red
seedless grapes
4 tbsp maple syrup

- Preheat the oven to 190°C (170° fan) / 375F / gas 5 and line 6 cardboard loaf trays with paper cases.
- Combine the flour, sugar, butter, eggs and vanilla extract in a bowl and whisk together for 2 minutes or until smooth.
- Fold in the grapes then divide the mixture between the cases and drizzle with maple syrup.
- Transfer the cakes to the oven and bake for 15 – 20 minutes.
- Test with a wooden toothpick, if it comes out clean, the cakes are done.

Blueberry and Maple Syrup Cakes

688

- Replace the grapes with 150 g of blueberries.

Apple Syrup Pancakes

Mango Syrup Pancakes 690

- Replace the apples with a large mango that has been peeled, stoned and finely chopped.

Pear and Syrup Pancakes 691

- Replace the apples with 2 large pears.

PREPARATION TIME 10 MINUTES

COOKING TIME 30 MINUTES

INGREDIENTS

2 eating apples, peeled, cored and finely chopped
250 ml / 9 fl. oz / 1 cup maple syrup
250 g / 9 oz / 1 ⅔ cups plain (all purpose) flour
2 tsp baking powder
2 large eggs
300 ml / 10 ½ fl. oz / 1 ¼ cups milk
2 tbsp butter

- Put the apple in a small saucepan with the maple syrup and simmer gently for 4 minutes.
- Mix the flour and baking powder in a bowl and make a well in the centre.
- Break in the eggs and pour in the milk then use a whisk to gradually incorporate all of the flour from round the outside.
- Melt the butter in a small frying pan then whisk it into the batter.
- Put the buttered frying pan back over a low heat. You will need a tablespoon of batter for each pancake and you should be able to cook 4 pancakes at a time in the frying pan.
- Spoon the batter into the pan and cook for 2 minutes or until small bubbles start to appear on the surface.
- Turn the pancakes over with a spatula and cook the other side until golden brown and cooked through.
- Repeat until all the batter has been used, keeping the finished batches warm in a low oven.
- Stack the pancakes, layering with the apple syrup as you go.

692

SERVES 6

Almond Meringue Pavlova

Pistachio Meringue Pavlova

693

- Replace the ground almonds in the meringue with ground pistachios and sprinkle the top with 2 tbsp of chopped pistachios before baking.

Hazelnut Meringue Pavlova

694

- Replace the almonds with ground hazelnuts and sprinkle the top with 2 tbsp of chopped hazelnuts before cooking.

PREPARATION TIME 30 MINUTES

INGREDIENTS

225 ml / 8 fl. oz / 1 cup double (heavy) cream
2 tbsp icing (confectioners') sugar
½ tsp vanilla extract
100 g / 3 ½ oz / ⅔ cup mixed summer berries

FOR THE ALMOND MERINGUE:
4 large egg whites
110g / 4 oz / 1 cup caster (superfine) sugar
1 tsp cornflour (cornstarch)
55 g / 2 oz / ½ cup ground almonds

- Preheat the oven to 140°C (120° fan) / 275F / gas 1 and oil and line a baking tray with greaseproof paper.
- Whisk the egg whites until stiff, then gradually whisk in half the sugar until the mixture is very shiny.
- Fold in the remaining sugar with the cornflour and ground almonds then spoon the mixture onto the baking tray.
- Bake the meringue for 1 hour or until crisp on the outside, but still a bit chewy in the middle.
- Leave to cool completely.
- Transfer the meringue to a serving plate and tie a ribbon round the side.
- Whip the cream with the icing sugar and vanilla until it just holds its shape, then spoon it into a piping bag fitted with a large star nozzle and pipe rosettes on top of the meringue.
- Arrange the berries on top of the cream and serve immediately.

Coffee Crème Caramel

695

SERVES 6

- Preheat the oven to 150°C (130° fan) / 300F / gas 2.
- Put 150 g of the sugar in a heavy-based saucepan and heat gently until it starts to turn liquid at the edges. Continue to heat and swirl the pan until the sugar has all melted and turned golden brown.
- Pour the caramel into a large crème caramel mould and leave to set, then butter the sides.
- Whisk the milk, eggs and vanilla extract with the remaining 25 g of sugar and stir in the espresso powder.
- Pour it into the mould, sit it in a roasting tin and pour boiling water around it to come halfway up the sides.
- Transfer the tin to the oven and bake for 50 minutes.
- Remove the mould from the tray and chill for 4 hours.
- Give the mould a vigorous shake to loosen the crème caramel, then turn it out onto a serving plate.

PREPARATION TIME 15 MINUTES

COOKING TIME 50 MINUTES

INGREDIENTS

175 g / 6 oz / ¾ cup caster (superfine) sugar
1 tbsp butter, softened
600 ml / 1 pint / 2 ½ cups whole milk
4 large eggs
1 tsp vanilla extract
1 tbsp instant espresso powder

Cinnamon Crème Caramel

696

- Replace the espresso powder with 2 tsp of ground cinnamon.

Peach and Coconut Swiss Roll

697

SERVES 6

- Preheat the oven to 180°C (160° fan) / 350F / gas 4 then grease and line a Swiss roll tin.
- Put all of the cake ingredients in a mixing bowl and whisk together with an electric whisk for 4 minutes or until pale and well whipped.
- Spoon into the tin and spread into an even layer.
- Bake for 15 - 20 minutes.
- Turn the cake out onto a sheet of greaseproof paper and discard the lining paper. Roll up the cake whilst warm, then leave to cool completely.
- Beat the butter with the icing sugar until smooth and well whipped. Fold in 2 tbsp of the desiccated coconut and add a few drops of water if the mixture is too stiff.
- Carefully unroll the cake and spread it with the buttercream then scatter over the peaches and re-roll.
- Spread the jam over the outside of the cake and sprinkle with the rest of the coconut before adding cake toppers.

PREPARATION TIME 45 MINUTES

COOKING TIME 15 – 20 MINUTES

INGREDIENTS

100 g / 3 ½ oz / ⅔ cup self-raising flour
1 tsp baking powder
100 g / 3 ½ oz / ½ cup caster (superfine) sugar
100 g / 3 ½ oz/ ½ cup butter, softened
2 large eggs
1 tsp coconut extract
2 tbsp desiccated coconut

TO DECORATE:

100 g / 3 ½ oz / ½ cup butter, softened
200 g / 7 oz / 2 cups icing (confectioners') sugar
50 g / 1 ¾ oz / ½ cup desiccated coconut
300 g / 10 ½ oz canned peaches, drained and chopped
300 g / 10 ½ oz / ¾ cup peach jam (jelly)
festive cake toppers to decorate

Raspberry and Coconut Swiss Roll

698

- Replace tinned peaches with 200 g of fresh raspberries and use raspberry jam in place of the peach jam.

699

SERVES 6

Apple, Sultana and Cinnamon Crumble

PREPARATION TIME 10 MINUTES

COOKING TIME 40 MINUTES

INGREDIENTS

3 eating apples, cored and diced
4 tbsp sultanas
3 tbsp runny honey
75 g / 2 ½ oz / ⅓ cup butter
50 g / 1 ¾ oz / ⅓ cup plain (all purpose) flour
2 tsp ground cinnamon
25 g / 1 oz / ¼ cup ground almonds
40 g / 1 ½ oz / ¼ cup light brown sugar

- Preheat the oven to 180°C (160° fan) / 350F / gas 4.
- Put the apples and sultanas in a baking dish and drizzle with honey.
- Rub the butter into the flour and stir in the cinnamon, ground almonds and brown sugar.
- Squeeze a handful of the mixture into a clump and then crumble it over the fruit. Use up the rest of the topping in the same way, then shake the dish to level the top.
- Bake the crumble for 40 minutes or until the topping is golden brown.

700

MAKES 24

Sweet Chocolate Profiteroles

PREPARATION TIME 1 HOUR 15 MINUTES

COOKING TIME 10 - 15 MINUTES

INGREDIENTS

55 g / 2 oz / ¼ cup butter, cubed
75 g / 2 ½ oz / ½ cup strong white bread flour, sieved
2 large eggs, beaten

225 ml / 8 fl. oz / 1 cup double (heavy) cream
2 tbsp icing (confectioners') sugar
½ tsp vanilla extract
150 g / 5 ½ oz dark chocolate (minimum 60 % cocoa solids), melted

- Preheat the oven to 200°C (180° fan) / 400F / gas 6.
- Line a baking tray with greaseproof paper and spray with a little water.
- Melt the butter with 150 ml water and bring to the boil.
- Immediately beat in the flour, off the heat, with a wooden spoon until it forms a smooth ball of pastry.
- Incorporate the egg a little at a time to make a glossy paste.
- Spoon the pastry into a piping bag fitted with a large plain nozzle and pipe 2.5 cm / 1" buns onto the baking tray.
- Bake for 20 minutes, increasing the temperature to 220°C (200° fan) / 425F / gas 7 halfway through.
- Transfer the choux buns to a wire rack and make a hole in the underneath of each one so the steam can escape. Leave to cool completely.
- Whip the cream with the icing sugar and vanilla until thick, then spoon it into a piping bag and fill the choux buns through the steam hole.
- Dip the top of each profiterole in melted chocolate and leave to set.

701

SERVES 6

Custard Brûlée Tart

- Preheat the oven to 200°C (180° fan) / 390F / gas 6.
- Rub the butter into the flour and add just enough cold water to bind.
- Chill for 30 minutes then roll out on a floured surface. Use the pastry to line a long rectangular tart case.
- Prick the pastry with a fork, line with clingfilm and fill with baking beans or rice.
- Bake for 10 minutes then remove the clingfilm and baking beans and cook for a further 8 minutes to crisp.
- Reduce the oven temperature to 160°C (140° fan) / 325F / gas 3.
- Whisk together the egg yolks, sugar, vanilla, cornflour and milk and strain it through a sieve into the case.
- Bake the tart for 30 minutes.
- Leave to cool completely then dust the top with icing sugar. Brûlée with a blow torch or under a hot grill.

PREPARATION TIME 40 MINUTES

COOKING TIME 55 MINUTES

INGREDIENTS

100 g / 3 ½ oz / ½ cup butter, cubed
200 g / 7 oz / 1 ⅓ cups plain (all purpose) flour
4 large egg yolks
75 g / 2 ½ oz / ⅓ cup caster (superfine) sugar
1 tsp vanilla extract
2 tsp cornflour (cornstarch)
450 ml / 16 fl. oz / 1 ¾ cups milk
3 tbsp icing (confectioners') sugar

Orange Cheesecake

702

SERVES 10-12

PREPARATION TIME 5 MINUTES

COOKING TIME 40 – 50 MINUTES

INGREDIENTS

600 g / 1 lb 5 oz / 2 ¾ cups cream cheese
100 ml / 3 ½ fl. oz / ½ cup soured cream

2 oranges, juiced and zest finely grated
175 g / 6 oz / ¾ cup caster (superfine) sugar
2 large eggs, plus 1 egg yolk
2 tbsp plain (all purpose) flour
fruit compote to serve

- Preheat the oven to 180°C (160° fan) / 350F / gas 4 and butter a 20 cm round spring-form cake tin.
- Whisk together all the ingredients until smooth.
- Spoon the cheesecake mixture into the tin and bake for 40 – 50 minutes or until the centre is only just set.
- Leave to cool completely in the tin then chill for 2 hours before unmoulding.
- Cut into slices and serve with the fruit compote.

Blueberry Clafoutis

703

SERVES 6

PREPARATION TIME I5 MINUTES

COOKING TIME 35 – 45 MINUTES

INGREDIENTS

75 g / 2 ½ oz / ⅓ cup caster (superfine) sugar
75 g / 2 ½ oz / ⅓ cup butter
300 ml / 10 ½ fl. oz / 1 ¼ cups whole

milk
2 large eggs
50 g / 1 ¾ oz / ⅓ cup plain (all purpose) flour
2 tbsp ground almonds
300 g / 10 ½ oz / 2 cups blueberries
granulated sugar for sprinkling

- Preheat the oven to 190°C (170° fan) / 375F / gas 5.
- Melt the butter in a saucepan and cook over a low heat until it starts to smell nutty.
- Brush a little of the butter around the inside of a baking dish then add a spoonful of the caster sugar and shake to coat.
- Whisk together the milk and eggs with the rest of the butter.
- Sift the flour into a mixing bowl with a pinch of salt, then stir in the ground almonds and the rest of the sugar.
- Make a well in the middle of the dry ingredients and gradually whisk in the liquid, incorporating all the flour from round the outside until you have a lump-free batter.
- Arrange the blueberries in the prepared baking dish, pour over the batter and sprinkle with granulated sugar.
- Bake the clafoutis for 35 – 45 minutes or until a skewer inserted in the centre comes out clean.

704

SERVES 8

Pomegranate and Pistachio Trifle

PREPARATION TIME 35 MINUTES

COOKING TIME 10 MINUTES

....

INGREDIENTS

600 ml / 1 pint / 2 ½ cups double
(heavy) cream
4 tbsp icing (confectioners') sugar
1 tbsp rose water
1 tbsp orange flower water
1 tsp lemon zest, finely grated
1 pomegranate, halved
300 g / 10 ½ oz Madeira cake,
crumbled
50 g / 1 ¾ oz / ½ cup ground
pistachio nuts
1 tbsp demerara sugar

- Whip the cream with the icing sugar, rose water and orange flower water until it forms soft peaks.
- Hold the pomegranate halves cut side down over a sieve in a bowl and hit the back with a wooden spoon to release the seeds.
- Arrange half of the cake in a glass bowl and drizzle with half of the pomegranate juice that has collected below the sieve.
- Sprinkle over some of the pomegranate seeds and top with a third of the cream. Sprinkle over half of the pistachio nuts and top with another third of the cream.
- Add the rest of the cake and pomegranate juice and sprinkle over a few more seeds then spoon over the rest of the cream.
- Sprinkle the top with the rest of the pistachios and the demerara sugar, then arrange the remaining pomegranate seeds in a ring round the edge.

Pomegranate and Date Trifle   **705**

- Omit the pistachio nuts and use 75 g of finely chopped dates instead.

706

MAKES 4

Pomegranate and Honey Yoghurt Pots

PREPARATION TIME 10 MINUTES

....

INGREDIENTS

1 pomegranate, halved
400 g / 14 oz / 2 ½ cups Greek
yoghurt
150 g / 5 ½ oz amaretti biscuits,
crushed
4 tbsp runny honey

- Hold the pomegranate halves cut side down over a sieve in a bowl and hit the back with a wooden spoon to release the seeds. Stir the seeds into the yoghurt.
- Divide ¾ of the biscuit crumbs between 4 glass pots and top with half of the pomegranate yoghurt mixture.
- Drizzle over the honey then top with the rest of the yoghurt and sprinkle over the remaining crumbs.

Pomegranate and Rose   **707**
Yoghurt Pots

- Stir 1 tbsp of rose water into the yoghurt with the pomegranate seeds.

708

MAKES 18 Cinnamon Crème Brûlée

- Pour the milk into a saucepan and bring to simmering point.
- Meanwhile, whisk the egg yolks with 75 g of the caster sugar, the cornflour and ground cinnamon until thick.
- Gradually incorporate the hot milk, whisking all the time, then scrape the mixture back into the saucepan.
- Stir the custard over a low heat until it thickens then divide it between 4 ramekins.
- Chill in the fridge for 25 minutes.
- Sprinkle the tops with the rest of the caster sugar then caramelise with a blow torch or under a hot grill.

PREPARATION TIME 35 MINUTES

COOKING TIME 10 MINUTES

INGREDIENTS

450 ml / 12 ½ fl. oz / 1 ¾ cups whole milk
4 large egg yolks
100 g / 3 ½ oz / ½ cup caster (superfine) sugar
2 tsp cornflour (cornstarch)
1 tsp ground cinnamon

Cardamom Crème Brûlée

709

- Replace the ground cinnamon with ground cardamom.

710

MAKES 24 Strawberry and Cinnamon Profiteroles

- Preheat the oven to 200°C (180° fan) / 400F / gas 6.
- Line a baking tray with greaseproof paper.
- Melt the butter with 150 ml water and bring to the boil.
- Immediately beat in the flour and cinnamon off the heat with a wooden spoon until it forms a smooth ball.
- Incorporate the egg gradually to make a glossy paste.
- Spoon the pastry into a piping bag and pipe 2.5 cm / 1" buns onto the baking tray.
- Bake for 20 minutes, increasing the temperature to 220°C (200° fan) / 425F / gas 7 halfway through.
- Transfer the choux buns to a wire rack and make a hole in the underneath of each one so the steam can escape.
- Whip the cream with the icing sugar and vanilla, then fold in the strawberries. Spoon it into a piping bag and fill the choux buns through the steam hole.
- Dust the profiteroles with cinnamon and icing sugar.

PREPARATION TIME 1 HOUR 15 MINUTES

COOKING TIME 10 - 15 MINUTES

INGREDIENTS

55 g / 2 oz / 1/4 cup butter, cubed
75 g / 2 ½ oz / ½ cup strong white bread flour, sieved
1 tsp ground cinnamon
2 large eggs, beaten

225 ml / 8 fl. oz / 1 cup double (heavy) cream
2 tbsp icing (confectioners') sugar, plus extra for sprinkling
½ tsp vanilla extract
100 g / 3 ½ oz strawberries, chopped
ground cinnamon for sprinkling

Apricot and Cardamom Profiteroles

711

- Use chopped fresh apricots instead of the strawberries and use ½ tsp of ground cardamom instead of the cinnamon.

712

MAKES 18 # Easy Melon Sorbet

PREPARATION TIME 5 HOURS 10 MINUTES

....

INGREDIENTS

2 charantais melons, halved
1 tbsp Midori liqueur
1 egg white, lightly beaten

- Scoop out and discard the seeds of the melons, then use a spoon to scrape out the flesh, reserving the empty shells.
- Roughly chop the flesh and put it in a freezer bag, then freeze for 4 hours or until solid.
- Transfer the frozen melon to a food processor and process for 2 minutes.
- Add the Midori and egg white and process to a smooth sorbet.
- Spoon the sorbet into a plastic tub with a lid and freeze for 1 hour.
- Fill the reserved melon shells with scoops of sorbet and serve immediately.

713

SERVES 4 # Chocolate Rice Pudding

PREPARATION TIME 5 MINUTES

COOKING TIME 1 HOUR 30 MINUTES

....

INGREDIENTS

50 g / 1 ¾ oz / 1/4 cup butter
110 g / 4 oz / ½ cup short grain rice
75 g / 2 ½ oz / ⅓ cup caster (superfine) sugar
25 g / 1 oz / 1/4 cup unsweetened cocoa powder
1.2 litres / 2 pints / 4 ½ cups whole milk

- Preheat the oven to 140°C (120° fan) / 275F / gas 1.
- Melt the butter in a cast iron casserole dish and add the rice, sugar and cocoa powder.
- Stir over a low heat for 2 minutes then gradually incorporate the milk and bring to a simmer.
- Cover the casserole dish and bake in the oven for 1 hour 30 minutes.
- Spoon the rice pudding into 4 kilner jars and serve hot or cold.

714

MAKES 6

Mini Raspberry and Almond Crumbles

- Preheat the oven to 180°C (160° fan) / 350F / gas 4.
- Mix the raspberries with the caster sugar and divide them between 6 ramekin dishes.
- Rub the butter into the flour and stir in the oats, brown sugar and flaked almonds.
- Crumble the mixture over the fruit then bake for 25 minutes or until the topping is golden brown.

PREPARATION TIME 10 MINUTES

COOKING TIME 25 MINUTES

INGREDIENTS

400 g / 14 oz / 2 ⅔ cups raspberries
4 tbsp caster (superfine) sugar
75 g / 2 ½ oz / ⅓ cup butter
50 g / 1 ¾ oz / ⅓ cup plain (all purpose) flour
25 g / 1 oz / 1/4 cup porridge oats
40 g / 1 ½ oz / 1/4 cup light brown sugar
50 g / 1 ¾ oz / ⅔ cup flaked (slivered) almonds

Mango and Coconut Crumble

715

SERVES 4

PREPARATION TIME 5 MINUTES

COOKING TIME 40 MINUTES

INGREDIENTS

2 ripe mangos, peeled, stoned and cubed
75 g / 2 ½ oz / ⅓ cup butter
50 g / 1 ¾ oz / ⅓ cup plain (all purpose) flour
25 g / 1 oz / 1/4 cup desiccated coconut
40 g / 1 ½ oz / 1/4 cup light brown sugar
50 g / 1 ¾ oz / ½ cup porridge oats

- Preheat the oven to 180°C (160° fan) / 350F / gas 4.
- Arrange the mango in a baking dish.
- Rub the butter into the flour and stir in the desiccated coconut, sugar and oats.
- Take a handful of the topping and squeeze it into a clump, then crumble it over the fruit.
- Repeat with the rest of the crumble mixture then bake for 40 minutes or until the topping is golden brown.

Pear and Chocolate Tart

716

SERVES 8

PREPARATION TIME 40 MINUTES

COOKING TIME 55 MINUTES

INGREDIENTS

100 g / 3 ½ oz / ½ cup butter, cubed
200 g / 7 oz / 1 ⅓ cups plain (all purpose) flour
400 g / 14 oz canned pear halves, drained and chopped
4 large egg yolks
75 g / 2 ½ oz / ⅓ cup caster (superfine) sugar
1 tsp vanilla extract
2 tsp cornflour (cornstarch)
2 tbsp unsweetened cocoa powder
450 ml / 16 fl. oz / 1 ¾ cups milk
edible flowers to garnish

- Preheat the oven to 200°C (180° fan) / 400F / gas 6.
- Rub the butter into the flour and add just enough cold water to bind.
- Chill for 30 minutes then roll out on a floured surface. Use the pastry to line a 23 cm round tart case.
- Prick the pastry with a fork, line with clingfilm and fill with baking beans or rice.
- Bake for 10 minutes then remove the clingfilm and baking beans and cook for a further 8 minutes to crisp.
- Reduce the oven temperature to 160°C (140° fan) / 325F / gas 3.
- Arrange the chopped pears in the pastry case.
- Whisk together the egg yolks, sugar, vanilla, cornflour, cocoa and milk and strain it through a sieve onto the pears.
- Bake the tart for 35 minutes or until the custard is just set in the centre.
- Leave to cool completely then garnish with edible flowers.

BAKING

717

MAKES 8-10

Coconut Sponge

PREPARATION TIME: 15 MINUTES

COOKING TIME: 35-45 MINUTES

INGREDIENTS

350 g / 12 oz / 1 ½ cup butter, softened
350 g / 12 oz / 1 ½ cup caster (superfine) sugar
6 large eggs, beaten
350 g / 12 oz / 1 ½ cups self-raising flour
2 tsp baking powder
100 g / 3 ½ oz / 1 cup desiccated coconut

TO DECORATE:

110 g / 4 oz / ½ cup butter, softened
225 g / 8 oz / 2 cups icing (confectioners') sugar
2 tbsp coconut cream
4 tbsp desiccated coconut
3 tbsp flaked coconut
edible silver leaf to decorate

- Preheat the oven to 180°C (160° fan) / 350F / gas 4 and grease and line 2 x 20 cm / 8" square cake tins with greaseproof paper.
- Cream the butter and sugar then gradually whisk in the eggs.
- Fold in the flour, baking powder and coconut then divide the mixture between the tins.
- Bake the cakes for 35 - 45 minutes.
- Transfer the cakes to a wire rack and leave to cool completely.
- To make the filling, beat the butter with a wooden spoon until light and fluffy then beat in the icing sugar a quarter at a time.
- Whisk in the coconut cream and half of the desiccated coconut, then whisk until smooth and well whipped.
- Trim the edges of the cakes to neaten, then sandwich them together with the coconut buttercream.
- Sprinkle the cake with the rest of the desiccated coconut and decorate with the flaked coconut and silver leaf.

Coconut and Lime Sponge

718

- Add the grated zest of 2 limes to the cake mixture and replace the coconut cream in the icing with 2 tbsp of lime juice.

719

MAKES 12

Cheese Scones

PREPARATION TIME 10 MINUTES

COOKING TIME 12-15 MINUTES

INGREDIENTS

75 g / 2 ½ oz / ⅓ cup butter, cubed
250 g / 9 oz / 1 ⅔ cups self-raising flour, plus extra for dusting
½ tsp mustard powder
¼ tsp cayenne pepper
150 ml / 5 ½ fl. oz / ⅔ cup milk, plus extra for brushing
100 g / 3 ½ oz / 1 cup Red Leicester cheese, grated

- Preheat the oven to 220°C (200° fan) / 425F / gas 7 and line a baking tray with greaseproof paper.
- Rub the butter into the flour with your fingertips until the mixture resembles fine breadcrumbs then stir in the mustard powder and cayenne pepper.
- Add the milk and ¾ of the cheese and mix together into a pliable dough.
- Turn the dough out onto a floured work surface and flatten it into a rectangle, 2 cm / 1 " thick.
- Use a round pastry cutter to stamp out the scones then transfer them to the baking tray.
- Brush the scones with milk, sprinkle with the rest of the cheese and bake for 12 – 15 minutes or until golden brown and cooked through.
- Transfer the scones to a wire rack to cool a little before serving.

Cheese and Thyme Scones

720

- Add 2 tbsp of fresh thyme leaves to the mixture when you add the mustard powder.

Victoria Sponge

721

SERVES 10

- Preheat the oven to 180°C (160° fan) / 350F / gas 4 and line 2 x 20 cm round loose-bottomed cake tins.
- Put all of the cake ingredients in a large mixing bowl and whisk until pale and well whipped.
- Divide the mixture between the 2 tins and level the tops with a spatula.
- Bake for 35 – 40 minutes. The cakes are ready when a toothpick inserted comes out clean.
- Transfer the cakes to a wire rack to cool completely.
- To make the buttercream, whisk the butter with an electric whisk then gradually add the icing sugar. Whisk until smooth and well whipped. If the mixture is too stiff add a tablespoon of warm water.
- Spread the buttercream onto one of the cakes with a palette knife and top with the raspberry jam.
- Place the second cake on top and dust with icing sugar.

PREPARATION TIME 10 MINUTES

COOKING TIME 35-40 MINUTES

INGREDIENTS

200 g / 7 oz / 1 ⅓ cups self-raising flour
200 g / 7 oz / ¾ cup caster (superfine) sugar
200 g / 7 oz / ¾ cup butter
4 large eggs
1 tsp baking powder
1 tsp vanilla extract

TO DECORATE:
100 g / 3 ½ oz / ½ cup butter, softened
200 g / 7 oz / 2 cups icing (confectioners') sugar, plus extra for dusting
300 g / 10 ½ oz / 1 ¼ cups raspberry jam (jelly)

Victoria Sandwich

722

- Leave out the buttercream and increase the quantity of jam to 400 g. Replace the dusting of icing sugar with a sprinkle of caster sugar.

Sultana Scones

723

MAKES 12

- Preheat the oven to 220°C (200° fan) / 425F / gas 7 and oil a large baking sheet.
- Sieve the flour into a bowl and rub in the butter until the mixture resembles fine breadcrumbs.
- Add the sultanas and stir in enough milk to bring the mixture together into a soft dough.
- Flatten the dough with your hands on a floured work surface until 2.5 cm / 1" thick.
- Use a pastry cutter to cut out 12 circles and transfer them to the prepared baking sheet.
- Bake in the oven for 10 – 15 minutes or until golden brown and cooked through.
- Transfer the scones to a wire rack to cool a little and serve warm.

PREPARATION TIME 10 MINUTES

COOKING TIME 10-15 MINUTES

INGREDIENTS

225 g / 8 oz / 1 ½ cups self-raising flour
55 g / 2 oz / ¼ cup butter
75 g / 2 ½ oz / ½ cup sultanas
150 ml / 5 fl. oz / ⅔ cup milk

Cranberry Scones

724

- Replace the sultanas with dried cranberries.

725

MAKES 12

Wholemeal Sesame and Honey Scones

Wholemeal Poppy Seed Scones

726

- Replace the sesame seeds with 2 tbsp of poppy seeds.

Honey and Almond Scones

727

- Replace the sesame seeds with flaked almonds.

PREPARATION TIME 10 MINUTES

COOKING TIME 12-15 MINUTES

INGREDIENTS

75 g / 2 ½ oz / ⅓ cup butter, cubed
150 g / 5 ½ oz / 1 cup self-raising flour, plus extra for dusting
100 g / 3 ½ oz / ⅔ cup wholemeal flour
150 ml / 5 ½ fl. oz / ⅔ cup milk, plus extra for brushing
4 tbsp runny honey
4 tbsp sesame seeds

- Preheat the oven to 220°C (200° fan) / 425F / gas 7 and line a baking tray with greaseproof paper.
- Rub the butter into the flours with your fingertips until the mixture resembles fine breadcrumbs.
- Pour in the milk and honey and mix together into a pliable dough.
- Turn the dough out onto a floured work surface and press it out into a rectangle, 2 cm thick.
- Use a round pastry cutter to stamp out the scones and transfer them to the baking tray.
- Brush the scones with milk and sprinkle with sesame seeds then bake for 12 – 15 minutes or until golden brown and cooked through.
- Transfer the scones to a wire rack to cool a little before serving.

728

SERVES 8

Golden Pineapple Upside-Down Cake

- Preheat the oven to 180°C (160° fan) / 350F / gas 4 and butter a 23 cm round spring-form cake tin.
- Sieve the flour and baking powder into a mixing bowl and add sugar, butter and eggs.
- Beat the mixture with an electric whisk for 4 minutes or until smooth and well whipped.
- Cut the pineapple into 8 wedges, then cut the wedges across into 1 cm slices.
- Arrange the pineapple around the sides and in the bottom of the cake tin and drizzle with honey.
- Spoon in the cake mixture and bake for 35 minutes or until a skewer inserted comes out clean.
- Leave the cake to cool for 20 minutes then turn out onto a serving plate and decorate with gold leaf.

PREPARATION TIME 15 MINUTES

COOKING TIME 35 MINUTES

INGREDIENTS

300 g / 10 ½ oz / 2 cups self-raising flour
2 tsp baking powder
250 g / 9 oz / 1 ¼ cups caster (superfine) sugar
250 g / 9 oz / 1 ¼ cups butter, softened
5 large eggs
1 pineapple, peeled
3 tbsp runny honey
edible gold leaf to decorate

Rum and Pineapple Cake

729

- When the cake comes out of the oven, pierce it all over with a skewer and drizzle with 3 tbsp of dark rum.

730

MAKES 12

Almond and Coconut Muffins

- Preheat the oven to 180°C (160° fan) / 350F / gas 4 and oil a 12-hole silicone muffin mould.
- Beat the egg in a jug with the oil and milk until well mixed.
- Mix together the flour, baking powder, sugar and ¾ of the almonds and coconut, then pour in the egg mixture and stir just enough to combine.
- Spoon the mixture into the mould, sprinkle with the remaining almonds and coconut then bake in the oven for 20 – 25 minutes.
- Test with a wooden toothpick, if it comes out clean, the muffins are done.
- Transfer the cakes to a wire rack and leave to cool completely.

PREPARATION TIME 10 MINUTES

COOKING TIME 20 – 25 MINUTES

INGREDIENTS

1 large egg
120 ml / 4 fl. oz / ½ cup sunflower oil
120 ml / 4 fl. oz / ½ cup milk
375 g / 12 ½ oz / 2 ½ cups self-raising flour, sifted
1 tsp baking powder
200 g / 7 oz / ¾ cup caster (superfine) sugar
4 tbsp flaked almonds (slivered almonds)
4 tbsp desiccated coconut

Almond and Coconut Mini Muffins

731

- Use the mixture to fill a 24-hole mini muffin mould and reduce the cooking time to 10 – 12 minutes.

732

SERVES 8

Wholemeal Treacle Tart

PREPARATION TIME 40 MINUTES

COOKING TIME 35 MINUTES

....

INGREDIENTS

350 g / 12 ½ oz / 1 cup golden syrup
2 lemons, zest and juice
100 g / 3 ½ oz / 1 ⅓ cups brown
breadcrumbs
clotted cream to serve

FOR THE PASTRY:

100 g / 3 ½ oz / ½ cup butter, cubed
and chilled
200 g / 7 oz / 1 ⅓ cups wholemeal
flour

- Preheat the oven to 200°C (180° fan) / 400F / gas 6.
- First make the pastry. Rub the butter into the flour until the mixture resembles fine breadcrumbs.
- Stir in just enough cold water to bring the pastry together into a pliable dough then chill for 30 minutes.
- Heat the golden syrup with the lemon zest and juice until runny then stir in the breadcrumbs.
- Roll out the pastry on a floured surface and use it to line a 23 cm round tart case.
- Spoon the filling into the pastry case and level the top.
- Bake for 25 – 30 minutes or until the pastry is cooked through underneath.
- Serve warm with clotted cream.

Wholemeal Ginger Treacle Tart   733

- Add 100 g of ginger cake crumbs to the filling and 1 tsp of ground ginger to the pastry.

734

SERVES 6

Apple Turnovers

PREPARATION TIME 2 MINUTES

COOKING TIME 10 MINUTES

....

INGREDIENTS

3 large cooking apples, peeled and
diced
3 tbsp caster (superfine) sugar
800 g / 1 lb 12 oz all-butter puff
pastry
1 egg, beaten

- Preheat the oven to 220°C (200° fan) / 425F / gas 7.
- Put the apples and sugar in a saucepan with 4 tablespoons of cold water.
- Put a lid on the pan then cook over a gentle heat for 10 minutes, stirring occasionally. Leave to cool.
- Roll out the pastry on a lightly floured surface and cut out 6 large circles with a fluted pastry cutter.
- Add a tablespoon of apple compote to the centre of each one and brush round the edge with egg.
- Fold the pastry in half and press the edges to seal then score a pattern into the top.
- Brush the turnovers with egg and bake for 18 minutes or until golden brown and cooked through.

Dairy Cream Apple Turnovers   735

- Sprinkle the turnovers liberally with granulated sugar before baking. Cool after cooking then split them open along the join and pipe whipped cream into the cavity.

736

MAKES 12

Prune and Pecan Cupcakes

- Preheat the oven to 190°C (170° fan) / 375F / gas 5 and grease a 12-hole silicone cake mould with oil.
- Combine the flour, sugar, butter, eggs and pecans in a bowl and whisk together for 2 minutes or until smooth.
- Divide the mixture between the moulds and press 3 prunes into the top of each one.
- Transfer the mould to the oven and bake for 15 – 20 minutes.
- Test with a wooden toothpick, if it comes out clean, the cakes are done.

PREPARATION TIME 10 MINUTES

COOKING TIME 15 – 20 MINUTES

INGREDIENTS

110 g / 4 oz / 1 cup self-raising flour, sifted
110 g / 4 oz / ½ cup caster (superfine) sugar
110 g / 4 oz / ½ cup butter, softened
2 large eggs
75 g / 2 ½ oz / ⅔ cup pecan nuts, chopped
36 prunes, stoned

Banana and Pecan Cupcakes

737

- Replace the prunes with chunks of banana and drizzle the cakes with honey when they come out of the oven.

738

SERVES 4

Pineapple Crumble

- Preheat the oven to 180°C (160° fan) / 350F / gas 4.
- Arrange the pineapple in a baking dish.
- Rub the butter into the flour and stir in the ground almonds and sugar.
- Take a handful of the topping and squeeze it into a clump, then crumble it over the fruit.
- Repeat with the rest of the crumble mixture then bake for 40 minutes or until the topping is golden brown.

PREPARATION TIME 5 MINUTES

COOKING TIME 40 MINUTES

INGREDIENTS

1 pineapple, peeled, cored and cut into chunks
75 g / 2 ½ oz / ⅓ cup butter
50 g / 1 ¾ oz / ⅓ cup plain (all purpose) flour
25 g / 1 oz / ¼ cup ground almonds
40 g / 1 ½ oz / ¼ cup caster (superfine) sugar

Pineapple and Ginger Crumble

 739

- Finely chop 3 pieces of stem ginger and scatter over the pineapple. Add 1 tsp ground ginger to the crumble topping when you add the sugar.

740

SERVES 8

Walnut Tart

PREPARATION TIME 40 MINUTES

COOKING TIME 45 MINUTES

....

INGREDIENTS

400 g / 14 oz / 2 ⅓ cups dark brown sugar
200 g / 7 oz / ⅔ cup golden syrup
200 g / 7 oz / 1 cup butter
2 tsp vanilla extract
6 large eggs, beaten
300 g / 10 ½ oz / 1 ½ cups walnut halves

FOR THE PASTRY:

150 g / 5 ½ / ⅔ cup butter, cubed and chilled
300 g / 10 ½ oz / 2 cups plain (all purpose) flour

- First make the pastry. Rub the butter into the flour then add just enough cold water to bind the mixture together into a pliable dough.
- Roll out the pastry on a floured surface and use it to line a large rectangular tart case then chill in the fridge for 30 minutes.
- Preheat the oven to 180°C (160° fan) / 350F / gas 4.
- Put the sugar, golden syrup, butter and vanilla extract in a saucepan and stir it over a low heat to dissolve the sugar.
- Leave the mixture to cool for 10 minutes then beat in the eggs.
- Pour the mixture into the pastry case and arrange the walnuts on top, then bake the tart for 45 – 50 minutes.

Walnut and Ginger Tart

741

- Finely chop 4 pieces of stem ginger and stir it in with the eggs.

742

SERVES 4

Stewed Apple with Meringue

PREPARATION TIME 5 MINUTES

COOKING TIME 20 MINUTES

....

INGREDIENTS

3 large cooking apples, peeled and diced
3 tbsp light brown sugar
½ tsp ground cinnamon

FOR THE MERINGUE:

4 large egg whites
110 g / 4 oz / ½ cup caster (superfine) sugar
2 tbsp flaked (slivered) almonds

- Preheat the oven to 200°C (180° fan) / 400F / gas 6.
- Put the apples, sugar and cinnamon in a saucepan with 4 tablespoons of cold water.
- Put a lid on the pan then cook over a gentle heat for 10 minutes, stirring occasionally.
- Taste the apple and stir in a little more sugar if it is too sharp then scrape the mixture into a baking dish.
- Whisk the egg whites until stiff, then gradually add the sugar and whisk until the mixture is thick and shiny.
- Spoon the meringue on top of the apple and make it into peaks with the back of the spoon.
- Sprinkle the top with flaked almonds then bake for 10 minutes or until the peaks of the meringue are toasted.

Apple Meringue Pie

743

- Spoon the apple filling into a cooked pastry case and top with the meringue before baking.

744

SERVES 8

Chocolate Tart

Vanilla Stewed Prunes **745**

- Put 250 g of prunes in a
  saucepan with 200 ml apple
  juice and a vanilla pod, split
  lengthways. Simmer gently for
  8 minutes then leave to cool.

Chocolate and **746**
Pistachio Tart

- Replace the ground almonds
  with ground pistachio nuts.

PREPARATION TIME 35 MINUTES

COOKING TIME 35 MINUTES

INGREDIENTS

225 g / 8 oz / 2 ¼ cups ground
almonds
225 g / 8 oz / 1 cup butter, softened
225 g / 8 oz / 1 cup caster (superfine)
sugar
3 large eggs
2 tbsp unsweetened cocoa powder,
plus extra for dusting
75 g / 2 ½ oz milk chocolate, grated
3 tbsp plain (all purpose) flour
icing (confectioners') sugar for
dusting
vanilla-stewed prunes to serve

FOR THE PASTRY:
100 g / 3 ½ oz / ½ cup butter, cubed
and chilled
200 g / 7 oz / 1 ⅓ cups plain (all
purpose) flour
1 egg, beaten
2 tbsp caster (superfine) sugar

- First make the pastry. Rub the butter into the flour until
  the mixture resembles fine breadcrumbs.
- Stir in just enough cold water to bring the pastry
  together into a pliable dough then chill for 30 minutes.
- Preheat the oven to 200°C (180° fan), 390 F, gas 6.
- Roll out the pastry on a floured surface and use it to line
  a 23 cm round tart case.
- Prick the pastry with a fork, line with clingfilm and fill
  with baking beans or rice.
- Bake for 10 minutes then remove the clingfilm and
  baking beans.
- Whisk together the almonds, butter, sugar, eggs, cocoa,
  chocolate and flour until smoothly whipped then spoon
  the mixture into the pastry case.
- Bake the tart for 25 minutes or until the filling is cooked
  through and the pastry is crisp underneath.
- Dust the tart with a little cocoa and icing sugar and
  serve with vanilla-stewed prunes.

747

MAKES 36

Chocolate and Walnut Fudge

PREPARATION TIME 15 MINUTES

COOKING TIME 45 MINUTES

INGREDIENTS

300 ml / 10 ½ fl. oz whole milk
100 g / 3 ½ oz butter
350 g / 12 oz caster (superfine) sugar
3 tbsp unsweetened cocoa powder
100 g / 3 ½ oz / ⅔ cup walnuts,
roughly chopped

- Oil an 18 cm / 7 " square cake tin.
- Put the milk, butter, caster sugar and cocoa in a large, heavy-based saucepan and stir over a low heat to dissolve the sugar.
- Increase the temperature a little and bring to the boil.
- Boil the mixture for 35 minutes or until it reaches 115°C / 240F on a sugar thermometer, stirring constantly.
- Take the pan off the heat and stir in the walnut pieces, then continue to stir for a further 10 minutes while it cools.
- Scrape the mixture into the prepared tin and level the surface with a palate knife.
- Leave the fudge to cool completely then turn it out of the tin and cut it into squares with a sharp knife.

Chocolate and Cherry Fudge

748

- Replace the walnuts with 100 g of halved glace cherries.

749

MAKES 12

Hot Cross Buns

PREPARATION TIME 2 HOURS 30 MINUTES

COOKING TIME 15 – 20 MINUTES

INGREDIENTS

55 g / 2 oz / ¼ cup butter, cubed
400 g / 14 oz / 2 ⅔ cups strong white bread flour, plus extra for dusting
½ tsp easy blend dried yeast
4 tbsp caster (superfine) sugar
1 tsp fine sea salt
2 tsp mixed spice
100 g / 3 ½ oz / ½ cup mixed dried fruit
4 tbsp plain (all purpose) flour
1 egg, beaten
softened butter for spreading

- Rub the butter into the bread flour and stir in the yeast, sugar, salt and spice. Stir the dried fruit into 280 ml of warm water and stir it into the dry ingredients.
- Knead the mixture on a lightly oiled surface for 10 minutes or until the dough is smooth and elastic.
- Leave the dough to rest, covered with the mixing bowl, for 1 – 2 hours or until doubled in size.
- Shape the dough into 12 buns and transfer to a greased baking tray, cover and leave to prove for 45 minutes.
- Preheat the oven to 220°C (200° fan) / 425F / gas 7.
- Mix the plain flour with just enough water to make a thick paste and spoon it into a piping bag.
- Brush the buns with egg and pipe a cross on top of each.
- Bake for 15 – 20 minutes or until golden brown.
- Leave to cool on a wire rack then split in half and sandwich back together with butter.

Simnel Easter Buns

750

- Add 150 g marzipan in small cubes to the dough when you add the dried fruit.

Tarte Tatin

751

SERVES 8

- Preheat the oven to 220°C (200° fan) / 425F / gas 7.
- Melt the butter and sugar together in a frying pan then add the apples and cook gently for 15 minutes or until they start to caramelise.
- Turn off the heat and arrange the apples, curved side down in a single layer.
- Roll out the pastry on a floured surface and cut out a circle the same size as the frying pan.
- Lay the pastry over the fruit and tuck in the edges, then transfer the pan to the oven and bake for 25 minutes or until the pastry is golden brown and cooked through.
- Using oven gloves, put a large plate on top of the frying pan and turn them both over in one smooth movement to unmold the tart.

PREPARATION TIME 10 MINUTES

COOKING TIME 40 MINUTES

INGREDIENTS

3 tbsp butter, softened and cubed
4 tbsp soft light brown sugar
5 apples, peeled, cored and quartered
250 g / 9 oz all-butter puff pastry

Apple and Blackberry Tarte Tatin

752

- Add 100 g of blackberries to the apple before topping with the pastry.

Apple and Raisin Rock Cakes

753

MAKES 12

- Preheat the oven to 200°C (180° fan) / 390F / gas 6 and grease a large baking tray.
- Rub the butter into the flour until the mixture resembles fine breadcrumbs then stir in the sugar, raisins and apple.
- Beat the egg with the milk and stir it into the dry ingredients to make a sticky dough.
- Use a dessert spoon to portion the mixture onto the baking tray, leaving the surface quite rough.
- Bake the rock cakes for 15 minutes then transfer them to a wire rack and leave to cool.

PREPARATION TIME 2 HOURS 30 MINUTES

COOKING TIME 10 – 12 MINUTES

INGREDIENTS

100 g / 3 ½ oz / ½ cup butter
200 g / 7 oz / 1 ⅓ cups self-raising flour
100 g / 3 ½ oz / ½ cup caster (superfine) sugar
100 g / 3 ½ oz / ½ cup raisins
50 g / 1 ¾ oz / ½ cup dried apple pieces
1 large egg
2 tbsp milk

Apple and Cinnamon Rock Cakes

754

- Omit the raisins and add 1 tsp of ground cinnamon to the flour.

755

SERVES 8

Chocolate and Apple Upside-Down Cake

Chocolate and Pear Upside-Down Cake

756

- Replace the apple with 2 large pears.

Spicy Chocolate Upside Down Cake

757

- Add ½ a tsp of ground ginger and ½ a tsp of ground cinnamon to the mixture for a spicy finish.

PREPARATION TIME 15 MINUTES

COOKING TIME 35 MINUTES

INGREDIENTS

300 g / 10 ½ oz / 2 cups self-raising flour
3 tbsp unsweetened cocoa powder
2 tsp baking powder
250 g / 9 oz / 1 ¼ cups caster (superfine) sugar
250 g / 9 oz / 1 ¼ cups butter, softened
5 large eggs
3 apples, peeled, cored and sliced

- Preheat the oven to 180°C (160° fan) / 350F / gas 4 and butter a 23 cm round spring-form cake tin.
- Sieve the flour, cocoa and baking powder into a mixing bowl and add the sugar, butter and eggs.
- Beat the mixture with an electric whisk for 4 minutes or until smooth and well whipped.
- Cut the pineapple into 8 wedges, then cut the wedges across into 1 cm slices.
- Arrange the apple in the cake tin then top with the cake mixture and bake for 35 minutes or until a skewer inserted comes out clean.
- Leave the cake to cool for 20 minutes then turn out onto a serving plate.

758

SERVES 8

Chocolate and Raspberry Marble Cake

- Preheat the oven to 170°C (150° fan) / 325F / gas 3 and oil and line a 20 cm / 8" round spring-form cake tin.
- Melt the dark chocolate, cocoa and butter together in a saucepan, then leave to cool a little.
- Whisk the sugar and eggs together with an electric whisk for 3 minutes or until very light and creamy.
- Pour in the chocolate mixture and sieve over the flour, then fold everything together until evenly mixed.
- Make the white chocolate mixture in the same way, folding in the ground almonds with the flour at the end.
- Put alternate spoonfuls of each mixture into the prepared tin, scattering in the raspberries as you go.
- Bake for 35 – 40 minutes or until the outside is set, but the centre is still quite soft, as it will continue to cook as it cools.
- Dust the top with icing sugar just before serving.

Chocolate and Cherry Marble Cake

759

- Stone 150 g of black cherries and use in place of the raspberries.

PREPARATION TIME 25 MINUTES

COOKING TIME 15 – 20 MINUTES

INGREDIENTS

55 g / 2 oz dark chocolate, minimum 60% cocoa solids, chopped
40 g / 1 ½ oz / ⅓ cup unsweetened cocoa powder, sifted
110 g / 4 oz / ½ cup butter
225 g / 7 ½ oz / 1 ¼ cups light brown sugar
2 large eggs
55 g / 2 oz / ½ cup self-raising flour
150 g / 5 ½ oz / 1 cup raspberries

FOR THE WHITE CHOCOLATE MIXTURE:

55 g / 2 oz white chocolate, chopped
110 g / 4 oz / ½ cup butter
225 g / 7 ½ oz / 1 ¼ cups light brown sugar
2 large eggs
55 g / 2 oz / ½ cup self-raising flour
2 tbsp ground almonds
icing (confectioners') sugar

760

SERVES 10

Chocolate and Cream Sponge

- Preheat the oven to 180°C (160° fan) / 350F / gas 4 and grease and line 2 x 20 cm round loose-bottomed cake tins.
- Put all of the cake ingredients in a large mixing bowl and whisk with an electric whisk for 4 minutes or until pale and well whipped.
- Divide the mixture between the 2 tins and level the tops with a spatula.
- Bake for 35 – 40 minutes. The cakes are ready when a toothpick inserted comes out clean.
- Transfer the cakes to a wire rack to cool completely.
- Whip the cream with the icing sugar until it forms soft peaks, then sandwich it between the cakes.
- Dust the top of the cake with icing sugar just before serving.

Chocolate Chip and Cream Sponge

761

- Add 150 g of chocolate chips to the cake mixture before baking.

PREPARATION TIME 15 MINUTES

COOKING TIME 35 – 40 MINUTES

INGREDIENTS

200 g / 7 oz / 1 ⅓ cups self-raising flour
200 g / 7 oz / ¾ cup caster (superfine) sugar
200 g / 7 oz / ¾ cup butter
4 large eggs
1 tsp baking powder
3 tbsp unsweetened cocoa powder

TO DECORATE:

300 g / 10 ½ fl. oz / 1 ¼ cups double (heavy) cream
2 tbsp icing (confectioners') sugar, plus extra for dusting

762

SERVES 6

Mini Upside-Down Pavlovas

PREPARATION TIME 30 MINUTES

COOKING TIME 45 MINUTES

....

INGREDIENTS

100 g / 3 ½ oz / ⅔ cup strawberries, halved
100 g / 3 ½ oz / ⅔ cup raspberries
100 g / 3 ½ oz / ⅔ cup redcurrants
4 tbsp runny honey
225 ml / 8 fl. oz / 1 cup double (heavy) cream
2 tbsp icing (confectioners') sugar
½ tsp vanilla extract

FOR THE MERINGUE:

4 large egg whites
110g / 4 oz / 1 cup caster (superfine) sugar
1 tsp cornflour (cornstarch)
1 tbsp unsweetened cocoa powder

- Preheat the oven to 140°C (120° fan) / 275F / gas 1 and oil and line a baking tray with greaseproof paper.
- Whisk the egg whites until stiff, then gradually whisk in half the sugar until the mixture is very shiny.
- Fold in the remaining sugar and the cornflour then spoon the mixture onto the baking tray in 6 large dollops.
- Bake the meringues for 45 minutes or until they are crisp on the outside, but still a bit chewy in the middle.
- Leave to cool completely.
- Divide the berries between 6 serving plates and drizzle with honey.
- Whip the cream with the icing sugar and vanilla until it just holds its shape, then spoon it on top of the fruit.
- Hold a heart-shaped stencil just above each meringue and dust over the cocoa, then sit them on top of the cream.

Individual Upside-Down Peach Pavlovas 763

- Replace the berries with 6 stoned, sliced peaches.

764

MAKES 20

Spiced Shortbread Hearts

PREPARATION TIME 20 MINUTES

COOKING TIME 12 – 15 MINUTES

....

INGREDIENTS

175 g / 6 oz / 1 ¼ cups plain (all purpose) flour
1 tsp mixed spice
75 g / 2 ½ oz / ⅓ cup caster (superfine) sugar
150 g / 5 oz / ⅔ cup butter, cubed

- Preheat the oven to 180°C (160° fan) / 350F / gas 4 and line a baking tray with greaseproof paper.
- Mix together the flour, mixed spice and caster sugar in a bowl, then rub in the butter.
- Knead gently until the mixture forms a smooth dough then roll out on a lightly floured surface to 5 mm thick.
- Use a heart-shaped cookie cutter to cut out the biscuits and spread them out on the baking tray.
- Bake the biscuits for 12 - 15 minutes, turning the tray round halfway through.
- Transfer the biscuits to a wire rack and leave to cool.

Spiced Icing with Dried Fruit 765

- Mix 200 g icing sugar and ½ tsp mixed spice with just enough boiling water and pink food colouring to make a thick icing. Ice the biscuits and sprinkle with chopped dried fruit.

766

SERVES 6

Strawberry and Kiwi Pavlova

- Preheat the oven to 140°C (120° fan) / 275F / gas 1 and oil and line a baking tray with greaseproof paper.
- Whisk the egg whites until stiff, then gradually whisk in half the sugar until the mixture is very shiny.
- Fold in the remaining sugar and the cornflour then spoon the mixture onto the baking tray.
- Bake the meringue for 1 hour or until crisp on the outside, but still a bit chewy in the middle.
- Leave to cool completely.
- Whip the cream with the icing sugar and vanilla until it just holds its shape, then spoon it on top of the meringue.
- Arrange the strawberries and kiwi on top of the cream and serve straight away.

PREPARATION TIME 30 MINUTES

COOKING TIME 1 HOUR

INGREDIENTS

225 ml / 8 fl. oz / 1 cup double (heavy) cream
2 tbsp icing (confectioners') sugar
½ tsp vanilla extract
100 g / 3 ½ oz / ⅔ cup strawberries, halved
2 kiwis, peeled, quartered and sliced

FOR THE MERINGUE:
4 large egg whites
110g / 4 oz / 1 cup caster (superfine) sugar
1 tsp cornflour (cornstarch)

Kiwi and Pomegranate Pavlova 767

- Replace the strawberries with the seeds from a large pomegranate.

768

MAKES 12

Mince Pies

- Rub the butter into the flour until the mixture resembles fine breadcrumbs. Stir in just enough cold water to bring the pastry together into a pliable dough.
- Leave the pastry to chill the fridge for 30 minutes.
- Preheat the oven to 200°C (180° fan) / 400F / gas 6.
- Roll out the pastry on a floured surface and cut out 24 circles. Use 12 of the circles to line a 12-hole cupcake tin and cut a star out of the centre of the other 12.
- Fill the pastry cases ¾ full with mincemeat then top with the pastry lids, sealing the edges with a little beaten egg.
- Brush the pies with egg and sprinkle with granulated sugar then bake for 12 - 15 minutes.

PREPARATION TIME 1 HOUR

COOKING TIME 12 – 15 MINUTES

INGREDIENTS

150 g / 5 ½ oz / ⅔ cup butter, cubed and chilled
300 g / 10 ½ oz / 1 ½ / 2 cups plain (all-purpose) flour
225 g / 8 oz / 1 cup mincemeat
1 egg, beaten
2 tbsp granulated sugar

Boozy Mince Pies 769

- Pour 1 tsp of brandy into the top of each pie when they come out of the oven.

Apple and Redcurrant Samosas

770

SERVES 6

PREPARATION TIME 25 MINUTES

COOKING TIME 12 - 15 MINUTES

INGREDIENTS

1 bramley apple, peeled and diced
100 g / 3 ½ oz / ⅔ cup redcurrants
50 g / 1 ¾ oz / ¼ cup brown sugar
25 g / 1 oz / ⅓ cup breadcrumbs
225 g / 8 oz filo pastry
100 g / 3 ½ oz / ½ cup butter, melted

- Preheat the oven to 180°C (160° fan) / 350F / gas 4 and grease a large baking tray.
- Toss the apple and redcurrants with the sugar and breadcrumbs.
- Cut the pile of filo sheets in half then take one halved sheet and brush it with melted butter.
- Arrange a tablespoon of the filling at one end and fold the corner over, then triangle-fold it up.
- Transfer the samosa to the baking tray and repeat with the rest of the filo and filling, then brush with any leftover butter.
- Bake the samosas for 12 – 15 minutes or until the pastry is crisp and golden brown.

Apple and Sultana Samosas

771

- Replace the redcurrants with 75 g of sultanas and add ½ tsp of mixed spice to the filling.

Pistachio and Walnut Brownies

772

MAKES 8

PREPARATION TIME 25 MINUTES

COOKING TIME 15 – 20 MINUTES

INGREDIENTS

110 g / 4 oz milk chocolate, chopped
85 g / 3 oz / ¾ cup unsweetened cocoa powder, sifted
225 g / 8 oz / 1 cup butter
450 g / 1 lb / 2 ½ cups light brown sugar
4 large eggs
110 g / 4 oz / 1 cup self-raising flour
75 g / 2 ½ oz / ½ cup pistachio nuts, chopped
75 g / 2 ½ oz / ½ cup walnuts, chopped
icing (confectioners') sugar for dusting

- Preheat the oven to 160°C (140° fan) / 325F / gas 3 and oil and line a 20 cm x 20 cm / 8" x 8" square cake tin.
- Melt the chocolate, cocoa and butter together in a saucepan, then leave to cool a little.
- Whisk the sugar and eggs together with an electric whisk for 3 minutes or until very light and creamy.
- Pour in the chocolate mixture and sieve over the flour, then fold everything together with the nuts until evenly mixed.
- Scrape into the tin and bake for 35 – 40 minutes or until the outside is set, but the centre is still quite soft.
- Leave the brownie to cool completely before cutting into 8 rectangles and dusting with icing sugar.

Pistachio and Cherry Brownies

773

- Replace the walnuts with 75 g of halved glace cherries.

774

SERVES 8

Sticky Toffee Pecan Tart

Sticky Toffee Pear Tart

775

- Omit the pecans and arrange 3 sliced pears on top of the toffee sauce before pouring over the cake mixture.

Sticky Toffee Walnut Tart

776

- Replace the pecans with halved walnuts.

PREPARATION TIME 40 MINUTES

COOKING TIME 45 MINUTES

....

INGREDIENTS

200 g / 7 oz / 1 ¼ cup dark brown sugar
100 g / 3 ½ oz / ⅓ cup golden syrup
100 g / 3 ½ oz / ½ cup butter
1 tsp vanilla extract
3 large eggs, beaten
3 tbsp plain (all purpose) flour
300 g / 10 ½ oz / 1 ½ cups pecan halves

FOR THE PASTRY:
150 g / 5 ½ / ⅔ cup butter, cubed and chilled
300 g / 10 ½ oz / 2 cups plain (all purpose) flour

FOR THE TOFFEE SAUCE:
100 g / 3 ½ oz / ½ cup butter
100 g / 3 ½ oz / ½ cup muscovado sugar
100 g / 3 ½ oz / ⅓ cup golden syrup
100 ml / 3 ½ fl. oz / ½ cup double (heavy) cream

- First make the pastry. Rub the butter into the flour then add just enough cold water to bind the mixture together into a pliable dough.
- Roll out the pastry on a floured surface and use it to line a 23 cm round tart case then chill for 30 minutes.
- Put all of the toffee sauce ingredients in a small saucepan and stir over a low heat until the sugar dissolves. Bring to the boil then take off the heat.
- Preheat the oven to 180°C (160° fan) / 350F / gas 4.
- Put the sugar, golden syrup, butter and vanilla extract in a saucepan and stir it over a low heat to dissolve the sugar.
- Leave the mixture to cool for 10 minutes then beat in the eggs and flour.
- Spoon half of the toffee sauce into the pastry case then pour in the cake mixture.
- Arrange the pecans on top, then bake the tart for 40 minutes.
- Leave the tart to cool for 10 minutes, then transfer to a serving plate and spoon over the rest of the toffee sauce.

777

SERVES 8

Banana and Walnut Loaf Cake

PREPARATION TIME 10 MINUTES

COOKING TIME 55 MINUTES

....

INGREDIENTS

3 very ripe bananas
100 g / 3 ½ oz / ½ cup soft light
brown sugar
2 large eggs
125 ml / 4 ½ fl. oz / ½ cup sunflower
oil
225 g / 8 oz / 1 ½ cups plain (all
purpose) flour
1 tsp bicarbonate of (baking) soda
75 g / 2 ½ oz / ⅔ cup walnuts,
chopped

• Preheat the oven to 160°C (140° fan) / 325F / gas 3 and
  line a loaf tin with greaseproof paper.
• Mash the bananas roughly with a fork then whisk in the
  sugar, eggs and oil.
• Sieve the flour and bicarbonate of soda into the bowl
  and add the chopped walnuts. Stir just enough to evenly
  mix all of the ingredients together.
• Scrape the mixture into the loaf tin and bake for 55
  minutes or until a skewer inserted comes out clean.
• Transfer the cake to a wire rack and leave to cool
  completely.

778

SERVES 8

Pear and Almond Tart

PREPARATION TIME 40 MINUTES

COOKING TIME 35 MINUTES

....

INGREDIENTS

110 g / 4 oz / ½ cup butter, cubed and
chilled
225 g / 8 oz / 1 ½ cups plain (all
purpose) flour
2 pears, very thinly sliced
3 tbsp flaked (slivered) almonds

FOR THE FRANGIPANE:
55 g / 2 oz / ½ cup ground almonds
55 g / 2 oz / ¼ cup caster
(superfine) sugar
55 g / 2 oz / ¼ cup butter, softened
1 large egg
1 tsp almond essence

• Rub the butter into the flour then add just enough cold
  water to bind the mixture together into a pliable dough.
• Roll out the pastry on a floured surface and use it to line
  a 23 cm / 9 " round tart case.
• Leave the pastry to chill the fridge for 30 minutes.
• Preheat the oven to 200°C (180° fan) / 400F / gas 6.
• Line the pastry case with clingfilm and fill it with
  baking beans, then bake for 15 minutes.
• To make the frangipane, combine the ground almonds,
  sugar, butter, egg and almond essence in a bowl and
  whisk together for 2 minutes or until smooth.
• When the pastry case is ready, remove the clingfilm and
  baking beans and fill the case with frangipane.
• Top with the sliced pears, sprinkle with flaked almonds
  and bake for 15 – 20 minutes.

SERVES 9

Raspberry Jam Cake

- Preheat the oven to 180°C (160° fan) / 350F / gas 4 and butter a 20 cm square cake tin.
- Sieve the flour and baking powder into a mixing bowl and add sugar, butter and eggs.
- Beat the mixture with an electric whisk for 4 minutes or until smooth and well whipped.
- Spread the raspberry jam in the cake tin and spoon the cake mixture on top.
- Level the top with a palette knife and bake for 25 minutes or until a skewer inserted comes out clean.
- Leave the cake to cool for 10 minutes before turning out onto a plate.
- Cut the cake into 9 squares and top each one with 2 raspberries.

PREPARATION TIME 15 MINUTES

COOKING TIME 25 MINUTES

INGREDIENTS

100 g / 3 ½ oz / ⅔ cup self-raising flour
1 tsp baking powder
100 g / 3 ½ oz / ½ cup caster (superfine) sugar
100 g / 3 ½ oz / ½ cup butter, softened
2 large eggs
450 g / 1 lb / 2 cups raspberry jam (jelly)
18 fresh raspberries to garnish

Moist Chocolate Cake

780

SERVES 8

PREPARATION TIME 15 MINUTES

COOKING TIME 35 - 40 MINUTES

INGREDIENTS

250 g / 9 oz / 1 ⅔ cups self-raising flour
1 tsp bicarbonate of (baking) soda
2 tbsp unsweetened cocoa powder

200 g / 8 ½ oz / ⅔ cup golden syrup
125 g / 4 ½ oz / ½ cup butter
125 g / 4 ½ oz / ¾ cup dark brown sugar
2 large eggs, beaten
240 ml / 8 fl. oz / 1 cup milk

- Preheat the oven to 180°C (160° fan) / 350F / gas 4 and grease and line 23 cm round cake tin.
- Sieve the flour, bicarbonate of soda and cocoa into a bowl.
- Put the golden syrup, butter and brown sugar in a small saucepan and boil gently for 2 minutes, stirring to dissolve the sugar.
- Add the butter and sugar mixture to the flour with the eggs and milk and fold it all together until smooth.
- Scrape the mixture into the prepared tin and bake for 35 - 40 minutes. The cake is ready when a toothpick inserted comes out with just a few sticky crumbs clinging to it.
- Transfer the cake to a wire rack to cool completely.

Lemon Drizzle Cake

781

SERVES 8

PREPARATION TIME 25 MINUTES

COOKING TIME 15 – 20 MINUTES

INGREDIENTS

175 g / 6 oz / 1 ¼ cups self-raising flour, sifted
1 tsp baking powder
175 g / 6 oz / ¾ cup caster (superfine) sugar

175 g / 6 oz / ¾ cup butter, softened
3 large eggs
2 lemons, zest finely grated

FOR THE SOAKING SYRUP:
2 lemons, juiced
3 tbsp caster (superfine) sugar
3 tbsp icing (confectioners') sugar

- Preheat the oven to 180°C (160° fan) / 350F / gas 4 and oil and line a 23 cm round cake tin with greaseproof paper.
- Combine the flour, baking powder, sugar, butter, eggs and lemon zest in a bowl and whisk together for 2 minutes or until smooth.
- Scrape the mixture into the tin and level the top then bake for 35 - 45 minutes or until a toothpick inserted comes out clean.
- Mix the lemon juice with the caster sugar and icing sugar and spoon it all over the cake when it comes out of the oven.
- Leave the cake to soak up the juice and cool in its tin for 20 minutes then transfer it to a wire rack and leave to cool completely.

782

SERVES 10-12

Blueberry Cheesecake

PREP TIME: 25 MINUTES

COOKING TIME: 40 – 50 MINUTES

INGREDIENTS

200 g / 7 oz digestive biscuits, crushed
50 g / 1 ¾ oz / ¼ cup butter, melted
600 g / 1 lb 5 oz / 2 ¾ cups cream cheese
150 ml / 5 fl. oz / ⅔ cup soured cream
175 g / 6 oz / ¾ cup caster (superfine) sugar
2 large eggs, plus 1 egg yolk
2 tbsp plain (all purpose) flour
1 tsp vanilla extract
100 g / 3 ½ oz / ⅔ cup blueberries

FOR THE BLUEBERRY TOPPING:
100 g / 3 ½ oz / ⅓ cup blueberry jam (jelly)
200 g / 7 oz blueberries

- Preheat the oven to 180°C (160° fan) / 350F / gas 4 and grease a 20 cm round spring-form cake tin.
- Mix the biscuit crumbs with the butter and press into an even layer in the bottom of the tin.
- Bake the biscuit layer for 5 minutes or until firm.
- Whisk together the remaining ingredients until smooth.
- Spoon the cheesecake mixture on top of the biscuit base and bake for 40 – 50 minutes or until the centre is only just set.
- Leave to cool completely in the tin.
- To make the topping, heat the jam in a small saucepan until runny then stir in the blueberries and spoon on top of the cheesecake.
- Transfer the tin to the fridge and chill for 2 hours before unmoulding and cutting into slices.

Raspberry and White Chocolate Cheesecake

 783

- Replace the blueberries with raspberries and the blueberry jam with raspberry jam. Add 100 g of chopped white chocolate to the filling before baking.

784

SERVES 8

Coconut Charlotte

PREPARATION TIME 10 MINUTES

COOKING TIME 35 – 40 MINUTES

INGREDIENTS

200 g / 7 oz / 1 ⅓ cups self-raising flour
200 g / 7 oz / ¾ cup caster (superfine) sugar
200 g / 7 oz / ¾ cup butter
4 large eggs
1 tsp baking powder
1 tsp coconut extract
2 tbsp desiccated coconut

TO DECORATE:
200 g / 7 oz / 1 cup butter, softened
1 tsp coconut extract
400 g / 14 oz / 4 cups icing (confectioners') sugar
16 langues de chat biscuits
3 tbsp desiccated coconut

- Preheat the oven to 180°C (160° fan) / 350F / gas 4 and line 2 x 20 cm round loose-bottomed cake tins.
- Put all of the cake ingredients in a large mixing bowl and whisk until pale and well whipped.
- Divide the mixture between the 2 tins and level the tops with a spatula.
- Bake for 35 – 40 minutes. The cakes are ready when a toothpick inserted comes out clean.
- Transfer the cakes to a wire rack to cool completely.
- To make the buttercream, whisk the butter and coconut extract with an electric whisk then gradually add the icing sugar. Whisk until smooth and well whipped. If the mixture is too stiff add a tablespoon of warm water.
- Sandwich the cakes together with buttercream and spread the rest over the top and sides.
- Stick the langues de chat biscuits round the edge of the cake and sprinkle the top with coconut.

Coconut and Raspberry Charlotte

785

- Top the cake with 150 g of fresh raspberries and sprinkle with icing sugar instead of the desiccated coconut.

786

SERVES 8

Madeira Cake

- Preheat the oven to 160°C (140° fan) / 325F / gas 3 and line a large loaf tin with greaseproof paper.
- Combine the flour, ground almonds, sugar, butter, eggs and lemon zest in a bowl and whisk together for 2 minutes or until smooth.
- Scrape the mixture into the tin and level the top then bake for 55 minutes or until a toothpick inserted comes out clean.
- Transfer to a wire rack and leave to cool completely.

PREPARATION TIME 10 MINUTES

COOKING TIME 55 MINUTES

INGREDIENTS

200 g / 7 oz / 1 ⅓ cups self-raising flour, sifted
50 g / 1 ¾ oz / ½ cup ground almonds
175 g / 6 oz / ¾ cup caster (superfine) sugar
175 g / 6 oz / ¾ cup butter, softened
3 large eggs
1 lemon, zest finely grated

Chocolate Madeira Cake

787

- Replace the lemon zest with 2 tbsp unsweetened cocoa powder.

788

SERVES 8

Tea and Almond Cake

- Preheat the oven to 180°C (160° fan) / 350F / gas 4 and line a 23 cm round cake tin with non-stick baking paper.
- Sieve the flour into a mixing bowl and rub in the butter until it resembles fine breadcrumbs then stir in the sugar.
- Lightly beat the egg with the tea and stir it into the dry ingredients until just combined then scrape the mixture into the tin.
- Mix the almonds with the tea leaves and granulated sugar and sprinkle it over the top, then bake for 55 minutes or until a skewer inserted comes out clean.
- Transfer the cake to a wire rack and leave to cool completely.

PREPARATION TIME 15 MINUTES

COOKING TIME 55 MINUTES

INGREDIENTS

225 g / 8 oz / 1 ½ cups self raising flour
100 g / 3 ½ oz / ½ cup butter, cubed
100 g / 3 ½ oz / ½ cup brown sugar
1 large egg
75 ml / 2 ½ fl. oz / ⅓ cup strong milky tea
75 g / 2 ½ oz / 1 cup flaked almonds (slivered almonds)
1 tbsp tea leaves
1 tbsp granulated sugar

Tea and Hazelnut Cake

789

- Replace the almonds with roughly chopped hazelnuts (cob nuts).

790

SERVES 8

Coconut and Chocolate Chip Loaf Cake

PREPARATION TIME 15 MINUTES

COOKING TIME 55 MINUTES

INGREDIENTS

225 g / 8 oz / 1 cup butter, softened
225 g / 8 oz / 1 cup caster (superfine) sugar
4 large eggs, beaten
225 g / 8 oz / 1 ½ cups self-raising flour
2 tbsp desiccated coconut, plus extra for sprinkling
100 g / 3 ½ oz milk chocolate chips

- Preheat the oven to 180°C (160° fan) / 350F / gas 4 and grease and line a loaf tin with greaseproof paper.
- Cream together the butter and sugar until well whipped then gradually whisk in the eggs, beating well after each addition.
- Sift over the flour then fold it in with the coconut and chocolate chips.
- Scrape the mixture into the tin and bake for 55 minutes or until a skewer inserted in the centre comes out clean.
- Turn the loaf out onto a wire rack and leave to cool completely before sprinkling with more coconut and slicing.

Vanilla and Chocolate Chip Loaf Cake

 791

- Omit the coconut and add 1 tsp of vanilla extract to the cake mixture.

792

MAKES 4

Mini Bread and Butter Puddings

PREPARATION TIME 15 MINUTES

COOKING TIME 20 MINUTES

INGREDIENTS

8 slices white bread
3 tbsp butter, softened
250 ml / 9 fl. oz / 1 cup milk
200 ml / 7 fl. oz / ¾ cup double (heavy) cream
4 large egg yolks
75 g / 2 ½ oz / ¼ cup runny honey
½ tsp ground cinnamon
cinnamon sticks to garnish

- Spread the bread with butter and lay 2 slices in 4 small buttered baking dishes.
- Whisk the milk, cream, eggs, honey and cinnamon together and divide it between the dishes, then leave to soak for 10 minutes.
- Preheat the oven to 180°C (160° fan) / 350F / gas 4.
- Bake the puddings for 20 minutes or until the tops are golden brown.

Chocolate Bread and Butter Puddings

 793

- Add 2 tbsp cocoa powder to the milk mixture and sprinkle 50 g of chocolate chips between the slices of bread.

794

SERVES 6

Chocolate and Coconut Swiss Roll

Chocolate and Orange Swiss Roll

795

- Replace the coconut in the cake mixture with the grated zest of an orange. Spread a layer of marmalade on top of the buttercream before rolling up.

Chocolate and Lime Swiss Roll

796

- Add the juice of ½ a lime and mix in the grated zest of a lime before cooking.

PREPARATION TIME 45 MINUTES

COOKING TIME 15 – 20 MINUTES

....

INGREDIENTS

100 g / 3 ½ oz / ⅔ cup self-raising flour
1 tsp baking powder
100 g / 3 ½ oz / ½ cup caster (superfine) sugar
100 g / 3 ½ oz/ ½ cup butter
2 large eggs
1 tsp coconut extract
2 tbsp desiccated coconut

TO DECORATE:

100 g / 3 ½ oz / ½ cup butter, softened
200 g / 7 oz / 2 cups icing (confectioners') sugar, plus extra for dusting
1 tbsp unsweetened cocoa powder
2 tbsp desiccated coconut

- Preheat the oven to 180°C (160° fan) / 350F / gas 4 and grease and line a Swiss roll tin.
- Put all of the cake ingredients in a large mixing bowl and whisk them together with an electric whisk for 4 minutes or until pale and well whipped.
- Spoon the mixture into the tin and spread into an even layer with a palette knife.
- Bake for 15 - 20 minutes or until the cake is springy to the touch.
- Turn the cake out onto a sheet of greaseproof paper and peel off the lining paper. Roll up the cake whilst warm, using the greaseproof paper to help you.
- Leave the cake to cool completely.
- Whisk the butter with an electric whisk then gradually add the icing sugar and cocoa powder until smooth and well whipped. If the mixture is too stiff add a tablespoon of warm water.
- Carefully unroll the cake and spread it with half the buttercream before rerolling.
- Spread the rest of the buttercream over the cake then sprinkle with coconut.

797

SERVES 8

Fruity Panettone

Chocolate Panettone
798

- Replace the mixed dried fruit with dark chocolate chips and replace the candied peel with white chocolate chips.

Chocolate Orange Pannetone
799

- Add 4-6 drops of orange oil when you mix in the chocolate chips.

PREPARATION TIME 4 HOURS 30 MINUTES

COOKING TIME 40 MINUTES

....

INGREDIENTS

250 g / 9 oz / 1 ¼ cups butter, cubed
400 g / 14 oz / 2 ⅔ cups strong white bread flour
2 ½ tsp easy blend dried yeast
4 tbsp caster (superfine) sugar
1 tsp fine sea salt
4 large eggs, plus 3 egg yolks
75 g / 2 ½ oz / ⅓ cup mixed dried fruit
50 g / 1 ¾ oz / ¼ cup candied peel, finely chopped
icing (confectioners') sugar for dusting

- Rub the butter into the flour then stir in the yeast, sugar and salt. Beat the whole eggs and yolks together and stir into the dry ingredients with the mixed fruit and peel.
- Knead the very soft dough on a lightly oiled surface with 2 plastic scrapers for 10 minutes or until smooth and elastic.
- Leave the dough to rest in a lightly oiled bowl, covered with oiled clingfilm, for 2 hours or until doubled in size.
- Knead the mixture briefly again, then transfer it to a 20 cm round cake tin lined with a paper case.
- Cover with oiled clingfilm and leave to prove for 2 hours or until doubled in size.
- Meanwhile, preheat the oven to 180°C (160° fan) / 350F / gas 4.
- Remove the clingfilm and bake the Panettone for 40 minutes or until golden brown and cooked through.
- Leave to cool completely on a wire rack before peeling away the paper case and dusting with icing sugar.

800
MAKES 12 Millionaire's Shortbread

- Make the caramel layer in advance. Put the unopened can of condensed milk in a saucepan of water and simmer for 3 hours, adding more water as necessary to ensure it doesn't boil dry. Leave the can to cool.
- Preheat the oven to 180°C (160° fan) / 350F / gas 4 and line a 20 cm square cake tin with greaseproof paper.
- Mix the flour and sugar, then rub in the butter.
- Knead gently until the mixture forms a smooth dough then press it into the bottom of the tin in an even layer.
- Bake the shortbread for 20 minutes, turning the tray round halfway through. Leave to cool.
- Open the can of condensed milk and beat until smooth. Spread it over the shortbread and chill for 1 hour.
- Put the chocolate and butter in a bowl set over a pan of simmering water. Stir until melted and smooth.
- Pour over the caramel layer and leave to cool.

PREPARATION TIME: 20 MINUTES

COOKING TIME: 3 HOURS 20 MINUTES

INGREDIENTS

225 g / 8 oz / 1 ½ cups plain (all purpose) flour
75 g / 2 ½ oz / ⅓ cup caster (superfine) sugar
150 g / 5 oz / ⅔ cup butter, cubed

FOR THE TOPPING:
400 g / 14 oz can of condensed milk
200 g / 7 oz milk chocolate, chopped
50 g / 1 ¾ oz / ½ cup butter

White Chocolate Millionaire's Shortbread
801

- Replace the milk chocolate and butter mixture with 200 g of melted white chocolate.

802
SERVES 10 Raspberries and Cream Sponge

- Preheat the oven to 180°C (160° fan) / 350F / gas 4 and grease and line 2 x 20 cm round loose-bottomed cake tins.
- Put all of the cake ingredients in a large mixing bowl and whisk with an electric whisk for 4 minutes or until pale and well whipped.
- Divide the mixture between the 2 tins and level the tops with a spatula.
- Bake for 35 – 40 minutes. The cakes are ready when a toothpick inserted comes out clean.
- Transfer the cakes to a wire rack to cool completely.
- Whip the cream with the icing sugar until it forms soft peaks, spread ⅔ of it over one of the cakes.
- Press the raspberries into the cream then top with the other cake and spread the rest of the cream on top.
- Crush the freeze-dried raspberries to a powder with a pestle and mortar then sprinkle over the cake.

PREPARATION TIME 15 MINUTES

COOKING TIME 35 – 40 MINUTES

INGREDIENTS

200 g / 7 oz / 1 ⅓ cups self-raising flour
200 g / 7 oz / ¾ cup caster (superfine) sugar
200 g / 7 oz / ¾ cup butter
4 large eggs
1 tsp baking powder
1 tsp vanilla extract

TO DECORATE:
300 g / 10 ½ fl. oz / 1 ¼ cups double (heavy) cream
2 tbsp icing (confectioners') sugar
200 g / 7 oz / 1 ⅓ cups raspberries
1 tbsp freeze-dried raspberry pieces

Blueberries and Cream Sponge
803

- Replace the raspberries with blueberries and use crystallised violets instead of the freeze-dried raspberries.

804

MAKES 12

Wholemeal Scones with Cream and Jam

PREPARATION TIME 25 MINUTES

COOKING TIME 10 – 15 MINUTES

INGREDIENTS

55 g / 2 oz / ¼ cup butter
225 g / 8 oz / 1 ½ cups self-raising wholemeal flour
150 ml / 5 fl. oz / ⅔ cup milk
200 g / 7 oz / ¾ cup clotted cream
200 g / 7 oz / ¾ cup raspberry jam (jelly)

- Preheat the oven to 220°C (200° fan) / 425F / gas 7 and oil a large baking sheet.
- Rub the butter into the flour until the mixture resembles fine breadcrumbs.
- Stir in enough milk to bring the mixture together into a soft dough.
- Flatten the dough with your hands on a floured work surface until 2.5 cm / 1" thick.
- Use a pastry cutter to cut out 12 circles and transfer them to the prepared baking sheet.
- Bake in the oven for 10 – 15 minutes or until golden brown and cooked through.
- Transfer the scones to a wire rack to cool a little.
- Split open the scones then sandwich them back together with clotted cream and jam.

Wholemeal Marmalade Scones

 805

- Add the grated zest of an orange to the scone dough and replace the jam with marmalade.

806

MAKES 12

Cherry Scones

PREPARATION TIME 25 MINUTES

COOKING TIME 10 – 15 MINUTES

INGREDIENTS

225 g / 8 oz / 1 ½ cups self-raising flour
55 g / 2 oz / ¼ cup butter
75 g / 2 ½ oz / ½ cup glace cherries, chopped
150 ml / 5 fl. oz / ⅔ cup milk
1 egg, beaten

- Preheat the oven to 220°C (200° fan) / 425F / gas 7 and oil a large baking sheet.
- Sieve the flour into a bowl and rub in the butter until the mixture resembles fine breadcrumbs.
- Add the glace cherries and stir in enough milk to bring the mixture together into a soft dough.
- Flatten the dough with your hands on a floured work surface until 2.5 cm / 1" thick.
- Use a pastry cutter to cut out 12 circles and transfer them to the prepared baking sheet and brush with beaten egg.
- Bake in the oven for 10 – 15 minutes or until golden brown and cooked through.
- Transfer the scones to a wire rack to cool a little and serve warm.

Cherry and Almond Scones

807

- Add 75 g of flaked almonds to the scone dough.

MAKES 36 Jam Sandwich Biscuits

- Cream together the sugar, butter and lemon zest until well whipped then stir in the flour and ground almonds.
- Bring the mixture together into a ball with your hands then wrap in clingfilm and refrigerate for 45 minutes.
- Preheat the oven to 140°C (120° fan) / 275F / gas 1 and line 2 baking sheets with greaseproof paper.
- Roll out the dough on a lightly floured surface to 5 mm thick. Use an oval fluted pastry cutter to cut out 72 biscuits, rerolling the trimmings as necessary.
- Use a small round cutter to cut the centre out of 36 of the biscuits.
- Transfer the biscuits to the prepared trays and bake in batches for 25 – 30 minutes.
- Transfer the biscuits to a wire rack and leave to cool.
- Sandwich the plain biscuits and centre-less biscuits together in pairs with the jam.

PREPARATION TIME 1 HOUR 15 MINUTES

COOKING TIME 25 – 30 MINUTES

INGREDIENTS

150 g / 5 ½ oz / ⅔ cup caster (superfine) sugar
350 g / 12 oz / 1 ½ cups butter, softened
1 lemon, zest finely grated
300 g / 10 ½ oz / 2 cups plain (all purpose) flour
150 g / 5 ½ oz / 1 ½ cups ground almonds
250 g / 9 oz / 1 cup raspberry jam (jelly)

Lemon Curd Sandwich Biscuits 809

- Replace the jam with lemon curd.

810

SERVES 6 Almond and Honey Cheesecake

- Preheat the oven to 180°C (160° fan) / 350F / gas 4 and grease a 20 cm x 30 cm rectangular loose-bottomed cake tin.
- Mix the biscuit crumbs with the butter and press into an even layer in the bottom of the tin.
- Bake the biscuit layer for 5 minutes or until firm.
- Whisk together the remaining filling ingredients until smooth.
- Spoon the cheesecake mixture on top of the biscuit base and bake for 40 minutes.
- Drizzle the top with honey and scatter with flaked almonds then return the tin to the oven for 5 – 10 minutes or until the almonds are golden and the centre is only just set.
- Leave to cool completely in the tin then chill for 2 hours before unmoulding and cutting into 6 squares.

PREPARATION TIME 25 MINUTES

COOKING TIME 40 – 50 MINUTES

INGREDIENTS

200 g / 7 oz digestive biscuits, crushed
50 g / 1 ¾ oz / ¼ cup butter, melted
600 g / 1 lb 5 oz / 2 ¾ cups cream cheese
150 ml / 5 fl. oz / ⅔ cup soured cream
200 ml / 7 fl. oz / ⅔ cup runny honey
2 large eggs, plus 1 egg yolk
2 tbsp plain (all purpose) flour
1 tsp almond extract

FOR THE ALMOND TOPPING
2 tbsp runny honey
50 g / 1 ¾ oz / ⅔ cup flaked almonds (slivered almonds)

Almond, Honey and Ginger Cheesecake 811

- Replace the digestive biscuits with ginger nut biscuits and add 3 finely chopped pieces of stem ginger to the almond topping.

812

SERVES 8

Pecan and Maple Syrup Cheesecake

PREPARATION TIME 25 MINUTES

COOKING TIME 40 – 50 MINUTES

INGREDIENTS

200 g / 7 oz digestive biscuits, crushed

50 g / 1 ¾ oz / ¼ cup butter, melted

600 g / 1 lb 5 oz / 2 ¾ cups cream cheese

150 ml / 5 fl. oz / ⅔ cup soured cream

2 large eggs, plus 1 egg yolk

2 tbsp plain (all purpose) flour

100 ml / 3 ½ fl. oz / ⅓ cup maple syrup

75 g / 2 ½ oz / ⅓ cup caster (superfine) sugar

FOR THE PECAN TOPPING:

3 tbsp maple syrup

75 g / 2 ½ oz / ⅔ cup pecan nuts, roughly chopped

- Preheat the oven to 180°C (160° fan) / 350F / gas 4 and grease a 23 cm round spring-form cake tin.
- Mix the biscuit crumbs with the butter and press into an even layer in the bottom of the tin.
- Bake the biscuit layer for 5 minutes or until firm.
- Whisk together the cream cheese, soured cream, eggs, egg yolk and flour until smooth. Divide the mixture between 2 bowls and beat the maple syrup into one half. Pour it into the tin and level the surface.
- Beat the caster sugar into the second bowl, then spoon it into the tin and level the surface.
- Bake the cheesecake for 40 minutes then drizzle the top with maple syrup, scatter with pecans and return the tin to the oven for 5 – 10 minutes or until the centre is only just set.
- Leave to cool completely in the tin then chill for 2 hours.

Walnut and Treacle Cheesecake   **813**

- Replace the pecans with walnuts and use treacle instead of maple syrup in the filling and topping, reducing the quantity by half.

814

SERVES 8

Iced Lemon Sponge

PREPARATION TIME 25 MINUTES

COOKING TIME 15 – 20 MINUTES

INGREDIENTS

175 g / 6 oz / 1 ¼ cups self-raising flour, sifted

1 tsp baking powder

175 g / 6 oz / ¾ cup caster (superfine) sugar

175 g / 6 oz / ¾ cup butter, softened

3 large eggs

2 lemons, zest finely grated

FOR THE SOAKING SYRUP:

2 lemons, juiced

3 tbsp caster (superfine) sugar

3 tbsp icing (confectioners') sugar

FOR FILLING AND ICING:

250 ml / 9 fl. oz / 1 cup double (heavy) cream

150 g / 5 ½ oz / 1 ½ cups icing (confectioners') sugar

2 – 4 tsp lemon juice

- Preheat the oven to 180°C (160° fan) / 350F / gas 4 and line a 23 cm round cake tin with greaseproof paper.
- Combine the flour, baking powder, sugar, butter, eggs and lemon zest and whisk together until smooth.
- Scrape the mixture into the tin and level the top then bake for 35 - 45 minutes.
- Mix the lemon juice with the caster sugar and icing sugar and spoon it all over the cake when it comes out of the oven.
- Leave the cake to soak up the juice and cool in its tin for 20 minutes then transfer it to a wire rack and leave to cool completely.
- Whip the cream until stiff then slice the cake in half horizontally and sandwich it back together with the cream.
- Mix the icing sugar with enough lemon juice to make a thick icing, then spread it over the top of the cake.

Lemon Cream Cupcakes   **815**

- Bake the cake mixture in 12 muffin cases, reducing the cooking time to 15 minutes. Scoop out the centres and fill with whipped cream, then replace the cake and spread with lemon icing.

816
MAKES 18

Orange and Ginger Hot Cross Buns

Orange and Cardamom Hot Cross Buns

817

- Replace the ground ginger with 1 tsp of ground cardamom.

Chocolate Orange Hot Cross Buns

818

- Replace the sultanas with chocolate chips and add as you knead the dough.

PREPARATION TIME 2 HOURS 30 MINUTES

COOKING TIME 15 – 20 MINUTES

INGREDIENTS

55 g / 2 oz / ¼ cup butter, cubed
400 g / 14 oz / 2 ⅔ cups strong white bread flour, plus extra for dusting
½ tsp easy blend dried yeast
4 tbsp caster (superfine) sugar
1 tsp fine sea salt
2 tsp ground ginger
100 g / 3 ½ oz / ½ cup candied orange peel, finely chopped
50 g / 1 ¾ oz / ¼ cup sultanas
80 ml / 3 fl. oz / ⅓ cup orange juice
4 tbsp plain (all purpose) flour
1 egg, beaten
softened butter for spreading

- Rub the butter into the bread flour and stir in the yeast, sugar, salt and ground ginger. Mix the candied peel and sultanas with the orange juice and 200 ml of warm water, then stir it into the dry ingredients.
- Knead the mixture on a lightly oiled surface for 10 minutes or until the dough is smooth and elastic.
- Leave the dough to rest, covered with the mixing bowl, for 1 – 2 hours or until doubled in size.
- Shape the dough into 12 buns and transfer to a greased baking tray, then cover and leave to prove for 45 minutes.
- Preheat the oven to 220°C (200° fan) / 425F / gas 7.
- Mix the plain flour with just enough water to make a thick paste and spoon it into a piping bag.
- Brush the buns with egg and pipe a cross on top of each one.
- Bake for 15 – 20 minutes or until golden brown and cooked through.
- Leave to cool on a wire rack then split in half and spread thickly with butter.

819

SERVES 4

Cheese Soufflé

Goats' Cheese and Thyme Soufflé

820

- Replace the Cheddar with 100 g of goats' cheese in small cubes. Replace the Worcestershire sauce with 2 tbsp of fresh thyme leaves.

Mimolette and Tarragon Soufflé

821

- Replace the cheddar with 100g of Mimolette and add 2 tbsp of chopped tarragon.

PREPARATION TIME 20 MINUTES

COOKING TIME 25 MINUTES

....

INGREDIENTS

3 tbsp butter
75 g / 2 ½ oz / ¾ cup Parmesan , finely grated
2 tbsp plain flour
600 ml / 1 pint / 2 ½ cups milk
¼ tsp freshly grated nutmeg
2 tsp Worcestershire sauce
1 tsp mustard powder
6 large eggs, separated
100 g / 3 ½ oz / 1 cup Gruyere, grated
100 g / 3 ½ oz / 1 cup mature Cheddar, grated

- Preheat the oven to 200°C (180° fan) / 400F / gas 6. Use 1 tbsp of the butter to grease a baking dish, then add half of the Parmesan and shake to coat the sides.
- Melt the rest of the butter in a saucepan then stir in the flour.
- Gradually whisk in the milk a little at a time until it is all incorporated then stir in the nutmeg, Worcestershire sauce and mustard powder.
- Cook the sauce over a low heat, stirring constantly, until the mixture thickens. Beat vigorously to remove any lumps.
- Take the pan off the heat and beat in the egg yolks and ¾ of the Gruyere and Cheddar and the rest of the Parmesan.
- Whisk the egg whites until they form stiff peaks, then fold them into the cheese mixture.
- Spoon the soufflé into the prepared dish and sprinkle with the rest of the cheese, then bake for 10 minutes.
- Reduce the oven temperature to 180°C (160° fan) / 350F / gas 4 and bake for a further 15 minutes or until well risen and golden brown.

822

SERVES 8

Cherry and Custard Tart

- Preheat the oven to 200°C (180° fan) / 390F / gas 6.
- Rub the butter into the flour and add just enough cold water to bind.
- Chill for 30 minutes then roll out on a floured surface. Use the pastry to line a 23 cm round tart case.
- Prick the pastry with a fork, line with clingfilm and fill with baking beans or rice.
- Bake for 10 minutes then remove the clingfilm and baking beans and cook for a further 8 minutes to crisp.
- Reduce the oven temperature to 160°C (140° fan) / 325F / gas 3.
- Whisk the egg yolks, sugar, vanilla, cornflour and milk and strain it through a sieve into the pastry case.
- Arrange the cherries on top then bake for 35 minutes or until the custard is just set in the centre.
- Leave to cool completely before slicing.

PREPARATION TIME 40 MINUTES

COOKING TIME 55 MINUTES

....

INGREDIENTS

100 g / 3 ½ oz / ½ cup butter, cubed
200 g / 7 oz / 1 ⅓ cups plain (all purpose) flour
4 large egg yolks
75 g / 2 ½ oz / ⅓ cup caster (superfine) sugar
1 tsp vanilla extract
2 tsp cornflour (cornstarch)
450 ml / 16 fl. oz / 1 ¾ cups milk
20 cherries, stoned

Plum and Custard Tart

823

- Halve and stone 6 small plums and arrange them in the pastry case before pouring in the custard.

824

SERVES 6

Raspberry Gateau Breton

- Preheat the oven to 180°C (160° fan) / 350F / gas 4 and butter a 20 cm x 30 cm loose-bottomed cake tin.
- Rub the butter into the flour then stir in the sugar.
- Beat 5 egg yolks and stir into the dry ingredients.
- Mix the mixture into a soft dough and divide it in two.
- Press one half into the bottom of the cake tin.
- Mash the raspberries into the jam with a fork then spread it on top of the base, leaving a clear border round the outside.
- Roll the remaining dough between 2 sheets of greaseproof paper then peel away and lay it on top of the raspberries.
- Press it into the edges to form an even layer.
- Brush the top of the gateau with the final egg yolk then score a pattern on top with the handle of a teaspoon.
- Bake the gateau for 40 – 45 minutes.
- Cool before unmolding and cutting into 6 squares.

PREPARATION TIME 15 MINUTES

COOKING TIME 40 - 45 MINUTES

....

INGREDIENTS

250 g / 9 oz / 1 ¼ cups butter, cubed
250 g / 9 oz / 1 ⅔ cups plain (all purpose) flour
250 g / 9 oz / 1 ¼ cups caster (superfine) sugar
6 large egg yolks
100 g / 3 ½ oz / ⅔ cup raspberries
175 g / 6 oz / ½ cup raspberry jam (jelly)

Apricot Gateau Breton

825

- Replace the raspberries and jam with 3 stoned chopped apricots, blended to a paste with 175 g of apricot jam.

826

SERVES 8

Pecan Pie

PREPARATION TIME 40 MINUTES

COOKING TIME 45 MINUTES

INGREDIENTS

200 g / 7 oz / 1 ¼ cup dark brown sugar
100 g / 3 ½ oz / ⅓ cup golden syrup
100 g / 3 ½ oz / ½ cup butter
1 tsp vanilla extract
3 large eggs, beaten
3 tbsp plain (all purpose) flour
1 tsp mixed spice
300 g / 10 ½ oz / 1 ½ cups pecan halves
softly whipped cream to serve

FOR THE PASTRY:
150 g / 5 ½ / ⅔ cup butter, cubed and chilled
300 g / 10 ½ oz / 2 cups plain (all purpose) flour

- First make the pastry. Rub the butter into the flour then add just enough cold water to bind the mixture together into a pliable dough.
- Roll out the pastry on a floured surface and use it to line a 23 cm round tart case then chill for 30 minutes.
- Preheat the oven to 180°C (160° fan) / 350F / gas 4.
- Put the sugar, golden syrup, butter and vanilla extract in a saucepan and stir it over a low heat to dissolve the sugar.
- Leave the mixture to cool for 10 minutes then beat in the eggs, flour and mixed spice.
- Pour the mixture into the pastry case and arrange the pecans on top, then bake the tart for 40 minutes.

Pecan and Ginger Pie

827

- Replace the mixed spice with 1 tsp ground ginger and add 3 finely chopped pieces of stem ginger to the filling.

828

MAKES 4

Mini Apple Clafoutis

PREPARATION TIME 10 MINUTES

COOKING TIME 25 MINUTES

INGREDIENTS

2 eating apples, peeled, cored and sliced
250 ml / 9 fl. oz / 1 cup apple juice
75 g / 2 ½ oz / ⅓ cup caster (superfine) sugar
75 g / 2 ½ oz / ⅓ cup butter
300 ml / 10 ½ fl. oz / 1 ¼ cups whole milk
1 lemon, zest finely grated
2 large eggs
50 g / 1 ¾ oz / ⅓ cup plain (all purpose) flour
2 tbsp ground almonds
icing (confectioners') sugar for dusting

- Preheat the oven to 190°C (170° fan) / 375F / gas 5.
- Put the apples in a small saucepan with the apple juice and simmer gently for 10 minutes. Drain well.
- Melt the butter in a saucepan and cook over a low heat.
- Brush a little of the butter around the inside of 4 small baking dishes then sprinkle with caster sugar.
- Whisk together the milk, lemon zest and eggs with the rest of the butter.
- Sift the flour into a mixing bowl, then stir in the ground almonds and the rest of the sugar.
- Make a well in the middle of the dry ingredients and whisk in the liquid, incorporating all the flour from round the outside until you have a lump-free batter.
- Arrange the apple slices in the dishes. Pour in the batter.
- Bake the clafoutis for 25 minutes.
- Sprinkle with icing sugar just before serving.

Mini Pear Clafoutis

829

- Replace the apples with 2 peeled and sliced pears.

830

SERVES 6

Pear and Lemon Samosas

- Preheat the oven to 180°C (160° fan) / 350F / gas 4 and grease a large baking tray.
- Toss the pears and lemon zest with the sugar and breadcrumbs.
- Cut the pile of filo sheets in half then take one halved sheet and brush it with melted butter.
- Arrange a tablespoon of the filling at one end and fold the corner over, then triangle-fold it up.
- Transfer the samosa to the baking tray and repeat with the rest of the filo and filling, then brush with any leftover butter.
- Bake the samosas for 12 – 15 minutes or until the pastry is crisp and golden brown.

PREPARATION TIME 25 MINUTES

COOKING TIME 12 - 15 MINUTES

INGREDIENTS

3 pears, peeled, cored and diced
1 lemon, zest finely grated
50 g / 1 ¾ oz / ¼ cup light brown sugar
25 g / 1 oz / ⅓ cup breadcrumbs
225 g / 8 oz filo pastry
100 g / 3 ½ oz / ½ cup butter, melted

Pear and Cranberry Samosas

831

- Add 75 g of dried cranberries to the filling.

832

MAKES 18

Chocolate and Pistachio Whoopee Pies

- Preheat the oven to 190°C (170° fan) / 375F / gas 5 and line 2 large baking trays with non-stick baking mats.
- Combine the flour, ground pistachios, cocoa, baking powder, sugar, butter, eggs and vanilla extract in a bowl and whisk together for 2 minutes or until smooth.
- Spoon the mixture into a piping bag and pipe 18 walnut-sized domes onto each tray.
- Transfer the trays to the oven and bake for 10 – 15 minutes. The mixture should spread a little and the cakes will be ready when springy to the touch.
- Leave the cakes to cool on the tray then lift them off with a palette knife.
- Mix the chocolate spread with all but 1 tbsp of the ground pistachios.
- Sandwich the cakes together in pairs with the filling and sprinkle over the rest of the ground pistachios.

PREPARATION TIME 30 MINUTES

COOKING TIME 10 – 15 MINUTES

INGREDIENTS

75 g / 2 ½ oz / ½ cup self-raising flour, sifted
30 g / 1 oz / ¼ cup ground pistachio nuts
2 tbsp unsweetened cocoa powder
2 tsp baking powder
110 g / 4 oz / ½ cup caster (superfine) sugar
110 g / 4 oz / ½ cup butter, softened
2 large eggs
1 tsp vanilla extract

FOR THE FILLING:
200 g / 7 oz / 1 cup chocolate spread
50 g / 1 ¾ oz / ½ cup ground pistachio nuts

Chocolate and Almond Whoopee Pies

833

- Use ground almonds in the place of the ground pistachios and use a few drops of almond extract instead of the vanilla.

834

MAKES 18

Coffee Whoopee Pies

PREPARATION TIME 30 MINUTES

COOKING TIME 10 – 15 MINUTES

INGREDIENTS

110 g / 4 oz / ⅔ cup self-raising flour
1 tbsp instant espresso powder
1 tsp baking powder
110 g / 4 oz / ½ cup caster (superfine) sugar
110 g / 4 oz / ½ cup butter, softened
2 large eggs

FOR THE FILLING:
100 g / 3 ½ oz / ½ cup butter, softened
200 g / 7 oz / 2 cups icing (confectioners') sugar
1 tbsp instant espresso powder

- Preheat the oven to 190°C (170° fan) / 375F / gas 5 and line 2 large baking trays with non-stick baking mats.
- Combine the flour, espresso powder, baking powder, sugar, butter and eggs in a bowl and whisk together for 2 minutes or until smooth.
- Spoon the mixture into a piping bag and pipe 18 walnut-sized domes onto each tray.
- Transfer the trays to the oven and bake for 10 – 15 minutes. The mixture should spread a little whilst cooking and the cakes will be ready when springy to the touch.
- Leave the cakes to cool on the tray then lift them off with a palette knife.
- Beat the butter with the icing sugar and espresso powder until smooth, adding a few drops of water if it is too stiff.
- Sandwich the cakes in pairs with the buttercream.

Mocha Whoopee Pies

 835

- Add 1 tbsp of unsweetened cocoa powder to the cake mixture and buttercream.

836

SERVES 8

Marble Loaf Cake

PREPARATION TIME 10 MINUTES

COOKING TIME 40-50 MINUTES

INGREDIENTS

100 g / 3 ½ oz / ⅔ cup self-raising flour
1 tsp baking powder
50 g / 1 ¾ oz / ½ cup ground almonds
150 g / 5 ½ oz / ⅔ cup caster (superfine) sugar
150 g / 5 ½ oz / ⅔ cup butter, softened
3 large eggs
2 tbsp unsweetened cocoa powder

- Preheat the oven to 180°C (160° fan) / 350F / gas 4 and grease and line a loaf tin with greaseproof paper.
- Sieve the flour and baking powder into a mixing bowl then add the ground almonds, sugar, butter and eggs and whisk with an electric whisk for 4 minutes or until pale and well whipped.
- Divide the mixture into 2 bowls. Mix the cocoa powder with 2 tbsp hot water until smooth and stir it into one of the bowls.
- Spoon the mixtures into the tin, alternating between chocolate and plain, then draw a knife through the middle to marble.
- Bake for 45 - 50 minutes - the cake is ready when a toothpick inserted comes out clean.
- Transfer the cake to a wire rack to cool completely before slicing.

Chocolate Orange Marble Loaf Cake

837

- Add the finely grated zest and juice of an orange to the cake mixture before dividing.

Apple, Coconut and Pistachio Pie

Pear and Coconut Pie 839

- Use pears in place of the apples and omit the pistachio nuts.

Mango, Pistachio and Coconut Pie 840

- Use the same weight in firm mango instead of apples.

PREPARATION TIME 45 MINUTES

COOKING TIME 45 MINUTES

INGREDIENTS

125 g / 4 ½ oz / ½ cup caster (superfine) sugar
3 tbsp desiccated coconut
800 g / 12 oz bramley apples, peeled, cored and diced
2 tbsp sultanas
1 egg, beaten
50 g / 1 ¾ oz / ½ cup sweetened shredded coconut
25 g / 1 oz / ¼ cup pistachio nuts, finely chopped

FOR THE PASTRY:

300 g / 10 ½ oz / 2 cups plain (all purpose) flour
150 g / 5 ½ oz / ⅔ cup butter, chilled

- Sieve the flour into a bowl then grate in the butter and mix well.
- Mix in enough cold water to form a pliable dough then wrap it in clingfilm and chill for 30 minutes.
- Preheat the oven to 190°C (170° fan) / 375F / gas 5 and butter a 23 cm round pie tin.
- Mix the sugar and coconut together in a bowl then toss with the apples and sultanas.
- Roll out half of the pastry and use it to line the prepared pie tin.
- Pack the apples into the pastry case and wet the rim with water.
- Roll out the rest of the pastry, lay it over the apples and press down round the outside to seal.
- Cut away the excess pastry and crimp the edges with your fingers.
- Cut 2 holes in the lid for the steam to escape then bake for 45 minutes or until the pastry is cooked through underneath.
- Sprinkle the top with the shredded coconut and pistachio nuts.

841

SERVES 8

Blueberry Frangipane Tart

Raspberry Frangipane Tart

842

- Replace the blueberries with raspberries.

Blackcurrant Frangipane Tart

843

- Replace the blueberries with the same weight of blackcurrants and add an additional 30g of sugar to the filling mixture.

PREPARATION TIME 40 MINUTES

COOKING TIME 45 MINUTES

INGREDIENTS

55 g / 2 oz / ½ cup ground almonds
55 g / 2 oz / ¼ cup caster (superfine) sugar
55 g / 2 oz / ¼ cup butter, softened
1 large egg
1 tsp almond essence
225 g / 8 oz / 1 ½ cups blueberries

FOR THE PASTRY:
110 g / 4 oz / ½ cup butter, cubed and chilled
225 g / 8 oz / 1 ½ cups plain (all purpose) flour

- Rub the butter into the flour then add just enough cold water to bind the mixture together into a pliable dough.
- Roll out the pastry on a floured surface and use it to line a 23 cm / 9 " round tart case.
- Leave the pastry to chill the fridge for 30 minutes.
- Preheat the oven to 200°C (180° fan) / 400F / gas 6.
- Line the pastry case with clingfilm and fill it with baking beans, then bake for 15 minutes.
- Combine the ground almonds, sugar, butter, egg and almond essence in a bowl and whisk together for 2 minutes or until smooth, then fold in the blueberries.
- When the pastry case is ready, remove the clingfilm and baking beans and fill the case with the blueberry mixture.
- Transfer the tin to the oven and bake for 30 minutes. or until just set in the centre.

844

SERVES 6 Strawberry Swiss roll

- Preheat the oven to 180°C (160° fan) / 350F / gas 4 and grease and line a Swiss roll tin.
- Put all of the ingredients, except the jam, in a large mixing bowl and whisk together with an electric whisk for 4 minutes or until pale and well whipped.
- Spoon the mixture into the tin and spread into an even layer with a palette knife.
- Bake for 15 - 20 minutes or until the cake is springy to the touch.
- Turn the cake out onto a sheet of greaseproof paper and peel off the lining paper.
- Spread the cake with jam then roll it up tightly and leave to cool before slicing.

PREPARATION TIME 15 MINUTES

COOKING TIME 15 – 20 MINUTES

INGREDIENTS

100 g / 3 ½ oz / ⅔ cup self-raising flour
1 tsp baking powder
100 g / 3 ½ oz / ½ cup caster (superfine) sugar
100 g / 3 ½ oz/ ½ cup butter
2 large eggs
1 tsp vanilla extract
350 g / 12 oz / 1 cup strawberry jam

Marmalade Swiss Roll

845

- Replace the strawberry jam with marmalade and use the grated zest of an orange instead of the vanilla extract.

846

MAKES 12 Apple and Hazelnut Rolls

- Combine flour, yeast, caster sugar and salt. Stir the oil into 280 ml water then stir into the dry ingredients.
- Knead the dough on an oiled surface until smooth.
- Leave the dough to rest in a lightly oiled bowl, covered with clingfilm, for 1 – 2 hours.
- Knead the dough for 2 minutes, then roll into a rectangle.
- Cream the brown sugar and butter together and stir in the apple and hazelnuts.
- Spread the mixture over the dough and roll it up tightly.
- Cut into 12 slices and arrange in a round cake tin.
- Cover the rolls with oiled clingfilm and leave to prove for 1 hour or until doubled in size.
- Preheat the oven to 220°C (200° fan) / 425F / gas 7.
- Brush the rolls with egg then transfer the tray to the top shelf of the oven and bake for 35 minutes.
- Leave to cool before breaking into individual rolls.

PREPARATION TIME 2 HOURS 30 MINUTES

COOKING TIME 35 MINUTES

INGREDIENTS

400 g / 14 oz / 2 ⅔ cups strong white bread flour
½ tsp easy blend dried yeast
4 tbsp caster (superfine) sugar
1 tsp fine sea salt
1 tbsp olive oil
75 g / 2 ½ oz / ½ cup dark brown sugar
25 g / ¾ oz / 1/8 cup butter, softened
1 eating apple, peeled and grated
50 g / 1 ¾ oz / ½ cup hazelnuts (cob nuts), chopped
1 egg, beaten

Pear and Walnut Rolls

847

- Replace the apple with a grated pear and use chopped walnuts instead of hazelnuts.

848

SERVES 8

Lemon and Honey Tart

PREPARATION TIME 40 MINUTES

COOKING TIME 55 MINUTES

INGREDIENTS

100 g / 3 ½ oz / ½ cup butter, cubed
200 g / 7 oz / 1 ⅓ cups plain (all purpose) flour
2 large egg yolks
75 ml / 2 ½ fl. oz / ¼ cup runny honey
1 tsp cornflour (cornstarch)
225 ml / 8 fl. oz / ¾ cup milk
50 g / 1 ¾ oz / ⅓ cup candied lemon peel, finely chopped
3 thin lemon slices, quartered

- Preheat the oven to 200°C (180° fan) / 390F / gas 6.
- Rub the butter into the flour and add just enough cold water to bind.
- Chill for 30 minutes then roll out on a floured surface. Use the pastry to line a 23 cm round tart case.
- Prick the pastry with a fork, line with clingfilm and fill with baking beans or rice.
- Bake for 10 minutes then remove the clingfilm and baking beans and cook for a further 8 minutes to crisp.
- Reduce the oven temperature to 160°C (140° fan) / 325F / gas 3.
- Whisk together the egg yolks, honey, cornflour, milk and candied peel and pour it into the pastry case.
- Float the lemon slices on top then bake for 25 minutes or until the filling is just set in the centre.
- Leave to cool completely before slicing.

Orange and Maple Syrup Tart 849

- Replace the honey with maple syrup. Use candied orange peel instead of the lemon peel and float orange slices on top instead of lemon.

850

SERVES 8

Flourless Hazelnut Torte

PREPARATION TIME 15 MINUTES

COOKING TIME 45 MINUTES

INGREDIENTS

300 g / 10 ½ oz / 2 ½ cups hazelnuts (cob nuts)
250 g / 9 oz / 1 ¼ cups caster (superfine) sugar
1 tsp ground cinnamon
3 large eggs, separated

- Preheat the oven to 160°C (140° fan) / 325F / gas 3 and line a 23 cm round spring-form cake tin with greaseproof paper.
- Put the hazelnuts in a food processor with 3 tablespoons of the sugar and the cinnamon and process until finely ground.
- Put the rest of the sugar in a bowl with the egg yolks and whisk with an electric whisk for 4 minutes or until the mixture is very thick and creamy. Fold in the ground hazelnuts.
- Whisk the egg whites to stiff peaks in a separate bowl, making sure that the bowl and whisk are clean.
- Stir a big spoonful of egg white into the torte mixture then fold in the rest, retaining as much air as possible.
- Scrape into the prepared tin and bake for 45 minutes.
- Transfer the tin to a wire rack and leave to cool completely before unmoulding.

Hazelnut and Orange Torte 851

- Add the finely grated zest of an orange to the egg yolks before whisking.

852

SERVES 8

Sultana Sponge Cake

- Preheat the oven to 180°C (160° fan) / 350F / gas 4 and oil and line a 23 cm round cake tin with greaseproof paper.
- Combine the flour, baking powder, sugar, butter, eggs, lemon zest and sultanas in a bowl and whisk together for 2 minutes or until smooth.
- Scrape the mixture into the tin and level the top then bake for 35 - 45 minutes or until a toothpick inserted comes out clean.
- Transfer the cake to a wire rack and leave to cool completely, then remove the greaseproof paper and dust lightly with icing sugar.
- Cut into wedges and serve with blueberry and orange relish.

PREPARATION TIME 10 MINUTES

COOKING TIME 35 - 40 MINUTES

INGREDIENTS

175 g / 6 oz / 1 ¼ cups self-raising flour, sifted
1 tsp baking powder
175 g / 6 oz / ¾ cup caster (superfine) sugar
175 g / 6 oz / ¾ cup butter, softened
3 large eggs
1 lemon, zest finely grated
50 g / 1 ¾ oz / ¼ cup sultanas
50 g / 1 ¾ oz / ¼ cup golden sultanas
icing (confectioners') sugar for dusting
blueberry and orange relish to serve.

Blueberry and Orange Relish

853

- Put 250 g of blueberry jam in a saucepan with the juice of an orange and stir over a low heat until bubbling and smoothly combined. Leave to cool.

854

MAKES 8

Croissants

- Mix 50 g of the flour with the yeast and 75 ml of warm water and leave somewhere warm for 1 hour.
- Whisk the egg yolks with the milk, cream, sugar and salt, then slowly incorporate it into the yeast mixture.
- Mix in the butter cubes and remaining flour, then knead briefly on a floured surface.
- Roll out the dough, then fold into thirds and roll again. Fold it into thirds then chill for 30 minutes.
- Repeat the rolling, folding and chilling twice more.
- Roll the dough into a square, cut into quarters and cut each one diagonally into 2 triangles. Roll into croissant shapes, then transfer them to a lined baking tray. Cover the croissants with clingfilm and leave to rise for 1 hour.
- Preheat the oven to 200°C (180° fan) / 400F / gas 6.
- Brush the croissants with egg white and bake for 30 minutes, reducing the heat to 180°C (160° fan) / 350F / gas 4 after the first 10 minutes.

PREPARATION TIME 4 HOURS

COOKING TIME 30 MINUTES

INGREDIENTS

350 g / 12 oz / 2 ⅓ cups strong white bread flour
1 tsp easy blend yeast
2 large eggs, separated
75 ml / 2 ½ fl. oz / ⅓ cup milk
50 ml / 1 ¾ fl. oz / ¼ cup double (heavy) cream
2 tbsp caster (superfine) sugar, plus extra for dusting
1 tsp salt
250 g / 9 oz / 1 ¼ cups butter, chilled and cubed

Pain au Chocolat

855

- Add 1 tbsp of chopped dark chocolate to each croissant before rolling up.

856

MAKES 12

Coffee and Chocolate Chip Muffins

PREPARATION TIME 10 MINUTES

COOKING TIME 20 – 25 MINUTES

INGREDIENTS

1 large egg
120 ml / 4 fl. oz / ½ cup sunflower oil
120 ml / 4 fl. oz / ½ cup milk
375 g / 12 ½ oz / 2 ½ cups self-raising flour, sifted
1 tsp baking powder
200 g / 7 oz / ¾ cup caster (superfine) sugar
1 tbsp instant espresso powder
75 g / 2 ½ oz / ½ cup chocolate chips

- Preheat the oven to 180°C (160° fan) / 350F / gas 4 and line a 12-hole muffin tin with paper cases.
- Beat the egg in a jug with the oil and milk until well mixed.
- Mix the flour, baking powder, sugar, espresso powder and chocolate chips in a bowl, then pour in the egg mixture and stir just enough to combine.
- Spoon the mixture into the cases, then bake in the oven for 20 – 25 minutes.
- Test with a wooden toothpick, if it comes out clean, the muffins are done.
- Transfer the cakes to a wire rack and leave to cool completely.

Mocha Muffins

857

- Add 2 tbsp cocoa powder to the flour before combining with the other ingredients.

858

SERVES 8

Light Fruit Cake

PREPARATION TIME 15 MINUTES

COOKING TIME 55 MINUTES

INGREDIENTS

225 g / 8 oz / 1 ½ cups self raising flour
100 g / 3 ½ oz / ½ cup butter, cubed
100 g / 3 ½ oz / ½ cup caster (superfine) sugar
1 large egg
75 ml / 2 ½ fl. oz / ⅓ cup milk
75 g / 2 ½ oz / 1 cup raisins
75 g / 2 ½ oz / 1 cup glace cherries, chopped
75 g / 2 ½ oz / 1 cup mixed candied peel, chopped
icing (confectioners') sugar for dusting

- Preheat the oven to 180°C (160° fan) / 350F / gas 4 and line a loaf tin with non-stick baking paper.
- Sieve the flour into a mixing bowl and rub in the butter until it resembles fine breadcrumbs then stir in the sugar.
- Lightly beat the egg with the milk and stir it into the dry ingredients with the fruit until just combined then scrape the mixture into the tin.
- Bake the cake for 55 minutes or until a skewer inserted comes out clean.
- Transfer the cake to a wire rack and leave to cool completely then sprinkle with icing sugar.

Glace-Iced Light Fruit Cake

859

- Sieve 150 g of icing sugar into a bowl and stir in just enough water to make a thick, spreadable icing. Spoon the icing over the cake and decorate with glace cherries.

860

MAKES 12

Banoffee Pie

Banoffee Lime Pie

861

- Add the juice and finely grated zest of a lime to the cream before whipping.

Coconut Banoffee Pie

862

- Add 4 tbsp of desiccated coconut to the cream as you are whipping.

PREPARATION TIME 45 MINUTES

COOKING TIME 3 HOURS 20 MINUTES

INGREDIENTS

400 g / 14 oz can of condensed milk
110 g / 4 oz / ½ cup butter, cubed and chilled
225 g / 8 oz / 1 ½ cups plain (all purpose) flour
3 bananas, chopped
300 ml / 10 ½ fl. oz / 1 ¼ cups double (heavy) cream
25 g / 1 oz dark chocolate

- Put the unopened can of condensed milk in a saucepan of water and simmer for 3 hours, adding more water as necessary to ensure it doesn't boil dry. Leave to cool completely.
- Rub the butter into the flour then add just enough cold water to bind the mixture together into a pliable dough.
- Roll out the pastry on a floured surface and use it to line a 23 cm / 9 " round tart case.
- Leave the pastry to chill for 30 minutes.
- Preheat the oven to 200°C (180° fan) / 400F / gas 6.
- Line the pastry case with clingfilm and fill it with baking beans, then bake for 15 minutes.
- Remove the clingfilm and beans and return to the oven until golden brown and crisp. Leave to cool.
- Open the can of condensed milk and beat the caramel until smooth then stir in the banana.
- Spoon the mixture into the pastry case and level the top.
- Whip the cream until it holds its shape, then spoon on top of the caramel layer.
- Grate over the chocolate before serving.

MAKES 6

Chocolate Custard Pots

863

Mint Chocolate Custard Pots

864

- Stir 1 tbsp of finely shredded mint leaves into the custard at the end before spooning into the pots.

Chocolate Orange Custard Pots

865

- Add ½ tsp of orange extract instead of vanilla and the zest of half an orange as the mixture starts to thicken.

PREPARATION TIME 10 MINUTES

COOKING TIME 10 MINUTES

INGREDIENTS

450 ml / 12 ½ fl. oz / 1 ¾ cups whole milk
4 large egg yolks
75 g / 2 ½ oz / ⅓ cup caster (superfine) sugar
1 tsp cornflour (cornstarch)
1 tsp vanilla extract
2 tbsp unsweetened cocoa powder

- Put the milk in a saucepan and bring to simmering point.
- Whisk the egg yolks with the caster sugar, cornflour, vanilla extract and cocoa until thick.
- Gradually incorporate the hot milk, whisking all the time, then scrape the mixture back into the saucepan.
- Stir the custard over a low heat until it thickens then divide between 6 small glass ramekins.
- Serve warm or chill in the fridge for 2 hours and serve cold.

SERVES 8 866

Chocolate Custard Tart

- Preheat the oven to 200°C (180° fan) / 390F / gas 6.
- Rub butter into the flour and add cold water to bind.
- Chill for 30 minutes then roll out on a floured surface. Use the pastry to line a 23 cm round tart case.
- Prick the pastry with a fork, line with clingfilm and fill with baking beans or rice.
- Bake for 10 minutes then remove the clingfilm and baking beans and cook for a further 8 minutes to crisp.
- Reduce the oven temperature to 160°C (140° fan) / 325F / gas 3.
- Whisk together the egg yolks, sugar, vanilla, cornflour, cocoa and milk and strain it through a sieve into the pastry case.
- Bake the tart for 35 minutes.
- Leave to cool completely then hold a stencil over the tart and dust with icing sugar.

PREPARATION TIME 40 MINUTES

COOKING TIME 55 MINUTES

INGREDIENTS

100 g / 3 ½ oz / ½ cup butter, cubed
200 g / 7 oz / 1 ⅓ cups plain (all purpose) flour
4 large egg yolks
75 g / 2 ½ oz / ⅓ cup caster (superfine) sugar
1 tsp vanilla extract
2 tsp cornflour (cornstarch)
2 tbsp unsweetened cocoa powder
450 ml / 16 fl. oz / 1 ¾ cups milk
icing (confectioners') sugar for dusting

Mint Chocolate Custard Tart 867

- Add a few drops of peppermint essence to the custard before baking.

868

MAKES 36

Waffle Biscuits

- Beat all the ingredients together until smooth.
- Heat a pizzelle iron on the hob until very hot, then add a heaped teaspoon of batter to each waffle indent and close the two halves together.
- Cook the waffles for 30 seconds to 1 minute or until cooked through.

PREPARATION TIME 10 MINUTES

COOKING TIME 1 MINUTE

INGREDIENTS

110 g / 4 oz / ½ cup butter, softened
3 large eggs, beaten
150 g / 5 ½ oz / ⅔ cup caster (superfine) sugar
2 tsp baking powder
225 g / 8 oz / 1 ½ cups self-raising flour

Lemon Waffle Biscuits 869

- Add the finely grated zest of a lemon to the batter.

870

SERVES 8-10

Carrot and Walnut Cake

PREPARATION TIME 25 MINUTES

COOKING TIME 40-45 MINUTES

INGREDIENTS

175 g / 6 oz / 1 cup soft light brown sugar
2 large eggs
150 ml / 5 fl. oz / ⅔ cup sunflower oil
175 g / 6 oz / 1 ¼ cups stoneground wholemeal flour
3 tsp baking powder
2 tsp ground cinnamon
1 orange, zest finely grated
200 g / 7 oz / 1 ⅔ cups carrots, washed and coarsely grated
100 g / 3 ½ oz / ¾ cup walnuts, chopped, plus extra for decorating

FOR THE ICING:

110 g / 4 oz / ½ cup cream cheese
55 g / 2 oz / ¼ cup butter, softened
110 g / 4 oz / 1 cup icing (confectioners') sugar
1 tsp vanilla extract

- Preheat the oven to 190°C (170° fan) / 375F / gas 5 and line a 23 cm square cake tin with greaseproof paper.
- Whisk the sugar, eggs and oil together for 3 minutes.
- Fold in the flour, baking powder and cinnamon, followed by the orange zest, carrots and walnuts.
- Scrape into the tin and bake for 40 - 45 minutes.
- Test with a wooden toothpick, if it comes out clean, the cake is done.
- Transfer the cake to a wire rack and leave to cool.
- To make the icing, beat the cream cheese and butter together with a wooden spoon until light and fluffy then beat in the icing sugar a quarter at a time.
- Add the vanilla extract then use a whisk to whip the mixture for 2 minutes or until smooth and light.
- Spread the icing over the cake and sprinkle with some more chopped walnuts.

Carrot and Sultana Cake

 871

- Replace the walnuts with 100 g of sultanas.

872

SERVES 8

Apple, Orange and Sultana Cake

PREPARATION TIME 15 MINUTES

COOKING TIME 55 MINUTES

INGREDIENTS

225 g / 8 oz / 1 ½ cups self raising flour
100 g / 3 ½ oz / ½ cup butter, cubed
100 g / 3 ½ oz / ½ cup caster (superfine) sugar
1 large egg
50 ml / 1 ¾ fl. oz / 1/4 cup milk
1 orange, juiced and zest pared into a long strip
75 g / 2 ½ oz / 1 cup sultanas
1 apple, thinly sliced

- Preheat the oven to 180°C (160° fan) / 350F / gas 4 and line a 23 cm round cake tin with non-stick baking paper.
- Sieve the flour into a mixing bowl and rub in the butter until it resembles fine breadcrumbs then stir in the sugar.
- Lightly beat the egg with the milk and orange juice and stir it into the dry ingredients until just combined then scrape the mixture into the tin.
- Arrange the apple slices on top, then bake for 55 minutes or until a skewer inserted comes out clean.
- Transfer the cake to a wire rack and leave to cool completely then top with the strip of orange zest.

Apple, Lemon and Cranberry Cake

873

- Replace the orange with lemon and use dried cranberries in place of the sultanas.

874

MAKES 8

Orange Pain au Chocolat

- Mix 50 g of the flour with the yeast and 75 ml of warm water and leave somewhere warm for 1 hour.
- Whisk the egg yolks with the milk, cream, sugar and salt, then slowly incorporate it into the yeast mixture.
- Mix in the butter cubes and remaining flour, then knead briefly on a floured surface.
- Roll out the dough, then fold into thirds and roll again. Fold it into thirds then chill for 30 minutes.
- Repeat the rolling, folding and chilling twice more.
- Roll out the dough and cut it into 8 rectangles. Arrange the chocolate in 2 lines across each rectangle, then roll them up and transfer to a lined baking tray.
- Cover the pastries with oiled clingfilm to rise for 1 hour.
- Preheat the oven to 200°C (180° fan) / 400F / gas 6.
- Brush with egg white and bake for 30 minutes, reducing the heat to 180°C (160° fan) / 350F / gas 4 after 10 minutes.

PREPARATION TIME 4 MINUTES

COOKING TIME 30 MINUTES

INGREDIENTS

350 g / 12 oz / 2 ⅓ cups strong white bread flour
1 tsp easy blend yeast
2 large eggs, separated
75 ml / 2 ½ fl. oz / ⅓ cup milk
50 ml / 1 ¾ fl. oz / 1/4 cup double (heavy) cream
2 tbsp caster (superfine) sugar, plus extra for dusting
1 tsp salt
250 g / 9 oz / 1 1/4 cups butter, chilled and cubed
200 g / 7 oz orange-flavoured chocolate, chopped

Mint Pain au Chocolat

875

- Replace the orange-flavoured chocolate with mint-flavoured chocolate.

876

MAKES 1 LOAF

Stollen

- Rub the butter into the bread flour and stir in the yeast, sugar, salt and spice. Stir the dried fruit and egg into 250 ml of warm water and stir into the dry ingredients.
- Knead on a lightly oiled surface for 10 minutes.
- Leave the dough to rest, covered with a lightly oiled bowl, for 1 – 2 hours or until doubled in size.
- Dust the work surface with icing sugar and press the dough out into a rectangle.
- Shape the marzipan into a rectangle and roll it up inside the dough.
- Transfer the stollen to a greased baking tray and leave to prove, covered, for 45 minutes.
- Preheat the oven to 220°C (200° fan) / 430F / gas 7.
- Bake for 35 – 40 minutes or until the underneath sounds hollow when tapped.
- Leave to cool completely on a wire rack then dust liberally with icing sugar.

PREPARATION TIME 2 HOURS 30 MINUTES

COOKING TIME 35 – 40 MINUTES

INGREDIENTS

55 g / 2 oz / 1/4 cup butter, cubed
400 g / 14 oz / 2 ⅔ cups strong white bread flour, plus extra for dusting
½ tsp easy blend dried yeast
4 tbsp caster (superfine) sugar
1 tsp fine sea salt
2 tsp mixed spice
100 g / 3 ½ oz / ½ cup mixed dried fruit
1 egg, beaten
300 g / 10 ½ oz marzipan
icing sugar to dust

Chocolate Stollen

877

- Add 2 tbsp of cocoa powder to the bowl when you add the spices, then add 100 g of chopped chocolate when you roll up the marzipan.

878

**MAKES
1 LOAF**

Spiced Wholemeal Bread

Spiced Wholemeal Raisin Bread

879

- Add 150 g of raisins to the dough when you add the water.

Fruity Spiced Bread

880

- Add 4 tbsp of candied mixed peel to the dough when you add the water.

PREPARATION TIME 2 HOURS 30 MINUTES

COOKING TIME 35 – 40 MINUTES

INGREDIENTS

200 g / 7 oz / 1 ⅓ cups strong white bread flour, plus extra for dusting
200 g / 7 oz / 1 ⅓ cups stoneground wholemeal flour
½ tsp easy blend dried yeast
1 tbsp caster (superfine) sugar
1 tsp fine sea salt
½ tsp ground cloves
½ tsp ground nutmeg
½ tsp ground star anise
½ tsp ground cardamom
½ tsp ground cinnamon
1 tbsp sunflower oil

- Mix together the flours, yeast, sugar, salt and spices. Stir the oil into 280 ml of warm water and stir it into the bowl.
- Knead on a lightly oiled surface for 10 minutes or until the dough is smooth and elastic.
- Leave the dough to rest, covered with oiled clingfilm, for 1 – 2 hours or until doubled in size.
- Knead the dough for 2 more minutes, then shape it into a loaf.
- Transfer the loaf to a greased baking tray and cover again with oiled clingfilm. Leave to prove for 1 hour or until doubled in size.
- Meanwhile, preheat the oven to 220°C (200° fan) / 425F / gas 7.
- When the dough has risen, slash the top with a sharp knife.
- Transfer the tray to the top shelf of the oven then quickly throw a small cupful of water onto the floor of the oven and close the door.
- Bake for 35 – 40 minutes or until the loaf sounds hollow when tapped.

881

SERVES 8

Coconut and Raisin Cake

- Preheat the oven to 180°C (160° fan) / 350F / gas 4 and line a loaf tin with non-stick baking paper.
- Sieve the flour into a mixing bowl and rub in the butter until it resembles fine breadcrumbs then stir in the sugar and coconut.
- Lightly beat the egg with the milk and stir it into the dry ingredients with the raisins until just combined then scrape the mixture into the tin.
- Bake the cake for 55 minutes or until a skewer inserted comes out clean.
- Transfer the cake to a wire rack and leave to cool completely then sprinkle with desiccated coconut.

PREPARATION TIME 15 MINUTES

COOKING TIME 55 MINUTES

INGREDIENTS

225 g / 8 oz / 1 ½ cups self raising flour
100 g / 3 ½ oz / ½ cup butter, cubed
100 g / 3 ½ oz / ½ cup caster (superfine) sugar
3 tbsp desiccated coconut, plus extra for sprinkling
1 large egg
75 ml / 2 ½ fl. oz / ⅓ cup milk
75 g / 2 ½ oz / 1 cup raisins

Coconut and Cherry Cake

882

- Replace the raisins with halved glace cherries.

883

MAKES 12

Portuguese Custard Tarts

- Preheat the oven to 200°C (180° fan) / 390F / gas 6.
- Roll out the pastry on a floured surface and cut out 12 circles with a pastry cutter.
- Use the circles to line a 12-hole cupcake tin.
- Mix the rest of the ingredients together in a jug, then pour it into the pastry cases.
- Transfer the tin to the oven and bake for 25 minutes or until the pastry is golden brown and cooked through underneath.

PREPARATION TIME 15 MINUTES

COOKING TIME 25 MINUTES

INGREDIENTS

450 g / 1 lb all-butter puff pastry
2 large egg yolks, beaten
50 g / 1 ¾ oz / 1/4 cup caster (superfine) sugar
2 tsp cornflour (cornstarch)
225 ml / 8 fl. oz / ¾ cup milk
½ lemon, zest finely grated
½ tsp ground cinnamon

Spiced Chocolate Custard Tarts

884

- Omit the lemon zest and add 1 tbsp of cocoa powder and 1 tsp of ground mixed spice to the filling.

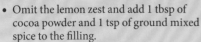

BASICS

885

SERVES 4

Creamy Green Peppercorn Sauce

PREPARATION TIME 2 MINUTES

COOKING TIME 5 MINUTES

INGREDIENTS

300 ml / 10 ½ fl. oz / 1 ¼ cups double (heavy) cream
1 tbsp Dijon mustard
1 clove of garlic, crushed
2 tbsp green peppercorns in brine, drained
lemon juice to taste

- Put all of the ingredients in a small saucepan and stir over a low heat until it starts to boil.
- Reduce the temperature a little and simmer for 2 minutes, stirring all the time.
- Turn off the heat and taste the sauce for seasoning, adding salt, pepper or lemon juice as necessary.

Creamy Caper Sauce

886

- Replace the green peppercorns with 2 tbsp of baby capers that have been drained and rinsed.

887

SERVES 4

Spiced Apple Compote

PREPARATION TIME 2 MINUTES

COOKING TIME 10 MINUTES

INGREDIENTS

3 large cooking apples, peeled and diced
3 tbsp brown sugar
1 tsp mixed spice

- Put the apples, sugar and spice in a saucepan with 4 tablespoons of cold water.
- Put a lid on the pan then cook over a gentle heat for 10 minutes, stirring occasionally.
- The compote is ready when there are no defined cubes of apple left in the mixture.
- Taste the compote and stir in a little more sugar if it is too sharp.

Spiced Pear Compote

888

- Replace the apples with 4 large ripe pears.

889

SERVES 4

Potato Wedges

- Preheat the oven to 220°C (200° fan) / 425F / gas 7.
- Put the oil in a large roasting tin and heat in the oven for 5 minutes.
- Carefully tip the potato wedges into the pan and turn to coat in the oil, then season well with salt and black pepper.
- Bake the wedges for 35 – 40 minutes, turning them every 15 minutes, until golden brown on the outside and fluffy within.
- Sprinkle with a little more sea salt and serve with spiced tomato salsa.

PREPARATION TIME 5 MINUTES

COOKING TIME 35 – 40 MINUTES

INGREDIENTS

4 tbsp olive oil
800 g / 1 lb 12 oz medium potatoes, cut into wedges

Potato Wedges and Salsa

890

- Simmer 2 chopped spring onions, 1 chopped red chilli, 100 g skinned cherry tomatoes, 1 tsp caster sugar, 2 tbsp red wine vinegar and ½ tsp black peppercorns together for 5 minutes.

891

1 LOAF

Hazelnut and Sultana Bread

- Mix together the flours, yeast, sugar, salt, hazelnuts and sultanas. Stir the butter into 280 ml of warm water.
- Stir the liquid into the dry ingredients then knead on a lightly oiled surface for 10 minutes.
- Leave the dough to rest, covered with oiled clingfilm, for 1 – 2 hours or until doubled in size.
- Knead the dough for 2 minutes, then shape into a loaf.
- Transfer the loaf to a greased baking tray and cover again with oiled clingfilm. Leave to prove for 1 hour.
- Preheat the oven to 220°C (200° fan) / 425F / gas 7.
- When the dough has risen, slash the top with a knife and dust with flour.
- Transfer the tray to the top shelf of the oven then quickly throw a small cupful of water onto the floor of the oven and close the door.
- Bake for 35 – 40 minutes.

PREPARATION TIME 2 HOURS 30 MINUTES

COOKING TIME 35 – 40 MINUTES

INGREDIENTS

200 g / 7 oz / 1 ⅓ cups strong white bread flour, plus extra for dusting
200 g / 7 oz / 1 ⅓ cups stoneground wholemeal flour
½ tsp easy blend dried yeast
1 tbsp caster (superfine) sugar
1 tsp fine sea salt
100 g / 3 ½ oz hazelnuts (cob nuts), chopped
100 g / 3 ½ oz sultanas
1 tbsp butter, melted

Walnut and Raisin Bread

892

- Replace the hazelnuts with walnuts and use raisins instead of the sultanas.

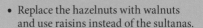

893

SERVES 8

Olive, Mushroom and Ham Loaf Cake

PREPARATION TIME 10 MINUTES

COOKING TIME 55 MINUTES

INGREDIENTS

300 g / 10 ½ oz / 2 cups self-raising flour
2 tsp baking powder
250 g / 9 oz / 1 ¼ cups butter, softened
5 large eggs
75 g / 2 ½ oz / ½ cup green olives, pitted and halved
50 g / 1 ¾ oz / ⅔ cup mushrooms, diced
75 g / 2 ½ oz ham, cubed

- Preheat the oven to 180°C (160° fan) / 350F / gas 4 and line a large loaf tin with non-stick baking paper.
- Sieve the flour and baking powder into a mixing bowl and add the butter and eggs.
- Beat the mixture with an electric whisk for 4 minutes or until smooth and well whipped.
- Fold in the olives, mushrooms and ham then scrape the mixture into the loaf tin.
- Bake for 55 minutes or until a skewer inserted comes out clean.
- Transfer the cake to a wire rack and leave to cool completely before serving.

Olive, Mushroom and Ham Cupcakes
894

- Line a 12-hole cupcake tin with paper cases and spoon in the cake mixture. Reduce the cooking time to 25 minutes.

895

SERVES 8

English Mint Sauce

PREPARATION TIME 10 MINUTES

INGREDIENTS

25 g / 1 oz / 1 ½ cups mint leaves, finely chopped
4 tbsp white wine vinegar
4 tbsp runny honey

- Put the chopped mint in a bowl and pour over 4 tablespoons of boiling water.
- Stir in the vinegar and honey with a large pinch of salt then leave to cool to room temperature.

Lamb and Mint Sauce
896

- Drizzle a little of the mint sauce over slices of hot roast lamb.

897

SERVES 4

Rice Pudding with Apricot Jam

Rice Pudding with Marmalade

898

- Replace the vanilla in the rice pudding with the finely grated zest of an orange and top with a spoonful of marmalade instead of the apricot jam.

Rice Pudding with Raspberry Jam

899

- Replace the apricot jam with raspberry jam and mix in 4-6 tbsp fresh raspberries before serving.

PREPARATION TIME 5 MINUTES

COOKING TIME 1 HOUR 30 MINUTES

....

INGREDIENTS

50 g / 1 ¾ oz / ¼ cup butter
110 g / 4 oz / ½ cup short grain rice
75 g / 2 ½ oz / ⅓ cup caster (superfine) sugar
1 vanilla pod, seeds only
1.2 litres / 2 pints / 4 ½ cups whole milk
4 tbsp apricot jam

- Preheat the oven to 140°C (120° fan) / 275F / gas 1.
- Melt the butter in a cast iron casserole dish and add the rice, sugar and vanilla seeds.
- Stir over a low heat for 2 minutes then gradually incorporate the milk and bring to a simmer.
- Cover the casserole dish and bake in the oven for 1 hour 30 minutes.
- Spoon the rice pudding into 4 bowls and top each one with a spoonful of apricot jam.

MAKES
500ML

Redcurrant Jelly

PREPARATION TIME 2 MINUTES

COOKING TIME 5 MINUTES

INGREDIENTS

450 g / 1 lb / 2 cups granulated sugar
450 g / 1 lb / 3 cups redcurrants

- Preheat the oven to 110°C (90° fan) / 225F / gas ¼.
- Put the sugar in a heatproof bowl and transfer it to the oven along with 2 small glass jars.
- Put the redcurrants in a large saucepan and cover with a lid. Heat gently for 10 minutes or until the redcurrants have burst and cooked down into a puree.
- Stir in the warmed sugar to dissolve then increase the heat and boil for 8 minutes.
- Pour the mixture into a muslin-lined colander set over a bowl to strain out the stalks and seeds.
- Ladle the jelly into the prepared jars while it's still hot, then seal the jars with clean lids or waxed paper.

Cumberland Sauce 901

- Boil 200 g of redcurrant jelly with 2 tbsp of port and the finely grated zest and juice of an orange and a lemon for 2 minutes, then cool.

 902

SERVES 4

Cherry Compote

PREPARATION TIME 2 MINUTES

COOKING TIME 12 MINUTES

INGREDIENTS

450 g / 1 lb cherries, stoned
50 g / 1 ¾ oz / ¼ cup caster (superfine) sugar
3 tbsp kirsch
½ tsp arrowroot

- Put the cherries and sugar in a saucepan with the kirsch.
- Put a lid on the pan then cook over a gentle heat for 10 minutes, stirring occasionally, until the cherries are soft.
- Slake the arrowroot with 1 tablespoon of cold water, then stir it into the compote. Continue to stir over a medium heat until the compote thickens.

Cherry and Almond Compote 903

- Replace the kirsch with amaretto and stir in 50 g of flaked almonds after the arrowroot.

904

SERVES 4

Saffron and Cardamom Rice Pudding

- Preheat the oven to 140°C (120° fan) / 275F / gas 1.
- Melt the butter in a cast iron casserole dish and add the rice, sugar and cardamom pods.
- Stir over a low heat for 2 minutes then gradually incorporate the milk, stir in the saffron and bring to a simmer.
- Cover the casserole dish and bake in the oven for 1 hour 30 minutes.

PREPARATION TIME 5 MINUTES

COOKING TIME 1 HOUR 30 MINUTES

INGREDIENTS

50 g / 1 ¾ oz / ¼ cup butter
110 g / 4 oz / ½ cup short grain rice
75 g / 2 ½ oz / ⅓ cup caster (superfine) sugar
4 cardamom pods
1.2 litres / 2 pints / 4 ½ cups whole milk
a large pinch of saffron

Orange and Cardamom Rice Pudding

905

- Omit the saffron and add the grated zest and juice of an orange when you add the milk.

906

SERVES 4

Creamy Rosemary Sauce

- Heat the butter in a small saucepan and fry the shallot, garlic and rosemary for 5 minutes without colouring.
- Pour in the wine and boil until reduced to 2 tbsp of liquid.
- Add the cream and simmer gently for 2 minutes then taste and adjust the seasoning as necessary.

PREPARATION TIME 2 MINUTES

COOKING TIME 5 MINUTES

INGREDIENTS

1 tbsp butter
1 shallot, very finely chopped
1 clove of garlic, crushed
1 tbsp rosemary leaves, finely chopped
150 ml / 5 ½ fl. oz / ⅔ cup dry white wine
300 ml / 10 ½ fl. oz / 1 ¼ cups double (heavy) cream

Creamy Madeira Sauce

907

- Replace the rosemary with ½ tsp of cracked black pepper and replace the white wine with 200 ml of Madeira.

908

MAKES
750 G

Mincemeat

Apricot and Date Mincemeat

909

- Replace half of the mixed fruit with 100 g chopped dried apricots and 75 g of chopped, stoned medjool dates.

Nutty Mincemeat

910

- Add 50g of chopped lightly toasted hazelnuts and 50 g of toasted chopped almonds.

PREPARATION TIME: 5 MINUTES

MARINATING TIME: OVERNIGHT

....

INGREDIENTS

350 g / 12 oz / 1 ¾ cups mixed dried fruit
1 large apple, peeled & grated
1 lemon, juiced and zest finely grated
1 orange, juiced and zest finely grated
100 g / 3 ½ oz / ½ cup soft brown sugar
100 g / 3 ½ oz / ⅔ cup suet
½ tsp freshly grated nutmeg
½ tsp ground cinnamon
½ tsp ground cloves
½ tsp ground ginger
50 ml / 1 ¾ fl. oz / ¼ cup brandy
50 ml / 1 ¾ fl. oz / ¼ cup port

- Mix all of the ingredients together in a large bowl and leave to marinate in the fridge overnight.

911

SERVES 4 # Carrots with Raisins and Almonds

- Separate the bulbs of the onions from the green leaves and slice both.
- Fry the bulb of the onions in the oil for 2 minutes then stir in the carrots, ras el hanout and mint and fry for 2 more minutes.
- Add the orange juice and raisins and bring to the boil, then turn down the heat add a lid and simmer very gently for 15 minutes.
- Taste the carrots and adjust the seasoning then stir in the almonds and the green part of the onions.

PREPARATION TIME 5 MINUTES

COOKING TIME 20 MINUTES

INGREDIENTS

2 salad onions
2 tbsp olive oil
4 carrots, cut into batons
1 tsp ras el hanout spice mix
½ tsp dried mint
300 ml / 10 ½ fl. oz / 1 ¼ cups orange juice
3 tbsp raisins
2 tbsp flaked (slivered) almonds

Braised Carrots with Cumin
912

- Spice the carrots with 1 tsp crushed cumin seeds instead of the ras el hanout and omit the raisins.

913

SERVES 4 # Stewed Apricots

- Put the apricots and sugar in a saucepan with the grape juice and apricot brandy.
- Put a lid on the pan then simmer over a gentle heat for 10 minutes or until the apricots are tender but still holding their shape.

PREPARATION TIME 2 MINUTES

COOKING TIME 12 MINUTES

INGREDIENTS

20 apricots, halved and stoned
50 g / 1 ¾ oz / ¼ cup caster (superfine) sugar
250 ml / 9 fl. oz / 1 cup white grape juice
3 tbsp apricot brandy

Stewed Apricots with Almond Cream
914

- Whip 300 ml double cream with 2 tbsp of icing sugar, 2 tbsp of amaretto and 75 g of crushed amaretti biscuits. Serve with the apricots.

915

SERVES 4

Smoked Mackerel and Carrot Salad

PREPARATION TIME 10 MINUTES

INGREDIENTS

2 tbsp mayonnaise
2 tbsp plain yoghurt
1 tsp Dijon mustard
½ tsp cracked black pepper
1 shallot, thinly sliced
4 carrots, julienned
2 smoked mackerel fillets, flaked
2 tbsp dill, roughly chopped

- Mix the mayonnaise with the yoghurt, mustard and pepper and season to taste with salt.
- Add the shallot, carrots and mackerel to the bowl and toss together then divide the mixture between 4 bowls and sprinkle with dill.

Mackerel and Red Cabbage Salad

916

- Replace the carrots with half a very thinly shredded red cabbage.

917

SERVES 4

Cracked Black Pepper Potato Wedges

PREPARATION TIME 5 MINUTES

COOKING TIME 35 – 40 MINUTES

INGREDIENTS

4 tbsp olive oil
800 g / 1 lb 12 oz medium potatoes, cut into wedges
1 tsp cracked black pepper

- Preheat the oven to 220°C (200° fan) / 425F / gas 7.
- Put the oil in a large roasting tin and heat in the oven for 5 minutes.
- Carefully tip the potato wedges into the pan and turn to coat in the oil, then sprinkle with the cracked pepper and season with salt.
- Bake the wedges for 35 – 40 minutes, turning them every 15 minutes, until golden brown and cooked through.

Poppy Seed Potato Wedges

918

- Replace the cracked pepper with 1 tbsp of poppy seeds.

919

SERVES 4

Stewed Rhubarb with Orange

- Put the rhubarb, sugar and orange juice and zest in a saucepan.
- Put a lid on the pan then simmer over a gentle heat for 10 minutes or until the rhubarb has cooked down to a soft compote.

PREPARATION TIME 2 MINUTES

COOKING TIME 10 MINUTES

INGREDIENTS

450 g / 1 lb rhubarb, chopped
50 g / 1 ¾ oz / ¼ cup caster (superfine) sugar
1 orange, juiced and zest finely grated

Stewed Rhubarb with Vanilla

 920

- Omit the orange juice and zest and add a split vanilla pod and a splash of water to the rhubarb before cooking.

921

SERVES 4

Gratin Dauphinoise

- Preheat the oven to 180°C (160° fan) / 350F / gas 4.
- Blanch the potatoes in boiling salted water for 5 minutes then drain well and dry off with a clean tea towel.
- Rub the inside of a baking dish with the halved garlic clove then smear the inside thickly with half of the butter.
- Pour the cream into a big mixing bowl and season well with salt and pepper. Tip in the potatoes and stir well to coat, then tip the lot into the baking dish and level the top.
- Dot over the rest of the butter then bake for 1 hour 30 minutes or until the potatoes are completely tender when you insert a skewer in the centre.

PREPARATION TIME 15 MINUTES

COOKING TIME 1 HOUR 35 MINUTES

INGREDIENTS

450 g / 1 lb maris piper potatoes, thinly sliced
1 clove of garlic, halved
50 g / 1 ¾ oz / ¼ cup butter, softened
800 ml / 1 lb 12 oz / 3 ¼ cups double (heavy) cream

Parsnip Dauphinoise

 922

- Replace the potatoes with an equal weight of parsnips and add a heaped teaspoon of Dijon mustard to the cream.

923

MAKES 175 ML

Homemade Mayonnaise

PREPARATION TIME 5 MINUTES

....

INGREDIENTS

1 large egg yolk
1 tsp Dijon mustard
2 tbsp lemon juice
150 ml / 5 ½ fl. oz / ⅔ cup
sunflower oil

- Whisk the egg yolk, mustard and 1 tablespoon of the lemon juice together with a pinch of salt until smoothly combined.
- Keep whisking as you slowly add the olive oil, drop by drop.
- When the mixture gets very thick, whisk in the rest of the lemon juice, then continue to add the oil in a thin trickle until it is all incorporated.
- Taste the mayonnaise and adjust the seasoning with a little more salt or lemon.

Basil Mayonnaise

924

- Put the finished mayonnaise in a liquidiser with a handful of basil leaves and blend until smooth.

925

SERVES 4

Stewed Apricots with Lemon Verbena

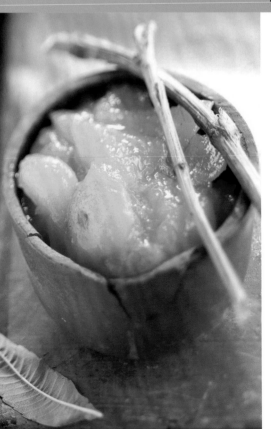

PREPARATION TIME 2 MINUTES

COOKING TIME 12 MINUTES

....

INGREDIENTS

20 apricots, peeled, stoned and sliced
50 g / 1 ¾ oz / ¼ cup caster
(superfine) sugar
100 ml / 3 ½ fl. oz / ½ cup white
grape juice
a small bunch lemon verbena, tied
with string

- Put the apricots and sugar in a saucepan with the grape juice and verbena.
- Put a lid on the pan then simmer over a gentle heat for 8 minutes or until the apricots are tender but still holding their shape.
- Remove the lid and cook , stirring occasionally, until the liquid evaporates and the apricots are really soft.
- Remove the verbena before serving.

Apricot and Lemon Verbena Sundae

926

- Layer the stewed apricots in a sundae glass with vanilla ice cream and cubes of lemon drizzle cake. Top with whipped cream and garnish with a lemon verbena leaf.

927

SERVES 6

Vanilla Custard

Bay Leaf Custard

928

- Replace the vanilla pod with 2 fresh bay leaves.

Chocolate Custard

929

- As the custard thickens add 100g dark chocolate broken into small pieces and stir constantly until melted.

PREPARATION TIME 25 MINUTES

COOKING TIME 10 MINUTES

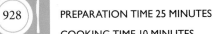

INGREDIENTS

450 ml / 12 ½ fl. oz / 1 ¾ cups whole milk
1 vanilla pod, split lengthways
4 large egg yolks
75 g / 2 ½ oz / ⅓ cup caster (superfine) sugar

- Combine the milk and vanilla pod in a saucepan and bring to simmering point, then turn off the heat and leave to infuse for 20 minutes.
- Whisk the egg yolks with the caster sugar until thick.
- Gradually incorporate the hot milk, whisking all the time, then scrape the mixture back into the saucepan.
- Stir the custard over a low heat until it just starts to thicken, then put the base of the pan in cold water and continue to stir until the custard cools a little and the danger of curdling has passed.

930

SERVES 6

Mashed Swede

PREPARATION TIME 5 MINUTES

COOKING TIME 35 MINUTES

INGREDIENTS

900 g / 2 lb swede, peeled and cubed
150 g / 5 ½ oz / ⅔ cup butter, cubed
¼ tsp nutmeg, freshly grated
chopped parsley to garnish

- Cook the swede in boiling salted water for 30 minutes or until tender all the way through.
- Tip the swede into a colander and leave to drain.
- Put the saucepan back on the heat and melt the butter, then take it off the heat, add the swede and mash with a potato masher.
- Stir in the nutmeg then season to taste with salt and plenty of black pepper.
- Spoon into serving bowls and sprinkle with parsley.

Mashed Swede with Horseradish

931

- Add 2 tsp of horseradish sauce to the swede instead of the nutmeg.

932

SERVES 4

Roasted New Potatoes

PREPARATION TIME 5 MINUTES

COOKING TIME 55 MINUTES

INGREDIENTS

800 g / 1 lb 12 oz new potatoes,
halved if large
6 tbsp olive oil
Szechwan pepper and rosemary salt
to season
soured cream for dipping

- Preheat the oven to 200°C (180° fan) / 400F / gas 6.
- Boil the potatoes in salted water for 10 minutes then drain well and leave to steam dry for 2 minutes.
- Put the oil in a large roasting tin in the oven to heat for 2 minutes.
- Add the potatoes to the roasting tin and stir to coat in the oil.
- Roast the potatoes for 45 minutes or until golden brown then sprinkle with Szechwan pepper and rosemary salt.
- Serve with soured cream for dipping.

Szechwan Pepper and Rosemary Salt

933

- Mix 2 tbsp sea salt flakes with 2 tsp dried rosemary and 2 tsp crushed Szechwan peppercorns. Leave to infuse for 2 days, then use for seasoning.

934

SERVES 4

Banana and Mango Compote

- Put the mango, banana and grape juice in a saucepan then cover with a lid and cook over a gentle heat for 10 minutes, stirring occasionally.
- Blend to a smooth puree, then add honey to taste.

PREPARATION TIME 5 MINUTES

COOKING TIME 10 MINUTES

INGREDIENTS

2 mangos, peeled and cubed
2 bananas, peeled and chopped
200 ml / 7 fl. oz / ¾ cup white grape juice
1 – 2 tbsp runny honey

Banana and Mango Breakfast Pots | 935

- Spoon the compote into glasses and top with a layer of Greek yoghurt and a sprinkling of granola.

936

SERVES 4

Pear and Lemon Compote

- Put the pears and sugar in a saucepan with 4 tablespoons of cold water.
- Put a lid on the pan then cook over a gentle heat for 10 minutes, stirring occasionally.
- The compote is ready when there are no defined cubes of pear left in the mixture.
- Stir in the lemon juice and leave to cool.

PREPARATION TIME 2 MINUTES

COOKING TIME 10 MINUTES

INGREDIENTS

4 pears, peeled and diced
2 tbsp caster (superfine) sugar
1 lemon, juiced

Pear and Banana Compote | 937

- Add 2 sliced bananas to the pears before cooking.

938

SERVES 4

Strawberry Compote

Strawberry and Apple Compote

 939

- Add a chopped bramley apple to the strawberries and double the amount of sugar.

Strawberry and Raspberry compote

 940

- Replace half the strawberries with raspberries for a more tart flavour.

PREPARATION TIME 2 MINUTES

COOKING TIME 10 MINUTES

....

INGREDIENTS

250 g / 10 ½ oz / 1 ⅔ cups strawberries, chopped
2 tbsp caster (superfine) sugar
1 lemon, juiced

- Put the strawberries and sugar in a saucepan.
- Put a lid on the pan then cook over a gentle heat for 10 minutes, stirring occasionally.
- The compote is ready when there are no defined cubes of strawberry left in the mixture.
- Stir in the lemon juice and leave to cool.

941

SERVES 4

Apple, Banana and Nutmeg Compote

- Put the apples, banana, sugar and nutmeg in a saucepan with 4 tablespoons of cold water.
- Put a lid on the pan then cook over a gentle heat for 10 minutes, stirring occasionally.
- Blend the compote until smooth then spoon into bowls and sprinkle with a little more nutmeg.

PREPARATION TIME 2 MINUTES

COOKING TIME 10 MINUTES

INGREDIENTS

2 large cooking apples, peeled and diced
2 bananas, peeled and chopped
3 tbsp brown sugar
½ tsp nutmeg, freshly grated, plus extra for sprinkling

Apple, Pear and Nutmeg Compote

942

- Replace the bananas with a chopped pear.

943

MAKES
4 JARS

Apple and Sultana Chutney

- Put the cloves, cinnamon and bay in a square of muslin, then fold up the sides and tie with string.
- Put it in a large preserving pan with the rest of the ingredients and 1 tsp of salt and bring to the boil.
- Turn down the heat a little and simmer for 1 hour, stirring occasionally, or until you can make a trench with the spoon that doesn't immediately fill up with liquid.
- Discard the spice bag and decant the chutney into sterilised jars. Seal while hot.

PREPARATION TIME 5 MINUTES

COOKING TIME 1 HOUR

INGREDIENTS

6 cloves
1 cinnamon stick
1 bay leaf
2 onions, chopped
2 bramley apples, peeled and diced
4 eating apples, peeled and diced
100 g / 3 ½ oz / ½ cup sultanas
1 tbsp grated ginger
400 ml / 14 fl. oz / 1 ⅔ cups white wine vinegar
400 g / 14 oz / 1 ¾ cups caster (superfine) sugar

Pear and Sultana Chutney

944

- Replace the eating apples with 4 pears, peeled and diced.

945

SERVES 4

Cinnamon and Honey Porridge

PREPARATION TIME 4 MINUTES

COOKING TIME 8 MINUTES

....

INGREDIENTS

600 ml / 1 pint / 2 ½ cups whole milk, plus extra to serve
125 g / 4 ½ oz / 1 ¼ cups rolled porridge oats
½ tsp ground cinnamon
4 tbsp runny honey, plus extra to serve

- Mix the milk with the oats and cinnamon. Stir the mixture over a medium heat until it starts to simmer.
- Add the honey and a pinch of salt then reduce the heat to its lowest setting and continue to stir for 4 minutes.
- Divide the porridge between 4 bowls and allow everyone to add their own milk and honey to taste.

946

MAKES 700 ML

Strawberry Jam

PREPARATION TIME 10 MINUTES

COOKING TIME 30 – 45 MINUTES

....

INGREDIENTS

450 g / 1 lb / 2 cups granulated sugar
450 g / 1 lb / 3 cups strawberries, quartered
1 lemon, juiced

- Preheat the oven to 110°C (90° fan) / 225F / gas ¼.
- Put the sugar in a heatproof bowl and transfer it to the oven along with 2 glass jars.
- Put the strawberries and lemon juice in a large saucepan and cover with a lid. Heat gently for 10 minutes or until they simmer and soften in the juice they produce.
- Stir in the warmed sugar to dissolve then increase the heat and boil until the mixture reads 107°C / 225F on a sugar thermometer.
- Leave the jam to cool and thicken for 10 minutes then ladle into the prepared jars and seal with clean lids or waxed paper.

947

MAKES 2 JARS

Lemon Curd

- Dissolve the cornflour in the lemon juice and put it in a saucepan with the rest of the ingredients.
- Stir constantly over a medium heat to melt the butter and dissolve the sugar. After 6 or 7 minutes the mixture should thicken.
- Continue to stir until it starts to bubble then spoon it into sterilised jars and seal with clean lids or waxed paper.

PREPARATION TIME 5 MINUTES

COOKING TIME 5 MINUTES

INGREDIENTS

2 tsp cornflour (cornstarch)
4 lemons, juiced
4 large eggs, beaten
225 g / 8 oz / 1 cup butter
175 g / 6 oz / ¾ cup caster (superfine) sugar

Mixed Herb Mayonnaise

948

MAKES 175 ML

PREPARATION TIME 5 MINUTES

INGREDIENTS

1 large egg yolk
1 tsp Dijon mustard
2 tbsp lemon juice
150 ml / 5 ½ fl. oz / ⅔ cup sunflower oil

1 tbsp flat leaf parsley, finely chopped
1 tbsp chives, finely chopped
1 tbsp French tarragon, finely chopped

- Whisk the egg yolk, mustard and 1 tablespoon of the lemon juice together with a pinch of salt until smoothly combined.
- Keep whisking as you slowly add the olive oil, drop by drop.
- When the mixture gets very thick, whisk in the rest of the lemon juice, then continue to add the oil in a thin trickle until it is all incorporated.
- Taste the mayonnaise and adjust the seasoning with a little more salt or lemon then stir in the herbs.

Stewed Rhubarb and Strawberries

949

SERVES 6

PREPARATION TIME 2 MINUTES

COOKING TIME 10 MINUTES

INGREDIENTS

450 g / 1 lb rhubarb, chopped
200 g / 7 oz strawberries, halved
50 g / 1 ¾ oz / ¼ cup caster (superfine) sugar

1 orange, juiced

- Put the rhubarb, sugar and orange juice in a saucepan.
- Put a lid on the pan then simmer over a gentle heat for 10 minutes or until the fruit is very tender.

950

SERVES 4

Lavender and Honey Rice Pudding

PREPARATION TIME 25 MINUTES

COOKING TIME 1 HOUR 30 MINUTES

....

INGREDIENTS

1.2 litres / 2 pints / 4 ½ cups whole milk
3 sprigs of lavender
50 g / 1 ¾ oz / ¼ cup butter
110 g / 4 oz / ½ cup short grain rice
75 g / 2 ½ oz / ¼ cup runny honey, plus extra to serve

- Preheat the oven to 140°C (120° fan) / 275F / gas 1.
- Warm the milk in a saucepan with the lavender then leave to infuse for 20 minutes.
- Melt the butter in a cast iron casserole dish and add the rice.
- Stir over a low heat for 2 minutes then gradually incorporate the hot milk and honey.
- Cover the dish and bake in the oven for 1 hour 30 minutes.
- Discard the skin on top of the pudding and divide the rice between 4 warm bowls.
- Serve with extra honey to spoon over at the table.

Rose and Honey Rice Pudding   951

- Omit the lavender and add 1 tbsp of rose water to the milk.

952

SERVES 4

Mustard Sauce

PREPARATION TIME 20 MINUTES

COOKING TIME 45 MINUTES

....

INGREDIENTS

2 tbsp butter
2 tbsp plain (all-purpose) flour
600 ml / 1 pint / 2 ½ cups vegetable stock
2 tbsp Dijon mustard

- Melt the butter in a saucepan then stir in the flour.
- Gradually whisk in the stock a little at a time until it is all incorporated.
- Cook the sauce over a low heat, stirring constantly, until the mixture thickens. Beat vigorously to remove any lumps.
- Take the pan off the heat and stir in the mustard then season to taste with salt and pepper.

Parsley Liquor   953

- Omit the mustard and stir 4 tbsp of chopped parsley into the sauce at the end.

954

**MAKES
175 ML**

Tartar Sauce

- Whisk the egg yolk, mustard and 1 tablespoon of the lemon juice together with a pinch of salt until smoothly combined.
- Keep whisking as you slowly add the olive oil, drop by drop.
- When the mixture gets very thick, whisk in the rest of the lemon juice, then continue to add the oil in a thin trickle until it is all incorporated.
- Stir in the herbs, capers and gherkins then adjust the seasoning with a little more salt or lemon juice as necessary.

PREPARATION TIME 5 MINUTES

INGREDIENTS

1 large egg yolk
1 tsp Dijon mustard
2 tbsp lemon juice
150 ml / 5 ½ fl. oz / ⅔ cup sunflower oil
1 tbsp flat leaf parsley, finely chopped
1 tbsp French tarragon, finely chopped
1 tbsp capers, finely chopped
6 gherkins, finely chopped

Quick Tartar Sauce

955

- Stir the herbs, capers and gherkins into 200 g of shop-bought mayonnaise.

956

SERVES 4

Griddled Asparagus

- Soak 4 wooden skewers in a bowl of water for 20 minutes.
- Heat a griddle pan until smoking hot.
- Skewer 4 asparagus spears together with each skewer and brush them liberally with olive oil.
- Sprinkle with plenty of sea salt and black pepper, then cook for 4 minutes on each side on the griddle.
- Squeeze over the lemon and serve immediately.

PREPARATION TIME 25 MINUTES

COOKING TIME 8 MINUTES

INGREDIENTS

16 asparagus spears
3 tbsp olive oil
½ lemon

Roasted Asparagus

957

- Alternatively you can roast the asparagus at 200⁰C for 15 minutes, turning halfway through.

958
SERVES 4

Boiled Sprouts

PREPARATION TIME 15 MINUTES

COOKING TIME 5 - 6 MINUTES

INGREDIENTS

450 g / 1 lb Brussels sprouts

- Bring a large pan of salted water to the boil.
- Trim the bottom off each sprout and remove the outer leaves, then score a cross into the base to help them to cook more evenly.
- Tip the sprouts into the water and boil for 5 – 6 minutes or until cooked al dente.
- Drain well and season with salt and pepper

Buttered Sprouts 959
- Toss the sprouts with 2 tbsp of melted butter after draining.

960
SERVES 4

Apple and Lemon Compote

PREPARATION TIME 2 MINUTES

COOKING TIME 10 MINUTES

INGREDIENTS

2 large cooking apples, peeled and diced
2 eating apples, peeled and diced
3 tbsp caster (superfine) sugar
1 lemon, juiced and zest finely grated

- Put all of the ingredients in a saucepan, then cover with a lid and cook over a gentle heat for 10 minutes, stirring occasionally.
- The compote is ready when there are no defined cubes of apple left in the mixture.
- Taste the compote and stir in a little more sugar if it is too sharp.

Apple Fool 961
- Leave the compote to cool then fold it into 200 g of Greek Yoghurt and 200 ml whipped cream.

962

MAKES
400 G

Homemade Chocolate Spread

Homemade Chocolate Hazelnut Spread

963

- Heat the cream with 100 g of chopped, toasted hazelnuts then strain out the pieces through a sieve before adding the chocolate.

Salted Chocolate Spread

964

- Add ¾ tsp of Kosher salt at the same time as adding the chocolate.

PREPARATION TIME 5 MINUTES

COOKING TIME 45 MINUTES

INGREDIENTS

200 ml / 7 fl. oz / ¾ cup
double (heavy) cream
200 g / 7 oz dark chocolate,
minimum 60% cocoa solids,
chopped

- Heat the cream until it starts to simmer, then pour in the chopped chocolate and stir until the mixture has cooled and thickened.
- Leave to cool to room temperature for a spreadable consistency.

965

**MAKES
500 ML**

Barbecue Sauce

PREPARATION TIME 5 MINUTES

COOKING TIME 15 MINUTES

....

INGREDIENTS

2 tbsp olive oil
1 small onion, grated
3 cloves of garlic, crushed
1 tbsp ginger, finely grated
1 tsp mixed spice
200 ml / 7 fl. oz / ¾ cup tomato
passata
200 ml / 7 fl. oz / ¾ cup apple juice
3 tbsp dark brown sugar
3 tbsp balsamic vinegar
1 tbsp Worcester sauce
1 tbsp Dijon mustard

- Heat the oil in a saucepan and fry the onion, garlic and ginger for 3 minutes without colouring.
- Stir in the mixed spice then add the rest of the ingredients with a large pinch of salt and bring to the boil.
- Turn down the heat and simmer for 10 minutes or until the sauce is thick and smooth.
- Spoon into a jar and seal whilst warm.

Barbecue Chicken Wings

966

- Marinate 12 chicken wings in the sauce overnight then roast at 200°C for 45 minutes.

967

SERVES 4

Cauliflower Cheese

PREPARATION TIME 10 MINUTES

COOKING TIME 40 MINUTES

....

INGREDIENTS

400 g / 14 oz cauliflower, broken into
florets
2 tbsp butter
2 tbsp plain (all-purpose) flour
600 ml / 1 pint / 2 ½ cups milk
1 tbsp Dijon mustard
150 g / 5 ½ oz Cheddar cheese, grated

- Preheat the oven to 180°C (160° fan) / 350F / gas 4.
- Cook the cauliflower in boiling, salted water for 6 minutes or until al dente, then drain well.
- Melt the butter in a medium saucepan then stir in the flour.
- Gradually whisk in the milk a little at a time until it is all incorporated.
- Cook the sauce over a low heat, stirring constantly, until the mixture thickens. Beat vigorously to remove any lumps.
- Take the pan off the heat and stir in the cauliflower, mustard and half of the cheese. Season to taste with salt and pepper.
- Spoon the mixture into a baking dish and sprinkle over the rest of the cheese.
- Bake for 25 minutes or until the top is golden brown.

Cauliflower and Bacon Cheese

968

- Stir 4 chopped rashers of streaky bacon into the sauce with the cauliflower.

969 · MAKES 6 — Yorkshire Puddings

- Preheat the oven to 230°C (210° fan) / 450F / gas 8.
- Put a teaspoon of dripping into each hole of a deep 6-hole muffin tin and put it in the oven to heat.
- Put the flour in a large jug with a pinch of salt and make a well in the centre.
- Break in the eggs and pour in the milk then use a whisk to gradually incorporate all of the flour from round the outside.
- Carefully take the muffin tin out of the oven and immediately divide the batter between the holes.
- Return the tin to the oven and bake for 25 minutes without opening the oven door.
- Serve straight away.

PREPARATION TIME 5 MINUTES

COOKING TIME 25 MINUTES

INGREDIENTS

6 tsp beef dripping
75 g / 2 ½ oz / ½ cup plain (all purpose) flour
2 large eggs
100 ml / 3 ½ oz / ½ cup whole milk

Yorkshire Puddings with Golden Syrup · 970

- Any leftover puddings make a tasty dessert – drizzle with golden syrup and serve with pouring cream.

971 · MAKES 1 LOAF — White Cob Loaf

- Mix together the flour, yeast, sugar and salt. Stir the oil into 280 ml of warm water then stir it into the dry ingredients.
- Knead the mixture on a lightly oiled surface for 10 minutes or until smooth and elastic.
- Leave the dough to rest in an oiled bowl, covered with oiled clingfilm, for 1 – 2 hours or until doubled in size.
- Knead for 2 more minutes then shape the dough into a round loaf on an oiled baking tray.
- Cover with oiled clingfilm and leave to prove for 1 hour or until doubled in size.
- Preheat the oven to 220°C (200° fan) / 425F / gas 7.
- Dust the cob with flour then transfer the tray to the top shelf of the oven. Quickly throw a small cupful of water onto the oven floor and close the door.
- Bake for 35 - 40 minutes.
- Transfer to a wire rack and leave to cool.

PREPARATION TIME 2 HOURS 30 MINUTES

COOKING TIME 35 – 40 MINUTES

INGREDIENTS

400 g / 14 oz / 2 ⅔ cups strong white bread flour, plus extra for dusting
½ tsp easy blend dried yeast
1 tbsp caster (superfine) sugar
1 tsp fine sea salt
1 tbsp olive oil

Cheese Bread · 972

- Add 150 g grated Cheddar to the flour before adding the water and sprinkle the loaf with another 50 g of grated Cheddar instead of the flour just before baking.

973

MAKES 6

Summer Fruit Custard Pots

Apricot and Almond Custard Pots

974

- Replace the summer fruit with 4 stoned, chopped apricots and use ½ tsp of almond extract instead of the vanilla extract.

Pineapple Custard Pots

975

- Replace the summer fruit with crushed drained pineapple and sprinkle with 4 tbsp of desiccated coconut before mixing with the custard.

PREPARATION TIME 10 MINUTES

COOKING TIME 10 MINUTES

INGREDIENTS

450 ml / 12 ½ fl. oz / 1 ¾ cups whole milk
4 large egg yolks
75 g / 2 ½ oz / ⅓ cup caster (superfine) sugar
1 tsp cornflour (cornstarch)
1 tsp vanilla extract
150 g / 5 ½ oz / 1 cup mixed summer fruit
25 g / 1 oz / ⅓ cup flaked (slivered) almonds
6 sprigs of redcurrants to garnish
icing (confectioners') sugar for sprinkling

- Put the milk in a saucepan and bring to simmering point.
- Whisk the egg yolks with the caster sugar, cornflour and vanilla extract until thick.
- Gradually incorporate the hot milk, whisking all the time, then scrape the mixture back into the saucepan.
- Stir the custard over a low heat until it thickens then stir in the summer fruit and divide between 6 small jars.
- Top each one with a few flaked almonds, a sprig of redcurrants and a sprinkling of icing sugar.
- Serve warm or chill in the fridge for 2 hours and serve cold.

976
SERVES 6 # Lemon Custard

- Combine the milk and lemon zest in a saucepan and bring to simmering point, then turn off the heat and leave to infuse for 20 minutes. Strain the milk through a sieve to remove the lemon zest.
- Whisk the egg yolks with the caster sugar until thick. Gradually incorporate the hot milk, whisking all the time, then scrape the mixture back into the saucepan.
- Stir the custard over a low heat until it just starts to thicken, then put the base of the pan in cold water and continue to stir until the custard cools a little and the danger of curdling has passed.

PREPARATION TIME 25 MINUTES

COOKING TIME 10 MINUTES

INGREDIENTS

450 ml / 12 ½ fl. oz / 1 ¾ cups whole milk
2 lemons, zest grated
4 large egg yolks
75 g / 2 ½ oz / ⅓ cup caster (superfine) sugar

Lemon Custard Pots
977

- Add 2 tsp of cornflour to the egg yolks before whisking. Pour the custard into ramekins and chill in the fridge for 2 hours before serving.

978
MAKES 1 LOAF # Cinnamon and Raisin Bread

- Mix together the flour, yeast, sugar, cinnamon , salt and raisins. Stir the butter into 280 ml of warm water.
- Stir the liquid into the dry ingredients then knead on a lightly oiled surface for 10 minutes.
- Leave the dough to rest, covered with oiled clingfilm, for 1 – 2 hours or until doubled in size.
- Knead the dough for 2 minutes, then shape into a loaf.
- Transfer the dough to a greased loaf tin and cover again with oiled clingfilm. Leave to prove for 1 hour or until doubled in size.
- Preheat the oven to 220°C (200° fan) / 425F / gas 7.
- When the dough has risen, brush with beaten egg.
- Transfer the tin to the top shelf of the oven then quickly throw a small cupful of water onto the floor of the oven and close the door.
- Bake for 35 – 40 minutes.

PREPARATION TIME 2 HOURS 30 MINUTES

COOKING TIME 35 – 40 MINUTES

INGREDIENTS

400 g / 14 oz / 2 ⅔ cups strong white bread flour, plus extra for dusting
½ tsp easy blend dried yeast
1 tbsp caster (superfine) sugar
1 tsp ground cinnamon
1 tsp fine sea salt
100 g / 3 ½ oz / ½ cup raisins
1 tbsp butter, melted
1 egg, beaten

Cinnamon, Orange and Cranberry Bread
979

- Replace the raisins with dried cranberries and add the finely grated zest of an orange.

980

SERVES 4

Dill Dressing

PREPARATION TIME 5 MINUTES

INGREDIENTS

4 tbsp mayonnaise
4 tbsp plain yoghurt
2 tbsp lemon juice
2 tbsp fresh dill, finely chopped

- Mix all of the ingredients together and season to taste with salt and pepper.

Smoked Salmon with Dill Dressing

981

- For a simple starter, serve the dressing with slices of cold-smoked salmon and some toasted soda bread.

982

SERVES 4

Semolina Roasted Potatoes with Rosemary

PREPARATION TIME 5 MINUTES

COOKING TIME 55 MINUTES

INGREDIENTS

800 g / 1 lb 12 oz potatoes, cut into chunks
3 sprigs of rosemary
3 tbsp semolina (cream of wheat)
6 tbsp olive oil
wholegrain mustard sauce for dipping

- Preheat the oven to 200°C (180° fan) / 400F / gas 6.
- Boil the potatoes and rosemary in salted water for 10 minutes then drain well and leave to steam dry for 2 minutes.
- Toss the potatoes with the semolina to coat and season well with salt and pepper.
- Put the oil in a roasting tin in the oven to heat for 5 minutes. Add the potatoes to the roasting tin and spoon over the hot oil.
- Roast the potatoes for 45 minutes or until golden brown, turning every 15 minutes.
- Serve with wholegrain mustard sauce for dipping.

Wholegrain Mustard Sauce

983

- Mix 2 tbsp of mayonnaise with 2 tbsp of plain yoghurt and stir in 2 tsp of wholegrain mustard. Serve with the potatoes for dipping.

984

MAKES 450 ML

Tomato Pasta Sauce

- Heat the oil in a frying pan and fry the onion and garlic without colouring for 8 minutes.
- Stir in the canned tomatoes, oregano and 150 ml of water and simmer gently for 30 minutes.
- Remove and discard the oregano and season to taste with salt and pepper.
- Blend the sauce until smooth with a liquidiser or emersion blender, then reheat when ready to serve.

PREPARATION TIME 5 MINUTES

COOKING TIME 45 MINUTES

INGREDIENTS

4 tbsp olive oil
1 small onion, finely chopped
3 cloves of garlic, crushed
400 g / 14 oz / 1 ¾ cups canned tomatoes, chopped
a small bunch of oregano

Tomato Pizza Sauce

985

- Cook as above without adding the water. After blending, leave to cool to room temperature before using.

986

SERVES 4

Potato Wedges with Oregano

- Preheat the oven to 220°C (200° fan) / 425F / gas 7.
- Put the oil in a large roasting tin and heat in the oven for 5 minutes.
- Carefully tip the potato wedges and oregano into the pan and turn to coat in the oil, then season well with salt and black pepper.
- Bake the wedges for 45 minutes, turning them every 15 minutes, until golden on the outside and fluffy within, then spoon into a warm serving dish.

PREPARATION TIME 5 MINUTES

COOKING TIME: 35 – 40 MINUTES

INGREDIENTS

4 tbsp olive oil
800 g / 1 lb 12 oz medium potatoes, cut into wedges
a few sprigs of oregano

Parsnip Wedges with Oregano

987

- Replace the potatoes with 4 parsnips, halved and cut into wedges.

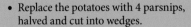

988

MAKES 2

Rustic Baguettes

PREPARATION TIME 2 HOURS 30 MINUTES

COOKING TIME 20 – 30 MINUTES

....

INGREDIENTS

350 g / 12 ½ oz / 1 ½ cups strong white bread flour, plus extra for dusting
50 g / 1 ¾ oz / ⅓ cup stoneground wholemeal flour
½ tsp easy blend dried yeast
1 tbsp caster (superfine) sugar
1 tsp fine sea salt
1 tbsp olive oil
280 ml / 9 ½ fl. oz / 1 cup warm water

- Mix the flours, yeast, sugar and salt. Stir the oil into the warm water then stir it into the dry ingredients.
- Knead on a lightly oiled surface for 10 minutes.
- Leave the dough to rest, covered with oiled clingfilm, for 1 – 2 hours or until doubled in size.
- Roll the dough into 2 long baguettes and squeeze the ends into a point.
- Transfer the baguettes to a greased baking tray then cover with oiled clingfilm and leave to prove for 1 hour.
- Preheat the oven to 220°C (200° fan) / 425F / gas 7.
- Dust the baguettes with a little flour and make diagonal slashes along the top with a sharp knife.
- Transfer the tray to the top shelf of the oven then quickly throw a small cupful of water onto the oven floor and close the door.
- Bake for 20 – 30 minutes.

Baguette Rolls

989

- Shape the dough into 8 long rolls and reduce the cooking time to 15 minutes.

990

MAKES 8

Granary Rolls

PREPARATION TIME 2 HOURS 30 MINUTES

COOKING TIME 20 - 25 MINUTES

....

INGREDIENTS

200 g / 7 oz / 1 ⅓ cups strong white bread flour, plus extra for dusting
200 g / 7 oz / 1 ⅓ cups malted granary flour
½ tsp easy blend dried yeast
1 tbsp caster (superfine) sugar
1 tsp fine sea salt
3 tbsp sunflower seeds
3 tbsp hemp seeds
1 tbsp sunflower oil

- Mix the flours, yeast, sugar, salt and seeds. Stir the oil into 280 ml of warm water and stir it into the bowl.
- Knead on a lightly oiled surface for 10 minutes.
- Leave the dough to rest, covered with oiled clingfilm, for 1 – 2 hours or until doubled in size.
- Knead the dough for 2 more minutes, then shape into 8 large rolls.
- Transfer the rolls to a greased baking tray and cover again with oiled clingfilm. Leave to prove for 1 hour.
- Preheat the oven to 220°C (200° fan) / 425F / gas 7.
- When the dough has risen, slash the tops with a sharp knife.
- Transfer the tray to the top shelf of the oven then quickly throw a small cupful of water onto the floor of the oven and close the door.
- Bake for 20 - 25 minutes.

Walnut Rolls

991

- Replace the seeds with 100 g of chopped walnuts.

992

SERVES 4

Hummus

Sundried Tomato Hummus

993

- Add 150 g of sundried tomatoes in oil to the food processor with the chickpeas.

Chilli Hummus

994

- Add a finely minced de-seeded red chilli for a more spicy flavour.

PREPARATION TIME 10 MINUTES

INGREDIENTS

400 g / 14 oz / 2 ⅔ cups canned chickpeas (garbanzo beans), drained
6 tbsp olive oil
1 tbsp tahini paste
1 lemon, juiced
1 clove of garlic, crushed
¼ tsp ground cumin
coriander (cilantro) leaves to garnish
pita bread for dipping

- Reserve a few chickpeas for a garnish and put the rest in a food processor with the other ingredients, except for the cumin and coriander.
- Blend to a smooth puree, then season to taste with salt and pepper.
- Spoon into a bowl and sprinkle with cumin. Garnish with coriander leaves and the reserved chickpeas and serve with pita bread for dipping.

995

SERVES 4

Roasted Carrot Hummus

Broad Bean Hummus

996

- Boil 300 g of frozen broad beans for 6 minutes, then drain well and add to the food processor in place of the roasted carrots.

Red Pepper and Carrot Hummus

997

- Add a roughly diced large red pepper to the roasting tin halfway through cooking and blend with the ingredients.

PREPARATION TIME 15 MINUTES

COOKING TIME 30 MINUTES

INGREDIENTS

3 large carrots, diced
4 tbsp olive oil
1 tbsp tahini paste
1 lemon, juiced
1 clove of garlic, crushed
grissini for dipping

- Preheat the oven to 190°C (170° fan) / 375F / gas 5.
- Toss the carrots with the olive oil in a large roasting tin and season with salt and pepper.
- Roast the carrots for 30 minutes or until tender, stirring half way through.
- Transfer the carrots to a food processor with the rest of the ingredients and blend to a smooth puree.
- Season to taste with salt and pepper and serve with grissini for dipping.

998

**MAKES
700 ML**

Apricot Jam

- Mix the apricots and sugar together and leave to macerate for 4 hours or overnight.
- Transfer the mixture to a large saucepan and heat gently whilst stirring to dissolve the sugar then add the almond extract.
- Increase the heat and boil without stirring until the mixture reads 107°C / 225F on a sugar thermometer.
- Leave the jam to cool and thicken for 10 minutes then ladle into the sterilised jars and seal with clean lids or waxed paper.

PREPARATION TIME 4 HOURS

COOKING TIME 30 – 45 MINUTES

INGREDIENTS

450 g / 1 lb / 2 cups granulated sugar
450 g / 1 lb / 3 cups apricots, stoned and chopped
½ tsp almond extract

Apricot and Almond Jam

999

- Stir 50 g of flaked almonds into the jam once it's reached 107°C.

1000

**MAKES
500 ML**

Blackberry Jelly

- Preheat the oven to 110°C (90° fan) / 225F / gas ¼.
- Put the sugar in a heatproof bowl and transfer it to the oven along with 2 small glass jars.
- Put the blackberries and lemon juice in a large saucepan and cover with a lid. Heat gently for 10 minutes or until the blackberries have burst and cooked down into a puree.
- Stir in the warmed sugar to dissolve then increase the heat and boil for 8 minutes.
- Pour the mixture into a muslin-lined colander set over a bowl to strain out the seeds.
- Ladle the jelly into the prepared jars while it's still hot, then seal with clean lids or waxed paper.

PREPARATION TIME 15 MINUTES

COOKING TIME 20 MINUTES

INGREDIENTS

450 g / 1 lb / 2 cups granulated sugar
450 g / 1 lb / 3 cups blackberries
2 lemons, juiced

Blackberry and Apple Jelly

1001

- For a better set, add 1 finely chopped bramley apple to the blackberries before cooking.

Blood Orange and Mace Marmalade

PREPARATION TIME 30 MINUTES

COOKING TIME I HOUR 30 MINUTES

INGREDIENTS

300 g / 10 ½ oz blood oranges, halved
300 g / 10 ½ oz Seville oranges, halved
6 whole mace
900 g / 2 lb / 4 cups granulated sugar

- Squeeze the juice from the oranges, reserving any pulp and seeds.
- Put the empty orange skins in a muslin bag with the mace and the reserved pulp and seeds and tie securely with string.
- Put the fruit juice and muslin bag in a preserving pan with 2 litres of water and leave to steep for 4 hours or overnight.
- Put the preserving pan over a high heat and boil for 1 hour.
- Preheat the oven to 110°C (90° fan) / 225F / gas ¼ and put the sugar in a heatproof bowl inside along with 3 glass jars.
- Squeeze out the muslin bag and discard, then stir in the warmed sugar until completely dissolved.
- Skim off any scum that rises to the surface, then increase the heat and boil until a sugar thermometer reads 107°C / 225F.
- Ladle the marmalade into the prepared jars while it's still hot, then seal the jars with clean lids or waxed paper.

Homemade Yoghurt

PREPARATION TIME 9 HOURS

COOKING TIME 5 MINUTES

INGREDIENTS

600 ml / 1 pint whole milk
50 g / 1 ¾ oz / ½ cup powdered milk
2 tbsp plain live yoghurt

- Put the milk in a saucepan and heat until it starts to simmer.
- Take the pan off the heat and whisk in the milk powder, then allow the mixture to cool until it reaches 38° / 100F on a sugar thermometer.
- Whisk in the live yoghurt then pour the mixture into a thermos flask and seal it well with a lid.
- Leave the yoghurt to ferment, without disturbing, for 8 hours, then chill in the fridge until ready to use.

1004
SERVES 4
Braised Peas with Lettuce

- Heat the oil in a large cast iron casserole dish and brown the onions all over. Sear the little gems on the cut sides, then add the peas to the pan and season with salt and pepper.
- Pour in the wine and bring to the boil, then add the stock and simmer for 5 minutes.

PREPARATION TIME 5 MINUTES

COOKING TIME 25 MINUTES

INGREDIENTS

2 tbsp olive oil
8 small salad onions, peeled
2 little gem lettuces, halved
400 g / 14 oz / 2 ⅔ cups peas, defrosted if frozen
175 ml / 6 fl. oz / ⅔ cup dry white wine
175 ml / 6 fl. oz / ⅔ cup good quality vegetable stock

Homemade Peanut Butter

1005
MAKES 1 JAR

PREPARATION TIME 5 MINUTES

COOKING TIME 15 MINUTES

INGREDIENTS

200 g / 7 oz / 1 ½ cups peanuts, shelled
1 tbsp caster (superfine) sugar
½ tsp sea salt

- Preheat the oven to 180°C (160° fan) / 350F / gas 4.
- Spread the peanuts out in a shallow roasting tin and toast them in the oven for 20 minutes, stirring occasionally.
- Leave to cool for 5 minutes then transfer the peanuts to a food processor with the sugar, salt and 3 tbsp of boiling water.
- Blend the peanuts to your preferred consistency, then spoon the peanut butter into a jar and leave to cool completely.

White Sauce with Nutmeg

1006
SERVES 4

PREPARATION TIME 20 MINUTES

COOKING TIME 45 MINUTES

INGREDIENTS

2 tbsp butter
2 tbsp plain (all-purpose) flour
600 ml / 1 pint / 2 ½ cups milk
¼ tsp freshly grated nutmeg

- Melt the butter in a saucepan then stir in the flour.
- Gradually whisk in the milk a little at a time until it is all incorporated.
- Cook the sauce over a low heat, stirring constantly, until the mixture thickens. Beat vigorously to remove any lumps.
- Take the pan off the heat and stir in the nutmeg then season to taste with salt and pepper.

Index

Index

Index

Index